A Legal Guide to Security and Emergency Management for State and Local Governments

Ernest B. Abbott and Otto J. Hetzel, Editors

Section of State and
Local Government Law

AMERICAN BAR ASSOCIATION
Defending Liberty
Pursuing Justice

09   08   07   06   05   5   4   3   2   1

Library of Congress Cataloging in Publication Data

Homeland security and emergency management : legal issues for state and local governments / edited by Ernest B. Abbott and Otto J. Hetzel.
    p. cm.
  Includes index.
  ISBN 1-59031-593-6
  1. National security—Law and legislation—United States. 2. Emergency management—Law and legislation—United States. I. Abbott, Ernest B. II. Hetzel, Otto J.

KF4850.H65 2005
344.7305′32—dc22   2005024148

CONTENTS

ABOUT THE EDITORS

Ernest B. Abbott is founder and principal of FEMA Law Associates, PLLC, a firm providing legal services to the emergency management community with particular emphasis on the laws and regulations governing preparedness, response, recovery, and mitigation programs of the Department of Homeland Security. Mr. Abbott served as general counsel of the Federal Emergency Management Agency during the Clinton administration and also has held senior legal and policy positions in both the private sector (with Tenneco Energy in Houston) and the public sector (with the U.S. Environmental Protection Agency and Interstate Commerce Commission). He is a graduate of Swarthmore College (B.A. with high honors), Harvard Law School (J.D. magna cum laude), and Harvard's Kennedy School of Government (M.P.P.). Mr. Abbott currently heads the American Bar Association's (ABA) Multisection Homeland Security Task Force and is on its Task Force on Hurricane Katrina. He is on the governing council of the ABA's Section of State and Local Government Law and is a founder and chair of its Committee on Homeland Security and Emergency Management.

Otto J. Hetzel practices law in Washington, D.C., and is a professor of law emeritus at Wayne State University Law School in Michigan, where he taught for more than thirty years. In his law practice, he advises local governments and private sector contractors in dealing with federal agencies and complying with federal legislation, agency regulations, Office of Management and Budget circulars, and federal acquisition requirements. He speaks frequently on homeland security issues and has published extensively. He is an author of two law school texts, *Legislative Law and Statutory Interpretation* and *Housing and Community Development*, both in third editions. His column, "Washington's Labyrinthine Ways," published for twenty years for the ABA's Section of State and Local Government Law, commented on activities in Congress and federal agencies and on homeland security matters. He served on the section's council and is a founder and vice chair of its Committee on Homeland Security and Emergency Management. He also is on the Homeland Security Committee of the ABA's Section on Administrative Law and Regulatory Practice. Earlier, he served as associate general counsel of the U.S. Department of Housing and Community Development and as a deputy attorney general of the state of California, where he handled a variety of law enforcement and regulatory matters. He has a J.D. from Yale Law School, an LL.M. from Harvard Law School, and a B.A. from the Pennsylvania State University.

ABOUT THE CONTRIBUTORS

Arthur P. Berg is counsel to Palmer & Dodge, LLC, specializing in matters involving airports. He was the lead federal regulatory and appellate lawyer for the Port Authority of New York and New Jersey until 2002. In that capacity, he was involved in nearly one hundred litigated matters and personally argued many of the Port Authority's major appeals, including successfully arguing to the U.S. Supreme Court that airports were nonpublic fora and that therefore the Port Authority could constitutionally ban the Hare Krishna from soliciting donations in airport terminals. Other successful cases include holdings by the U.S. Court of Appeals for the Third Circuit that the Port Authority's ban on newspaper vending machines at its airports was proper, and by the Second Circuit that the Port Authority's perimeter rule at LaGuardia Airport banning nonstop flights of more than 1500 miles was valid. At the Port Authority, he also rendered opinions on major issues such as airport rates and charges, developed litigation strategy, provided comments on proposed federal legislative issues as well as Department of Transportation and Federal Aviation Administration (FAA) rules and regulations, and coordinated regulatory and environmental policies involving Port Authority airports with the FAA. In 1990, he received the Airport Council International (ACI) Distinguished Service Award for extraordinary work as chair of the Legal Committee in developing, articulating, and promoting ACI policies, particularly on aircraft noise and passenger facility charges. In 1998, he received the Port Authority Executive Director's Award of Achievement for obtaining FAA approval to use passenger facility charges to finance the Airtrain link to JFK International Airport. He has an LL.B. from St. John's University Law School and a B.A. from St. John's University. He is admitted to practice in New York, the U.S. Supreme Court, and the Federal Courts of Appeals for the D.C., Second, Third, and Eleventh Circuits.

Alfred O. Bragg III was the assistant general counsel of the Florida Division of Emergency Management for many years. He was active and instrumental in many National Emergency Management Association legal, legislative, and EMAC committee activities. He drafted Governor Jeb Bush's executive orders to engage state resources in disasters and prepared presidential disaster declaration requests, emergency requests, Small Business Administration disaster declaration requests, and others as needed. He received a J.D. from the University of Georgia School of Law after graduating from Duke University with a B.A. in English literature and a minor in Russian language. He was a member of the Georgia bar for thirty-four years and the Florida bar for twenty-nine years until his death on April 2, 2005. He grew up in Columbus, Georgia.

Alan Cohn is an attorney with Akin Gump Strauss Hauer & Feld, LLP, in Washington, D.C. Mr. Cohn represents clients in matters involving domestic preparedness, emergency response, disaster recovery, and other homeland security–related issues, in addition to his practice in labor and employment law. He is chair of the Legal Issues Working Group of the National Urban Search and Rescue Response System Advisory Committee, which advises the Federal Emergency Management Agency (FEMA), and is a member of the Fairfax County, Virginia, Urban Search and Rescue Task Force. He has been involved in emergency services for the past fifteen years. Mr. Cohn is a graduate of Columbia University (A.B.) and the Georgetown University Law Center (J.D. cum laude). Mr. Cohn is vice chair for programs of the American Bar Association's (ABA) Section of State and Local Government Law Committee on Homeland Security and Emergency Management.

John Copenhaver is president and CEO of DRI International and president of the Global Partnership for Preparedness. Previously he was a senior vice president of Marsh Risk Consulting, chairman and CEO of the Contingency Management Group, a senior advisor to the IBM International Crisis Response Team, and director of business continuity services for BellSouth Corp. He was appointed by President Clinton as regional director of FEMA's Region IV in 1997 and served as chair of the Atlanta Federal Executive Board in 2000–2001. He provided on-scene assistance in the response and recovery efforts to the City of New York after the 9/11 attacks and to the governments of El Salvador and Peru after the 2001 earthquakes. He was appointed to the CEM Commission of the International Association of Emergency Managers in November 2003 and to the editorial advisory boards of *Contingency Planning and Management* and the *Disaster Resource Guide.* He has a J.D. from the University of Georgia School of Law and a B.S. from Brown University. He is a member of the Georgia bar.

Jean Cox currently is senior counsel at Carr Public Affairs, Inc., in Albany, New York, where her practice focuses on homeland security and emergency management matters. She spent eight years as the primary legal counsel to the New York State Emergency Management Office (SEMO), where she was integral to that agency's role in leading New York's response to numerous disasters, both natural events and the terrorist attacks of 9/11. At SEMO, she was the liaison to Congress and the New York legislature concerning all aspects of emergency management. She often acted as director of New York's Emergency Operations Center during declared disasters, in which capacity she supervised staff; communicated with state and federal legislators; and coordinated the activities of federal agencies, other New York agencies, and other states. Earlier, she served as counsel to New York State Senator Nicholas A. Spano and the New York Senate Labor Committee, was an attorney and lobbyist with the firm of Bond, Schoeneck & King, and acted as senior management services coordinator for the New York Assembly Republican minority and the New York Senate Mental Hygiene Committee. She is a graduate of Albany Law School and the State University of New York College at Plattsburgh. Admitted to the New York bar and related federal courts, she was the former chair of the National Emergency Management Association's Legal Committee.

Diane Donley has been with FEMA's Office of General Counsel for five years, handling litigation and program law matters. Currently she is involved with various response issues in the event of a presidentially declared disaster or emergency and the activation of the National Disaster Medical System. She is on one of FEMA's national response teams and has been deployed to a number of disasters, including the World Trade Center, the Pentagon, and the aftermath of the space shuttle Columbia explosion. Ms. Donley spent ten years at the U.S. Department of Justice, litigating cases concerning toxic torts, large commercial contracts, bankruptcy, civil fraud, and violations of environmental statutes. She also was in private practice, primarily handling environmental law, commercial contracts, and bankruptcy law matters, and she has worked for nonprofit hazardous waste mediation and environmental firms. She created and taught a course in toxic torts at the George Washington University National Law Center. In addition, she worked in the Executive Office of the President for the council on Environmental Quality, where she developed transportation policies for the Council and monitored agency compliance with the National Environmental Policy Act. She has a master's degree in urban and regional planning, a J.D. from Catholic University, and a B.A. from Wellesley College. A member of the District of Columbia and Virginia bars, she has published several articles on transportation planning and water quality management and has served as a professional mediator for the U.S. courts.

Dwight H. Merriam is the founding member and senior partner of the Land Use Group at Robinson & Cole, LLP, a multioffice general practice firm. He represents developers, governments, landowners, and advocacy groups in land development and conservation issues. He has a J.D. from Yale Law School, a master's degree in regional planning from the University of North Carolina, and a B.A. cum laude from the University of Massachusetts. He is a fellow and past president of the American Institute of Certified Planners, a former director of the American Planning Association (APA), and a former chair of APA's Planning and Law Division. He is also a member of the American College of Real Estate Lawyers and a Counselor of Real Estate, and he teaches land use law at Vermont Law School. He is on the governing council of the ABA's Section of State and Local Government Law, and his two most recent books are *The Complete Guide to Zoning* (2005) and *Eminent Domain Use and Abuse: Kelo in Context* (Mary Massaron Ross, coeditor) (2005).

H. Crane Miller is a general attorney with FEMA's Office of the General Counsel, currently concentrating on legal issues related to the Defense Production Act and on urban search and rescue matters. He has had extensive experience with international, regulatory, and legislative matters for FEMA. His nearly twenty-five years of federal service includes time in the Department of the Navy's Office of General Counsel; as assistant general counsel of the Smithsonian Institution; as legal advisor to the Commission on Marine Science, Engineering, and Resources in the Executive Office of the President; and as counsel to the Oceans and Atmosphere Subcommittee of the U.S. Senate Committee on Commerce. He also has spent twenty years in private law practice. He is the author, coauthor, or editor of more than forty research papers and publications on legal and community development issues related to riverine and coastal flooding, hurricanes, earthquakes, and other natural disasters, and has served on several commissions and panels of the National Academy of Sciences.

William C. Nicholson is an assistant professor at North Carolina Central University's Department of Criminal Justice. He has extensive experience in and knowledge of homeland security and emergency management law. Previously he taught a course on terrorism and emergency law as an adjunct professor at Widener University School of Law and one on homeland security law and policy at the University of Delaware. Mr. Nicholson served as general counsel to the Indiana State Emergency Management Agency, the Indiana Department of Fire and Building Services, and the Public Safety Training Institute, as well as for seven related public safety boards and commissions. He has published numerous articles and speaks on terrorism and emergency law. He has published two books, *Emergency Response and Emergency Management Law* (2003) and *Homeland Security Law and Policy* (2005).

Robert A. Sedler is Distinguished Professor of Law and member of the Academy of Scholars at Wayne State University in Detroit, Michigan, where he teaches constitutional law and conflict of laws. Before coming to Wayne State in 1977, he was a professor of law at the University of Kentucky. Professor Sedler received his A.B. and his J.D. from the University of Pittsburgh. He has litigated a large number of civil rights and civil liberties cases and has written on the American federal system and on the relationship between federal and state power. In the aftermath of 9/11, Professor Sedler has spoken and written extensively on the subject of civil liberties and the war on terrorism. He has published many works in his fields, including a monograph on American constitutional law as part of the International Encyclopedia of Laws series in 1994 that was updated in 2000 and 2005.

David A. Trissell has served as general counsel of FEMA and associate general counsel for Emergency Preparedness and Response (EP&R) in the Department of Homeland Security (DHS) since October 2004. He directs FEMA's sixty-five attorneys and serves as principal legal advisor to the DHS undersecretary for EP&R. Previously he was a senior trial attorney at FEMA and in that post was responsible for litigating a number of significant cases. Before that he worked at the U.S. Department of Justice, Environment and Natural Resources Division, General Litigation Section, where he handled mainly environmental and Fifth Amendment takings cases. He is the author of two articles involving seminal takings matters: *Tabb Lakes Ltd. v. United States*, at 4 Fed. Cir. Bar J. 219

(Summer 1994); and, *M&J Coal Company and Mononga Development Company v. United States*, at 5 Fed. Cir. Bar J. 255 (Summer 1995). He clerked with U.S. Magistrate Judge Bana B. Blasdel (W.Dist. Okla.) while in law school. His B.A. in journalism and J.D. are from the University of Oklahoma. He is admitted to the Oklahoma and U.S. Court of Federal Claims bars.

Joe D. Whitley is a partner with Alston & Bird, both in its Atlanta and Washington, D.C., offices. From August 2003 to May 2005, he served as first general counsel of DHS. Before that he was associate attorney general in the U.S. Department of Justice. Mr. Whitley is unique in having been appointed to serve as a U.S. attorney in two different federal districts: President Reagan appointed him for the Middle District of Georgia in Macon, and President George H. W. Bush appointed him for the Northern District of Georgia in Atlanta. Mr. Whitley was previously a partner at Alston & Bird, where he served as head of its Government Enforcement and Investigations Group. His practice concentrated on government investigations, environmental and health care fraud, and complex civil litigation. He received his undergraduate and law degrees from the University of Georgia. Mr. Whitley served on the council of the ABA's Criminal Justice Section and as vice chair of its Committee for Governmental Affairs. He also chaired annual seminars and institutes for the section.

Rufus C. Young, Jr., is Of Counsel to Burke, Williams & Sorensen, LLP, in the California firm's San Diego office, where he formerly was a senior partner. He is head of the firm's homeland security practice, advising clients on matters ranging from water system vulnerability, risk assessments, and security protocols to planning and liability issues. A retired U.S. Marine Corps colonel, he has a master of laws degree in environmental law (with highest honors) from the George Washington University National Law Center, a J.D. from the University of San Diego School of Law, and a B.A. from San Diego State University. He is a member of the core faculty of the American Law Institute–ABA advanced-level annual program, the Land Use Institute.

David Zocchetti is general counsel for the California Governor's Office of Emergency Services (OES). For more than nineteen years he has served OES in several capacities, including chief of the Planning Section and manager of the Hazardous Material Unit. He also has served as the senior consultant to the California Assembly's Select Committee on Hazardous Materials, Pipeline, Chemical Plant, and Refinery Safety. He has a B.A. and a M.A. in environmental planning from California State University–Sacramento, and a J.D. from the University of the Pacific McGeorge School of Law.

FOREWORD

by Joe D. Whitley

In the aftermath of the 9/11 terrorist attacks, Congress created a new Department of Homeland Security (DHS), bringing together in one Department 22 different agencies with vast and sometimes disparate responsibilities. The Homeland Security Act of 2002 directed the DHS Secretary to take steps to prevent the next act of terrorism and to prepare America for the consequences of an attack if it could not be prevented. Congress also tasked this new Department with coordinating federal assistance to state and local governments responding to natural or accidental catastrophic events such as those caused by hurricanes, earthquakes, tornados, floods, fires, accidental release of toxic substances, or a pandemic flu outbreak. The Federal Emergency Management Agency (FEMA), which had coordinated federal assistance in both natural and non-natural major disasters, was made a central component of the new Department, and the Secretary of DHS was charged with building an improved all-hazards response capability.

Fortunately, since the creation of DHS through this writing in late 2005, no terrorist attacks have occurred within the United States to test the nation's catastrophic response capability. Yet the one-two punch of Hurricanes Katrina and Rita on the Gulf States—and the well publicized difficulties in response to these disasters at all levels of government—clearly demonstrate the need for greater coordination and response integration between state and local governments and the federal civil and military authorities in catastrophic events generally.

We can expect many analyses of the Katrina/Rita responses over the next several years—and of how federal, state, and local responders can improve response capabilities, coordination, and programs to reduce short- and long-term human, social, environmental, and economic impacts. But what is absolutely clear even now is that the nation demands effective advance preparation and planning for emergency management that is coordinated at all levels of government, and that preparation, planning, and response require that all levels of government understand the legal framework of emergency management and the laws that govern agency actions in homeland security and emergency management. These materials assembled by its Editors Ernie Abbott and Otto Hetzel, two well regarded and knowledgeable experts in the field of disaster prevention, relief, and mitigation, provide a solid basis for state and local government officials and their legal counsel to prepare to meet their emergency management responsibilities.

This book's coverage is a very timely and useful compendium of work by authors who have a unique appreciation of the roles of DHS, states, and local governments, including cities and counties, in the dynamic and changing field of emergency management and disaster relief. In particular the thorough "work in progress" represented by the Checklist Appendix prepared by the Editors, provides critical guidance for those who must prepare for these catastrophic events.

As the first General Counsel of DHS, my mission was to develop a common legal culture among the nearly 1,500 attorneys at DHS while at the same time preserving the distinct legal expertise developed by FEMA lawyers over the years. I would have found a book like this indispensable as a tool to prepare and train my DHS legal teams' appreciation of many of the topics in it that will be encountered by those in federal, state, and local governments and the private sector with infrastructure roles as well. It is a worthy and useful companion to a growing body of legal writing in the field of Homeland Security Law in 2005 and will be helpful in the years ahead. My advice to anyone who must exercise responsibility or advise those who will do so regarding homeland security and emergency management issues is to make sure this text is in your library if you plan to function effectively in this legal area.

INTRODUCTION AND OVERVIEW

by Ernest B. Abbott and Otto J. Hetzel

The fundamental responsibility of government is the protection of the lives, health, and welfare of its people. After the terrorist attacks of September 2001, the United States has devoted unprecedented attention—as well as substantial public and private resources—to protecting our homeland from potential terrorist catastrophic events. Hurricane Katrina's awesome landfall in 2005—and the media and public outcry over stumbling by federal, state, and local responders—will require the expenditure of hundreds of billions of dollars for recovery and will trigger efforts to improve our defenses to natural catastrophes as well.

The nation's massive homeland security efforts build upon an "all hazards" system of emergency response. This response system is activated whenever catastrophe strikes, whether its source is a natural event such as an earthquake, hurricane, or epidemic, an accidental release at a chemical plant, or the intentional detonation of an explosive device. Thus, even though actual terrorist events within our borders fortunately have been quite rare, the national response system is utilized 50 or more times a year for major disaster events, and even more often for smaller events. This response system has developed its own body of law—statutes, regulations, and published policies—that specifies government authority to take emergency actions, affects its potential liabilities, and authorizes reimbursement to state and local governments. Counsel for state and local governments must be prepared to apply these legal authorities during emergencies, and can do so effectively only if they prepare in advance.

Our country has adopted many security measures—including some that are controversial in an open society—to protect our population and infrastructure from terrorist attacks. We have reorganized our domestic and foreign intelligence services to focus on identifying and interdicting terrorists and the use of weapons of mass destruction. We have spent billions of dollars to help train, equip, and provide exercises for federal and state responders. Quite simply, there are new rules with which state and local governments must comply in maintaining public safety and protecting infrastructure. Their lawyers must be familiar with these rules.

Our federal system is a critical feature of homeland security. In this system, the federal government has responsibility for the national defense, for interstate commerce, taxation, and expenditures for the public welfare—but state and local governments have primary responsibility for protection of the public health and welfare. State and local governments almost always will be the first to respond to any catastrophic event. Local police, fire safety, and emergency management personnel are the first on the scene and have 'incident command' responsibility at virtually every event that threatens public health and safety in their communities. This was true on September 11, 2001, both in New York and at the Pentagon, and it was true on August 29, 2005, when Hurricane Katrina devastated the coastlines of Louisiana, Mississippi, and Alabama. Success in responding to catastrophic events requires coordination of these first local responders' resources with the support needed from other local jurisdictions, other states, and many federal government agencies. Representing state and local governments in emergencies requires a thorough understanding of both the legal and practical underpinnings of federalism. It also helps to know the acronyms.

In short, homeland security and emergency management are now such important responsibilities of state and local governments that their lawyers must understand the management systems that are being generated to respond to these threats, whether the causes are terrorist-created or natural in source. Legal counsel need to know and anticipate what these problems may be and how they will respond. A working knowledge of how these issues may affect their client's interests is essential.

Just as law enforcement and emergency response teams must develop contingency plans so they can act expeditiously to prevent use of a biological, chemical, radiological, or nuclear weapon, and then deal with the aftermath, lawyers must be ready to counsel their clients on a wide variety of legal issues. Legal counsel must be prepared to provide professional advice regarding the full extent of their jurisdictions' authority to deal with these matters, the legal powers available to mobilize the resources needed, and the legal viability of the measures needed to protect affected populations.

In particular, lawyers for state and local governments must be familiar with the different legal rules, authorities, prohibitions, and liabilities that apply when governments respond to catastrophic events. And, counsel must be ready with new forms to authorize governmental bodies to take action, and they must draft new—or interpret previously executed—cooperation agreements so that their client governments can work together effectively in a disaster environment. This is likely to be an environment in which many different federal, state, local, private, and nonprofit entities must work together, often in dangerous and chaotic conditions.

The breadth of the issues impacted by homeland security—intelligence, prevention, and preparedness programs—is extraordinary. The effects reach far into our nation's economy. The scope of emergency management law is similarly daunting. Arguably, emergency management law encompasses the law applicable to *all* government actions and authority, *as modified* by the authorities and exemptions activated in particular kinds of emergency events. Lawyers practicing emergency management law face the additional challenge that advice must be given immediately, most likely in the face of imminent threats to life and property, and when the basic elements of a working law office (power, communications, computer, and staff) may be unavailable.

This book provides a number of windows into homeland security and emergency management law—covering the basic structure of the emergency management system and presenting detailed analyses of specific areas—such as applying for federal preparedness funds, negotiating intergovernmental agreements, applying for disaster assistance, and managing the impact of catastrophic events. These are matters with which every state and local government lawyer should be familiar. We do not cover every issue. We do provide, as an Appendix, a checklist of the legal issues that lawyers must be prepared to face so they can research their own circumstances and authorities, and have completed in advance most of the legal work that will be required when an emergency occurs. This brief volume is intended to give its readers invaluable insight in the best ways to represent their clients in this area that is so critical for them and for the nation. It can be used as a starting point for legal counsel to prepare for tasks that are liable to stretch their capabilities considerably unless they prepare in advance.

Overview

This book has two parts. Part I explores issues that jurisdictions encounter in preventing, mitigating, and preparing a community for catastrophic conditions. These issues are encountered every day in the "pre-disaster" environment. They generally are not addressed in the chaos of an actual emergency. Prevention and mitigation activities aim to prevent a catastrophic event from occurring in the first place (by intercepting and arresting terrorists, for example, or by reducing the vulnerability of a structure to damage from high winds or explosives). Preparedness activities aim to develop resources (such as responders with necessary equipment, training, exercises, and surge medical capacity) that can be activated quickly and effectively when the need arises. Lawyers play important roles in both areas.

Part II addresses issues encountered when coping with an actual catastrophic event. During the response phase of a disaster, multiple levels of government must coordinate and execute emergency operation plans and take immediate action to save lives, protect property, and meet basic human needs. When conditions have stabilized, efforts turn to reconstituting normal functions, restoring services, and repairing and rebuilding damaged and destroyed property. At this point, critical determinations will be required for which legal counsel is essential: determining which government and private entities will absorb losses caused by the disaster and those that will bear the cost of response.

Although Part II deals with post-event phases of emergency management, these materials stress that **a lawyer's success in representing a jurisdiction as it responds to and recovers from a terrorist attack or natural catastrophe will largely depend on actions taken in advance of the event.** The massive resources available in emergencies from other communities, other states, the federal government, and even other countries will arrive more quickly if mutual aid agreements are negotiated in advance. Handling influxes of donated goods and services must be anticipated and planned for in advance. Potential civil liabilities can be minimized only if advance attention is paid to the kinds of actions to be taken in emergencies. Provisions in mutual aid agreements and in the design of emergency response plans should be drafted, where possible, to take advantage of such doctrines as sovereign immunity and Good Samaritan laws as applied to emergency requirements. Communities will lose eligibility for federal reimbursement of the cost of removing debris or repairing damaged facilities if they are not aware in advance of federal rules governing disaster assistance grants—and are prepared to follow them.

Preparedness/Prevention

Until the attacks on the World Trade Center and Pentagon in 2001, one of the primary methods of emergency management was to make readily available to the public risk information; to give the public the information it needed to protect itself. This method built on the philosophy of open government and the generally permissive access to information reflected in the post-Watergate enactment of the federal and state Freedom of Information Acts and Open Meetings laws. In Chapter 1, David Zocchetti, counsel to the California Governor's Office of Emergency Management, relates how the threat of terrorism—and a desire to withhold from terrorists a roadmap of our nation's vulnerabilities—has reduced availability of risk information and created conflicts among various policies and requirements governing disclosure of information.

A principal focus of the nation's homeland security effort has been on the protection of critical infrastructure from attack. Each type of infrastructure presents its own issues. State and local governments—including public authorities such as airports, maritime ports, utilities, and transit systems—are deeply involved in the legal ramifications of all types of infrastructure. Potential infrastructure vulnerability varies widely, given the physical differences obvious even from these few examples: pipelines, electric lines, airports, roads, tunnels, water and electrical grids, and transit systems. The strategies appropriate and being implemented to protect each type of infrastructure are similarly varied—with impacts dependent on each infrastructure industry's financial and regulatory system. In Chapter 2, Arthur Berg examines the challenges faced by airports in complying with a broad new range of homeland security initiatives and requirements. These measures have required substantial investments, extensive modification of operations, and are presenting new challenges in customer service.

In Chapter 3, Professor Robert Sedler reviews the constitutional authority of congressional acts that frequently affect state regulatory requirements and require expenditure of state funds in areas applicable to homeland security, such as the Patriot Act and the Homeland Security Act. He analyzes the constitutional limits of federal powers to impose financial burdens on state jurisdictions—in order to comply with federal requirements—in excess of funds provided by the federal government. A recent example is provided of Congress overriding state powers without using the carrot of access to funds to gain compliance. States normally issue drivers' licenses and personal identification cards. In its 2004 Intelligence Reforms and Terrorism Prevention Act, Congress set federal standards for the issuance of such forms of identification, but states were still authorized to determine who was eligible. No longer: in May 2005, concerned about controlling the use of such documents by aliens, Congress repealed the 2004 law and enacted a new version that as a practical matter requires states to use federal standards in issuing drivers' licenses and personal identification cards and in verifying eligibility for them. The federal requirements are enforced by limiting acceptance of state identification cards by federal agencies—at airport security checkpoints, for example, or to enter federal facilities—to those that comply with federal standards. Thus, if states fail to comply with the federal standards, this would limit significantly the identification value of such licenses and cards to those obtaining them.

Traditionally, government approaches to public health emergencies have not been integrated with state and local emergency management efforts. Public health officials have used their considerable emergency powers, which are based on the state's police powers, to disrupt transmission of communicable disease, while emergency management officials have exercised separate emergency authority, again derived from the police power, to meet emergency needs and to restore basic services after catastrophic events. In Chapter 4, Professor William Nicholson shows how the public health emergency system works in tandem with, and as part of, the National Response Plan and National Incident Management System, and provides an overview of the legal issues that community public health officials face in preparing for serious outbreaks of communicable diseases.

The most effective actions that state and local communities can take to protect themselves from the impact of catastrophic events are through adoption of the codes and ordinances that govern the siting and construction of the structures our citizens live, work, and play in. Adoption and enforcement of building codes requiring structures to meet seismic standards in an earthquake zone, requiring structures to withstand hurricane force winds along the Atlantic and Gulf coasts, and prohibiting construction in floodplains except in accordance with flood plain management regulations, will make communities disaster resistant and save countless lives and economic hardship. Rufus Young and Dwight Merriam demonstrate in Chapter 5 how communities can also use building codes to protect against terrorist attacks—and common criminals.

Chapter 6 concludes the section on preparedness and prevention, with practical information on the many different federal grants available to states and communities so they can build preparedness against terrorist attacks. These sources of support are of critical importance to already strapped state and local governments. Quite simply, it is expensive to train, equip, and exercise first responders to be ready for their new mission of responding to attacks on our homeland, particularly given the special requirements applicable to interdicting the variety of potential weapons of mass destruction. The over-time costs of providing public safety for society and critical infrastructure place significant burdens on these levels of government, which must respond to federal requirements regarding preparedness levels when increased threats are perceived. Alan Cohn provides a detailed review of federal preparedness grants and grant policies to help every community identify which programs to apply for, and tells them how to apply.

Response and Recovery

Al Bragg introduces the response and recovery section with an extensive case study of what state and local government lawyers need to anticipate in responding to and recovering from catastrophic events. He offers his reflections on his recent experiences as chief counsel for Florida's Office of Emergency Management during the 2004 Hurricane season. That was the year four major hurricanes struck Florida in the space of six weeks. He describes the legal and operational environment in which he had to operate, and demonstrates how pre-disaster planning allowed him to provide needed legal advice in an extraordinarily chaotic and high-pressure environment.

In Chapter 8, David Trissell, FEMA's general counsel, and Diane Donley, a lawyer in that office, describe how the National Response Plan and the National Incident Management System (NIMS) work. These plans are of critical importance to all state and local governments. Not only will the federal government use these plans to coordinate all federal response activities to any natural or man-made "Incidents of National Significance," but all federal agencies are under express instruction to require states and local governments and public authorities to comply with the NIMS as a condition to any grant of federal funding for preparedness. Knowledge of these systems is essential for every state and local government lawyer.

One of the key elements of NIMS and of emergency management generally is mutual aid—that is, assistance provided by jurisdictions unaffected by a disaster to the communities (in the same or other states) beset by a catastrophic event. This assistance is almost always provided under written intergovernmental agreements. Chapter 9 is Alan Cohn's seminal discussion of the legal issues that must be addressed in these intergovernmental agreements, including a detailed review of the case law demonstrating the liabilities that communities face when mutual aid agreements are improperly drafted.

Jean Cox, counsel to the New York State Emergency Management Office during the September 11 attacks, highlights the importance of donations management during response to a significant disaster. While donations of goods and the services of volunteers may not appear to be resources for which government and its lawyers have responsibility, Chapter 10 demonstrates that planning for, staging, and coordinating these resources is absolutely critical to a jurisdiction's successful response effort. The New York experience is an essential roadmap to the preparedness required in each governmental jurisdiction. Significant liability and exposure issues and concomitant public affairs and political repercussions will occur if these issues are not properly handled from a legal perspective. Her organized advice is an excellent starting point for lawyers to deal with these issues that are frequently overlooked in advance planning.

Chapter 11 gives a careful review of the potential availability of a powerful national defense statute, the Defense Production Act, to help the federal, state, and local governments acquire critical goods and services to deal with incidents that pose severe threats to the nation and its citizens. Crane Miller, senior counsel for FEMA, reviews a little known statutory cross reference—under which the "national defense" is defined to include emergency preparedness, response, and recovery activities—and its implications for state and local emergency managers.

In Chapter 12, Ernest Abbott summarizes some dangerous shoals through which local and state governments and authorities must navigate to maintain their eligibility for significant disaster assistance should a catastrophe occur. This chapter provides critical guidance to help communities avoid adding a financial and political disaster, caused by violation of federal regulatory requirements or improperly characterizing eligible costs, to the physical damage from which they seek to recover.

Finally, John Copenhaver reminds us in Chapter 13 that emergency management is not just the province of government. In the United States, most property—including the critical infrastructure on which our security depends—is held by the private sector, most jobs are provided by that sector, and most resources for response and recovery reside there as well. Effective homeland security and emergency management planning requires a partnership between government and the private sector. State and local government lawyers must be aware of these realities during emergency planning and response. They also must be prepared to structure these public/private arrangements, and craft the necessary documents to reflect the private sector's role.

CHAPTER 1

Public Disclosure of Information by Emergency Services Agencies: A Post-September 11 Paradigm Shift

by David Zocchetti[1]

Introduction

Government agencies are trying to keep from public disclosure a computer program developed as part of a student's doctoral dissertation that gives exact precise locations of the infrastructure in U.S. communities. It appears that by using this program, a person can determine precisely, on a map, where phone lines, power transmission cables, and other elements of a city's lifelines are located—making them vulnerable to disruption.[2] Government officials believe that this computer program should be kept out of public circulation for fear that it could be a handy tool for facilitating a future attack against this country.[3] This is an interesting shift of governmental attitude.

Federal, state and local governments have generally encouraged development of systems that depict key lifelines critical to a community's operations. Using such systems, emergency planners can develop procedures for focusing resources in disasters, from earthquakes to chemical spills. Government officials historically have viewed the maps and data available through computer systems (particularly Geographic Information Systems) as critical to ensuring an effectively targeted emergency response. As these systems became more affordable, many emergency services and planning departments invested in them, even though they were surely not as advanced as the system developed by the doctoral student.[4]

This shift in the federal government's perspective on public disclosure of information is not unique. Government officials and legislators at all levels have been reassessing the efficacy of publicly disclosing information, particularly as it relates to emergency preparedness. The area of chemical safety programs presents one of the most dramatic and complex areas where government, prompted by law enforcement or industry, is reevaluating the appropriateness of public access to such information.

Where We Have Been

During the final decades of the twentieth century, legislators and policy makers directed their efforts toward promoting disclosure of public risk and the plans to mitigate it. It was generally assumed that people needed to know about chemical hazards in their communities. State[5] and federal[6] laws gave legal weight to this premise. Public disclosure, or "right-to-know," about hazards was assuming the mantle of a basic right.

Many people believed that, armed with knowledge about the chemicals and other hazards in their communities, members of the general public could make better decisions about where they lived, more coherently comment on land-use decisions, and better evaluate whether government and industry were adequately providing for their safety. Implicit in this rationale was the belief that the public could not rely on government and industry to ensure its welfare, and that public oversight, based on detailed information, was necessary.

Over time, legislators have added to the basic programs that required industry to simply disclose information. For example, it is no longer adequate for businesses to affirm that they have certain chemicals in various quantities. In some cases, they must comprehensively analyze the risk of catastrophic chemical releases to the environment and the resulting impacts on the community.[7] Businesses also must evaluate how systems could fail, and if that failure could lead to a mishap involving chemicals. Further, businesses often must consider a "worst-case" release scenario and the "off-site consequence" of such a release to the communities surrounding their facilities.[8] For the most part, the law ensures that this chemical risk information is available to the public.[9] Some states, like California, even require public hearings to circulate the results of these assessments.[10]

Public and legislative demand for heightened disclosure of chemical accident risk information was driven in part by some very dramatic disasters involving releases of chemicals into the environment. The intent was to avoid future chemical disasters through better prevention and planning.[11]

The trend toward heightened information disclosure in the emergency management field has not been limited to chemical safety, but rather has incorporated all types of hazards, both natural and technological, and this was being done at all levels of government.[12] For example, California requires residential real estate sellers to disclose to buyers any earthquake, fire, or potential flood information they may possess.[13]

The emergency management aspects of public disclosure are layered upon the more general federal and state laws that address the broader issues of openness in government and disclosure of information held by government agencies. Lawyers practicing in the area of government law realize that both the federal Freedom of Information Act (FOIA)[14] and its state equivalents[15] typically have a presumption that records and information held by governments are available to the public on request. Although these general laws contain numerous exemptions, the overarching principle is that the public has a right to information held by its government.[16]

The catastrophic events of September 11, 2001, compelled governments immediately to reevaluate how they viewed public information disclosure. This rethinking was not limited to the highly publicized areas of secret intelligence files and closed hearings for alleged terrorists. It also included information previously created or collected by the emergency management community, such as risk assessments, procedures, plans, and community profiles developed by emergency managers.[17] Government officials charged with providing the critical services of law enforcement, firefighting, medical and emergency rescue, hazardous material emergency response, public health, and myriad other emergency services, began to evaluate whether the information they had so carefully developed, and in some cases were compelled by law to provide to the public, should remain easily available to anyone who asked, including potential terrorists. Understandably, emergency response organizations and emergency responders would not want the information they collect or developed to decrease the safety of those they are sworn to protect.

Pre-9/11 Foreshadowing

Well before 9/11, increasing concerns about terrorism were beginning to shift attitudes about what information governments should make available to the public. In August 1999, President Clinton signed into law the Chemical Safety Information Site Security and Fuels Regulatory Relief Act.[18] Among other things, this new act imposed a moratorium on the electronic release of off-site consequence analyses developed by chemical companies and submitted to local agencies and the U.S. Environmental Protection Agency (EPA).[19] This law focused on public disclosure, via the Internet, of the off-site consequences to a community that could be expected if a chemical facility had an accident.

Originally, the government believed disclosing this information would encourage industry to initiate efforts to reduce the risks of accidents involving chemicals. This concept relied on analysis, knowledge of the risks, and potential public pressure to improve. However, the Federal Bureau of Investigation and other representatives of the law enforcement and intelligence communities raised the concern that releasing off-site consequence information electronically would "enable individuals anywhere in the world [to] anonymously search electronically for industrial facilities in the U.S. to target for the purposes of causing an intentional industrial chemical release," according to the EPA.[20]

The federal government's final rule implementing the act tries to establish a balance between secrecy and disclosure. Even though off-site consequence information cannot be displayed on the Internet, paper copies of the information can be made available at federal reading rooms scattered throughout the country. Reading rooms can provide any member of the public access to the off-site consequence information for up to ten facilities per month, allowing public access to this information for the vulnerability zones where people live and work.[21]

Interestingly, limitations on the release of chemical facility off-site conse-quence analyses apply only to the EPA. In fact, Congress was very precise in ensuring that the dissemination restrictions it created (and that would even-tually would be interpreted by the EPA and the U.S. Department of Justice) would not apply if "a state, under an existing law or a law yet to be enacted, were to require the submission of similar or even identical information about chemical releases . . . ."[22] Thus, states with chemical risk assessment programs that predated the Chemical Safety Information Site Security and Fuels Regula-tory Relief Act—such as California—or states with new programs that disclose off-site consequences of potential chemical mishaps, are still free to release the information as they deem appropriate.[23]

Before 9/11, some states were already heading toward less disclosure, as least as it applied to the general information held by public agencies. The state of Washington, for example, amended its Public Records Act to include an exemption for "specific and unique vulnerability assessments or specific and unique response plans, either of which is intended to prevent or mitigate criminal terrorist acts, the public disclosure of which would have a substantial likelihood of threatening public safety."[24] Following the State of Washington's lead, other states reduced disclosure, even before 9/11.

Post 9/11

The shift away from disclosure started before the 9/11 attacks, but the degree and pace accelerated after the attacks. One of the most immediate signs of this pre-9/11 policy shift came a month later, when Attorney General Ashcroft is-sued a memorandum to the heads of all federal agencies rescinding a memo-randum[25] in which his predecessor, Attorney General Reno, called for a strong presumption toward openness under FOIA. The new Attorney General's memorandum contains a much different tone, to wit,

> Any discretionary decision by your agency to disclose information protected un-der the FOIA should be made only after full and deliberate consideration of the in-stitutional, commercial, and personal privacy interests that could be implicated by disclosure of the information . . . [If your agency were to carefully consider FOIA requests and decide to withhold records, in whole or in part, you can be assured that the Department of Justice will defend your decisions unless they lack a sound legal basis or present an unwarranted risk of adverse impact on the ability of other agencies to protect other important records.[26]

General Ashcroft's memorandum certainly signaled a trend away from the presumption of openness established by General Reno. Although these memoranda are not legally binding or specifically directed at emergency man-agement-related information, they set the tone for information disclosure by federal agencies.

After 9/11, and consistent with policies expressed in General Ashcroft's memorandum, many public agencies under this new regime removed previously posted information from their public Web sites. This action was not limited to federal agencies; states removed information from their Web sites about power plants, electrical transmission lines, water resources, public buildings, landslide reports, and other types of information believed to aid potential terrorists.[27] There was little consistency to what agencies removed from their Web sites. The information generally contained facts about public infrastructure, critical facilities, or plans for responding to terrorist events. However, information on the Internet usually is archived, and can still be accessed after it is removed from Web sites, reducing the security benefit of removing information.[28]

In addition to removing information from the Internet, many state houses saw legislation introduced that would restrict public access to information or public meetings. Some of these efforts ran into significant opposition from politicians and members of the public who believed either that current law sufficiently protected records or that the legislative proposals went too far in limiting disclosure of otherwise public information. For example, a bill introduced in New York's legislature would have provided an exemption for maps, architectural drawings, operational plans or procedures, or other detailed information relating to utilities. The bill did not survive the legislative process, apparently succumbing to concerns that New York's public records laws already contained a general exemption from disclosure when a record could threaten people's lives and safety.[29]

A number of state-level legislative actions to limit public disclosure, however, were successful. For example:[30]

Idaho revised its public records law to exempt from disclosure emergency evacuation, escape, or other emergency response plans, vulnerability assessments, operation and security manuals, plans, blueprints or security codes, and other such records if disclosure would jeopardize the safety of persons or the public.[31]

Ohio amended its public records act to exempt security records that contain information used for protecting or maintaining security at public offices, as well as records intended to prevent, mitigate, or respond to terrorist acts, which would include vulnerability assessments, response plans, communications codes, specific intelligence information, investigative records, or security records classified by federal actions.[32]

Michigan amended its disclosure laws to protect information related to the security of persons or property—whether public or private—including buildings, public works, public water supply designs, ongoing security measures of a public body, capabilities and plans for responding to terrorist acts, emergency response plans, risk planning documents, threat assessments, and domestic preparedness strategies. Information remains protected unless disclosure would not impair a public body's ability to protect the security or safety of persons or property, or unless the public interest in disclosure outweighs the public interest in nondisclosure in the particular instance.[33]

California amended its public records act to exempt access to documents that local government has prepared to assess vulnerability to terrorist attacks or other criminal acts intended to disrupt the public agency's operations.[34]

Maryland amended its public information act to exclude response procedures or plans to prevent or respond to emergency situations, the disclosure of which would reveal vulnerability assessments, and specific tactics, emergency procedures, or security procedures; and building information (e.g., plans and security systems) specific to airports and other mass transit facilities, bridges, tunnels, emergency response facilities or structures, buildings where hazardous materials are stored, arenas, stadiums, waste and water systems, and any other building, structure, or facility (some public facilities, and facilities involved in previous disasters, would be excluded from this exemption).[35]

Several other states also have created exemptions to their public records acts, or have bills pending in their legislatures proposing exemptions.

The federal government has taken a different approach. Although Congress has not yet carved out a place for a new exemption within FOIA, it did create the Homeland Security Act of 2002 (HSA), which granted a specific exemption for certain material submitted to the new Department of Homeland Security and created a new class of information referred to as "unclassified but sensitive." Section 214 of the act created an exemption for "critical infrastructure information" voluntarily submitted to the federal government by a nongovernmental entity.[36] "Critical infrastructure information" would include "information not customarily in the public domain and related to the security of critical infrastructure or protected systems."[37] "Critical infrastructure" would include "systems and assets, whether physical or virtual, so vital to the United States that the incapacity or destruction of such systems and assets would have a debilitating impact on security, national economic security, national public health or safety, or any combination of those matters."[38]

Not only does the HSA exempt this information from disclosure under FOIA, it preempts similar state disclosure laws if the information is provided to the states. The HSA also grants a degree of civil immunity to entities that voluntarily submit information to the government.[39] Under this new exemption, it is plausible that government could—while intending to protect information about the risk to critical infrastructure—limit the flow of information necessary to protect the public from earthquakes, hurricanes, chemical spills, and other disasters. For example, an area of the electrical transmission system that is vulnerable to a terrorist bomb could also be the weak point in the system for earthquakes or wildfires.

Section 891 of the HSA addresses information sharing between governmental entities, and appears to establish a category of information that is unclassified but "sensitive" because of its source (e.g., human intelligence assets) or its nature (e.g., terrorist threat activity).[40] By adding this section to the law, Congress intended to encourage federal intelligence agencies to share relevant homeland security information that could be unclassified with state and local governments, while at the same time providing for the protection of sources and methods used to acquire such information. Congress apparently was responding to complaints by local governments—in particular law enforcement agencies—about the paucity of information flowing to them from their federal counterparts regarding threats to homeland security.

With these two limits on disclosure of information, Congress intended to create a legal environment in which companies would feel safe sharing with the government information about systems' vulnerabilities, and the federal government would be encouraged to share this information with other governmental entities. Congress may have been successful in protecting information from potential terrorists, but there are detractors to this shift.

Senators Leahy, Levin, Jeffords, Lieberman, and Byrd proposed a "Restore Freedom of Information Act," which would have narrowed the exemptions provided by the HSA.[41] This illustrates that some in Congress are still trying to seek the appropriate balance between public disclosure and confidentiality.[42]

For lawyers practicing at local and state levels of government, it should be noted that the federal statutory and regulatory actions could have impacts beyond issues of preemption. Some state public records acts have a bridging exemption to other laws that limit information disclosure. For example, California law exempts from disclosure requirements records that are "exempted or prohibited from release by federal or state law." Therefore, for a state like California, information such as that collected to administer federal homeland security grants—or otherwise developed to evaluate terrorist risk—may be excluded based upon the legal bridge between state law and the exclusions of the Federal Homeland Security Act.[43]

An Approach to Representing Clients on Homeland Security Information

First, review the law on a case-by-case basis. The importance of this basic legal practice cannot be overstated when addressing the area of public records disclosure. As this chapter illustrates, legislatures, administrative agencies, and the courts are all active in this area. Further, the interplay between state and federal law, as in the case of critical infrastructure and nuclear energy information, requires an awareness of developments in multiple legal arenas.

Evaluate what has already been disclosed. Under most state legal schemes for public records, any confidentiality privilege or exemption is eliminated, or at least seriously eroded, by disclosing information outside the confines of the governmental agency. It is important to consider the agency's policy about information handling. Because records are often released by the lowest ranking clerk, or from a remote office, determine whether any prior release of records was intentional or inadvertent. In some cases, releasing records to another governmental agency or private company under government contract would not jeopardize a privilege.

Determine the effects of release of any records where the confidentiality requirements were established by agreement. Also, be aware of restrictions that may apply from other jurisdictions. State, federal, and private sector grants may require recipients to adhere to certain information practices or laws of other jurisdictions. Keep in mind that the interaction between these agreements and local laws might jeopardize funding if the agreements are contrary to state or federal law.

Finally, use another basic legal practice: Review with your client the actual effect of penalties for disclosure or failure to disclose. Under most state and federal disclosure schemes, including FOIA, the redress for a governmental agency that declines to release a record is a form of writ requesting a court to review the agency's decision and there are no penalties for the agency or governmental official. On the other hand, under some of the so-called 3(b) exemptions to FOIA (referring to 5 U.S.C. 552(b)(3)(B)), there are significant penalties on covered individuals for their unauthorized release of records. For example, the federal Clean Air Act's prohibition on the release of chemical hazard information can carry very large organizational and personal fines.

Conclusion

At the beginning of the twenty-first century, legislators, governmental officials, and the general public are considering the correct balance between the public's right to know about the potential risks that could befall any community and the preparations their government has made to protect them from these same risks. Balanced against this is the need to keep information that could be used as a tool for terrorists out of the public domain. This is a departure from the two previous decades that witnessed a strong trend toward providing information to people to enhance their understanding of their surroundings and enable them to take action that could lessen their vulnerability to everything from earthquakes to chemical spills. Judging from the heightened momentum to adopt new laws in this area since 9/11, as well as the continued threats of terrorist action, it may be a long time before we shift back toward fuller disclosure.

As we lean toward nondisclosure, there is no doubt we should consider the potential costs. For many years, we have assumed that we could protect people, save lives, reduce injuries, and minimize the impacts to property and the environment by disclosing information about myriad natural and technological disasters, thus reducing the costs to individuals and their governments. This disclosure has been based on two premises: That more information in people's hands will encourage them to take protective measures (strap down their water heaters, move to a safer neighborhood, lobby their planning agencies, etc.), and provide them with a tool to hold their government accountable for addressing the disaster risks surrounding them. With terrorism, however, we may have encountered a risk under which more information in more people's hands may cost more in decreased levels of safety, because our assessments, plans, and many other types of records can be used against us.[44]

NOTES

1. The views and opinions in this paper are not intended to reflect the policies of the Office of Emergency Services or the state of California.

2. Laura Blumfield, *Dissertation Could Be Security Threat: Student's Maps Illustrate Concerns About Public Information*, WASH. POST, July 8, 2003.

3. *Id*. The article quotes Richard Clarke, the former White House counterterrorism coordinator, as saying that the student author of the program should "turn it in to his professor, get his grade—and then they both should burn it."

4. John O'Looney, Beyond Maps: GIS and Decision Making in Local Government 106-107, 110-111 (ESRI Press, 2000). *See also* Gary Amdahl, Disaster Response: GIS for Public Safety 165-211 (ESRI Press 2001).

5. Cal. Health & Safety Code § 25500-25545 (2005). This law established a statewide program for California that, in addition to requiring businesses and local governments to develop chemical inventories and emergency plans, required most of the information to be readily available to the public. California law allows exclusion of facility site maps and proprietary information from public disclosure if some specific criteria are met.

6. 42 U.S.C. § 11001-11050 (1986). This federal program built on similar programs in several states, including California and New Jersey, and added an element whereby emergency services personnel, the media, and the general public could participate in the planning process through Local Emergency Planning Committees.

7. 42 U.S.C. § 7412(r).

8. 40 C.F.R. Part 68.25.

9. *See id*. § 68.210.

10. Cal. Health & Safety Code § 25535.2.

11. U.S. Environmental Protection Agency, Chemical Emergency Preparedness and Prevention Office, Emergency Planning and Community Right-to-Know Act Overview (June 12, 2003), http://yosemite.epa.gov/oswer/ceppoweb.nsf/content/epcraOverview.htm. For example, well over two thousand people died or suffered serious injury from the accidental release of methyl isocyanate at a Union Carbide facility in Bhopal, India, in December 1983.

12. For example, Congress and the Federal Emergency Management Agency established a pre-disaster mitigation program in several communities with a key component being the development of maps to inform the general public about the risks of commonly recurring natural hazards, such as floods, hurricanes, and seismic events. *See* 42 U.S.C § 5133.

13. Cal. Civ. Code § 1102-1103 (2005).

14. For example, in the Electronic Freedom of Information Act Amendments of 1996, Pub. L. No. 104-231 (1996), Congress made a finding that FOIA was intended "to require agencies of the Federal Government to make certain agency information available for public inspection and copying and to establish and enable enforcement of the right of any person to obtain access to the records of such agencies, subject to statutory exemptions, for any public or private purpose . . . ."

15. For example, under California's Public Records Act (Cal. Gov't Code § 6250 (2005), the legislature declares, "information concerning the conduct of the people's business is a fundamental and necessary right of every person in the state."

16. FOIA contains approximately eight statutory exemptions, in addition to numerous exemptions contained in other program areas. California's Public Records Act contains approximately twenty seven specific statutory exemptions.

17. Eric Lichtblau, *Justice Dept. Lists Use of New Power to Fight Terror*, N.Y. Times, May 21, 2003, at A1.

18. Pub. L. No. 106-40, 113 Stat. 207 (1999).

19. 40 U.S.C. 7412(r)(7)(H).

20. Introduction to 40 C.F.R. Chapter IV, at 48108. These are the regulations that the EPA and the U.S. Department of Justice adopted to implement restrictions on the release of off-site consequence analyses.

21. *Id.* The rule did not preclude dissemination of all off-site information on the Internet. For example, the EPA still could electronically make available information about the passive and active mitigation systems that the facility considered when developing its off-site consequence analysis. Apparently, the EPA believes this information would not significantly assist potential terrorists and would assist the public in evaluating the facility's efforts to reduce the potential for an off-site release of hazardous chemicals. (*See id.,* at 48125, 48133.)

22. 145 Cong. Rec. H6083 (daily ed. July 21, 1999) (statement of Rep. Dingell).

23. State and local governments would still be limited in the release of information by other requirements of federal law. For example, federal law prohibits the release of any proprietary information contained in materials a chemical facility submits. 42 U.S.C. 11042.

24. 2002 Wash. Sess. Laws, ch. 172, § 1.

25. Attorney General Janet Reno, *FOIA Memorandum of October 1993*, XIV U.S. Dep't of Justice FOIA Update, No. 3. In her memorandum, General Reno stated, "The Department will no longer defend an agency's withholding of information merely because there is a substantial legal basis for doing so. Rather, in determining whether or not to defend a nondisclosure decision, we will apply a presumption of disclosure."

26. Attorney General John Ashcroft, *FOIA Memorandum of October 2001*, XIX U.S. Dep't of Justice FOIA Update, No. 4.

27. Gil Shochat, *State Agencies Pull Information From Web*, The Reporters Committee for Freedom of the Press, Fall 2002, at 41.

28. A number of organizations, such as an entity known as Internet Archive, systematically archive large parts of the information on the Internet. Also, many individual Internet users download substantial portions of Web sites to their own computer systems.

29. Mimi Moon, *States also limit access in wake of 9/11*, 26 The News Media and the Law, No. 1, at 28 (Winter 2002).

30. These summaries do not include all the details of the individual state code, e.g., the exemptions to the exemption. They are provided to give the reader a general sense of the type of records some states have chosen to exempt from public dissemination.

31. Idaho Code Ann. § 9-340B(4)(b).

32. Ohio Rev. Code Ann. § 149.433(A).

33. Mich. Comp. Laws § 15.243.

34. Cal. Gov't Code § 6254(aa). California law provides a general exemption from disclosure that predates the 9/11 incidents and allows for nondisclosure when the public interest in confidentiality clearly outweighs the public's interest in disclosure. (*See also*, Cal. Gov't Code § 6255.)

35. Md. Code Ann., State Gov't § 10-618.

35. 6 U.S.C.A. § 132. This also is referred to as the Critical Infrastructure Information Act of 2002.

36. 6 C.F.R. § 29.2.

37. *Id.*

38. 6 C.F.R. § 29.8(d).

39. The Homeland Security Information Sharing Act, 6 U.S.C.A. §§ 481-482, requires the development of procedures to implement the process of sharing sensitive security information. As of this writing, procedures have not been promulgated, but President Bush has delegated the responsibility to the Secretary of Homeland Security. (*See* Exec. Order No. 13,311, 68 Fed. Reg. 45,149 (July 29, 2003).)

40. *Restore FOIA Bill: An Important Step in Fixing the Homeland Security Act*, OMB Watch, March 12, 2003, *available at* http://www.ombwatch.org/article/articleview/1378 (last visited Sept. 23, 2005).

41. *Id.*

42.   CAL. GOV'T CODE § 6254(k).

43.   Implicit in this question is the assumption that the information collected and the actions taken by people and governments to protect themselves from disasters other than terrorist acts are similar to the actions they might take in reducing vulnerability to terrorism. This is probably a fair assumption given the paucity of unique actions that individuals can take to protect themselves from terrorism. Even the actions of state and local governments—except for increased law enforcement presence, efforts toward better intelligence collection, some specialized equipment first responders can use to detect terrorist acts, and additional personnel protection for those responders—seems limited to the same types of actions taken to prepare for earthquakes, hurricanes, and chemical spills.

CHAPTER 2

Protecting Airports: A Review of Security Measures Used to Protect the Nation's Airports and Challenges Airports Have Faced Because of the Increased Security Regulations

by Arthur P. Berg[1]

Introduction

Almost all commercial airports in the United States are owned and operated by states, counties, cities, and independent governmental authorities.[2] Public entities operate airports with the goal of providing affordable air service to as many destinations as possible for the traveling public, and especially for residents of the communities around them.[3] Airport directors are accountable to their boards, local governments, and communities to financially manage the airport and maintain competitive air service.[4]

The Aviation and Transportation Security Act (ATSA),[5] enacted shortly after the events of 9/11, made significant changes to airport security operations. The ATSA created the Transportation Security Administration (TSA) to oversee aviation security.[6] The ATSA listed numerous duties and powers of the under secretary of the TSA to ensure aviation security. The Homeland Security Act of 2002[7] brought the TSA under the authority of the newly created Department of Homeland Security (DHS).[8]

The Responsibilities and Authority
of the Transportation Security Administration (TSA)

The TSA is responsible for aviation security, as well as related research and development activities.[9] It has been given extensive powers and duties, among them the major responsibility of screening passengers and cargo—which includes day-to-day operations; training, hiring, and testing screeners; and developing standards for hiring screeners.[10] The TSA also is in charge of assessing and distributing intelligence information, assessing threats to transportation and developing plans for dealing with those threats, enforcing security regulations, undertaking research and development activities, inspecting and maintaining security facilities, overseeing the implementation of airport security measures, requiring background checks for screening personnel and for individuals with access to secure areas, and much more.[11]

One of the TSA's duties is to manage security information.[12] Congress instructed the TSA to enter into memoranda of understanding with other agencies to share or cross-check data on individuals identified on federal agency databases who may pose a risk to transportation or national security.[13] It also is responsible for establishing procedures to notify the Federal Aviation Administration (FAA), state and local law enforcement officials, and airport or airline security officials of the identity of individuals known to pose a safety risk.[14] In addition, the TSA is responsible—in consultation with others—for establishing policies that require air carriers to use governmental information to identify people who may be a security risk and, once identified, to take appropriate action.[15] In pursuing these objectives, the TSA shall consider the views of the National Transportation Safety Board.[16]

During a national emergency, the TSA has additional responsibilities.[17] It is authorized to coordinate domestic transportation, to coordinate and oversee the transportation-related responsibilities of other federal departments and agencies (excluding the military and defense departments), and to coordinate and provide notice to government agencies about threats to transportation.[18] The TSA also can issue regulations or security directives without notice or comment if such a regulation or order is necessary to protect transportation security.[19]

The TSA also is authorized to make acquisitions and to accept transfers of funds from other federal agencies.[20] The TSA may acquire any real or personal property or services as it deems necessary.[21]

Employees of the TSA or of other federal agencies may serve as law enforcement officers of the TSA.[22] Such officers may make arrests without warrants when there is probable cause.[23] They also may carry firearms, and seek and execute warrants.[24]

The TSA is also responsible for the deployment of federal air marshals.[25] While it may provide for marshals on every passenger flight,[26] the TSA should provide them on every flight that the secretary has determined to be a high security risk, giving priority to nonstop, long distance flights.[27] In addition, the TSA is responsible for the training, supervision, and equipment of federal air marshals.[28] Air carriers must provide seats for marshals at no cost to the government, and shall provide—on a space-available basis—no-cost seats to off-duty marshals who are going home.[29] The TSA may enter into agreements with federal, state, and local agencies allowing trained law enforcement personnel to carry a firearm and be ready to assist federal air marshals.[30]

The TSA also is involved in the training of air carrier crew members.[31] Air carriers shall carry out basic security training to prepare crew members for potential threat conditions.[32] The training program is subject to the approval of the TSA, and the TSA shall monitor training programs and order air carriers to modify them to reflect new or different threats.[33] The TSA is also responsible for developing a voluntary self-defense training program for flight and cabin crew members.[34]

The TSA, in consultation with other agencies, shall also make regulations to protect passengers and property against violence and piracy.[35] When making such regulations, the TSA shall consider whether a regulation is consistent with protecting passengers and with the public interest, and shall require a uniform procedure for searching and detaining passengers that ensures their safety and courteous and efficient treatment.[36]

The TSA also is responsible for developing and carrying out a program to research and develop procedures and technologies to protect against terrorist acts.[37] This program shall expand the research, development, and implementation of technologies and procedures to confront terrorist threats.[38] The TSA may make grants to research facilities and may make cooperative agreements with governmental authorities.[39]

Additionally, the TSA must biennially submit a report to Congress on the effectiveness of procedures to screen passengers and property and a summary of the assessments conducted by the TSA.[40]

Security Measures Imposed on Airports, TSA's Role in Implementing and Overseeing These Measures, and the Status of Implementing Them

Airport Perimeter and Access Control

The TSA has various obligations, responsibilities, and authority relating to airport perimeter and access control.[41] After consulting with the airport operator and law enforcement authorities, the TSA may deploy personnel to secure areas of the airport in order to counter risks to aircraft operations or to meet national security concerns.[42] In deciding where to deploy such personnel, the security needs of air traffic control facilities, parked aircraft, aircraft servicing equipment, aircraft supplies, automobile parking areas within airport perimeters, and access and transition areas at airports shall be considered.[43] Counsel for airport operators will have an opportunity to impact TSA decisions on such issues. The TSA also may deploy federal law enforcement personnel to meet security concerns by entering into an agreement with the head of a federal law enforcement agency.[44]

The TSA also has the duty to establish procedures to protect the safety and integrity of all persons providing services related to passenger or intrastate air transportation, of all supplies placed aboard such aircraft, and of all persons providing such supplies.[45] These responsibilities are likely to have significant cost implications for airport operators and air carriers. For instance, the TSA may require the use of biometric or other technology that positively identifies employees and law enforcement officers entering secure areas.[46] Actual procedures used at airports are to be assessed and tested for compliance with access control requirements. Enforcement actions are to be taken when there is noncompliance with the access control requirements.[47]

The TSA also is responsible for working with airport operators and air carriers to strengthen access control points in secured areas—such as air traffic control areas, maintenance areas, crew lounges, baggage handling areas, concessions, and catering delivery areas—to ensure the security of passengers and aircraft, and is responsible for considering the use of technologies to identify individuals based on their unique characteristics.[48] Additionally, the TSA shall recommend to airport operators and air carriers commercially available measures to prevent access to secure areas of the airport by unauthorized persons, and shall provide airports with a twelve-month deployment strategy for currently available technology.[49] The TSA also shall establish pilot programs in no less than twenty airports to test and evaluate new and emerging technology for providing access control and other security protections for secure areas.[50]

Additionally, the TSA is responsible for reducing the risks posed by airport workers. The TSA shall require screening or inspection of all individuals, goods, vehicles, and equipment before such items enter a secured area of an airport, and shall prescribe requirements for such screening or inspection that are at least as protective as screening procedures for passengers and baggage.[51] The TSA shall direct air carriers and airports to develop security awareness programs for employees, ground crews, air carrier agents, and other individuals employed at the airport.[52] Vendors with direct access to the airfield and aircraft also will be required to develop security programs.[53] Additionally, the TSA is responsible for issuing regulations requiring employment investigations, including criminal history records checks for screeners, flight crew members, or individuals seeking unescorted access to "secure identification display areas" (SIDA) of the airport,[54] which it has already done.[55] The TSA may not employ screeners and individuals who have unescorted access to secure areas who have been criminally convicted of a disqualifying offense in the previous ten-year period.[56]

The TSA has been working on both access control and perimeter security. It has issued new security directives to better control access to SIDAs within the airport.[57] These directives include reducing the number of operational doors that lead from a public area to a SIDA, enhancing security—such as through closed circuit television and contract security guards—and limiting the number of vendor employees working in the SIDA who have unescorted access.[58] The TSA also has been exploring the threat of "man portable air defense systems" (MANPADs) as part of its strategy to improve perimeter security. The Department of Homeland Security has entered into an agreement with several contractors to test prototypes and determine whether a counter-MANPAD technology could be deployed to address the threats to commercial aircraft.[59]

A June 2004 report by the Government Accountability Office (GAO) described the steps the TSA has taken to improve perimeter and access control security, as well as areas in which further steps can and should be taken to improve security.[60] The TSA has been evaluating the security of airport perimeters and the controls limiting access into secured areas through vulnerability and compliance inspections at various airports, and has identified some security concerns.[61] Where the TSA found noncompliance with security requirements, it addressed most issues through counseling, but some cases warranted administrative action and civil penalties.[62] The GAO noted, though, that the TSA has not assessed the effectiveness of the penalties, developed a plan for completing the assessments, or determined how the results of the security evaluations will be used to improve security.[63]

The TSA has provided some airports with funds to improve perimeter and access control security.[64] It also has been evaluating technologies such as biometric identification systems, but the GAO noted that the TSA has not developed a plan for implementing new technologies or balancing the costs and usefulness of these technologies with the security needs of airports.[65] Moreover, the GAO noted that the TSA has not fully complied with the ATSA requirements.[66] The TSA has not required fingerprint-based criminal history checks for all airport workers.[67] Nor does the TSA require security-awareness training for all airport workers, even though these are ATSA requirements.[68] The TSA also has not required vendors with direct access to the airfield and aircraft to develop security programs.[69] The TSA has said that the costs of such measures and the time-consuming requirements of the rule-making process have kept it from implementing these measures.[70]

Screening of Passengers and Property

The TSA also is responsible for the screening of passengers and property, including carry-on and checked baggage, and other articles that are carried onto an aircraft.[71] Screening must take place before boarding and generally must be performed by federal government employees.[72] Uniformed federal personnel of the TSA shall supervise all screening operations.[73] The law requires that a system must be established to screen all checked baggage at airports.[74] According to the law, the TSA shall take action to ensure that explosive detection systems (EDS) are deployed, and that baggage is screened by such systems.[75] The law provides that until EDSs are available, alternative means to screen checked baggage—such as matching bags to people, manual searches, canine searches, and other means approved by the TSA—shall be used to screen checked baggage.[76]

The TSA also may order the deployment of law enforcement personnel authorized to carry firearms at each airport security screening location to ensure passenger safety and national security.[77] It shall, at least, order one law enforcement officer at each airport security screening location, and shall order more law enforcement personnel at the largest airports if additional deployments appear necessary to protect passenger safety and national security.[78] The TSA also shall designate and station a federal security manager at each airport.[79] The manager shall oversee the screening of passengers and property at airports.[80]

ATSA has established standards for the training and employment of screening personnel.[81] The TSA must establish a hiring and training program for screening personnel, and shall review and revise as necessary any rules or regulations related to hiring security screening personnel.[82] The law lists some specific qualifications for individuals to be hired by the United States as security screening personnel.[83] Such individuals must undergo background checks, and must be determined not to pose a threat to national security.[84] The TSA also will develop an examination that such individuals must take, and those examined must perform at least on a satisfactory level.[85] Once hired, the TSA must conduct annual proficiency reviews of screeners.[86] The TSA may enter into an agreement with other agencies to assist in the training of security personnel.[87] The TSA shall develop a training plan, including minimum hours of classroom instruction and minimum hours of on-the-job instruction that security screeners must complete successfully.[88] Such a plan must include certain minimum requirements.[89] Security screeners must undergo training in the use of equipment they may operate, and training to ensure they are proficient in the most up-to-date technology.[90]

EVALUATING A PILOT PRIVATE SCREENING ALTERNATIVE. ATSA required a two-year pilot program in which airports would review the use of private screeners in place of federal screeners.[91] In November 2002, the TSA entered into private screening contracts for two-year pilot screening programs at San Francisco International, Kansas City International, Greater Rochester International, Jackson Hole, and Tupelo Airports.[92] The report that compared the private screeners' performance against that of the TSA's federal screeners found that (1) there was no evidence that any of the privately screened airports performed below the average level of federalized airports, (2) costs for privately screened operations were not significantly different from the estimated federal screening costs at the same airport, and (3) at the larger airports, passengers had less confidence in private screening operations but their average wait time was slightly shorter.[93]

The Department of Homeland Security's Office of the Inspector General (OIG) reviewed the TSA's role in the pilot program.[94] The OIG found that the level of the TSA's involvement limited any role that the contractors may have had in improving aspects of the program because the TSA had to evaluate and approve applicants through assessment centers established ad hoc for that purpose.[95] Additionally, when contractors needed more staff, they were forced to wait for the TSA to reestablish an assessment center.[96] These problems resulted in understaffing, excessive overtime, and poor morale.[97] Another problem was that local TSA officials managed and monitored the contractors, but when these local officials needed guidance there was no central authority at the TSA to consult, resulting in different guidance being provided on similar issues at the various sites.[98] Further, the TSA had neither developed nor implemented standards to compare private with federalized screeners' performance.[99] The OIG ultimately recommended that the TSA develop a plan to compare the performance of federal and private screeners, and that the TSA establish greater flexibility to test new methods.[100]

AIRPORT OPT-OUT PRIVATE SCREENING OPTION. ATSA established that at the end of the two-year pilot program—on November 19, 2004—any airport may apply to have the screening of passengers and property at airports be carried out by a qualified private screening company.[101] Under the opt-out program, the contractors must meet the employment and compensation standards and performance requirements that apply to federal security screeners, though there is some flexibility in the types of benefits and compensation packages that may be offered.[102] There is no limit to the number of airports that can submit applications.[103] Funding for the private security contractors comes from the same pool as the funding for federal screening operations nationwide.[104] An airport can form a private company to apply to be a qualified vendor and bid on contacts.[105] An airport company that contracts with TSA to provide screening may subcontract with another TSA-approved screening services provider.[106] It is unclear how many airports will be approved for participation in the opt-out program.[107]

Under this opt-out, or Screening Partnership Program, the TSA administrator retains important controls over the screening process. First, any airport opt-out is subject to the approval of the administrator.[108] Second, the contract is entered into between the private security company and the TSA; the airport is not a party to the contract.[109] Third, the TSA continues to provide federal security directors to oversee the screening process.[110] Finally, the administrator is authorized to terminate any contract if the company has failed repeatedly to comply with any standard, regulation, or law.[111]

Under the opt-out program, although it is the airport that initially applies to participate, the airport's involvement is very limited.[112] The TSA must ensure that the screening company meets federal standards. The TSA establishes the "qualified vendors list," as outlined in the Guidance on Screening Partnership Program (guidance).[113] The guidance states that the airport will participate in the selection of the screening company, but exact parameters of that involvement appear to consist of only an advisory role.[114] Once an application is approved and a contractor is selected, the contract is entered into between the TSA and the screening company, and the screening company is paid with federal funds.[115] The supervision of the screening program is conducted by federal agents.[116] In fact, of the twenty operational elements of the screening program identified in the guidance, only one—performance evaluation—is identified as a responsibility of the airport.[117] Even that responsibility is shared with the TSA.[118] Finally, the TSA retains the authority to terminate the contract if the screening company fails to perform its obligations.[119]

POTENTIAL PRIVATE LIABILITY UNDER OPT-OUT PRIVATE SCREENING OPTION. It is unclear whether an airport that has opted out could be liable for mistakes made by private screeners.[120] Undoubtedly, an airport choosing to opt out is at greater risk of liability than an airport using federal screeners. However, it is likely that an airport's risk of liability will be limited. One reason is because, as discussed above, the federal government still retains substantial control of screening, even under an opt-out program. But possible claims could include that the airport knew or should have known that private screeners would be less reliable or less effective than federal screeners.

The 2002 Support Anti-terrorism by Fostering Effective Technologies Act (SAFETY Act) may help protect airports from liability.[121] The SAFETY Act was passed to encourage the development and use of technology against terrorism by limiting liability that sellers of qualified anti-terrorism technology products and services could incur.[122] Airports could be protected under the SAFETY Act because DHS has determined that screening is considered a service relating to qualified anti-terrorism technology. If airports are protected by the SAFETY Act, they could not incur punitive damages, and noneconomic damages would have to be awarded proportional to the percentage of responsibility of the defendant. Any award would be reduced by the amount of collateral source compensation received by the plaintiff, such as life insurance.[123] In addition, the SAFETY Act has been interpreted by DHS to limit causes of action to those who sell qualified anti-terrorism technology products or services.[124] This could be important. Airports are not themselves providing screening services and, therefore, likely would be protected under the SAFETY Act. Although the SAFETY Act has the potential to provide protection to airports that opt out, in the absence of favorable court rulings to that effect there is no guarantee of such protection. Also, at the present time there would appear to be no way that an airport could condition its opt-out on the selection by TSA of a screening company that had SAFETY Act approval. Based on TSA's control over private screeners and the potential for protection under the SAFETY Act, an airport's risk of liability for opting out of the federal program would appear to be relatively low. Nevertheless, even a low risk of liability would be unacceptable to most airports because the potential for damages is enormous in the event of a terrorist attack.

POLICIES AND PROCEDURES OF THE OPT-OUT PROGRAM. The TSA has been developing key procedures and policies related to the opt-out program.[125] The TSA has released guidelines describing the process for determining how and when private screening contractors will be evaluated and selected for the program.[126] The TSA has been developing internal guidance for managing the opt-out program, and has been communicating with interested parties to solicit information relating to the program and to provide these parties with information about the program.[127] The TSA also has been developing measures to assess the airports that participate in the opt-out program, as well as individual contractors performing screening services.[128] It is also considering the option of a partial opt-out program, although there are concerns with the operational and legal challenges that such a program could present.[129]

The TSA has outlined the procedures to follow in implementing the opt-out program. As mentioned above, airports could begin submitting applications for participating in the opt-out program on November 19, 2004.[130] The TSA is responsible for developing lists of qualified potential contractors.[131] To be a qualified contractor, the contractor must pass both ATSA and TSA requirements.[132] Contractors must prove they are qualified screening companies—meaning they are privately owned and controlled by United States citizens—and must provide benefits and compensation not less than the level provided by the federal government.[133] Contractors also must agree that federal government employees will be given a hiring preference and demonstrate their financial capability.[134]

After the TSA approves airports for the opt-out program, it is responsible for issuing a request for proposals to prequalified potential contractors, and then selecting private contractors for the opt-out program.[135] Those invited to submit a request for proposal will be awarded a "basic ordering agreement" when they are selected to participate in the opt-out program.[136] The TSA will select private contractors for the opt-out program based on business management, technical merit, past performance, and cost.[137]

DEPLOYMENT OF CHECKED BAGGAGE SCREENING SYSTEMS. The ATSA required the TSA to screen all checked baggage with explosive detection systems by December 31, 2002.[138] When it became clear that this deadline would not be met, the Homeland Security Act of 2002 extended the deadline for airports to screen all baggage for explosives to December 31, 2003.[139] The TSA continued to face challenges in meeting that deadline.[140]

In order to satisfy the requirement of deploying equipment to screen 100 percent of checked baggage for explosives, the TSA deployed two types of screening equipment: Explosives detection systems (EDS), which use computer-aided tomography X-rays to recognize explosives, and (2) Explosives trace detection (ETD), which uses chemical analysis to detect the vapors and residues of explosives.[141] From November 2001 to September 2004, the TSA obligated about $2.5 billion for procuring and installing explosive detection equipment and for making associated airport modifications to accommodate such equipment.[142] The TSA placed 1,200 EDS machines and 6,000 ETD machines at airports across the county.[143] However, much of this equipment was placed in airport lobbies, and was not integrated with the airports' baggage conveyor systems because of the costs of such integrated equipment and because of the costs of making airport modifications to accommodate such equipment.[144] (Such integrated systems often are referred to as "in-line" systems.) Additionally, the TSA often chose to deploy ETD machines instead of EDS machines.[145]

Numerous operational problems resulted from using stand-alone EDS machines and ETD machines, rather than in-line EDS machines. First, in comparison with in-line EDS machines, the stand-alone machines require more screeners to work them and result in fewer bags screened per hour.[146] This is due to the fact that the stand-alone machines require that screeners obtain the passenger's baggage, lift the bags onto the machines, appropriately screen the bags, and then return the bags to the air carriers.[147] In-line EDS machines are attached to an airport's baggage conveyor system and, therefore, such automated screening requires less human labor.[148] The least efficient machines are the ETD machines, since the screener needs to manually screen the baggage by swabbing an area of the bag and then placing the swab in the ETD machine.[149] Thus, the stand-alone machines have resulted in operational inefficiencies because they are more labor and time-intensive. Other problems that have resulted from using stand-alone machines, which often were located in airport lobbies, were passenger congestion and associated security concerns.[150] Additionally, stand-alone machines that require screeners to carry passengers' bags have resulted in an increase in workplace injuries.[151]

A March 2005 GAO report assessed the TSA's progress in deploying checked baggage screening systems. The report discussed that a significant impediment to installing in-line EDS machines is the lack of resources.[152] (This issue is further discussed in the section of this chapter entitled "Challenges Facing the Airports.") The GAO recommended initiatives that the TSA should implement in the deployment of screening systems. The GAO recommended that the TSA conduct a systematic analysis for determining where to install in-line EDS machines or, if in-line EDS machines are not economically feasible, where to replace less-efficient ETD machines with stand-alone EDS machines.[153] Where installing in-line EDS machines may not be economically feasible, stand-alone EDS machines are often a better alternative to ETD machines since stand-alone EDS machines can screen more bags an hour and require less human labor than ETD machines.[154] The GAO suggested that the TSA determine which airports would most benefit from the installation of new checked baggage equipment.[155]

Air Cargo Operations

Under ATSA, the TSA is to provide for screening of all property, cargo, carry-on, and checked baggage carried onto passenger aircraft, and is to establish a system to screen or ensure the security of freight carried in all-cargo aircraft as soon as possible.[156] The TSA created the Known Shipper Program, which prohibits the operator of passenger aircraft from accepting cargo from shippers who were unknown.[157] Congress has recognized that this program need not be carried out by a federal government employee, but rather may be carried out by aircraft carriers.[158] The TSA conducted analyses of internal and external threats, risk vulnerability assessments, and security measures currently in place, to assess and decide how to enhance air cargo security.[159] The TSA has submitted a notice of proposed rulemaking that contains measures to enhance the security of air cargo.[160]

The TSA's proposed rule would strengthen air cargo security in a variety of ways. The new rule would require security threat assessments for individuals with unescorted access to cargo.[161] It would also codify cargo screening requirements and strengthen the Known Shipper Program.[162] It would require aircraft operators to prevent unauthorized access to the operational area of the aircraft while loading and unloading cargo.[163] The proposed rule would also establish a security program specific to aircraft carriers in all-cargo operations with aircraft of a maximum certificated takeoff weight of more than 45,500 kilograms.[164] Additionally, the rule would enhance security requirements for indirect air carriers, and would strengthen foreign air carriers' security requirements.[165] Finally, the rule would require aircraft carriers under a full or all-cargo program to accept cargo only from the shipper directly or from an entity with a comparable security program.[166]

The TSA also has taken other steps to improve cargo security. The TSA has increased the number of air cargo security inspectors and is developing a Freight Assessment System to identify elevated-risk cargo that should be inspected.[167] The TSA also is pursuing research and development opportunities relating to new technologies that could be used to screen air cargo.[168]

General Aviation

General aviation security measures include various activities, aircraft types, and airports.[169] It covers aircraft operated for recreational, business, instructional, corporate, air taxi and tours, and miscellaneous other uses such as medical services and aerial observation.[170] Under ATSA, some of the TSA's security responsibilities with respect to commercial aviation also apply to general aviation.[171] These provisions include receiving, assessing, and distributing intelligence information, assessing threats related to transportation security, developing policies, plans, and strategies for dealing with such threats, enforcing security-related regulations and requirements, and overseeing the implementation—and ensuring the adequacy—of security measures.[172]

Some provisions relate to general aviation specifically, although not many. One requirement in the ATSA that specifically applied to general aviation was that foreign student pilots seeking aircraft training undergo a background check when the aircraft weighed 12,500 pounds or more.[173] The Department of Justice issued regulations requiring that flight training providers ensure that foreigners seeking training in aircraft of 12,500 pounds or more submit a Department of Justice Flight Training Candidate Checks Program form and get fingerprinted.[174] The Foreign Terrorist Tracking Task Force performs the background check, and then notifies the flight-training provider whether the student has been cleared and may begin training.[175] The Vision 100—Century of Aviation Reauthorization Act (Vision 100) transferred responsibility for conducting background checks to the TSA and changed the background check requirement so that all foreign student pilots must receive background checks.[176]

ATSA also directed the TSA to promulgate new rules for charter operations.[177] According to the regulations, the "twelve-five rule" requires scheduled or charter services of 12,500 pounds or more to implement security procedures similar to those of scheduled commercial airlines, and the "private charter rule" requires private charters using aircraft of 45,500 kilograms or more—or that have 61 or more seats—to implement many of the same security procedures that the major airlines have.[178] However, the GAO has found that the TSA faces challenges in monitoring compliance with these regulations, and that only selected requirements have been expanded from commercial air carriers to public and private charter aircraft.[179]

The FAA and the TSA also have implemented various regulations relating to the screening and validation of pilot and student pilot identities.[180] Individuals interested in serving as flight crew members must complete fingerprint-based criminal history records checks.[181] All pilots must carry and present picture identification along with pilot certificates.[182] Additionally, the FAA may suspend, revoke, or refuse to issue an airman certificate to anyone if the TSA determines that such a person is a threat to transportation security.[183]

The GAO's November 2004 report on general aviation security lists numerous observations relating to the present state of general aviation security.[184]

First, it found that the TSA and other federal agencies have not conducted an overall systematic assessment of threats to general aviation.[185] While the TSA has conducted a limited assessment of threats and vulnerability assessments at selected airports, a systematic assessment has not been conducted.[186] The TSA intends to implement a risk management approach to assess threats and is developing an online vulnerability self-assessment tool, but has not developed a plan to implement this tool.[187]

Second, while the TSA has been working with industry associations to develop security guidelines and distribute security information, the security information distributed by the TSA is often not received and is overly general.[188] Third, the TSA and the FAA could take further steps to enhance security.[189] For example, while there are regulations concerning flight training programs, there are limitations in the process for inspecting these programs.[190]

The GAO also noted that a lack of funds may hinder the TSA's efforts to establish new security efforts at general aviation airports.[191] These airports have used some federal funds to make security improvements, but have had to fund most security improvements on their own.[192]

The GAO reported the status of several other general aviation security measures. While the TSA and the FAA have implemented airspace restrictions, they have not established procedures for reviewing these restrictions.[193] Various general aviation stakeholders have taken measures to enhance aviation security.[194] Industry associations have worked with the TSA to launch the Airport Watch Program and the TSA Access Certificate Program.[195] Some states have provided funding or established further security regulations.[196] Many general aviation airports have also taken the initiative to enhance security, such as by installing fencing and lighting.[197] The GAO recommended that a plan be developed for implementing a risk management approach to identify threats and vulnerabilities, that specific actions to be taken be communicated in as specific a manner as is possible, and that a process be instituted to review and reevaluate flight restrictions.[198]

Other Security Measures Being Undertaken by TSA

A measure being tested in a pilot program at selected airports across the country is the Registered Traveler Program.[199] According to the Registered Traveler Program, participants will submit their personal information to the TSA, such as address, phone numbers, date of birth, and biometric data, including a fingerprint and/or an iris scan.[200] A security assessment of these participants will be conducted.[201] Individuals participating in the program will pass through a biometric kiosk and go through primary screening, but they generally will be able to avoid secondary screening.[202] The purpose of the program is to ease congestion, reduce wait time, and to use screeners more efficiently and effectively.[203] One criticism of the program is that the TSA currently uses different technologies at different airports so that a registered traveler is only a registered traveler in one airport.[204] As of February 2005, the results of the registered traveler program were in the process of being analyzed.[205]

The TSA also has been developing a passenger prescreening program called Secure Flight.[206] Secure Flight will identify passengers flying domestically who pose a security risk and who should receive further screening.[207] Secure Flight will replace the current Computer-Assisted Passenger Prescreening System (CAPPS I).[208] Under Secure Flight, the TSA will assume the responsibility for checking airline passengers' names against expanded terrorist watch lists.[209] This is a function currently assumed by each airline individually.[210] By consolidating this function within the federal government, the TSA hopes to apply more consistent internal procedures and allow for more consistent response procedures.[211] The TSA and the Department of Homeland Security expect that the Secure Flight Program will improve security, reduce screening time, and protect privacy and civil liberties.[212]

The GAO issued a report in March 2005, which summarized its assessment of the development and implementation of the Secure Flight Program. The GAO found that the TSA was making progress and taking specific steps to address issues related to development and testing, system effectiveness, program management, and privacy protections.[213] However, the GAO also found that the TSA had not completed or fully addressed these issues.[214] The TSA had completed only initial tests and had not made key policy decisions.[215] More specifically, the TSA had drafted a number of key documents, but had not finalized them.[216] The TSA also had not met deadlines relating to the Secure Flight Program.[217] Additionally, key testing relating to the effectiveness of the Secure Flight Program had been undertaken, but still had to be finalized and assessed by the time of the report.[218] Oversight policies, performance measures, security plans, and life cycle cost estimates also were unfinished at the time of the report.[219] The TSA has recognized the potential privacy issues with the Secure Flight Program that could adversely affect the public, and has made progress in addressing privacy issues (such as through developing a redress process for those who believe they were treated inappropriately).[220] However, the redress process has to be more clearly defined, and the TSA has to address international privacy concerns.[221] Therefore, the GAO was unwilling to attest to the viability of the Secure Flight Program until further steps were taken.[222] In sum, the GAO found that while the TSA has made progress, much remains to be addressed.[223]

Paying for Space at Airports

With the increased security measures, the TSA has been using more space and more utilities at airports. It has agreed to pay airports for some of these costs.[224] According to its appropriations statute, the TSA may not demand free utilities, maintenance, or expenses but may acquire rent-free checkpoint space.[225] Since Congress did not define what checkpoint space is, the TSA has defined the term to mean both passenger and checked baggage space.[226] Therefore, the TSA may use passenger and checked baggage space without paying rent.[227] However, the TSA will pay for the maintenance of its EDS equipment and for the associated power backup and supplemental air conditioning necessary to run that equipment.[228]

The TSA is to reimburse airports for utility and janitorial costs.[229] The TSA does this through license agreements.[230] The agreement contains various provisions relating to the TSA's authority, purpose, use of property, and much more. Once both parties have signed the document, reimbursement will be retroactive to the effective date.[231] Exhibit 1 to the basic agreement must contain the floor plans that identify the locations where the TSA conducts screening operations, including the areas where the screening equipment lies and the necessary area around the machines to carry out the screening duties.[232]

Exhibit 2 to the basic license agreement addresses electrical consumption. The airport may choose to place meters on the screening equipment and the TSA will pay the utility invoice, or the "checked baggage equipment power consumption chart" will be attached to the agreement.[233] Charges for checkpoint lighting and air conditioning are common area costs that the airport would provide whether the TSA was present or not. Therefore, the TSA will consider paying these costs only when it and its employees are the only entities benefiting from these things.[234]

Exhibit 3 to the basic agreement addresses janitorial costs. It often will be easier for the airport to use existing janitorial services and be reimbursed accordingly.[235] If the airport's offer of janitorial services at checkpoints is competitive and fair, reimbursement for such services may be included in the license agreement.[236] The janitorial exhibit will be included in the basic agreement when in-house services perform janitorial services.[237]

Another important document is the Standard Operating Procedures for Utilities and Janitorial Services. The federal security director at the airport must nominate an employee to be the "contracting officers technical representative."[238] This person must receive training, and will be responsible for the day-to-day administration of the license agreement.[239]

Financing of Security Measures

To finance the above measures, the TSA has implemented security fees. It is responsible for the collection and regulation of the fees. One such fee is the September 11th Security Fee.[240] This $2.50 fee is imposed on passengers of all flights that originate in the United States.[241] This fee assists in defraying such costs as: paying screeners, managers, and federal law enforcement personnel deployed at screening locations; performing background investigations of personnel; financing the federal air marshals program; security research and development; paying federal security managers and federal law enforcement; financing security-related improvements; and training pilots and flight attendants.[242]

Another source of fees is the Aviation Security Infrastructure Fee. The TSA has the authority to charge airlines a fee to pay for the costs of providing civil aviation security service.[243] Airlines pay the TSA one-twelfth per month of their year 2000 screening costs.[244]

Passenger facility fees or charges also assist in paying for security-related expenses. Passenger facility fees are imposed by airports with FAA approval in amounts of one, two, or three dollars per passenger, or may be imposed in the amount of $4.00 or $4.50 per passenger if certain conditions are met.[245] These fees are used to fund airport projects involving airport development, planning, terminal development, and similar projects.[246]

Grants to airports have been an important source of funding for security-related projects. One example is the Airport Improvement Program (AIP).[247] In fiscal year 2002, AIP grants awarded for security projects were used to fund projects in the areas of access control, perimeter fencing, surveillance and fingerprinting equipment, and other security projects, such as terminal modifications.[248] In fiscal year 2003, $491 million was provided for security-related AIP projects.[249] The TSA also provides some security funding directly to airport operators through grants.[250]

An important source of funding for airport security improvement projects is the Vision 100 legislation,[251] which established the Federal Aviation Security Capital Fund. Congress authorized up to $500 million for airport security for each of the four fiscal years from 2004 through 2007.[252] Passenger security fees are to provide half of the total amount ($250 million) and up to another $250 million will come from authorized appropriations.[253] Of the mandatory $250 million, it is expected that $125 million in discretionary grants will be distributed.[254] The other $125 million will be made available in a manner such that 40 percent is distributed to large hub airports, 20 percent to medium hub airports, and 15 percent to small and nonhub airports.[255] The remaining 25 percent is to be allocated based on relative aviation security risks.[256]

Impact of the Intelligence Reform and Terrorism Prevention Act of 2004

On December 17, 2004, the Intelligence Reform and Terrorism Prevention Act of 2004 (IRTPA)—a response to issues raised by the National Commission on Terrorist Attacks Upon the United States (9/11 Commission)[257]—was signed into law.[258] It includes various provisions relating to aviation security.[259] The IRTPA addresses EDS equipment installation, research, and development.[260] It authorizes, but does not appropriate, an additional $150 million per year for three years to fund expiring and new letters of intent that will allow airports to install EDS.[261] The reimbursement period for these letters of intent would be up to ten years.[262] The IRTPA requires the TSA to submit to Congress a schedule to expedite the installation and use of in-line baggage screening equipment at airports, with an estimate of the impact that such equipment, facility modification, and baggage conveyor placement will have on staffing needs and levels.[263] The IRTPA also requires that a schedule be submitted for replacing trace-detection equipment with EDS equipment.[264] It also states that the secretary of homeland security—in consultation with air carriers and airport operators and others—shall submit to the appropriate congressional committees a proposed formula for cost-sharing among the federal government, states, local governments, and the private sector for projects to install in-line baggage screening equipment.[265] These are to reflect the benefits each entity derives from the projects, and should include recommendations for an equitable, feasible, and expeditious system for defraying the costs of the in-line baggage screening equipment, and the results of a review of innovative financing approaches and possible costs savings associated with the installation of in-line baggage screening equipment.[266] Additionally, the IRTPA authorizes $100 million for the research and development of "improved explosive detection systems."[267]

Various other security issues at airports are also addressed in the IRTPA. It authorizes $250 million for the research and installation of systems to detect biological, radiological, and explosive materials at airports[268] It requires the TSA to establish performance standards for the use of biometrics and access control systems, and authorizes $20 million for research and development of biometric technology that can be used for aviation security.[269] The IRTPA also requires the TSA to develop standards for determining staffing levels at security checkpoints within ninety days.[270] Additionally, it requires the Department of Homeland Security to develop and implement a National Strategy for Transportation Security.[271] The IRTPA also authorizes $200 million per year for three years to improve cargo security and $100 million per year for research and development of cargo security technology.[272] Under the IRTPA, the FAA is to establish a process for conducting airworthiness and safety certification of missile defense systems for commercial aircraft, and it calls on the president to pursue efforts to limit the availability, transfer, and proliferation of MANPADS worldwide.[273]

Challenges Facing the Airports

Airports face many security challenges. Some of the greatest among these challenges have been summarized and presented to Congress in statements that airport interest groups have made in the last two years before House and Senate aviation subcommittees, have been discussed at the Worldwide Conference on Current Challenges in International Aviation, and have been mentioned in GAO reports.

One challenge is the need to move the EDS equipment out of the airports' crowded terminals and place it "in-line," as part of the airports' integrated baggage system.[274] Leaving such equipment in airport terminals causes congestion and increases the number of TSA personnel required to screen baggage. The impediment to moving this equipment is that the cost of moving it out of airport terminals—while unknown—is estimated, nationally, to be somewhere between $3 billion and $5 billion.[275] This money is required to fund projects to accommodate in-line EDS equipment, such as projects to reinforce flooring, make electrical upgrades, and construct new facilities.[276] There have been attempts to address the need for additional funding.[277] The Vision-100 legislation authorized up to $500 million a year for four years to fund EDS equipment installation and other airport security improvements.[278] However, significantly less than that has actually been appropriated for EDS installation.[279]

The Vision-100 legislation also reaffirmed the letter of intent (LOI) process.[280] This process allows airports to fund projects for which the federal government commits to reimbursement over the course of several years.[281] Four categories of projects are covered by LOIs: replacement of baggage conveyor systems related to aviation security; reconfiguration of terminal baggage areas for EDS installation; installation of EDS equipment behind ticket counters, in baggage sorting areas, or in line with baggage handling systems; and other airport security improvement projects.[282] There were nine LOI airport recipients as of October 2004.[283] These include Hartfield Atlanta International, Logan International, Denver International, Dallas/Fort Worth International, McCarran International, Los Angeles International/Ontario International, Phoenix Sky Harbor International, and Seattle-Tacoma International.[284] The fiscal year 2005 Department of Homeland Security Appropriations legislation, however, reduced the percentage of federal funds provided under LOIs from 90 to 75 percent at large and medium hub airports.[285]

Moreover, while LOIs are an important initiative, many airports do not have LOIs and are desperately in need of funds to address the challenge of EDS installation.[286] While LOIs are the principal funding method for modifying airport facilities, the TSA and airport operators have used other methods to fund airport modification projects to accommodate the installation of in-line explosive detection systems. The TSA has used transaction agreements to fund smaller airport modification projects.[287] Airport operators also have used AIP grants to fund facility modifications.[288]

However, the availability of funding is limited. The president's fiscal year 2005 and 2006 budget requests, and the fiscal year 2005 Department of Homeland Security Appropriations Act, do not include or provide for further funding for LOIs.[289] Moreover, the availability of AIP funds for financing the installation of baggage screening systems is currently limited by prohibitions that appear in the 2004 and 2005 Consolidated Appropriations Act.[290]

Thus, a key challenge to airports is acquiring the funds needed to move EDS equipment out of overcrowded lobbies. While the federal government has taken steps to provide some funding, a long-term solution to the EDS problem is lacking at many airports across the country.[291] In addition, TSA screening staff (capped at 45,000 full-time employees) are not used effectively, resulting in long lines at passenger and baggage screening checkpoints.[292] The lack of a long-term solution to the EDS problem, combined with the cap on the TSA screening workforce, likely will result in longer lines for airport customers.[293]

The airport industry has presented several recommendations related to the problem of baggage screening. First, the industry suggests that the TSA help fund the enormous sum of money required to place the EDS equipment in line at the nation's airports.[294] If the government would commit to pay back more airports over time (through LOIs), many airports would likely pay the upfront costs.[295] Second, the industry suggests that the TSA work to harmonize regulations so that bags could move freely between some nations.[296] Third, the TSA should fund research and development of more efficient baggage and passenger screening systems.[297]

A March 2005 GAO report also presented recommendations for the deployment of checked baggage screening systems. The GAO suggested that the TSA determine the total costs of installing in-line EDS equipment.[298] The GAO also recommended that the TSA conduct a systematic analysis of airports to prioritize which airports should receive in-line EDS equipment based on an assessment of costs and benefits, and—where such systems simply are not feasible—whether stand-alone EDS equipment could and should replace less-efficient ETD systems.[299]

Another challenge facing airports is staffing at airport security screening checkpoints.[300] At some airports, there are many TSA employees at security checkpoints, while at others there are not enough TSA screeners and wait times delay passengers.[301] TSA often has not had the necessary number of checkpoints open and properly staffed, resulting in wait times for some that can reach one to two hours.[302] Thus, a key challenge facing airports is staffing and the ability to address staffing problems at the local level where the problems and potential solutions are best understood. A November 2004 GAO report related the concerns of airport operators, who said they would not opt out of using federal screeners in 2004 because they needed additional information regarding the flexibility that private contractors would have, for example, to deploy screeners where they are needed most at airports.[303] It should be noted that as of February 2005, the TSA had begun implementing a more localized system to hire screeners by creating twenty local hiring centers around the country to serve as focal points for local hiring activities.[304] Only time will tell if the concerns related to staffing problems are ameliorated by this endeavor.

The airport industry has presented several recommendations regarding passenger screening. First, the TSA should create an institutional mechanism whereby airports and airlines can consult with the TSA on passenger screening issues.[305] Second, each airport's federal security director should have the authority to hire, schedule, assess, and train screeners at the local level.[306] Local flexibility could address these workforce problems.[307] Each airport has a unique situation and local flexibility could ensure that these problems are addressed more effectively. Third, the TSA should institute performance indicators that can measure security and customer service, and compare performance at TSA-operated airports against airports where private contractors conduct screening operations.[308]

While some of the biggest problems facing airports are placing EDS equipment in line and addressing screener staffing concerns, other security challenges face airports. Such challenges include improving airport perimeter access security, controlling access to secure areas, screening those with airfield access, securing cargo areas, securing general aviation operations, and much more.[309]

Airports face not only the challenges described above, but also the financial strain related to the increased security measures.[310] Airports' operating costs have increased, requiring many airport staff members to be on extended overtime.[311] There also has been financial drain because of the requirements for emergency contracts for security equipment and services.[312] These financial difficulties were compounded by the fact that fewer people flew after 9/11, resulting in less revenue—large airports derive most of their money from passenger facility charges, concessions from vendors, parking, and airline rates and charges.[313] And the smaller airports have had the most severe financial difficulties since September 11.[314]

Federalism: The Need to Use Local Airport Experience

A challenge for airports is exercising some of the responsibilities that tra-ditionally were local responsibilities at a time when federal regulation has increased.[315] Airports are interested in ensuring that federal resources and standards are guided by local experience and management.[316] Airport person-nel understand their configurations, layouts and opportunities better than the federal government.[317] They have experience arranging for local law enforce-ment presence and for establishing the parking plans at airports.[318] Airports also have experience with perimeter security, access control, and terminal security.[319] They believe they have performed these functions well, and that providing for these responsibilities at the local level will allow the TSA to focus on its central missions of baggage and passenger screening and coordinating and distributing intelligence information.[320] By allowing the airports—the entities that traditionally have administered these areas—to manage these security concerns, resources can be allocated more effectively, and the most effective security measures can be implemented.[321] Moreover, keeping these responsibilities at the local level allows for use of security measures that are geared toward the needs of the specific airport involved.[322]

A related challenge is ensuring that the TSA and the airports operate with a cooperative and coordinated approach to security.[323] Airports would like to ensure that local experience is not ignored, and that the roles of local airport security officials and TSA's federal security directors stationed at the airports are predictable, complimentary and not in conflict.[324] Creating a more balanced federal-local partnership is a challenge and goal of the airport industry.[325] Air-port interest groups have pointed out that airports, as public institutions, serve the community and the national aviation system by ensuring competitive, safe, and secure environments for the public.[326] Moreover, airports traditionally have been responsible for the safety and security of airports and individuals using them.[327] Since the mission of the TSA and the airports—to ensure safety and security for the airports and the public—is the same, a coordinated and cooperative approach to securing the nation's airports makes sense.[328]

As public bodies, airports have the incentive to undertake security respon-sibilities.[329] One specific area where airports have suggested that there should be a more coordinated approach is in the planning for baggage screening con-figurations.[330] Airport operators have felt ignored in the past, and airport inter-est groups suggest that ignoring airport operators has cost the TSA time and millions of dollars. They also say this has cost airports money because they have needed to perform design and engineering work while the TSA's plan-ning was delayed or not feasible.[331] The objective is to create an environment where the roles and tasks undertaken by airports and the federal government are coordinated, predictable, complementary, and best use the knowledge and resources of each entity.

The airport industry has made several recommendations related to im-proving security management. First, the federal government should coordi-nate with state and local governments to define roles and responsibilities so that the federal role of ensuring airport security does not conflict with local airport management.[332] Second, the TSA should continue to delegate operational and managerial responsibilities to its local federal security directors.[333] Third, risk-based assessments should be made so that the TSA can prioritize the scarce dollars available for aviation security.[334]

Lessons for Other Types of Government-Operated Infrastructure Facilities

There are several lessons that state and local authorities can learn from the relationship between the TSA and the local airports, and the challenges faced by these airports. First, implementing massive projects requires enormous sums of money. When the federal government requires that state and local governments undertake massive projects, there is likely to be tension over what funds the federal government will provide. One potential solution is to have the federal government offer to contribute some money now and offer to reimburse local governments over a period of time for expenditures, if the local governments agree to front the money for the improvements. Such a solution, however, will work only to the extent the federal government commits to its role. All parties will have to work to find creative funding solutions. Ultimately, however, both federal and state/local governments need to be realistic about the costs involved in large-scale improvement projects, and need to negotiate a long-term solution to the funding problems that any such projects will present.

Second, state and local entities should be included, if not deferred to, as the appropriate entities to address problems with which they have extensive experience. When the federal government increases regulation and oversight in an area traditionally controlled at the local level, and then ignores the experience of state and local authorities, the increased federal presence is likely to cause friction and be less effective. These local authorities may understandably be concerned with the increased federal presence because local institutions that have been handling the problems are more likely to understand better the problems and the solutions specific to that locality.

Third, both state/local and federal authorities need to have a cooperative and coordinated approach to accomplishing massive projects, such as securing government-operated transportation facilities. It is imperative that federal agencies consult with local authorities that often have expertise and resources and, if consulted, can save federal agencies time and money. In fact, with cooperation, a better solution is likely to result that is satisfactory to all parties involved. Moreover, when both state/local and federal authorities must be involved, the roles of both can come into conflict especially if their roles are not clear. Each entity's role needs to be clarified and communicated clearly.

In order to alleviate the tension likely to arise when federal agencies work with state and local authorities—especially on massive projects where federal involvement is necessary—open communication is critical through designated channels about conflicts and issues arising in areas where the federal and state or local presence overlap. In that way, the knowledge and resources that each group bring to the table can be used to define clearly the roles assumed by each.

Conclusion

Airports face many challenges in securing their facilities and protecting the public. With the substantial increases in security that have developed from the need to combat the escalation of terrorism, a major challenge is how to facilitate travel for the public while increasing security measures. One area that needs immediate attention is how to facilitate the moving of EDS equipment out of airport terminals to improve security and reduce passenger wait times. This is an endeavor estimated to cost billions of dollars. Along with this challenge is the need to provide adequate staffing at security screening checkpoints. Both of these important improvements will benefit from more effectively involving local governments in solutions currently being engineered by the federal government. To date, the experience of those who have traditionally exercised local responsibilities has not been utilized effectively. Their local experience may better equip them to handle certain challenges, especially those involving knowledge of local conditions. While the solutions must be national in keeping with the potential exposure, better involving those at the local level and giving them responsibilities also will assist in more effectively allocating scarce governmental resources at all levels.

Several lessons can be learned from the TSA-local government airport relationship. First, everyone must be realistic and creative in finding long-term solutions to funding problems. Second, federal officials need to realize that sometimes state and local entities may be better suited to addressing problems at any specific location, particularly those problems that were traditionally local responsibilities. Finally, both federal and local government should take a cooperative and coordinated approach so as to use the available resources in the most efficient manner possible.

NOTES

1. The author wishes to thank Kara Krolikowski, an associate at Palmer & Dodge LLP, for her very able assistance in researching and writing this article.

2. *Hearing on H.R. 2115, The Vision 100—Century of Aviation Reauthorization Act Before the H. Subcommittee on Aviation, Committee on Transportation and Infrastructure*, 108th Cong. (2d Sess. 2004) (statements of Bonnie Allin, President & CEO, Tucson Airport Authority, James E. Bennett, President & CEO, Metropolitan Washington Airports Authority, and Charles M. Barclay, President, American Association of Airports Executives, on behalf of Airports Council International—North America and the American Association of Airports Executives), www.aaae.org/government/100_AAAE_ACI-NA_Legislative_Affairs/400_Congressional_Testimony/0401deregulation.pdf.

3. *See id.*

4. *Id.*

5. Airport Transportation Security Act, Pub. L. No. 107-71, 115 Stat. 597 (2001).

6. 49 U.S.C.A. § 114 (West Supp. 2004); Transportation Security Administration, Report to Congress on Transportation Security, at 2 (Mar. 31, 2003), www.tsa.gov/public/display?theme=76&content=090005198009d38d (Mar. 31, 2003).

7. Homeland Security Act of 2002, Pub. L. No. 107-296, 116 Stat. 2135 (2002).

8. 49 U.S.C.A. § 114 (West Supp. 2004); Transportation Security Administration, Report to Congress on Transportation Security, at 2 (Mar. 31, 2003), www.tsa.gov/public/display?theme=76&content=090005198009d38d.

9. 49 U.S.C.A. § 114.

10. *Id.*

11. *Id.*

12. *Id.*

13. *Id.*

14. *Id.*

15. *Id.*

16. *Id.*

17. *Id.*

18. *Id.*

19. *Id.*

20. *Id.*

21. *Id.*

22. *Id.*

23. *Id.*

24. *Id.*

25. 49 U.S.C.A. § 44917 (West Supp. 2004).

26. *Id.*

27. *Id.*

28. *Id.*

29. *Id.*

30. *Id.*

31. 49 U.S.C.A. § 44918 (West Supp. 2004).

32. *Id.*

33. *Id.*

34. *Id.*

35. 49 U.S.C.A. § 44903 (West Supp. 2004).

36. *Id.*

37. 49 U.S.C.A. § 44912 (West Supp. 2004).

38. *Id.*

39. *Id.*

40. 49 U.S.C.A. § 44938 (West Supp. 2004).

41. 49 U.S.C.A. § 44903.

42. *Id.*

43. *Id.*

44. *Id.*

45. *Id.*

46. *Id.*

47. *Id.*

48. *Id.*

49. *Id.*

50. *Id.*

51. *Id.*

52. *Id.*

53. *Id.*

54. 49 U.S.C.A. § 44936 (West Supp. 2004).

55. *See* 49 C.F.R. §§ 1542.209, 1544.229, 1544.230.

56. 49 U.S.C.A. § 44936.

57. Scott Dalton, Office of Chief Counsel, Transportation Security Administration, Presentation at Transportation Security Administration Current Issues: AAAE Basics of Airport Law (Oct. 24, 2004).

58. *Id.*

59. *Id.*

60. U.S. Gov't Accountability Office, Aviation Security: Further Steps Needed to Strengthen the Security of Commercial Airport Perimeters and Access Controls, GAO-04-728, www.gao.gov/docsearch/featured/airptsec.html (2004).

61. *Id.* at 1.

62. *Id.* at 12.

63. *Id.* at 1, 12, 16.

64. *Id.* at 1.

65. *Id.*

66. *Id.*

67. *Id.*

68. *Id.*

69. *Id.*

70. *Id.*

71. 49 U.S.C.A. § 44901 (West Supp. 2004).

72. *Id.*

73. *Id.*

74. *Id.*

75. *Id.*

76. *Id.*

77. *Id.*

78. *Id.*

79. 49 U.S.C.A. § 44933 (West Supp. 2004).

80. *Id.*

81. 49 U.S.C.A. § 44935 (West Supp. 2004).

82. *Id.*

83. *Id.*

84. *Id.*

85. *Id.*

86. *Id.*

87. *Id.*

88. *Id.*

89. *Id.*

90. *Id.*

91. Security screening pilot program, 49 U.S.C. § 44919 (West Supp. 2004); Pub. L. No. 107-71, 115 Stat. 611.

92. Press Release, Transportation Security Administration, DHS Delivers Guidance for Screening Partnership Program: Plan Available for Airports Considering Private Security Screeners (June 23, 2004), www.tsa.gov/public/display?theme=244&content=0900051980 0b18a4; Press Release, Transportation Security Administration, TSA Releases Performance Report on Contract Screeners at Five U.S. Airports (April 22, 2004), www.tsa.gov/public/interapp/press_release/press_release_0412.xml.

93. Press Release, Transportation Security Administration, TSA Releases Performance Report on Contract Screeners at Five U.S. Airports (April 22, 2004), www.tsa.gov/public/interapp/press_release/press_release_0412.xml.

94. DEPARTMENT OF HOMELAND SECURITY, OFFICE OF THE INSPECTOR GENERAL, TRANSPORTATION SECURITY ADMINISTRATION REVIEW OF THE TSA PASSENGER AND BAGGAGE SCREENING PILOT PROGRAM, OIG-04-47 (2004), www.dhs.gov/dhspublic/interapp/editorial/editorial_0334.xml.

95. *Id.* at 4.

96. *Id.*

97. *Id.*

98. *Id.*

99. *Id.*

100. *Id.*

101. Security screening opt-out program, 49 U.S.C. § 44920(a) (West Supp. 2004); Pub. L. No. 107-71, 115 Stat. 612.

102. 49 U.S.C. §§ 44920(c)-(d); TRANSPORTATION SECURITY ADMINISTRATION, SCREENING PARTNERSHIP PROGRAM: SPP FREQUENTLY ASKED QUESTIONS, www.tsa.gov/public/interapp/editorial/editorial_1752.xml.

103. Press Release, Transportation Security Administration, DHS Delivers Guidance for Screening Partnership Program: Plan available for Airports Considering Private Security Screeners (June 23, 2004), www.tsa.gov/public/display?theme=244&content=09000519800b18a4.

104. *Id.*

105. *Id.*

106. Scott Dalton, Office of Chief Counsel, Transportation Security Administration, Presentation at Transportation Security Administration Current Issues: AAAE Basics of Airport Law (Oct. 24, 2004).

107. TRANSPORTATION SECURITY ADMINISTRATION, SCREENING PARTNERSHIP PROGRAM: SPP FREQUENTLY ASKED QUESTIONS, *www.tsa.gov/public/interapp/editorial/editorial_1752.xml*.

108. 49 U.S.C. § 44920(b).

109. *Id.* at § 44920(a).

110. *Id.* at § 44920(e).

111. *Id.* at § 44920(f).

112. 49 U.S.C. §§ 44920(a)-(f).

113. 49 U.S.C. § 44920(d); TRANSPORTATION SECURITY ADMINISTRATION, GUIDANCE ON SCREENING PARTNERSHIP PROGRAM, at 10 (June 2004), www.tsa.gov/public/display?theme=244&content=09000519800cfe42.

114. TRANSPORTATION SECURITY ADMINISTRATION, GUIDANCE ON SCREENING PARTNERSHIP PROGRAM, at 11 (June 2004), www.tsa.gov/public/display?theme=244&content=09000519800cfe42.

115. TRANSPORTATION SECURITY ADMINISTRATION, SCREENING PARTNERSHIP PROGRAM: SPP FREQUENTLY ASKED QUESTIONS, www.tsa.gov/public/interapp/editorial/editorial_1752.xml; 49 U.S.C. § 44920(d).

116. 49 U.S.C. § 44920(e).

117. TRANSPORTATION SECURITY ADMINISTRATION, GUIDANCE ON SCREENING PARTNERSHIP PROGRAM, at 16 (June 2004), www.tsa.gov/public/display?theme=244&content=09000519800cfe42.

118. *Id.*

119. 49 U.S.C. § 44920(f).

120. TRANSPORTATION SECURITY ADMINISTRATION, SCREENING PARTNERSHIP PROGRAM: SPP FREQUENTLY ASKED QUESTIONS, www.tsa.gov/public/interapp/editorial/editorial_1752.xml.

121. Support Anti-Terrorism by Fostering Effective Technologies Act of 2002, 6 U.S.C. §§ 441-444 (2004).

122. 6 C.F.R. § 25.3 (2003).

123. 6 U.S.C. § 442(b) (2004).

124. Regulations Implementing the Support Anti-terrorism by Fostering Effective Technologies Act of 2002 (the Safety Act), 68 Fed. Reg. 59,684, 59,693 (Oct. 16, 2003).

125. U.S. Gov't Accountability Office, Aviation Security: Preliminary Observations on TSA's Progress to Allow Airports to Use Private Passenger and Baggage Screening Services, GAO-05-126, at 3 (Nov. 2004), www.gao.gov/docdblite/details.php?rptno=GAO-05-126.

126. *Id.*

127. *Id.*

128. *Id.* at 4.

129. Scott Dalton, Office of Chief Counsel, Transportation Security Administration, Presentation at Transportation Security Administration Current Issues: AAAE Basics of Airport Law (Oct. 24, 2004).

130. Transportation Security Administration, About TSA, Screening Partnership Program, Strategic Objectives and Approximate Program Timeline, www.tsa.gov/public/display?theme=244&content=09000519800cfe46.

131. *Id.*

132. Transportation Security Administration, About TSA, Screening Partnership Program, Combined Presolicitation/Synopsis for Screening Partnership Program (SSP), HSTSO1-04-Q-OPTOUT, at 1 (Nov. 4, 2004), www.tsa.gov/public/display?theme=244&content=09000519800d79ed.

133. *Id.* at 3.

134. *Id.*

135. Transportation Security Administration, About TSA, Screening Partnership Program, Strategic Objectives and Approximate Program Timeline, www.tsa.gov/public/display?theme=244&content=09000519800cfe46; U.S. Gov't Accountability Office, Aviation Security: Preliminary Observations on TSA's Progress to Allow Airports to Use Private Passenger and Baggage Screening Services, GAO-05-126, at 9 (Nov. 2004), www.gao.gov/docdblite/details.php?rptno=GAO-05-126.

136. Transportation Security Administration, About TSA, Screening Partnership Program, Combined Presolicitation/Synopsis for Screening Partnership Program (SSP), HSTSO1-04-Q-OPTOUT, at 2 (Nov. 4, 2004), www.tsa.gov/public/display?theme=244&content=09000519800d79ed.

137. Transportation Security Administration, About TSA, Screening Partnership Program, Screening Partnership Program Contracting Approach, at 7 (Nov. 4, 2004), www.tsa.gov/public/display?theme=244&content=09000519800d79ed.

138. Airport Transportation Security Act, Pub. L. No. 107-71, § 110, 115 Stat. 597, 615 (2001).

139. Homeland Security Act of 2002, Pub. L. No. 107-296, 116 Stat. 2135 (2002); U.S. Gov't Accountability Office, Aviation Security: Systematic Planning Needed to Optimize the Deployment of Checked Baggage Screening Systems, GAO-05-365, at 6 (March 2005), http://www.gao.gov.

140. U.S. Gov't Accountability Office, Aviation Security: Systematic Planning Needed to Optimize the Deployment of Checked Baggage Screening Systems, GAO-05-365, at 2 (March 2005), http://www.gao.gov.

141. *Id.* at 1.

142. *Id.* at 3.

143. *Id.*

144. *Id.* at 4.

145. *Id.*

146. *Id.*

147. *Id.* at 9.

148. *Id.*

149. *Id.* at 4, 9.

150. *Id.* at 4.

151. *Id.* at 22.

152. *Id.* at 4.

153. *Id.* at 5.

154. *Id.* at 44; Recently, Reveal Technologies CT-80 machines have been certified. *U.S. Department of Homeland Security, Transportation Security Administration, Hearing before the S. Committee on Commerce, Science, and Transportation,* at 2 (Feb. 15, 2005) (statement of David M. Stone), http://www.tsa.gov/public/display?theme=47&content=09000519800ffdcc. As of Spring 2005, the TSA was in the process of conducting pilots of these machines. *Id.* They are smaller, less costly, and more compact than EDS machines. *Id.*

155. *Id.*

156. Air Cargo Security Requirements, 69 Fed. Reg. 65,257-65,291 (Nov. 10, 2004) (to be codified at 49 C.F.R. § 1540); 49 U.S.C. §§ 44901(a), (f).

157. Air Cargo Security Requirements, 69 Fed. Reg. at 65,259.

158. *Id.*

159. Air Cargo Security Requirements, 69 Fed. Reg. at 65,258.

160. Air Cargo Security Requirements, 69 Fed. Reg. at 65,257-65,291.

161. Air Cargo Security Requirements, 69 Fed. Reg. at 65,262.

162. *Id.*

163. *Id.*

164. *Id.*

165. *Id.*

166. *Id.*

167. *U.S. Department of Homeland Security, Transportation Security Administration, Hearing before the S. Committee on Commerce, Science, and Transportation,* at 2 (Feb. 15, 2005) (statement of David M. Stone), http://www.tsa.gov/public/display?theme=47&content=09000519800ffdcc.

168. *Id.*

169. U.S. Gov't Accountability Office, Increased Federal Oversight is Needed but Continued Partnership with the Private Sector is Critical to Long-Term Success, at 6 (November 2004).

170. *Id.* at 6-8.

171. Pub. L. No. 107-71, § 101(a), 115 Stat. at 598; U.S. Gov't Accountability Office, General Aviation Security: Increased Federal Oversight is Needed but Continued Partnership with the Private Sector is Critical to Long-Term Success, GAO-05-144, at 14 (Nov. 2004), www.gao.gov/docsearch/featured/terrorism.html.

172. *Id.*

173. Pub. L. No. 107-71, § 113, 115 Stat. at 622.

174. 28 C.F.R. Part 105 (2004).

175. U.S. Gov't Accountability Office, General Aviation Security: Increased Federal Oversight is Needed but Continued Partnership with the Private Sector is Critical to Long-Term Success, GAO-05-144, at 26 (Nov. 2004), www.gao.gov/docsearch/featured/terrorism.html.

176. Vision 100-Century of Aviation Reauthorization Act, Pub. L. No. 108-176, § 612, 117 Stat. at 2572-74 (2003).

177. Pub. L. No. 107-71, § 132, 115 Stat. 635; U.S. Gov't Accountability Office, General Aviation Security: Increased Federal Oversight is Needed but Continued Partnership with the Private Sector is Critical to Long-Term Success, GAO-05-144, at 28 (Nov. 2004), www.gao.gov/docsearch/featured/terrorism.html.

178. 49 C.F.R. § 1544.101 (2004); U.S. Gov't Accountability Office, General Aviation Security: Increased Federal Oversight is Needed but Continued Partnership with the Private Sector is Critical to Long-Term Success, GAO-05-144, at 27-28 (Nov. 2004), www.gao.gov/docsearch/featured/terrorism.html.

179. U.S. Gov't Accountability Office, General Aviation Security: Increased Federal Oversight is Needed but Continued Partnership with the Private Sector is Critical to Long-Term Success, GAO-05-144, at 28-29 (Nov. 2004), www.gao.gov/docsearch/featured/terrorism.html.

180. *Id.* at 25.

181. *Id.*; 49 C.F.R §§ 1544.229, 1544.230 (2004).

182. U.S. Gov't Accountability Office, General Aviation Security: Increased Federal Oversight is Needed but Continued Partnership with the Private Sector is Critical to Long-Term Success, GAO-05-144, at 25 (Nov. 2004), www.gao.gov/docsearch/featured/terrorism.html; 14 C.F.R § 61.3 (2004).

183. U.S. Gov't Accountability Office, General Aviation Security: Increased Federal Oversight is Needed but Continued Partnership with the Private Sector is Critical to Long-Term Success, GAO-05-144, at 25 (Nov. 2004), www.gao.gov/docsearch/featured/terrorism.html; 14 C.F.R § 61.18; 49 C.F.R §§ 1540.115, 1540.117 (2004).

184. U.S. Gov't Accountability Office, General Aviation Security: Increased Federal Oversight is Needed but Continued Partnership with the Private Sector is Critical to Long-Term Success, GAO-05-144 (Nov. 2004), www.gao.gov/docsearch/featured/terrorism.html.

185. *Id.* at 3.

186. *Id.* at 3-4.

187. *Id.* at 4.

188. *Id.*

189. *Id.*

190. *Id.*

191. *Id.*

192. *Id.* at 39.

193. *Id.* at 4.

194. *Id.* at 5.

195. *Id.*

196. *Id.*

197. *Id.*

198. *Id.* at 52.

199. Transportation Security Administration, What is Registered Traveler?, www.tsa.gov/public/display?content=0Id.9000519800b4ddd.

200. *Id.*

201. *Id.*

202. *Id.*

203. *Id.*

204. *TSA seeks registered traveler program expansion,* CNN.com, Dec. 14, 2004, at 2, www.cnn.com/2004/TRAVEL/12/14/registered.travelers.ap/.

205. *U.S. Department of Homeland Security, Transportation Security Administration, Hearing before the S. Committee on Commerce, Science, and Transportation,* at 2 (Feb. 15, 2005) (statement of David M. Stone), http://www.tsa.gov/public/display?theme=47&content=09000519800ffdcc.

206. Press Release, Transportation Security Administration, TSA to Test New Passenger Pre-Screening System, "Secure Flight" to be Tested Before Year's End (Aug. 26, 2004), www.tsa.gov/public/display?theme=44&content=09000519800c6c77.

207. U.S. Gov't Accountability Office, Aviation Security: Secure Flight Development and Testing Under Way, but Risks Should be Managed as System is Further Developed, GAO-05-356, at 8, 11 (Mar. 2005), http://www.gao.gov.

208. *Id.* at 8.

209. Press Release, Transportation Security Administration, TSA to Test New Passenger Pre-Screening System, "Secure Flight" to be Tested Before Year's End (Aug. 26, 2004), www.tsa.gov/public/display?theme=44&content=09000519800c6c77; Scott Dalton, Office of Chief Counsel, Transportation Security Administration, Presentation at Transportation Security Administration Current Issues: AAAE Basics of Airport Law (Oct. 24, 2004).

210. Press Release, Transportation Security Administration, TSA to Test New Passenger Pre-Screening System, "Secure Flight" to be Tested Before Year's End (Aug. 26, 2004), www.tsa.gov/public/display?theme=44&content=09000519800c6c77.

211. Scott Dalton, Office of Chief Counsel, Transportation Security Administration, Presentation at Transportation Security Administration Current Issues: AAAE Basics of Airport Law (Oct. 24, 2004).

212. *Id.*

213. U.S. Gov't Accountability Office, Aviation Security: Secure Flight Development and Testing Under Way, but Risks Should be Managed as System is Further Developed, GAO-05-356, at 4 (Mar. 2005), http://www.gao.gov.

214. *Id.*

215. *Id.*

216. *Id.* at 4-5.

217. *Id.* at 5.

218. *Id.*

219. *Id.* at 6.

220. *Id.* at 7.

221. *Id.*

222. *Id.* at 61.

223. *Id.* at 16.

224. Information provided by Scott Dalton, Office of the Chief Counsel, TSA-2, Transportation Security Administration (Jan. 5, 2005).

225. Appropriations for the Department of Homeland Security for the Fiscal Year Ending September 30, 2004, Pub. L. No. 108-90, 117 Stat. 1155 (Oct. 1, 2003).

226. Information provided by Scott Dalton, Office of the Chief Counsel, TSA-2, Transportation Security Administration (Jan. 5, 2005).

227. *Id.*

228. *Id.*

229. *Id.*

230. *Id.*

231. *Id.*

232. *Id.* Queuing areas and exit lanes are not part of these areas. Generally, the beginning of the area is the table in front of the x-ray machine, and the end of the checkpoint area will be the tables at the end of the x-ray, the ETD machines, or the supervisor station, whichever is farthest. The checked baggage screening area will include the footprint of the screening equipment and the necessary area around the machines for carrying out duties. The screening area may include other areas when automated in-line EDS based systems are involved. *Id.*

233. *Id.*

234. *Id*.

235. *Id*.

236. *Id*.

237. *Id*.

238. *Id*.

239. *Id*.

240. Transportation Security Administration, September 11ᵗʰ Security Fees, www.tsa.gov/public/display?content=0900051980002dd4.

241. 49 C.F.R. § 1510.5 (2004).

242. 49 U.S.C.A. § 44940 (West Supp. 2004).

243. Pub. L. No. 107-71, § 118; Aviation Security Infrastructure Fees, Interim Final Rule, 67 Fed. Reg. 7,926 (Feb. 20, 2002) (to be codified at 49 C.F.R. pt. 1511); Transportation Security Administration, Aviation Security Infrastructure Fees (Air Carrier Fees), www.tsa.gov/public/interapp/editorial/editorial_0238.xml.

244. *Id*.

245. 49 U.S.C.A. § 40117 (West Supp. 2004).

246. *Id*.

247. U.S. Gov't Accountability Office, Aviation Security: Further Steps Needed to Strengthen the Security of Commercial Airport Perimeters and Access Controls, GAO-04-728, at 18 (June 4, 2004), www.gao.gov/docsearch/featured/airptsec.html.

248. *Id*.

249. *Id*.

250. *Id*. at 19.

251. Vision 100-Century of Aviation Reauthorization Act, Pub. L. No. 108-176, § 605, 117 Stat. 2490, §§ 2566-68 (2003).

252. U. S. Gov't Accountability Office, Aviation Security: Further Steps Needed to Strengthen the Security of Commercial Airport Perimeters and Access Controls, GAO-04-728, at 20 (June 4, 2004), www.gao.gov/docsearch/featured/airptsec.html; Pub. L. No. 108-176, § 605, 117 Stat. 2490, 2567.

253. *Id*.; The Intelligence Reform and Terrorism Prevention Act of 2004, Pub. L. No. 108-458, 118 Stat. 3638 (2004), increases the authorized appropriation for aviation security from Vision 100 from $250 million to $400 million for each of the fiscal years 2005 through 2007. However, the $250 million mandatory appropriation remains the same.

254. Scott Dalton, Office of Chief Counsel, Transportation Security Administration, Presentation at Transportation Security Administration Current Issues: AAAE Basics of Airport Law (Oct. 24, 2004); Pub. L. No. 108-176, § 605, 117 Stat. 2490, 2567.

255. *Id*.

256. *Id*.

257. National Commission on Terrorist Attacks Upon the United States, The 9/11 Commission Report: Final Report of the National Commission on Terrorist Attacks Upon the United States (2004).

258. Intelligence Reform and Terrorism Prevention Act of 2004, 108 Pub. L. No. 458, 118 Stat. 3638 (Dec. 17, 2004).

259. *Id*.

260. 108 Pub. L. No. 458, 118 Stat. 4019.

261. *Id*.

262. *Id*.

263. *Id*.

264. *Id*.

265. *Id*.

266. *Id*.

267. 108 Pub. L. No. 458, 118 Stat. 4024.

268. 108 Pub. L. No. 458, 118 Stat. 4013.

269. 108 Pub. L. No. 458, 118 Stat. 4011.

270. 108 Pub. L. No. 458, 118 Stat. 4023.

271. 108 Pub. L. No. 458, 118 Stat. 4001.

272. 108 Pub. L. No. 458, 118 Stat. 4052.

273. 108 Pub. L. No. 458, 118 Stat. 4026.

274. *Joint Statement on behalf of Airports Council International-North America (ACI-NA) and American Association of Airport Executives (AAAE): Hearing on Passenger and Baggage Screening Problems Before the H. Aviation Subcommittee*, 108th Cong. (2d Sess. 2004) (joint statement of David Z. Plavin, President, ACI-NA, and Todd Hauptli, Sr. Executive Vice President, AAAE), www.aaae.org/government/100_AAAE_ACI-NA_Legislative_Affairs/400_Congressional_Testimony/.

275. U.S. Gov't Accountability Office, Aviation Security: Systematic Planning Needed to Optimize the Deployment of Checked Baggage Screening Systems, GAO-05-365, at 29 (Mar. 2005), http://www.gao.gov.

276. *Joint Statement on behalf of Airports Council International-North America (ACI-NA) and American Association of Airport Executives (AAAE): Hearing on Passenger and Baggage Screening Problems Before the H. Aviation Subcommittee*, 108th Cong. (2d Sess. 2004) (joint statement of David Z. Plavin, President, ACI-NA, and Todd Hauptli, Sr. Executive Vice President, AAAE), www.aaae.org/government/100_AAAE_ACI-NA_Legislative_Affairs/400_Congressional_Testimony/.

277. *Id.*

278. *Id;* Vision-100 Century of Aviation Reauthorization Act, Pub. L. No. 108-176, 117 Stat. 2567 (2003).

279. Department of Homeland Security Appropriations Act 2005, Pub. L. No. 108-334, 118 Stat. 1304-05 (2004); Making Appropriations for the Department of Homeland Security for the Fiscal Year Ending September 30, 2005, and for Other Purposes, 108-774 (2004).

280. *Joint Statement on behalf of Airports Council International-North America (ACI-NA) and American Association of Airport Executives (AAAE): Hearing on Passenger and Baggage Screening Problems Before the H. Aviation Subcommittee*, 108th Cong. (2d Sess. 2004) (joint statement of David Z. Plavin, President, ACI-NA, and Todd Hauptli, Sr. Executive Vice President, AAAE), www.aaae.org/government/100_AAAE_ACI-NA_Legislative_Affairs/400_Congressional_Testimony/; Vision-100 Century of Aviation Reauthorization Act, Pub. L. No. 108-176, 117 Stat. 2566 (2003).

281. *Id.*

282. Scott Dalton, Office of Chief Counsel, Transportation Security Administration, Presentation at Transportation Security Administration Current Issues: AAAE Basics of Airport Law (Oct. 24, 2004); Vision-100 Century of Aviation Reauthorization Act, Pub. L. No. 108-176, 117 Stat. 2566 (2003).

283. Scott Dalton, Office of Chief Counsel, Transportation Security Administration, Presentation at Transportation Security Administration Current Issues: AAAE Basics of Airport Law (Oct. 24, 2004).

284. *Id.*

285. Department of Homeland Security Appropriations Act of 2005, Pub. L. No. 108-334, 118 Stat. 1304-05 (2004).

286. *Joint Statement on behalf of Airports Council International-North America (ACI-NA) and American Association of Airport Executives (AAAE): Hearing on Passenger and Baggage Screening Problems Before the H. Aviation Subcommittee*, 108th Cong. (2d Sess. 2004) (joint statement of David Z. Plavin, President, ACI-NA, and Todd Hauptli, Sr. Executive Vice President,

AAAE), www.aaae.org/government/100_AAAE_ACI-NA_Legislative_Affairs/400_Congressional_Testimony/.

287. U.S. Gov't Accountability Office, Aviation Security: Systematic Planning Needed to Optimize the Deployment of Checked Baggage Screening Systems, GAO-05-365, at 32 (Mar. 2005), http://www.gao.gov.

288. *Id.* at 33.

289. *Id.* at 35

290. *Id.* at 35-36.

291. *Statement of on behalf of ACI-NA and AAAE: Hearing on Financing/Deployment of Explosive Detection Systems Before the H. Aviation Subcommittee,* 108th Cong. (2d Sess. 2004) (statement of David Z. Plavin, President, ACI-NA), www.house.gov/transportation/aviation/02-12-04/plavinhauptli.html.

292. Stephen D. Van Beek, Ph.D., Executive Vice President, Policy, Airports Council International North America, Presentation to the Worldwide Conference on Current Challenges in International Aviation, Institute of Air & Space Law, McGill, University: Security and Airports: Assessing the Progress and Going Forward, at 8 (Sept. 25, 2004), www.acina.org/asp/pressdetail.asp?art=1000.

293. *Id.*

294. *Id.* at 9.

295. *Id.*

296. *Id.*

297. *Id.* at 10.

298. U.S. Gov't Accountability Office, Aviation Security: Systematic Planning Needed to Optimize the Deployment of Checked Baggage Screening Systems, GAO-05-365, at 5-6 (Mar. 2005), http://www.gao.gov.

299. *Id.*

300. *Joint Statement on behalf of Airports Council International-North America (ACI-NA) and American Association of Airport Executives (AAAE): Hearing on Passenger and Baggage Screening Problems Before the H. Aviation Subcommittee,* 108th Cong. (2d Sess. 2004) (joint statement of David Z. Plavin, President, ACI-NA, and Todd Hauptli, Sr. Executive Vice President, AAAE), www.aaae.org/government/100_AAAE_ACI-NA_Legislative_Affairs/400_Congressional_Testimony/.

301. *Id.*

302. Stephen D. Van Beek, Ph.D., Executive Vice President, Policy, Airports Council International North America, Presentation to the Worldwide Conference on Current Challenges in International Aviation, Institute of Air & Space Law, McGill, University: Security and Airports: Assessing the Progress and Going Forward, at 4 (Sept. 25, 2004), www.acina.org/asp/pressdetail.asp?art=1000.

303. U.S. Gov't Accountability Office, Aviation Security: Preliminary Observations on TSA's Progress to Allow Airports to Use Private Passenger and Baggage Screening Services, GAO-05-126, at 14 (Nov. 2004), www.gao.gov/docdblite/details.php?rptno=GAO-05-126.

304. *U.S. Department of Homeland Security, Transportation Security Administration, Hearing before the S. Committee on Commerce, Science, and Transportation,* at 3 (Feb. 15, 2005) (statement of David M. Stone), http://www.tsa.gov/public/display?theme=47&content=09000519800ffdcc.

305. Stephen D. Van Beek, Ph.D., Executive Vice President, Policy, Airports Council International North America, Presentation to the Worldwide Conference on Current Challenges in International Aviation, Institute of Air & Space Law, McGill, University: Security and Airports: Assessing the Progress and Going Forward, at 6 (Sept. 25, 2004), www.acina.org/asp/pressdetail.asp?art=1000.

306. *Id.*

307. *Joint Statement on behalf of Airports Council International-North America (ACI-NA) and American Association of Airport Executives (AAAE): Hearing on Passenger and Baggage Screening Problems Before the H. Aviation Subcommittee*, 108th Cong. (2d Sess. 2004) (joint statement of David Z. Plavin, President, ACI-NA, and Todd Hauptli, Sr. Executive Vice President, AAAE), www.aaae.org/government/100_AAAE_ACI-NA_Legislative_Affairs/400_Congressional_Testimony/.

308. Stephen D. Van Beek, Ph.D., Executive Vice President, Policy, Airports Council International North America, Presentation to the Worldwide Conference on Current Challenges in International Aviation, Institute of Air & Space Law, McGill, University: Security and Airports: Assessing the Progress and Going Forward, at 6 (Sept. 25, 2004), www.aci-na.org/asp/pressdetail.asp?art=1000.

309. AVIATION SECURITY ADVISORY COMMITTEE, AIRPORT OF THE FUTURE: THE TASK AHEAD (Sept. 30, 2004), www.tsa.gov/interweb/assetlibrary/Airport_of_the_future_ASAC.ppt; A new emerging technology being deployed and tested is explosive trace detection portals that can screen passengers for explosives. *U.S. Department of Homeland Security, Transportation Security Administration, Hearing before the S. Committee on Commerce, Science, and Transportation*, at 3 (Feb. 15, 2005) (statement of David M. Stone), http://www.tsa.gov/public/display?theme=47&content=09000519800ffdcc.

310. *State of Nation's Airports: Hearing Before the Subcomm. on Aviation of the S. Comm. On Commerce, Science & Transportation*, 108th Cong. (1st Sess. 2003) (statement of Woodie Woodward, Associate Administrator for Airports, Federal Aviation Administration), commerce.senate.gov/pdf/woodward022503.pdf.

311. *Id.*

312. *Id.*

313. *Id.*

314. *Id.*

315. *Joint Statement on behalf of Airports Council International-North America (ACI-NA) and American Association of Airport Executives (AAAE): Hearing on Passenger and Baggage Screening Problems Before the H. Aviation Subcommittee*, 108th Cong. (2d Sess. 2004) (joint statement of David Z. Plavin, President, ACI-NA, and Todd Hauptli, Sr. Executive Vice President, AAAE), *www.aaae.org/government/100_AAAE_ACI-NA_Legislative_Affairs/400_Congressional_Testimony/*.

316. *Id.*

317. *Id.*

318. *Efforts to Meet the Aviation and Transportation Security Act: Hearing on Aviation Security Before the Aviation Subcomm. of the S. Committee on Commerce, Science & Transportation*, 108th Cong. (1st Sess. 2003) (statement of Charles M. Barclay, President, American Association of Airport Executives, on behalf of ACI-NA and AAAE), www.commerce.senate.gov/hearings/testimony.cfm?id=716&wit_id=1924.

319. *9/11 Commission Report: Review of Aviation Security Recommendations: Hearing Before the House Aviation Subcomm.* (Aug. 25, 2004) (statement of Charles M. Barclay, President, American Association of Airport Executives, on behalf of ACI-NA and AAAE), www.house.gov/transportation/aviation/08-25-04/barclay.pdf.

320. *Id.*

321. *Id.*

322. *Id.*

323. *Efforts to Meet the Aviation and Transportation Security Act: Hearing on Aviation Security Before the Aviation Subcomm. of the S. Committee on Commerce, Science & Transportation*, 108th Cong. (1st Sess. 2003) (statement of Charles M. Barclay, President, American Asso-

ciation of Airport Executives, on behalf of ACI-NA and AAAE), *www.commerce.senate.gov/hearings/testimony.cfm?id=716&wit_id=1924.*

324. Stephen D. Van Beek, Ph.D., Executive Vice President, Policy, Airports Council International North America, Presentation to the Worldwide Conference on Current Challenges in International Aviation, Institute of Air & Space Law, McGill, University: Security and Airports: Assessing the Progress and Going Forward, at 11-13 (Sept. 25, 2004), www.acina.org/asp/pressdetail.asp?art=1000.

325. *Joint Statement on behalf of Airports Council International-North America (ACI-NA) and American Association of Airport Executives (AAAE): Hearing on Passenger and Baggage Screening Problems Before the H. Aviation Subcommittee,* 108th Cong. (2d Sess. 2004) (joint statement of David Z. Plavin, President, ACI-NA, and Todd Hauptli, Sr. Executive Vice President, AAAE), *www.aaae.org/government/100_AAAE_ACI-NA_Legislative_Affairs/400_Congressional_Testimony/.*

326. *Efforts to Meet the Aviation and Transportation Security Act: Hearing on Aviation Security Before the Aviation Subcomm.* of the S. Committee on Commerce, Science & Transportation, 108th Cong. (1st Sess. 2003) at 1 (Feb. 5, 2003) (statement of Charles M. Barclay, President, American Association of Airport Executives, on behalf of ACI-NA and AAAE), *www.commerce.senate.gov/hearings/testimony.cfm?id=716&wit_id=1924.*

327. *Id.*

328. *Id.*

329. *9/11 Commission Report: Review of Aviation Security Recommendations: Hearing Before the H. Aviation Subcomm.* (Aug. 25, 2004) (statement of Charles M. Barclay, President, American Association of Airport Executives, on behalf of ACI-NA and AAAE), www.house.gov/transportation/aviation/08-25-04/barclay.pdf.

330. *Efforts to Meet the Aviation and Transportation Security Act: Hearing on Aviation Security Before the Aviation Subcomm.* of the S. Committee on Commerce, Science & Transportation, 108th Cong. (1st Sess. 2003) (statement of Charles M. Barclay, President, American Association of Airport Executives, on behalf of ACI-NA and AAAE), *www.commerce.senate.gov/hearings/testimony.cfm?id=716&wit_id=1924.*

331. *Id.*

332. Stephen D. Van Beek, Ph.D., Executive Vice President, Policy, Airports Council International North America, Presentation to the Worldwide Conference on Current Challenges in International Aviation, Institute of Air & Space Law, McGill, University: Security and Airports: Assessing the Progress and Going Forward, at 14 (Sept. 25, 2004), www.acina.org/asp/pressdetail.asp?art=1000.

333. *Id.*

334. *Id.* at 15.

CHAPTER 3

The American Federal System and the "War on Terrorism"

by Robert A. Sedler

Introduction

In our American federal system, states and local governments function within a framework established by constitutional doctrine and principles. In the area of homeland security, this framework necessarily involves the interaction between federal and state responsibility. While the federal government has the responsibility to protect the nation against a terrorist attack, state and local governments also must protect the health and safety of their residents, so that in this area the exercise of federal power necessarily interacts with the exercise of state power. This chapter will discuss the constitutional principles applicable to federal and state power, and the interaction between federal power and state power in the "war on terrorism." In this connection, the chapter specifically will discuss the provisions of the USA Patriot Act (Patriot Act)[1] and the Homeland Security Act (HSA)[2] that directly relate to state and local governments.

The Constitutional Principles

Our federal system begins with the states. In American constitutional theory, upon Independence, the states succeeded to the sovereignty formerly exercised by the British Crown over domestic matters. State sovereignty is thus a "given" under our constitutional system. Each state has its own laws and its own courts, and possesses the general regulatory and taxation power.[3] As a constitutional matter then, every state can exercise full sovereignty over domestic matters, except to the extent that the Constitution prohibits or restricts a particular exercise of state sovereignty.

This means that each state has the constitutional responsibility to take all actions that are necessary to prevent "domestic terrorism" within its boundaries. When the horrific terrorist attack of 9/11 struck New York City, the state of New York—acting through New York City—made the first response by courageously trying to save the lives of people trapped in the burning buildings, by stopping the fires from spreading, and by controlling the movement of people and traffic in and out of the city. The terrorist attack violated the state's criminal laws, and the state has the constitutional power to prosecute anybody responsible for that attack. The state of New York and all other American states then have the constitutional power to take all actions necessary to prevent any future terrorist attacks within their borders, and are required to expend their own resources to do so.

The Constitution established a federal government with enumerated powers, imposed some limited restrictions on the exercise of state power,[4] and provided that, in the event of a conflict between the exercise of federal power and the exercise of state power, the exercise of federal power would prevail.[5] While, in theory, the federal government can exercise only those powers enumerated for it in the Constitution, as all lawyers know, these powers, particularly the power over interstate commerce, have been construed very broadly by the Supreme Court. The result has been that, today, there is virtually no activity that cannot constitutionally be subject to regulation by Congress in the exercise of its powers under Article I, Section 8, and other constitutional powers.[6]

However, since virtually none of the powers given to Congress under the Constitution are exclusive federal powers, the states—in the absence of federal preemption—are generally free to regulate the same matters regulated by Congress. Moreover, Congress has exercised its preemptive power with a high degree of respect for state sovereignty, and in practice federal preemption is only a modest restriction on the exercise of state power.[7]

Since state power is so extensive, and since the enumerated powers of Congress have been construed so broadly, it follows that the overriding feature of the American federal system with respect to domestic matters is *concurrent power*. Just as the federal government can exercise its power throughout the United States, each state—in the absence of federal preemption—can exercise comparable power within its boundaries. Both the federal government and the states then have the power to take action to prevent domestic terrorism. Further, as we will see, the provisions of the Patriot Act and the HSA provide for considerable federal/state cooperation in this struggle.

In terms of federal/state relations, the Supreme Court specifically has held that considerations of state sovereignty do *not* prevent Congress from regulating the "states as states," such as by requiring them to comply with federal minimum wages laws,[8] or prohibiting them from disclosing or selling information obtained from motor vehicle registrations.[9] The only constitutional restriction on the power of Congress to regulate the "states as states" is that Congress does not have the power to force the states to enact regulatory laws in accordance with federal standards. That is, Congress does not have the power to "commandeer state governments into the service of federal regulatory purposes," because this would be "inconsistent with the Constitution's division of authority between federal and state governments."

The leading case on this issue is *New York v United States*.[10] Congress had enacted a law regulating the disposal of low-level radioactive waste. The law imposed on the states the obligation to deal with the disposal of low-level waste generated within their borders, and provided a number of financial incentives for the states to do so—such as allowing a state to impose a surcharge on radioactive waste received from another state. But the law also contained a provision that if a state failed to provide for the disposal of all radioactive waste by a given date, the state would become the owner of the waste and would be liable for all harm caused by the state's failure to take prompt possession of the waste. The Court held that Congress did not have the constitutional power to compel the states to become the owners of the waste. This, said the Court, "crosses the line distinguishing encouragement from coercion, because it would force the states either to accept ownership of the waste or regulate its disposal according to instructions from Congress."[11] To the same effect is *Printz v. United States*,[12] holding that Congress lacked the power to require state and local law enforcement officers to conduct background checks on prospective handgun purchasers as part of a detailed federal scheme governing the distribution of handguns. Again, the Court emphasized that Congress may not "commandeer state regulation" by requiring the states to enact regulations in accordance with federal standards.

However, Congress may put pressure on the states to regulate in accordance with federal standards by the use of its preemption power and its spending power. Congress may provide that, if the states wish to continue regulating in a field where Congress could preempt state regulation, the states must enact regulations that accord with federal standards.[13] More significantly, Congress may impose restrictions on states and municipalities in its grant-in-aid programs as a condition for the receipt of federal funds, such as a provision in a federal highway program withholding 5 percent of the allocated highway funds from any state that did not prohibit the purchase of alcoholic beverages by persons under the age of twenty-one.[14] In both the preemption and funding situations, the states have a choice. In order to avoid complying with the federally imposed regulations, they can abandon state regulation or refuse federal funding. But if they choose to accept the conditions for continuation of regulation or accept the conditions for the receipt of the funds, there is no "coercion" for constitutional purposes, and so no violation of state sovereignty.

Once these principles are understood, it is clear that in these situations, there can be no such thing as an "unfunded mandate." Congress cannot mandate that the states regulate in accordance with federal standards or expend funds for federally mandated purposes. But Congress can impose conditions on continued state regulation in a field subject to preemption that requires the states to expend their own funds, or it can impose conditions for the receipt of federal funds that require the states to expend funds beyond those received from Congress. As long as the states have a choice to discontinue the state regulation or to refuse the federal funding, state and local governments have no basis for mounting a constitutional challenge.[15]

A final point involves the constitutionality of interstate cooperative arrangements. While Article I, Section 10 requires congressional approval of interstate compacts, for constitutional purposes, an interstate compact refers to only an agreement between states that may increase the political power of the involved states or interfere with federal supremacy. Congressional approval is not required for interstate cooperative agreements that do not have this effect, such as an agreement between states to promote regional banking.[16]

With these constitutional principles in mind, we may now turn our attention to a consideration of how the allocation of federal and state power plays out in the "war on terrorism," specifically in the provisions of the Patriot Act and the HSA.

Federal and State Power in the "War on Terrorism"

The provisions of the Patriot Act and the HSA are directed toward increasing the effectiveness of the federal government in the war on terrorism.

Since the states, in the exercise of their sovereignty over domestic matters, have the constitutional responsibility to take all actions that are necessary to prevent "domestic terrorism" within their boundaries, there was no need, in the wake of 9/11, for Congress to address state efforts to combat terrorism, and Congress did not do so. There are very few provisions in either the Patriot Act or the HSA that are directed toward the states, and most of them provide for cooperative ventures designed to assist the states or coordinate federal and state efforts in the war on terrorism. One set of provisions, contained in the Patriot Act, involves funding programs for state and local governments that are designed to prevent computer crime.[17] Another set of provisions—also contained in the Patriot Act—recognizes that state and local government officials may need access to foreign intelligence, and so provides for the establishment of a program that will help them identify and utilize foreign intelligence.[18] A third set of provisions in the Patriot Act, recognizing the role of state and local governments as the first responders to acts of terrorism, provides grants to state and local governments to improve their first response and terrorism prevention capabilities.[19]

The HSA likewise tries to promote federal/state cooperative arrangements in the war on terrorism. Among other things, the HSA: establishes a Directorate for Information Analysis and Infrastructure Protection in the Department of Homeland Security, which is to coordinate and cooperate with state and local governmental agencies in a number of ways;[20] gives the Under Secretary for Science and Technology the responsibility for establishing a system for transferring homeland security developments or technologies to federal, state, local government, and private sector entities;[21] establishes an Office for State and Local Government Coordination in the Office of the Secretary of Homeland Security that is directed to provide substantial assistance to state and local governments in the national strategy for combating terrorism and other homeland security activities;[22] and provides for the sharing of homeland security information between the federal and state governments.[23]

Turning now to federal preemption, we see that in the Patriot Act and the HSA, Congress has made little effort to preempt or control state action in the war on terrorism. Only two provisions appear to fall into this category. The first involves licenses to transport hazardous materials (HAZMAT licenses). Congress has directed that the states not issue or renew a license to any individual to operate a motor vehicle transporting in commerce a hazardous material unless the secretary of transportation has first determined that the individual does not pose a security risk warranting denial of the license.[24] The state must ask the U.S. attorney general to conduct a background records check of the individual seeking such a license, and upon completing the background check, the attorney general notifies the secretary of transportation of the results. The secretary of transportation then makes the determination of whether the individual requesting the license poses a security risk warranting denial of the license. The state is also directed to submit to the secretary of transportation such information as the secretary may require concerning each alien to whom the state has issued a HAZMAT license and other individuals to whom a HAZMAT license has been issued. Since Congress could constitutionally preempt state power to regulate the issuance of licenses to transport hazardous materials in interstate commerce, it can, as a condition of continued state regulation, impose conditions on the issuance of HAZMAT licenses.[25]

The second provision involves disclosure of critical infrastructure information. The HSA provides that information voluntarily submitted to a federal agency regarding the security of critical infrastructure and protected systems, analysis, warning, interdependency study, recovery, reconstitution, or other informational purpose, is exempt from disclosure under the federal Freedom of Information Act (FOIA).[26] The HSA also provides that, if this information is provided to a state or local government or agency, it shall not (1) be made available pursuant to any state or local law requiring disclosure of information or records, (2) be disclosed to any party by a state or local government agency without the written consent of the person or entity distributing the information, or (3) be used for any purpose other than protecting critical infrastructure or protected systems, or in furtherance of an investigation or the prosecution of a criminal act.[27] This is a permissible condition on the receipt of information by state or local governments, since states and local governments can refuse to accept this information from the federal government. The HSA specifically provides that it does not apply to critical infrastructure information independently obtained by a state or local governmental agency.[28]

The one area in which Congress, in waging the war on terrorism, has acted directly to override state power involves the issuance of drivers' licenses and personal identification cards. In 2004 Congress effectively set standards that the states must follow in issuing drivers' licenses and personal identification cards. However, in 2005 Congress repealed the 2004 law and enacted a new law that imposed more restrictions on the states. Under the 2005 law,[29] state-issued drivers' licenses and personal identification cards must comply with the federal standards to be accepted by a federal agency for any official purpose, such as identification at airport security. Obviously, the states will have to comply with these requirements, or their state-issued drivers' licenses and personal identification cards will become worthless. Licenses must be magnetized and machine-readable; contain a digital photograph of the licensee; and have physical security features designed to prevent tampering, counterfeiting, and duplication of the document for fraudulent purposes.

The most significant changes made by the 2005 law took away the power of the states, recognized in the 2004 law, to determine what categories of persons would be eligible to receive drivers' licenses and what the criteria for determining eligibility would be. The 2005 law takes this power away from the states and effectively prevents the states from issuing drivers' licenses to undocumented or "illegal" aliens, as is now done in eleven states. The law sets "minimum issuance standards," which require presentation and verification of specific information before a drivers' license or personal identification card can be issued. This specific information includes "evidence of lawful status," namely valid documentary evidence that the person is a U.S. citizen or national, is a lawfully admitted alien, or otherwise has immigration status that entitles the person to remain in the United States.[30] The law also contains rules relating to verification of documents and requires the states to enter into a memorandum of understanding with the secretary of homeland security no later than September 11, 2005, to use routinely the automated Systematic Alien Verification for Entitlements System to verify the legal status of applicants who are not U.S. citizens. Finally, the law imposes a number of other detailed requirements on the issuance of drivers' licenses and personal identification cards by the states and provides for federal grants to assist the states in complying with the standards imposed by the law.

In an effort to prevent the issuance of drivers' licenses and personal identification cards to illegal aliens, Congress has swept aside any pretense of concern for state sovereignty and has imposed stringent requirements on the states. This contrasts sharply with what Congress did in the Patriot Act and the HSA, where it made little effort to preempt or control state action.

So far, we have discussed preemption of state laws under the Patriot Act and the HSA, and the direct control imposed by Congress on state issuance of drivers' licenses and personal identification cards. There is also the possibility that some state and local anti-terrorism laws could be preempted by other federal laws that in and of themselves were not designed to deal with terrorism. Congress is deemed to have impliedly intended to preempt state law wherever there is a direct conflict between state law and federal law such that compliance with both the state and federal laws is a physical impossibility, or whenever the state law stands as an obstacle to the implementation of the full purposes of the federal law.[31] This issue arose very recently with respect to a District of Columbia law regulating the rail transport of certain ultrahazardous activities within a 2.2-mile zone around the Capitol. The law was challenged by a railroad on the ground that it interfered with the comprehensive federal regulation of hazardous materials by rail, in particular with the Hazardous Materials Transportation Act.[32] The district court, looking to the terms of this law and other federal laws relating to railroad safety, rejected the claim of implied preemption on the ground that the railroad could comply with both the applicable federal law and the District of Columbia law, so there was no conflict.[33] However, the court of appeals immediately stayed the enforcement of the law pending appeal,[34] immediately heard an emergency motion for injunction, and remanded the case to the district court with directions to enter a preliminary injunction prohibiting enforcement of the District of Columbia law.[35]

The appeals court concluded that the railroad had demonstrated a strong likelihood of prevailing on the merits, on the ground that the District of Columbia law was preempted by the Federal Railroad Safety Act (FRSA).[36] The court noted that the FRSA mandated that, throughout the United States, laws related to railroad safety "shall be nationally uniform to the extent practicable," and that, while the FRSA contained a "safe harbor" provision for state and local laws, the state or local law could not be incompatible with a federal regulation. The court went on to find that the District of Columbia law was incompatible with a regulation relating to the transportation of hazardous materials that had been issued by the department of transportation following the terrorist attacks of September 11 and subsequent threats related to hazardous materials.

The court specifically found that the federal regulation required a flexible, individually tailored approach, while the District of Columbia law was more restrictive. And, the court concluded, in any event, the vulnerability of hazardous material passing through the Capitol area would adequately be addressed by the standards set forth in the department of transportation regulation. This case serves as an illustration of the possibility of implied preemption of state and local laws directed against terrorist activity, here by the combination of a more general federal law and a specific regulation issued in response to the threat of terrorist activity within a particular jurisdiction.

Federal and State Power in the "War on Terrorism": A Retrospective

As pointed out above, there are very few provisions in either the Patriot Act or the HSA that are directed toward the states,[37] and most of them are cooperative ventures designed to assist the states or coordinate federal and state efforts in the war on terrorism. It is true that Congress has interfered seriously with the power of states to control the issuance of drivers' licenses. But while this measure is justified ostensibly in terms of national security (proponents noted that some of the nineteen hijackers in the September 11 attacks used drivers' licenses as identification when checking in at the airports), it would appear that the primary concern of Congress was to prevent the issuance of drivers' licenses to undocumented or illegal aliens. With this exception, Congress has made no effort to interfere with or supplant the states' constitutional power and responsibility to take all actions that are necessary to prevent "domestic terrorism" within the boundaries of each state. But as the horrific terrorist attacks of 9/11 demonstrate, preventing terrorism is a national problem, and it is the federal government that must have the primary responsibility to protect the nation from future terrorist attacks. By the enactment of the Patriot Act and the HSA, Congress has sought to exercise that responsibility.

As explained at the outset, the overriding feature of the American federal system with respect to domestic matters is concurrent power. Thus, while Congress has the primary responsibility to protect the nation from future terrorist attacks, the states not only have the responsibility to prevent "domestic terrorism," but also the responsibility to carry on the day-to-day functions of government. The exercise of federal power often impacts the states, which must deal with the collateral consequences that the exercise of federal power creates within states and localities. Nowhere is this impact more clear than in the war on terrorism. To quote Mr. Abbott,[38] as a result of many actions taken by the federal government to prevent a terrorist attack, "the freedom of the state to set its own priorities in protecting the public health and safety, and to identify and adopt systems best suited to its own history, economy, and geography is reduced."

One example is the financial burden imposed on state and local governments when the terrorist threat level is raised, since they must increase the police presence required in areas with potential terrorist targets.[39] Another example is the mandates issued by the Transportation Security Administration on airports and maritime ports requiring adoption of new passenger, baggage, and cargo screening measures with substantial direct and indirect costs that must be borne by states and local governments.[40] A third example is the conditions imposed on federal grant assistance, which require state and local governments to expend additional funds of their own.[41] These requirements lead Mr. Abbott to conclude that: "The threat of terrorism—exacerbated by the availability of weapons of mass destruction—has dramatically changed the environment of independence under which states and local governments must act to protect the public health and safety. Even though states retain the police power under the Constitution, and even though the Constitution and federal statutes give states the primary responsibility to protect the public health and safety, federal homeland security programs are dramatically centralizing authority in the federal government even while much of the economic and operational burden of homeland security resides with the states."[42]

Without necessarily agreeing that the situation is as dire as Mr. Abbott posits, it is worth noting that it is the inevitable result of the operation of the American federal system during the war on terrorism. The exercise of federal power to prevent a terrorist attack on the United States clearly impacts on the states that must deal with the collateral consequences that the exercise of federal power creates within the states and localities. As states deal with these collateral consequences, they must expend their own resources—usually far in excess of the financial assistance they receive from the federal government—and must alter their priorities in protecting the public health and safety. But this result is fully consistent with the constitutional structure of the American federal system. For the most part, Congress is not imposing any mandates, unfunded or otherwise, on the states.[43] Congress is exercising its powers under the Constitution, and the states' exercise of their powers are necessarily affected by Congress' exercise of its powers.

If this has resulted in a diminution of state power, the Constitution provides a remedy. That remedy lies in the structure of the federal government itself. As the Supreme Court explained in *Garcia v. San Antonio Metropolitan Transit Authority*,[44] the composition of the federal government was designed to protect the states from overreaching by Congress. The states set the qualifications for members of the House of Representatives and for voting for presidential electors, and are directly represented in the Senate. The underlying assumption here is that Congress will be responsive to the needs of the states, and will see to it that Congress does not impair the sovereignty of the states and their function in the American federal system. Stated simply, if the states need more funding and greater control in carrying out their responsibility to protect their citizens from "domestic terrorism," they must turn to Congress.

NOTES

1. Pub. L. No. 107-56, 115 Stat. 272 (2001).
2. Pub. L. No. 107-296, 116 Stat. 2135 (2002).
3. Local governments, it may be noted, do not possess any sovereignty, and for constitutional purposes are "creatures of the state" that can exercise only the power given to them by state legislatures.
4. These restrictions are contained in Article I, Section 10, and, among other things, prohibit the states from coining money, enacting any law impairing the obligations of contracts, and, without the consent of Congress, from taxing imports or exports or entering into an agreement with another state or foreign country.
5. Federal supremacy is provided in the Supremacy Clause of Art. I, § 6.
6. In recent years, the Supreme Court has imposed some limitations on the power of Congress to regulate purely local noneconomic activity. *See* U.S. v. Lopez, 514 U.S. 549 (1995) (the regulation of firearms near a school); U.S. v. Morrison, 529 U.S. 598 (2000) (violence against women having no connection to interstate commerce). However, in Gonzales v. Raich, 125 S.Ct. 2195 (2005), the Court came down strongly in favor of federal power by holding that Congress could prohibit the local cultivation and use of marijuana for medicinal purposes, as permitted by California law. The Court's holding was based on the fact that the production of marijuana for home consumption would have a substantial effect on the supply and demand in the national market for this illegal commodity. The effect of the decision basically limits Lopez and Morrison to their particular facts. The decision is also a blow to states' rights insofar as it enables federal law to preempt California's efforts to permit the use of medical marijuana.
7. As the Court emphasized in Medtronic, Inc v. Lehr, 518 U.S. 470 (1996), the application of preemption should be informed by "the assumption that the historic police powers of the States were not to be superseded by the Federal Act unless that was the clear and manifest purpose of Congress. As we will see, there is only very limited preemption under the USA Patriot Act and the HSA.
8. Garcia v. San Antonio Metro. Transit Auth., 469 U.S. 528 (1985).
9. Reno v. Condon, 528 U.S. 141 (2000). When Congress is regulating the "states as states," pursuant to a proper exercise of congressional power (such as under the commerce clause), for constitutional purposes, the states are in the same position as private entities subject to congressional regulation. This being so, Congress may require the states as well as private entities to bear the costs of complying with congressional regulations. While state and local governments strongly protest against so-called "federal unfunded mandates," they cannot assert any constitutional objection. Congress has tried to put some limits on the imposition of "federal unfunded mandates" in the Unfunded Mandates Reform Act of

1995, 28 U.S.C. §§ 658, 1531-32, but the Act appears to have had only a minimal effect. *See* Daniel E. Troy, *Recent Developments: Regulatory Reform & the 104th Congress: The Unfunded Mandates Reform Act of 1995*, 49 ADMIN. L. REV. 139 (1997); David S. Broder, *Those Unfinished Mandates*, WASH. POST, March 17, 2005, at A25.

10. 505 U.S. 144 (1992).

11. *Id.* at 175.

12. 521 U.S. 898 (1997).

13. Fed. Energy Comm'n v. Miss., 456 U.S. 742 (1982) (state utility regulation would not be preempted if state agreed to consider adopting proposed federal standards in such regulation); S.C. v. Baker, 485 U.S. 505 (1988) (state wishing to enact regulation in field where state regulation could be preempted must comply with federal standards). And, of course, the states must bear any additional costs connected with their enacting regulations that accord with federal standards.

14. S.D. v. Dole, 483 U.S. 203 (1987).

15. And as pointed out previously, where Congress can regulate the states as states, it is irrelevant that the states, like private entities, have to expend their own funds in order to comply with the federal regulation. *See supra* note 9.

16. Ne. Bancorp, Inc. v. Bd. of Governors of Fed. Reserve Sys., 472 U.S. 159 (1985). *See generally*, the discussion of intergovernmental cooperation *infra* Chapter 9, *Marshalling Resources*.

17. These include provisions: for the establishment of regional computer forensic laboratories to provide training for federal, state, and local law enforcement personnel involving computer-related crime; to assist federal, state, and local law enforcement personnel in enforcing laws relating to computer-related crime; and to facilitate the sharing of federal law enforcement expertise about computer-related crime with state and local law enforcement personnel. USA Patriot Act § 816, 28 U.S.C. § 509.

18. *Id.*

19. USA Patriot Act § 1005 (First Responders Assistance Act), 28 U.S.C. § 509; USA Patriot Act § 1014, 42 U.S.C. § 3711.

20. Homeland Security Act § 201, 6 U.S.C. § 121.

21. Homeland Security Act § 302, 6 U.S.C. § 182.

22. Homeland Security Act § 801, 6 U.S.C. § 361.

23. Homeland Security Act §§ 891-892, 6 U.S.C. § 482.This includes electronic wire and oral interception information, information revealing the threat of an actual or potential attack, and information from grand jury proceedings.

24. USA Patriot Act § 1012, 49 U.S.C. § 5103.

25. See the discussion, *supra*, note 13 and accompanying text.

26. Homeland Security Act § 214, 6 U.S.C. § 133.

27. *Id.*

28. *Id.* These provisions are discussed in more detail *infra* Chapter 1, *Public Disclosure of Information by Emergency Services Agencies: A Post September 11 Paradigm Shift*.

29. Pub. L. No. 109-13, 119 Stat. 311 (2005).

30. This includes nonimmigrant visa status, such as for students and authorized foreign workers, and asylum applicant status.

31. *See, e.g.*, Hisquierdo v. Hisquierdo, 439 U.S. 572 (1979) (where a federal law providing retirement benefits explicitly stated that the benefits would not be subject to legal attachment, a state could not apply its marital property law to require that a share of these benefits go to the other spouse upon divorce).

In some circumstances, Congress may have intended what is called "implied field preemption," in that Congress intended to "occupy the field" so as to leave no room for state regulation at all. It is difficult to think of any circumstances where "implied field preemption" would apply to exclude all state regulation in the war on terrorism.

32. 49 U.S.C. § 5101.

33. CSX Transp., Inc. v. Williams, CV Action No. 05-338 (EGS), 2005 U.S. Dist. LEXIS 6569, U.S. Dist. Ct. D.D.C. (Apr. 18, 2005).

34. 406 F.3d 667 (D.C. Cir. 2005).

35. 2005 U.S. App. LEXIS 7604 (May 3, 2005).

36. 49 U.S.C. §§ 20101-20153. The government has now sought a Section 215 order against a library in Connecticut, and the library has filed a federal court suit challenging the constitutionality of Section 215. *See* Editorial, *Excessive Powers*, N.Y. Times, Aug. 27, 2005; *ACLU Sues FBI over Record Request from Library Association Member*, Frontrunner (Bulletin News Network), Aug. 26, 2005.

37. State universities and state and local libraries potentially could be impacted by the federal government's invocation of Section 215 of the USA Patriot Act, 50 U.S.C. § 1861, which authorizes the Federal Bureau of Investigation to obtain an order from the Foreign Intelligence Surveillance Court requiring the production of a person's "records" in connection with an investigation to obtain foreign intelligence information. By its terms, the order could require a university to disclose student records or a library to disclose patron book or video borrowings. A suit challenging the constitutionality of Section 215 under the First and Fourth Amendments has been pending in the United States District Court for the Eastern District of Michigan for some time. Muslim Cmty. Ass'n of Ann Arbor v. Ashcroft, No. 03-72913 (E.D.Mich. filed July 20, 2003). In connection with this suit, Attorney General John Ashcroft filed an affidavit, stating that the Federal Bureau of Investigation had never sought a Section 215 order. Section 215 is scheduled to expire at the end of 2005 unless reauthorized by Congress.

38. Ernest B. Abbott, *Homeland Security in the 21st Century: New Inroads on the State Police Power*, 36 Urb. Law. 837 (2004).

39. *Id.*

40. *Id.*

41. *Id.*

42. *Id.*

43. Congress has effectively imposed a mandate on the states with respect to standards for the issuance of drivers' licenses and personal identification cards. Congress has provided for grants to the states to enable them to comply with the requirements; depending on the adequacy of the grants, this mandate will be either "funded" or "unfunded." *See* the discussion of the costs of compliance with the requirements in *States May Obey Driver's License Rules*, Associated Press, May 10, 2005.

44. 469 U.S. 528, 550-553 (1985).

CHAPTER 4

Preparedness
for Public Health Emergencies

by William C. Nicholson

Introduction

The September 11, 2001, terrorist attacks and the anthrax attacks that followed closely thereafter dramatically changed our national priorities. Innumerable experts across the country—from government, business, and academia—began to examine closely our capabilities for responding to different kinds of terrorist assaults. Preparedness concerns that had previously received only lip service suddenly were at the center of national attention. It was apparent that our health care and public health systems were not prepared for the potential use of weapons of mass destruction, nor for the onset of a communicable disease pandemic.

Potential medical response needs contrast markedly with our deteriorated national public health structure. In addition to improvements in the ability to deal with mass casualty events, assessment of the existing public health structure revealed the need for changes in its legal underpinnings. The major public health topics of legal interest include evolving standards, implications of increasing medical surge capacity, quarantine and evacuation issues, licensing of medical personnel and activities outside their certifying jurisdiction, and general liability concerns.

Defining Public Health Responders

Our nation's public health system encompasses far more than its principal governmental institutions, which are found in public health offices in all states and in many localities, as well as in the federal Centers for Disease Control and the United States Public Health Service Commissioned Corps.[1] Increasingly, all health care providers whether in private, nonprofit, or government entities—are being incorporated into the public health system. The trend toward encompassing all aspects of health care into the public health arena accelerated after the September 11, 2001, attacks.

The Homeland Security Act of 2002 (HSA)[2] includes "emergency medical, and related personnel, agencies, and authorities" in its definition of "emergency response provider."[3] On February 28, 2003, President Bush released Homeland Security Presidential Directive 5 (HSPD 5).[4] This directive commanded all federal agencies to take detailed steps for planning and incident management.[5] The document also directed that emergency responder performance standards be set, and established sanctions for responders who failed to conform to those standards.[6] The sanctions involve withholding of federal preparedness grant funds for noncompliant entities. Given the heavy reliance of the public health care system on federal support, it is highly unlikely that any entity receiving grant funds will refuse to comply.[7]

HSPD 5 also commands all federal agencies to collaborate with the Department of Homeland Security (DHS) to establish a National Response Plan (NRP) and a National Incident Management System (NIMS).[8] On the first anniversary of the DHS,[9] March 1, 2004, Secretary Tom Ridge announced publication of the adopted NIMS.[10] NIMS is the operational part of the NRP,[11] and it contains specific guidelines for emergency preparedness and response.

The NRP was adopted in November 2004.[12] The NRP includes in its first responder definition "public health, clinical care, and other skilled support personnel (such as equipment operators) who provide immediate support services during prevention, response, and recovery operations. First responders may include personnel from Federal, State, local, tribal, or nongovernmental organizations."[13]

Events of National Significance: Evolving Federal Preparedness Standards

Clearly, when medical service providers diagnose and treat afflicted persons, and isolate them from "healthy" residents, they are acting as "first responders" and have key responsibilities in public health emergencies. Initial actions by responders may include surveillance, testing processes, immunizations, prophylaxis, and isolation or quarantine for biological threats. The Department of Health and Human Services (HHS), together with state and local public health officials, will coordinate these efforts.[14]

The NRP has annexes that offer detailed information on how the federal government will assist in "incidents of national significance." The basic premise of the NRP is that such occurrences will be handled at the lowest possible level of government.[15] Assistance takes place through prevention, preparedness, response, and recovery from potential or actual events of national significance.[16] Federal assistance is structured around Emergency Support Functions (ESFs), the goal of which is to energize the precise components that can best address the incident's requirements.[17]

ESF #8, titled "Public Health and Medical Services Annex,"[18] defines the structure for federal assistance in the public health arena. ESF #8's lead agency is HHS, under general supervision of the assistant secretary for public health emergency preparedness (ASPHEP). ESF #8 resources can be activated through the Robert T. Stafford Act[19] or the Public Health Service Act[20] (pending the availability of funds) for federal-to-federal support, or in accordance with the memorandum for federal mutual aid included in the NRP Financial Management Support Annex. The core functional areas that comprise ESF #8 support include assessment of public health/medical needs (including behavioral health); public health surveillance; medical care personnel; and medical equipment and supplies.[21] ESF #8 details initial and continuing actions to provide these areas of support. It also details specific supporting actions to be taken by federal agencies in support of HHS.

As stated previously, HSPD 5 requires federal regulation of homeland security responders.[22] These requirements will be enforced through loss of funding for noncompliant "states, territories, tribes, and local entities."[23] Although these cuts could have begun in FY 2005, DHS issued guidance for compliance in FY 2005 that puts off such steps.[24]

NIMS mandates "establishing guidelines, protocols, and standards for planning, training, and exercises, personnel qualification and certification, equipment certification, and publication management."[25] National-level preparedness standards will be "maintained and managed" through a multijurisdictional, multidisciplinary center, using a collaborative process.[26] To achieve this end, NIMS establishes a NIMS Integration Center (NIC).[27]

NIMS outlines the NIC's nature in very approximate terms.[28] A variety of entities, including local, state, tribal, federal, private sector, and professional organizations may suggest changes in NIMS standards and other corrective actions.[29] The secretary of DHS, however, retains ultimate authority for alteration of NIMS standards.[30] In other words, other affected entities may put forward modifications, but their input is advisory only.

On another front, the National Commission on Terrorist Attacks Upon the United States (9/11 Commission) proposed that National Fire Protection Association's "Standard on Disaster/Emergency Management and Business Continuity Programs" (NFPA 1600),[31] be recognized as "the national preparedness standard" for government and business.[32] The commission further suggested that NFPA 1600 become the legal standard of care toward the public and employees.

On December 17, 2004, President Bush signed the Intelligence Reform and Terrorism Prevention Act of 2004 (IRTP Act).[33] The IRTP Act endorses NFPA 1600 as a "voluntary" national preparedness standard, and states that the sense of Congress is that the secretary of homeland security should promote voluntary adoption of standards such as NFPA 1600.[34]

NFPA 1600 iterates major requirements for planning, training, and conducting exercises. It sets up a shared set of norms for disaster management, emergency management, and business continuity programs. NFPA 1600 specifies ways to exercise plans, and catalogs resource organizations within the fields of disaster recovery, emergency management, and business continuity planning. NFPA 1600 requires that "[t]he program shall include, but shall not be limited to a(n):

1. strategic plan;
2. emergency operations/response plan;
3. mitigation plan;
4. recovery plan;
5. continuity plan."[35]

NFPA 1600 recommends that financial institutions and insurers consider compliance when evaluating creditworthiness and insurability. For those enterprises, compliance will result in better protection of their own assets. Therefore, they will likely adopt the proposal. The result would be that businesses or individuals not in compliance could find themselves facing significant increases in the costs of borrowing and insurance. For the health care industry, the cost and availability of insurance is already creating national concern. Similarly, this capital-intensive business cannot function without the availability of credit. In this manner, the federal government has created a system that relies on business pressure to encourage obedience with the standard.

NFPA 1600 also imposes a duty to adhere to current laws, policies, and industry practices.[36] Compliance, therefore, will be an evolving objective. The pressure for adoption of NFPA 1600 created by the IRTP Act will likely combine with the standard-setting power of DHS under NIMS to result eventually in broad acceptance of the standard throughout the public health community.

While the federal structure for public health preparedness may seem both daunting and all-inclusive, states also have requirements that must be obeyed.[37]

Legal Issues in Developing Medical Surge Capacity

Medical surge capacity (MSC) may be defined as increasing rapidly the health care system's ability to deal with a large number of patients in the aftermath of a terrorist attack or other mass casualty event. Prime challenges include increasing the number of available hospital beds, enlarging decontamination abilities, ensuring that a sufficient number of medical personnel show up after an event, and ensuring a sufficient supply of medicines.

Hospital capacity is a "critical element of homeland security."[38] The *Economist* stated in December 2001, that "All the doubts about money, co-ordination and politics will apply to the most worrying aspect of homeland security: the medical response. Though it has some of the best hospitals in the world, America (has) . . . largely eliminated (its) 'surge capacity' (the ability to cope with a flood of patients)."[39] In September 2003, Secretary Ridge stated that "We need, in our working with the Department of Health and Human Services and with mayors and folks in local communities, to . . . begin to build the capacity within each urban area to respond to a mass-casualty event."[40] Building MSC, however, will take both time and money.

Developing MSC involves making choices. The options available all require funding and a commitment to creative management. They may be summed up as: (1) crowd a larger number of patients into existing physical space; (2) augment treatment space by incorporating locations not normally utilized for emergency care; (3) push patients through the structure faster. It stands to reason that reducing the time a patient spends in the system by 25 percent will result in a 25 percent greater ability to treat patients; or increase patients' delays before they get medical care.[41] Rural hospitals in particular face many challenges as they consider how to weigh, and select among, these approaches.[42] Lack of funding is a very real consideration. Rural venues are not considered to be primary terrorist targets. Indeed, even the tasks of defining the term "rural" and delineating demarcation between rural and urban areas pose significant challenges. The lack of definition makes application for grant funds, evaluating services, and creating uniform policies difficult tasks.[43] Whether urban or rural, health system choices taken (or not taken) regarding MSC have significant potential legal effects.

One way to augment capacity is through portable hospitals similar to those used by the military. This is costly, but the federal government has shown itself willing to make such investments.[44]

Failure to appreciate the dimensions of the matter and make appropriate plans may result in liability. NIMS has planning requirements applicable to public health entities. Failure to comply with those requirements may result in liability if that failure is the proximate cause of injury.[45] Capacity must be evaluated and, if inadequate, reasonable goals for rectification must be set and complied with for planning to be considered sufficient. Every entity should evaluate achievable improvements and understand that the consequence of not implementing them may be liability.

The need to enhance the U.S. Food and Drug Administration surge capability for evaluating biological, chemical, and radiological threat agents by enhancing the Food Emergency Response Network is another challenge relevant to public health. While increases have been sought to augment this capacity, much remains to be done.[46]

Quarantine

The 2001 anthrax attacks and numerous copycat events—as well as the Severe Acute Respiratory Syndrome (SARS) epidemic—brought to the fore the question of whether existing powers for quarantine and evacuation were sufficient for the aftermath of a bioterrorism attack. The potential scope of isolation and quarantine—and the logistical complexity of large-scale quarantine—is daunting. Thus, even though only one uncooperative patient was physically detained in the United States to prevent the spread of SARS,[47] the city of Toronto experienced a much greater challenge, with over 39,000 people ordered to remain in quarantine.[48]

As a general matter, local responders will be faced with the issue of how to apply legal authorities to questions related to public health; this typically is a matter of state law.[49] To promote uniformity, the Centers for Disease Control and Prevention supported research into creation of a broadly accepted standard. The result was the Model State Emergency Health Powers Act (MSEHPA).[50] The National Association of Attorneys General endorsed reevaluation of state public health statutes and consideration of them in light of MSEHPA.[51] Their resolution encouraged the education of public health authorities and their counsel on the constitutional and statutory laws regarding public health response to assure the best response and preparedness in an emergency. MSEHPA's intent is to promote a "renewed focus on the prevention, detection, management, and containment of public health emergencies."[52] A substantial majority of states have modified their preexisting public health statutes after review of the recommended public health emergency powers in MSEHPA.

MSEHPA comes down strongly on the side of public health regulation, granting broad powers to states. States adopting MSEHPA provisions have given their governors broad powers to declare and enforce public health emergencies. MSEHPA also would allow adopting states to seize medical supplies and drugs, regardless of ownership, during a declared public health emergency. Authorities also could take possession of, utilize, and, if needed, destroy property.

MSEHPA has two goals regarding infectious disease: Effective detection and efficient response.[53] In terms of detection, MSEHPA positions pharmacies, hospitals, and outpatient service providers on the leading edge of the fight against bioterrorism. Most states and many local governments have long had, and exercised, authority to isolate or quarantine any person diagnosed with—or who has been in contact with—certain contagious diseases. MSEHPA includes a similar isolation and quarantine authority during public health emergencies. MSEHPA also contains provisions—based on preexisting state provisions—that allow officials to examine, vaccinate, and treat people during a public health emergency, and to isolate or quarantine them if they refuse.

Recognizing that any mandatory isolation, quarantine, examination, or treatment is a restriction on individual liberty triggering constitutional due process protections, MSEHPA includes the rights to notice and a hearing, and requires officials to demonstrate that their proposed restraint is the "least restrictive means" to prevent the spread of infectious disease. However, it also authorizes strong steps if needed. People could be tested forcibly for illness, and compelled to receive vaccinations.

A written directive from public health officials would be required for isolation and quarantine. An appeals process exists through the courts, which includes access to free legal counsel. The process commences with a court hearing for the state to show cause that its actions were taken properly. An individual would be required to demonstrate that the state breached conditions of the isolation or quarantine order. The appeals procedure would consume a period of days. The process attempts to balance the social goals served by police powers with individual freedom.

Critics have pointed out constitutional conflicts in the MSEHPA.[54] The broad powers that MSEHPA grants have been characterized as overly intrusive on important freedoms. Personal privacy is one of our most cherished constitutional rights. The privacy rule contained in the Health Information Portability and Accountability Act of 1996 (HIPAA)[55] respects this right by creating classes of protected health information. MSEHPA, in contrast, uses a "disclose now, obtain consent later" approach to this data. Indeed, under appropriate circumstances, authorities may be able to obtain, use, and even publicly release this information prior to complying with privacy regulations.[56] In so doing, MSEHPA adheres to a long line of preventative jurisprudence cases, many of which arose in the public health arena.[57] These cases recognize that in an emergency, the government must be granted leeway to create a strong and effective legal structure to combat major dangers such as bioterrorism.

ESF #8 tasks the Department of State with informing other nations of quarantine and isolation steps.

Evacuation

One of emergency response's most difficult characteristics is the reality that frequently a choice must be made between unambiguously ugly alternatives. On occasion, various plaintiffs will view the same act as mistaken on contradictory grounds. Evacuation is a prime illustration of this phenomenon.

State and local emergency management statutes and ordinances are the source for legal authorities to issue an evacuation order. These laws generally grant the head of government the authority to forcibly evacuate people from their homes and businesses.[58] Frequently, evacuation may be the most helpful move to ensure public safety. Common examples are evacuations from low-lying coastal areas in the path of a hurricane, a community in which a chemical tank car filled with chlorine gas has derailed, or a specific area to protect evidence as part of a criminal investigation. Evacuation, nonetheless, is expensive and logistically complex, it creates significant economic disruption to individuals and the economy, and it generates safety hazards of its own. Evacuation decisions force response officials to balance conflicting objectives in a chaotic environment to react effectively to the circumstances, while avoiding unnecessary disruption of daily life. Fortunately, while they do have major economic impacts and may be controversial and politicized after the fact, evacuation decisions rarely lead to liability. Public policy decisions, such as deciding whether and to what extent evacuation should take place, are the type of act that typically should be sheltered by discretionary function immunity.[59]

Every so often, individuals refuse to evacuate. No appealing alternatives are available at that juncture. Should authorities consume irreplaceable time convincing the intractable inhabitants to evacuate when other people need to be rescued? Is it a wise investment of inadequate responders to arrest and confine these people (thereby also running the risk of a possible false arrest lawsuit)? At that point, some jurisdictions demand that those declining to evacuate execute a "next of kin" document in order to preserve the information needed to notify their relatives following their death, with the implication that failure to leave will result in death. Such forms also contain waiver of liability language to lessen the probability that the government will be held responsible for the person's death. One frequent cause for a person's refusal to evacuate is that companion animals may not come with them to Red Cross shelters. Many jurisdictions are dealing with this matter by making preparatory arrangements for veterinarians to care for such animals.

Occasionally, vital tasks must be performed at an evacuated scene during the emergency. At that time, the mission's character and importance must be assessed to determine whether it is worthwhile to hazard lives and legal liability by allowing such action. To be safe from a legal standpoint, reentry should be permitted only when the risk has ended. If the scene harbors infectious organisms or other dangers, appropriate personal protective equipment must be utilized.

ESF #8 specifies the Department of Defense as a support agency for evacuations.[60]

Duty to Treat

One significant concern during a mass casualty event, particularly one resulting from terrorist activity, is whether health care workers will show up for work. Health care workers have justifiable concerns regarding cross contamination in chemical events, as well as infection from biological agents. The NRP's ESF #8 addresses their safety specifically.[61] It specifies the Department of Labor's (DoL) role—through the Occupational Safety and Health Administration—in coordinating the safety and health assets of cooperating agencies and the private sector with the goal of providing technical assistance and conducting worker exposure assessment, as well as responder and worker risk management within the Incident Command System.

Possible elements in this activity may include 24/7 site-safety monitoring; worker exposure monitoring; health monitoring; sampling and analysis; development and oversight of the site-specific safety and health plan; and personal protective equipment selection, distribution, training, and respirator-fit testing. These matters recall the kinds of issues that responders typically face in hazardous materials (HAZMAT) incidents, as well as the federal regulatory scheme that controls HAZMAT scenes.[62] This similarity is not mere coincidence, since every terrorist event also is likely to be a HAZMAT event.[63] The DoL provides personnel and management support related to worker safety and health in field operations during ESF #8 deployments.

While some commentators believe that health care workers have ethical obligations to respond when their professional services are needed, this is not a universal conclusion.[64] They have special training and expertise, but often are confronted with demands for service that are beyond their ability to respond. If shortages are the frequent rule in daily practice, in large-scale emergency situations the situation likely will be even more extreme. Local realities faced by the provider determine what constitutes a "reasonable" level of medical service, and a lack of resources may be a defense to a claim for malpractice.[65]

Enactment of the Emergency Medical Treatment and Active Labor Act (EMTALA)[66] obligated emergency room-equipped hospitals that accept federal funds to accept patients regardless of ability to pay. If emergency care must be given regardless of the patient's ability to pay on a normal day, it would appear difficult to avoid doing so during emergency response operations. The realities of triage and sometimes rough "battlefield medicine" most probably would dominate the aftermath of a mass casualty event.[67] Physicians and other members of the health care community have a great tradition of volunteering to assist patients under horrendous circumstances, and they frequently contribute their good works in the aftermath of emergencies. This is not, nor does it appear to be enforceable as, a universal characteristic.[68]

Licensing of Medical Personnel and Activities Working Outside the Licensing Jurisdiction

One matter that continues to be a thorn in the side of emergency response to large public health events is the issue of credentialing for visiting medical personnel when they leave their home jurisdictions to provide health care assistance.

The Emergency Management Assistance Compact (EMAC)[69] is the point of reference for interstate agreements. Each state has adopted its own variant of EMAC.[70] Under EMAC, state officers and employees with professional licenses and certifications from their own states are deemed to be licensed in the state in which they provide assistance.[71] However, this does not resolve all of the 'licensing' issues raised in a major incident, since some responders may not be officers or employees of the state. Reportedly, this subject caused such controversy during EMAC's drafting that the decision was made to permit each state to address the issue separately.[72] Nor does its resolve related 'privilege' and 'credentialing' issues, such as whether a hospital will grant an out-of-state physician hospital privileges. A number of organizations, including the National Emergency Management Association and the Centers for Disease Control and Prevention, are seeking to foster a uniform national approach to this issue.

The MSEHPA suggested that, during a public health emergency, the public health authority may require in-state health care providers to help with a variety of medical services and to "appoint and prescribe the duties of out-of-state emergency health care providers as may be reasonable and necessary to respond to the public health emergency."[73] This authority would empower the state to put aside all licensure requirements, permits, and fees for health care providers from other jurisdictions that otherwise would be required for them to practice within the state.[74] Provisions of this type already have been adopted in many states.[75]

More importantly, those who become federally certified under the authority of NIMS will receive nationwide credentialing as part of their official recognition.[76] This approach will do a great deal to diminish possible confusion after an emergency or disaster.

The EMAC web page also contains a pattern intrastate agreement.[77] Some states previously have created intrastate agreements. For example, Indiana's intrastate mutual aid program binds every political subdivision that does not opt out through adoption of an ordinance or resolution.[78]

Jurisdictions that call for mutual aid assistance must be aware of potential legal claims that might result from such action. Although model agreements like those considered above generally cover issues such as responsibility for injuries to members of the assisting unit, case law suggests that the requesting entity may be accountable for the workers' compensation claims of those injured during the response.[79]

Congress has decided to begin organizing the hodge-podge of mutual assistance compacts, with the goal of establishing recommended approaches to the matter. The IRTP Act amends the Stafford Act to establish a program to support the development of emergency preparedness compacts for acts of terrorism, disasters, and emergencies.[80] FEMA is tasked with identifying and cataloging existing emergency preparedness compacts for acts of terrorism, disasters, and emergencies at the state and local levels of government; disseminating to state and local governments examples of best practices in the development of emergency preparedness compacts and models of existing emergency preparedness compacts, including agreements involving interstate jurisdictions; and completing an inventory of federal response capabilities for acts of terrorism, disasters, and emergencies, making such inventory available to appropriate federal, state, and local government officials, and ensuring that such inventory is as current and accurate as practicable.[81]

Liability

A major concern of health care workers at all levels is potential liability and its possible impact on malpractice insurance. In recognition of these worries, various schemes have arisen to reassure these important first responders. They generally focus on making it more difficult to show that services provided during emergencies triggered liability, or on immunizing responders from liability altogether in an emergency situation. Another possibility is looking to various sources of insurance or indemnification for medical responses.

Immunities

Many states' legal schemes provide for lessened levels of duty during an emergency response. In states adopting the MSEHPA, any private person, corporation, or firm that provides advice or assistance at the state's request during a public health emergency may not be held liable for causing death or injury to a person, or for any property damage,[82] in the absence of gross negligence or willful misconduct.

In the aftermath of the September 11, 2001 attacks, some states have responded with increased immunities from malpractice liability in emergency situations. Florida, for example, enacted a MSEHPA-derived law providing immunities during emergencies. The need for this protection, however, was not universally acknowledged.[83]

Other states had already addressed the matter. Indiana, for example, deals with the topic in its emergency management statute, which similarly provides that liability will not attach to any emergency management worker, which includes health care workers,[84] absent gross negligence or willful misconduct.[85]

Malpractice Insurance

Medical malpractice insurance has become one of the most controversial public policy issues, even without the added impetus of a public health emergency. Premiums escalate constantly, while some physicians find themselves unable to purchase malpractice insurance for any price. The causes of this situation are complex and interrelated.[86] Insurers lay the responsibility for the situation on ever-rising numbers of lawsuits and mounting numbers of large jury awards.[87] Some companies no longer write malpractice insurance. Federal legislation allows members of the medical profession to consider alternatives such as captive insurance, risk retention groups, and purchasing groups. The insurance industry characterizes the cost of these options as "affordable"[88]

The potential changes in availability of malpractice insurance that may result from broad adoption of the standards contained in NFPA 1600, as discussed above, cannot be overstated. Failure to comply with NFPA 1600 may render an entity uninsurable. Such a situation could not be tolerated in the heavily insurance-driven, and risk-averse, health care industry. Medical malpractice coverage is vital to a physician's practice, and a rise in premium rates has a significant impact on total net income.[89]

One challenge in relying on malpractice insurance policies as a source of funds in the event of alleged malpractice is their scope. Typically, malpractice insurance is written to cover a specific physician working in a particular practice area. Further, policies may have restrictions on the locations at which they apply, being limited to the hospitals at which the doctor has privileges. These limitations may mean that coverage does not apply to actions taken as part of the response to an emergency event, where health care may be needed at the scene of the occurrence or at nearby triage centers that have been set up to receive the injured.

Good Samaritan Laws

Good Samaritan laws are often thought to provide blanket freedom for liability in emergency situations. In fact, the typical Good Samaritan law grants freedom for negligence liability alone to those whose activities fall under its purview. These laws, which vary by state, normally do not provide any protection to the emergency responder who is acting within the scope of his or her employment. The issue of scope of employment typically revolves around the issue of whether a responder has a preexisting duty to the patient. To illustrate, Good Samaritan law does not cover a paramedic who is dispatched to a vehicle accident while on duty. He or she would be covered if, while driving home from work after going off duty, the paramedic came upon an accident and rendered assistance to the victims. Occasionally, even a medical responder who has been dispatched to respond to a victim may be protected by not having a duty to that patient.[90]

On the federal level, a statute may provide significant protection to volunteer responders. In order to convince volunteers to partake in structured units that benefit emergency response and recovery, Congress passed the Volunteer Protection Act of 1997 (VPA)[91] to provide statutory immunity for people wanting to help through volunteer organizations. Congress found that people's readiness to volunteer was discouraged by the prospect of litigation resulting from their volunteer service.[92] This law preempts state laws that set a higher standard for volunteer liability than gross negligence.[93] States may opt out if desired.[94] As well as security from negligence lawsuits, punitive damages may not be allowed against a volunteer acting within the scope of his or her responsibilities to a nonprofit organization, even if the volunteer is negligent or grossly negligent.[95] Importantly, the immunity does not apply to the organization with which the volunteer is associated. [96]

The VPA does not excuse volunteers from liability for any damage caused while driving a vehicle.[97] This exclusion is significant since, according to some research, half the claims involving emergency response organizations concern vehicle accidents.[98] While the VPA changes the basis for a lawsuit, it probably does not affect administrative actions taken on the basis of negligence. Laws making negligent conduct that endangers persons a basis for administrative penalties[99] continue to be valid.

The limitations on the VPA render it largely useless as a shelter for many members of the professional health care community. The definition of volunteer has extreme limits on who it applies to, requiring that a person not be compensated more than $500 per year in order to preserve volunteer status.[100] Though it would be possible for members of the health care system to fit within the definition—particularly if their service during an emergency were uncompensated—there are limits on how long one can go without compensation, and some emergency events continue for extended periods. The protection from both negligence liability and punitive damages, however, is broad for those who can come within its ambit.

Indemnification

There also may be sources for indemnification for medical responses. On the federal level, the massive indemnification and limited awards provided by Congress in the wake of the September 11, 2001, attacks come immediately to mind.[101] Other federal indemnification has occurred with the swine flu vaccine, where the federal government assumed vicarious liability for all participants and limited awards.[102] Similarly, indemnification and limits on awards exist prospectively for nuclear power plant mishaps.[103]

A state also might act to indemnify health care workers and businesses in the wake of an emergency event, but the federal government is a much more likely source.

Of course, the proper source for compensation in the wake of an emergency situation would be the actual wrongdoer. That entity may be identifiable in the wake of a mass casualty event like the inadvertent chemical release at Bhopal, India. In the terrorism scenario, however, the culprit may be anonymous. Even if the bad actor's identity is known, however, the entity may be judgment proof. Al Qaeda is known to be the source of the September 11, 2001, attacks, yet that group has no identifiable assets to attach. Although its self-confessed leader, Osama bin Laden, at one time had significant personal assets, they likely have been either expended to support the Jihadist cause or hidden beyond the grasp of potential plaintiffs.

Conclusion

One result of the 9/11 attacks is evolving legal principles that affect all emergency responders as well as the private sector. Legal requirements for public health preparedness are in flux. Clearly, the team that is responsible for public health has grown steadily over the years. The standards that regulate public health responders are being reexamined as the system incorporates the lessons of 9/11. The total effect of the IRTP Act remains to be seen. The "voluntary" standards contained in NFPA 1600 may end up having a much greater effect than the mandates of law on the daily activities of responders. The significant funding that currently flows into public health preparedness has a momentum of its own.

Many barriers exist to increasing medical surge capacity. To the extent that devoting funding and raising prioritization can speed up the process, the federal government has devoted those resources to the effort.

Quarantine and evacuation issues have a long history. The MSEHPA addresses many of the public health issues that have arisen in the last twenty years or so, and proposes due process protections for quarantine and evacuation that were not spelled out in the preexisting quarantine laws of many states. Concerns regarding MSEHPA's impact on civil liberties have caused some authorities to view it with suspicion. While MSEHPA addresses licensing of medical personnel and activities outside their certifying jurisdiction, some jurisdictions have addressed the matter through other parts of their legal systems, such as emergency management.

Public health preparedness encompasses a number of general liability concerns. Different approaches address these important issues. At their essence, these approaches look to decreased levels of duty or immunities in an emergency situation. Malpractice insurance is facing difficult times, with constantly increasing premiums and ever fewer carriers. Its scope may be too limited to apply in an emergency situation. Immunities granted by Good Samaritan and similar laws may provide some protection under tightly delineated circumstances. Indemnification may be available from various sources for medical responses. The federal government appears to be the prime origin for such coverage.

Preparedness for public health emergencies is constantly increasing, which is an encouraging development. While we hope that these capabilities would never be required, our experience over the last several years—with anthrax, SARS, avian flu, and potential biological weapons in the hands of terrorists—has demonstrated that we cannot afford *not* to be prepared.

Notes

1. A primary mission of the Public Health Service is to "furnish health expertise in time of war or other national or international emergencies." The mission of the Commissioned Corps may be found at http://www.usphs.gov/html/mission.html.

2. Pub. L. No. 107-296 (2002).

3. 6 U.S.C. § 101(6).

4. Homeland Sec. Presidential Directive 5, Subject: Mgmt. of Domestic Incidents, http://www.whitehouse.gov/news/releases/2003/02/20030228-9.html (February 28, 2003) (HSPD 5).

5. *Id.*, at ¶ 3.

6. *Id.*, at ¶ 17b.

7. Even for-profit entities receiving federal preparedness funds ultimately may be covered by this obligation, although DHS has not yet sought to extend the NIMS obligation to them.

8. HSPD 5, at ¶ 19.

9. Press Release, White House, President Marks Homeland Security's Accomplishments at Year One (March 2, 2004), http://www.whitehouse.gov/news/releases/2004/03/20040302-2.html.

10. Press Release, Department of Homeland Security, Department of Homeland Security Secretary Tom Ridge Approves National Incident Management System (NIMS) (March 1, 2004), http://www.dhs.gov/dhspublic/display?content=3259 ("NIMS gives all of our Nation's responders the same framework for incident management and fully puts into practice the concept of, 'One mission, one team, one fight.'"). For more information on NIMS, *see* http://www.fema.gov/nims/; the actual NIMS document is available at http://www.dhs.gov/interweb/assetlibrary/NIMS-90-web.pdf.

11. HSPD 5, at ¶ 16.

12. http://www.rmfd.org/National%20Response%20Plan%20-%20Approved-Unsigned%20(16%20Nov%2004).pdf

13. NRP, at 66.

14. NIMS, at 68.

15. NRP, at 15.

16. *Id.*

17. NRP, at 27.

18. NRP Emergency Support Function #8—Public Health and Medical Services Annex.

19. Robert T. Stafford Disaster Relief and Emergency Assistance Act, 42 U.S.C. § 5121 (amended 2004). The pre-appropriated no-year funds in the Disaster Relief Fund are available for assisting state and local governments respond to incidents upon the president's declaration that the incident is a major disaster or emergency.

20. Public Health Service Act, 42 U.S.C. § 201 (amended 2004). This act authorizes the secretary of health and human services to declare a "Public Health Emergency," and then to take such steps as are necessary to control the emergency. However, the Public Health Emergency Fund generally does not have funds already appropriated for this purpose.

21. *Id.*

22. HSPD 5, at ¶ 16.

23. HSPD 5, at ¶ 20; DHS letter to governors *infra* note 24.

24. DHS Secretary Ridge laid out the NIMS adoption timetable and potential penalties in a letter to governors, http://www.fema.gov/txt/nims/letter_to_governors_09082004.txt.

25. NIMS, at 33.

26. NIMS, at 59. "The process for managing and maintaining the NIMS ensures that all users and stakeholders—including various levels of government, functional disciplines, and private entities—are given the opportunity to participate in NIMS Integration Center activities.

To accomplish this goal, the NIMS Integration Center will be multijurisdictional and multidisciplinary and will maintain appropriate liaison with private organizations."

27. NIMS, at 59-64.

28. NIMS, at 59-64.

29. NIMS, at 59. Revisions to the NIMS and other corrective actions can be proposed by: local entities (including their preparedness organizations, see Chapter III); state entities (including their preparedness organizations, see Chapter III); regional entities (including their preparedness organizations, see Chapter III); tribal entities (including their preparedness organization, see Chapter III); federal departments and agencies; private entities (including business and industry, volunteer organizations, academia, and other nonprofit and nongovernmental organizations); and NIMS-related professional associations.

30. HSPD 5, at ¶ 15.

31. NFPA 1600, Standard on Disaster/Emergency Management and Business Continuity Programs (Nat'l Fire Prot. Ass'n 2004), http://www.nfpa.org/PDF/nfpa1600.pdf?src=nfpa (NFPA 1600).

32. National Commission on Terrorist Attacks Upon the United States, The 9/11 Commission Report: Final Report of the National Commission on Terrorist Attacks Upon the United States 398 (2004). (9/11 Commission Report.)

33. Intelligence Reform and Terrorism Prevention Act of 2004, S. 2845 ENR, 108th Cong. (2004) (enrolled as agreed to or passed by both House and Senate), http://thomas.loc.gov/cgi-bin/query/D?c108:4:./temp/~c108150E9Q. (IRTP Act).

Press Release, White House, President Signs Intelligence Reform and Terrorism Prevention Act (December 17, 2004), http://www.whitehouse.gov/news/releases/2004/12/20041217-1.html.

34. IRPT Act § 7305(b) (Sense of Congress on Private Sector Preparedness).

35. NFPA 1600 § 5.7.1.

36. NFPA 1600 § 5.2.1 ("The disaster/emergency program shall comply with all applicable legislation, regulations, directives, policies, and industry codes of practice.")

37. *See, e.g.*, Fla. Stat. § 395.1056 (2004) (requiring hospitals to plan for terrorism events).

38. *Disaster Hospital Demonstrated in Nation's Capital to Show State-of-the-Art Preparedness for Terrorist Attack, Bio/Flu Crisis or Natural Disaster*, Business Wire (Dec. 8, 2004), http://home.businesswire.com/portal/site/altavista/index.jsp?ndmViewId=news_view&newsId=20041208005904&newsLang=en.

39. *Id.*

40. Remarks by Secretary Tom Ridge to the Council for Excellence in Government (September 16, 2003), http://www.dhs.gov/dhspublic/display?content=1597.

41. Agency for Healthcare Research and Quality, Bioterrorism and Health System Preparedness Issue Brief No. 3, AHRQ Pub. No. 04-P008. Optimizing Surge Capacity: Hospital Assessment and Planning (2004), http://www.ahrq.gov/news/ulp/btbriefs/btbrief3.htm.

42. *See generally,* Elin A. Gursky, Sc.D., *Hometown Hospitals: The Weakest Link? Bioterrorism Readiness in America's Rural Hospitals*, Report Commissioned by the National Defense University Center for Technology and National Security Policy (June 2004).

43. *Id.*, at 6.

44. *Disaster Hospital Demonstrated in Nation's Capital to Show State-of-the-Art Preparedness for Terrorist Attack, Bio/Flu Crisis or Natural Disaster*, Business Wire (Dec. 8, 2004), http:

//home.businesswire.com/portal/site/altavista/index.jsp?ndmViewId=news_view&ne
wsId=20041208005904&newsLang=en.

45. "Violation of a 'specific and mandatory' directive to prepare a plan would not be
discretionary under *Berkovitz v. United States*, 486 U.S. 531 (1988)." Ken Lerner, *Governmental Negligence Liability Exposure in Disaster Management*, 23 Urban Lawyer 333 (1991). "The
Government's failure to develop an adequate emergency plan and failure to give adequate
warning . . . is not comprehended in the conduct which Congress intended to protect
through enactment of . . . the [Federal] Tort Claims Act." *Coates v. U.S.*, 612 F. Supp. 592, 599
(C.D. Ill. 1985).

46. U.S. Food & Drug Administration, FDA's Budget Proposal for FY 2005 Requests
Increases for Food Safety, FDA Law Weekly (February 26, 2004).

47. Dee Ann Divis, *BioWar: Balancing Rights and Needs Legally*, United Press International (July 22, 2004).

48. Institute for Bioethics, Health Policy and Law, University of Louisville School of
Medicine, Quarantine and Isolation: Lessons from SARS, a Report to the Centers for Disease
Control (November 2003).

49. R. Clarke & W. Rudman, Council on Foreign Relations, Drastically Underfunded,
Dangerously Unprepared: Report of the Independent Task Force on Emergency Responders
(NY 2003).

50. Model State Emergency Health Powers Act (MSEHPA), http://
www.publichealthlaw.net/Resources/Modellaws.htm.

51. National Association of Attorneys General, *Resolution Urging States to Review Their
Public Health Laws* (December 2-6, 2003), http://www.publichealthlaw.net/Resources/
ResourcesPDFs/PHL%20NAAG.pdf.

52. MSEHPA, Preamble.

53. L. Gostin, J. Sapsin, & S. Teret, *et als.*, *The Model State Emergency Health Powers
Act: Planning for and Response to Bioterrorism and Naturally Occurring Infectious Diseases*, 288
JAMA 622-628 (2002).

54. *See, e.g.*, Julie Bruce, *Bioterrorism Meets Privacy: An Analysis of the Model State Emergency Health Powers Act and the HIPAA Privacy Rule*, 12 Annals Health L. 75 (2003); William
Martin, MPA, *Legal and Public Policy Responses of States to Bioterrorism*, 94 Am. J. Pub. Health,
No. 7, 1093 (July 2004); George J. Annas, *Puppy Love: Bioterrorism, Civil Rights, and Public
Health*, 55 Fla. L. Rev. 1171, 1184 (December 2003).

55. Standards for Privacy of Individually Identifiable Health Information, 45 C.F.R.
§ 164.500 (2004).

56. Bruce, at 77-78.

57. *Id.*, at 108-112.

58. *See, e.g.*, Ind. Code § 10-14-3-12(d) (2004). In addition to the governor's other powers, the governor may do the following while the state of emergency exists: ". . . (5) Assist
in the evacuation of all or part of the population from any stricken or threatened area in
Indiana if the governor considers this action necessary for the preservation of life or other
disaster mitigation, response, or recovery. (6) Prescribe routes, modes of transportation,
and destinations in connection with evacuation. (7) Control ingress to and egress from a
disaster area, the movement of persons within the area, and the occupancy of premises in
the area."

59. For extensive discussion of this subject, see Bruce A. Peterson & Mark E. Van Der
Weide, *Susceptible to Faulty Analysis: United States v. Gaubert and the Resurrection of Federal
Sovereign Immunity*, 72 Notre Dame L. Rev. 447 (1997).

60. For detailed discussion of Department of Defense assistance, *see* Gregory M.
Huckabee, Esq., *Partnering with the Department of Defense for Improved Homeland Security, in
Homeland Security Law and Policy*, Chapter 8 (William C. Nicholson, ed. [in press]); Gary

Cecchine, *et als.*, T<small>RIAGE FOR</small> C<small>IVIL</small> S<small>UPPORT</small>: U<small>SING</small> M<small>ILITARY</small> M<small>EDICAL</small> A<small>SSETS TO</small> R<small>ESPOND TO</small> T<small>ER-</small>
<small>RORIST</small> A<small>TTACKS</small> (National Defense Research Institute & Rand Health 2004).

61. ESF #8, Worker Health/Safety.

62. For detailed consideration of HAZMAT law standards in terrorism events, *see*
William C. Nicholson, *Legal Issues in Emergency Response to Terrorism Incidents Involving Haz-
ardous Materials: The Hazardous Waste Operations and Emergency Response ("HAZWOPER")
Standard, Standard Operating Procedures, Mutual Aid and the Incident Management System*, 9
W<small>IDENER</small> L. S<small>YMP.</small> J.,No. 2, 295 (2003).

63. *Id.*, at 295. ("Emergency responders frequently refer to terrorist attacks as 'hazardous materials (HAZMAT) incidents with an attitude.'")

64. Maxwell J. Mehlman, *The Patient-Physician Relationship in an Era of Scarce Resources:
Is There a Duty to Treat?*, 25 C<small>ONN.</small> L. R<small>EV.</small> 349, 352 (Winter 1993).

65. *Id.*, at 362-363.

66. Emergency Medical Treatment and Active Labor Act (EMTALA), 42 U.S.C.
§ 139.5.

67. Moreover, the secretary of health and human services can waive the "duty to
treat" requirement of EMTALA after declaring a public health emergency, although hospitals are still prohibited from discriminating in treatment decisions based on ability to pay.
42 U.S.C.A. § 1320b-5.

68. Gail B. Agrawal, *Resuscitating Professionalism: Self-Regulation in the Medical Market-
place*, 66 M<small>O.</small> L. R<small>EV.</small> 341, 386-395 (Spring 2001).

69. Interstate compacts require the consent of Congress under the U.S. Constitution.
Approval for EMAC was provided in 1996. Pub. L. No. 104-321, 110 Stat. 3877 (1996). For
current EMAC developments, *see* http://www.emacweb.org/.

70. *See, e.g.*, I<small>ND.</small> C<small>ODE</small> § 10-14-6 (2004) (Interstate Emergency Management and Disaster Compact).

71. *See* EMAC Article VI, 100 Stat. 3877, 3880 (1996), *available at* http://www.emacweb.
org/?564.

72. For one approach, *see, e.g.*, I<small>ND.</small> C<small>ODE</small> §§ 10-14-3-3, 10-14-3-15(b). Section 10-14-3-3
defines "emergency management worker" as any full-time or part-time paid, volunteer,
or auxiliary employee of the state; other states, territories, or possessions; the District of
Columbia; the federal government; any neighboring country; any political subdivision of
any of the foregoing entities; or any agency or organization performing emergency management services at any place in Indiana subject to the order or control of, or under a request
of, the state government or any political subdivision of the state. Under I<small>ND.</small> C<small>ODE</small> § 10-14-
3-15(b), any requirement for a license to practice any professional, mechanical, or other skill
does not apply to any authorized emergency management worker who, in the course of
performing duties as an emergency management worker, practices a professional, mechanical, or other skill during a disaster emergency.

73. MSEHPA § 608 (a)-(b).

74. *Id.*, at § 608(b)(2).

75. For example, the Florida Emergency Management Act not only allows the governor (or his delegate) to waive state medical licensing requirements during a state of
emergency, it gives him the authority to suspend the effect of *any* statute, rule, ordinance,
or order of any state, regional, or local governmental entity as needed to cope with the disaster. 14 F<small>LA.</small> S<small>TAT.</small> § 252.36 (2004).

76. NIMS, at 46. ("Personnel certification entails authoritatively attesting that individuals meet professional standards for the training, experience, and performance required
for key incident management functions. Credentialing involves providing documentation
that can authenticate and verify the certification and identity of designated incident managers and emergency responders.")

77. *See,* http://emacweb.org/docs/Wide%20Release%20Intrastate%20Mutual%20Ai
d.pdf.

78. IND. CODE § 10-14-3-10.6 (2004).

79. *See, e.g.,* Thomas v. Lisbon, 550 A.2d 894 (Conn. 1988).

80. IRTP Act § 7406. (Emergency Preparedness Compacts.)

81. *Id.*

82. MSEHPA § 804(b)(3).

83. George J. Annas, *Puppy Love: Bioterrorism, Civil Rights, and Public Health,* 55 FLA. L. REV. 1171, 1184 (December 2003). ("In the current so-called medical-malpractice crisis, it is not surprising that immunity for physicians acting in publicly declared emergencies has support in a strongly conservative state led by a very conservative governor.")

84. See discussion of definition of "emergency management worker" in IND. CODE § 10-14-3-3 *supra* note 48.

85. IND. CODE § 10-14-3-15(a) (2004). ("Any function under this chapter and any other activity relating to emergency management is a governmental function. The state, any political subdivision, any other agencies of the state or political subdivision of the state, or, except in cases of willful misconduct, gross negligence, or bad faith, any emergency management worker complying with or reasonably attempting to comply with this chapter or any order or rule adopted under this chapter, or under any ordinance relating to blackout or other precautionary measures enacted by any political subdivision of the state, is not liable for the death of or injury to persons or for damage to property as a result of any such activity."

86. *See generally, Third Annual Health Law Colloquium: Transcribed Speeches of Professors Barry Furrow and David Hyman,* 13 ANNALS HEALTH L. 521 (Summer 2004).

87. Joseph B. Treaster, *Malpractice Rates Are Rising Sharply: Health Costs Follow,* N.Y. TIMES, Sept. 10, 2001, at A1. ("Insurers blame rate hikes and policy considerations on what they describe as a rising tide of lawsuits and $1 million-plus jury awards.")

88. *See generally,* Robert W. Mulcahey and Nicole Williams Koviak, *Third Annual Health Law Colloquium: An Insurance Perspective on the Medical Malpractice Crisis,* 13 ANNALS HEALTH L. 607

(Summer 2004).

89. Dr. William P. Gunnar, *Is There an Acceptable Answer to Rising Medical Malpractice Premiums?* 13 ANNALS HEALTH L. 465, 470 (Summer 2004).

90. *See e.g.,* Clarken v. U.S., 791 F. Supp. 1029 (D. N.J. 1992) (medical responders at U.S. Military Academy found not to have duty toward persons staying at hotel on campus).

91. Pub. L. No. 105-19, 111 Stat. 218 *(codified at* 42 U.S.C.A. 14501-14505 (West Supp. III 2002)). As is the case with any type of tort reform, the VPA has borne significant criticism. *See e.g.,* Andrew F. Popper, *A One-Term Tort Reform Tale: Victimizing the Vulnerable,* 35 HARV. J. ON LEGIS. 123, 130-137 (Winter 1998). An underlying principle of tort law is that the threat of personal liability creates individual accountability, and thereby enhances the quality of goods and services. Accordingly, the common law imposes a minimum level of due care on people who choose to volunteer. The Volunteer Protection Act changes that standard and, in so doing, reduces the incentive to provide quality services. *Id.,* at 134-135 (footnotes omitted).

92. 42 U.S.C.S. § 14501. "The Congress finds and declares that—(1) the willingness of volunteers to offer their services is deterred by the potential for liability actions against them; (2) as a result, many nonprofit public and private organizations and governmental entities, including voluntary associations, social service agencies, educational institutions, and other civic programs, have been adversely affected by the withdrawal of volunteers from boards of directors and service in other capacities; (3) the contribution of these pro-

grams to their communities is thereby diminished, resulting in fewer and higher cost programs than would be obtainable if volunteers were participating; . . . ."

93. *Id.*, at § 14503(a)(3).

94. *Id.*, at § 14502(b). The opt-out authorization would apply only where all of the parties in a case were residents of the state in question.

95. *See* 42 U.S.C. §§ 14503 (a), (c), (e), 14504. The VPA's limits on punitive damages liability and joint and several liability for noneconomic damages are not limited to matters where the volunteer acted with a required license or were not caused by a motor vehicle. The prohibition on ordinary negligence actions and limits on punitive damages against volunteers do not apply to civil cases brought by a nonprofit or governmental entity against affiliated volunteers. The limitation is not contained in the provisions limiting noneconomic damages in joint and several liability cases.

96. *Id.*, at § 14503(c). The VPA does not provide any direct liability protections to the nonprofit organizations or government agencies.

97. *Id.*, at §§ 14503(a)(1), (2) & (3). The VPA also excludes from liability protection any specific misconduct constituting a crime of violence or international terrorism, hate crime, sexual offense, civil rights violation, or misconduct which is caused by the influence of alcohol or drugs in violation of state law, as well as volunteers performing services for groups responsible for federal hate crimes (e.g., crimes that manifest evidence of prejudice based on race, religion, sexual orientation, or ethnicity). *Id.*, at §§ 14503(f) & 14505(4). (Federal hate crimes are defined at 28 U.S.C. § 534 note).

98. *See, e.g.*, Soler, et als., *The Ten Year Malpractice Experience of a Large Urban EMS System*, 14 ANNALS EMERGENCY MED. 982, 985 (1985); Goldberg, et als., *A Review of Prehospital Care Litigation in a Large Metropolitan EMS System*, 19 ANNALS EMERGENCY MED. 557, 558 (1990).

99. *See e.g.*, 836 IND. ADMIN. CODE § 1-5-1(g)(4) (specifying negligent conduct endangering patients as a basis for imposing administrative penalties on emergency medical services personnel).

100. *Id.*, at § 14505 (6). "Volunteer" is defined as an individual (including a director or officer) performing services for a "nonprofit organization" or a governmental entity who does not receive compensation (other than reasonable expenses) in excess of $500 per year.

101. *See*, Erin G. Holt, *Note: The September 11 Victim Compensation Fund: Legislative Justice Sui Generis*, 59 N.Y.U. ANN. SURV. AM. L. 513 (2004).

102. *See*, National Swine Flu Immunization Program of 1976, Pub. L. No. 94-380, § 2(k)(1)(A)(i), 90 Stat. 1113 (1976).

103. *See*, Atomic Energy Act § 2210(e)(2) 42 U.S.C. § 2210(e)(2); Duke Power Co. v. Carolina Envtl. Study Group, 438 U.S. 59, 64-65 (1978) ("In its original form the Act limited the aggregate liability for a single nuclear incident to $500 million plus the amount of liability insurance available on the private market—some $ 60million in 1957."); Price-Anderson Amendments Act of 1988, Pub. L. No. 100-408, § 6(e)(C)(ii)(2), 102 Stat 1066 (1988). Specifically, the Price-Anderson Amendments Act directs that Congress shall "take whatever action is determined to be necessary (including approval of appropriate compensation plans and appropriation of funds) to provide full and prompt compensation to the public for all public liability claims resulting from a disaster of such magnitude."

CHAPTER 5

Homeland Security Begins at Home: Local Planning and Regulatory Review to Improve Security*

by Rufus Calhoun Young, Jr., and Dwight H. Merriam, FAICP

Introduction

The United States faces the threat of terrorist attacks. As with most risks, there are steps that can be taken to reduce the likelihood, and mitigate the impact, of such attacks. Many of these steps are the province of intelligence and law enforcement agencies and designated first responders. However, some, such as review of building design, lighting and landscaping plans, and the protection of heating, ventilating, and air conditioning systems, and parking facilities, to name a few, are or could be part of the process for land use review and approval.[1]

This chapter provides an outline of homeland security factors that merit consideration in the land use review and approval process. While these measures might be particularly appropriate for terrorist-sensitive facilities in an effort to make them less attractive and vulnerable to terrorist attacks, they also may be helpful for the security and safety of other facilities by reducing the threats posed by common criminals and vandals. The measures identified in this chapter should not be regarded as minimum standards for a given facility or class of facilities, nor as an exhaustive list of the universe of countermeasures. This is because the identification of appropriate measures for facility protection will depend on continuing site-specific analyses of perceived risks and the feasibility of the countermeasures.[2]

Private sector building owners and operators also have responsibilities with respect to homeland security. Private industry owns and operates approximately 85 percent of our critical infrastructures and key assets.[3] Rudolph Giuliani put it this way:

> And I would like to see more being done [in terms of securing the critical infra-structure of the country] on the private side. **Most buildings are run not by the government but by private companies. . . . I think we need a lot more participation from the private sector.** We have to think about how we are going to keep the people in this building secure. . . . Just think of the amount of money that the [New York Stock] exchange saved during the blackout by being able to come back the next day. Coming back in one day probably paid for the entire investment that the exchange made in its backup generators and duplication plan.[4]

According to President Bush's national strategy for protecting critical infrastructure and key assets: "For the most part, commercial owners and operators must be responsible for assessing and mitigating their specific facility vulnerabilities and practicing prudent risk management and mitigating measures."[5]

Identify Existing and Planned New Terrorist-Sensitive Facilities[6]

These may include:

- Airports
- Bridges
- Chemical plants
- Computer centers and Internet hubs
- Convention centers
- Cruise ship terminals
- Dams
- Government buildings (especially those with high traffic and symbolic recognition, including courthouses, jails, police stations, and post offices)
- Hospitals
- Hotels (especially those with symbolic recognition)
- Nuclear reactors
- Office buildings
- Ports
- Power plants
- Railroads, rail yards, and passenger terminals
- Schools
- Stadiums
- Shopping centers and restaurants
- Multifamily apartment buildings and planned urban developments
- Symbolic structures (for example, Statue of Liberty, Golden Gate Bridge)
- Transportation terminals (especially hazardous material freight facilities)
- Tunnels

- Wastewater plants and facilities
- Water utilities
- Others, particularly those with high concentrations of people, identified through site- and threat-specific analyses

Conduct Vulnerability Assessments of Terrorist-Sensitive Facilities

Basic Elements of Site-Specific Vulnerability Assessments

1. Identify the mission of the facility or system;
2. Identify sensitive vulnerable areas;
3. Assess the likelihood of terrorist or other criminal acts;
4. Identify avoidable events;
5. Identify possible defensive measures, including those that could be implemented through the exercise of land use controls; and
6. Develop and implement plans for the prudent reduction of risks.

Framework for Site-Specific Vulnerability Assessments

Approach and frame site plan review with proactive questions in the initial planning and plan review stages:

1. *Who* are the intended users of the site (staff, service crews, visitors, etc.)?
2. *What* types of activities can the users perform at the site (tasks, recreation, deliveries of benign or hazardous materials)?
3. *When* do users of the site arrive at and leave the site (schedules for public access, typical working hours, etc.)?
4. *Where* on the site can users go, and where can users enter the site (doors, lobbies, windows, outdoor walking paths, etc.)?
5. *How* can users get to the site (methods of access, circulation of roadways approaching site, etc.)?

Site plan review also should address the threats to which the specific site is susceptible. Risk management entails significant costs. Analyzing realistic threats and protecting against identifiable vulnerabilities *before building design begins*—and no later than the programming phase—will yield a defined, economical approach to site security. Consider:

1. What are the identifiable assets at the site that will require protection (people, information, tangible property, computer systems)?
2. What are the specific criminal/terrorist threats that present the greatest danger to the site and its assets?
3. What are the assets' greatest vulnerabilities that a criminal/terrorist could capitalize upon?
4. What are the most effective countermeasures that can be taken to protect against threat vulnerabilities?

Design site security provisions according to specific defensible layers:

1. *Public layer:* What are the potential threats and countermeasures for the site?
2. *Semi-public layer:* What are the potential threats and countermeasures for the building's architectural skin?
3. *Semi-private layer:* What are the potential threats and countermeasures for the sensitive areas within the building, beyond security check-in points?
4. *Private layer:* What are the potential threats and countermeasures for the inner core of critical people, information, and property?

RELATED RESOURCES:

- Randall Atlas, *Designing Against Terror: Site Security Planning and Design Criteria* (from ARCHITECTURAL GRAPHICS STANDARDS 1999 rev.), http://www.cpted-security.com/cpted4.htm.
- Randall Atlas, *Environmental Design That Prevents Crime* (from THE CONSTRUCTION SPECIFIER April 1999), http://www.cpted-security.com/cpted11.htm.

These informative articles contain several of the site plan-provisions detailed below, including specific considerations for implementing Defensible Space/Crime Prevention Through Environmental Design (CPTED) approaches to site planning.

Federal Requirements and Recommendations for Terrorist-Sensitive Facilities

1. Federal Requirements
   a. Title 12 U.S.C. § 1701n provides:
      Reduction of vulnerability of congested urban areas to enemy attack. The Department of Housing and Urban Development, and any other departments or agencies of the Federal Government having powers, functions, or duties with respect to housing under any law shall exercise such powers, functions, or duties in such manner as, consistent with the requirements thereof, will facilitate progress in the reduction of the vulnerability of congested urban areas to enemy attack.
   b. The Emergency Planning and Community Right-to-Know Act of 1986, 42 U.S.C. §§ 11001-11050, requires the establishment of state commissions, planning districts, and local committees to prepare emergency plans to address releases of extremely hazardous chemicals.
   c. Title IV of the Public Health Security and Bioterrorism Preparedness and Response Act of 2002 (Bioterrorism Act), Pub. L. No. 107-188, amended the Safe Drinking Water Act by adding a new § 1433, requiring assessments of the vulnerability to terrorist attack of water systems serving more than 3,300 persons.

RELATED RESOURCE:
http://www.epa.gov/safewater/security/community.html.

> d. Vulnerability assessments also are required for ports and transportation terminals.

RELATED RESOURCE:
Department of Transportation Hazardous Materials Regulations (HMR), 49 C.F.R. Parts 171-180; 68 Fed. Reg. 23,831 (May 5, 2003) (interim rule), http://hazmat.dot.gov/rules/68fr-23831.htm.

> 2. Federal Recommendations
> Recommendations by federal agencies and working groups may be found through the articles and links cited at the end of this chapter. Notable among these articles is:
> CENTERS FOR DISEASE CONTROL AND PREVENTION AND NATIONAL INSTITUTE FOR OCCUPATIONAL SAFETY AND HEALTH, DEPARTMENT OF HEALTH AND HUMAN SERVICES, GUIDANCE FOR PROTECTING BUILDING ENVIRONMENTS FROM AIRBORNE CHEMICAL, BIOLOGICAL, OR RADIOLOGICAL ATTACKS, DHHS (NIOSH) PUBLICATION NO. 2002-139, (May 2002), http://www.cdc.gov/NIOSH/bldvent/2002-139.html.

Vulnerability Assessment Coordination

Vulnerability assessments by local agencies should be coordinated with requirements for vulnerability assessments and preparedness measures established by the Environmental Protection Agency and the Department of Transportation.

RELATED RESOURCE:
Public Health Security and Bioterrorism Preparedness and Response Act of 2002, Pub. L. No. 107-188, http://www.epa.gov/safewater/security/community.html.

Prudent Threat-Reducing Land Use Measures for Building Owners, Operators, and Local Governments[7]

On-Site Measures

RELEVANT RESOURCES:

> ■ Barbara Nadel, *Better Safe: Planning Secure Environments*, AREA DEVELOPMENT: SITE AND FACILITY PLANNING (May 2001), http://www.areadevelopment.com/past/0501/features/better.html.
> ■ Patti Gallagher & Alex Krieger, *Security with Dignity*, URBAN LAND (March 2003), at 73, http://www.chankrieger.com/frames/aboutus/principals/security.htm (enhancing security and urban design in Washington, D.C.).

1. Site Perimeter Security
   Establish a secure site perimeter:
   a. Maintain site setbacks as far as possible from roadways and other routes providing rapid public access (The U.S. Department of State recommends at least one hundred feet).
   b. Provide an unobstructed view around the site.
   c. Limit and define lines of approach to the site: Avoid perpendicular avenues of approach and focus entrances through the use of clear directional signs.
   d. Avoid unnecessary signage that reveals site assets or calls unnecessary attention to site vulnerabilities.
   e. Maintain edges and boundaries of the site to clearly define desired circulation of people, cars, etc.
   The site perimeter defines public access to the site and serves as a critical first line of defense for entrance to more semi-public and semi-private areas of the site. Establishing a secure site perimeter is a crucial first step in any site plan. Apply common principles of property law: Physically and symbolically define the site to signify ownership and control and preserve property rights.
2. Landscaping
   a. *Security review.* Review landscaping requirements and design in light of security concerns.
   b. *Security consistency.* Revise landscaping requirements for consistency with security.
   c. *Security measures.* Require landscaping measures for site-specific security concerns.
      i.   Do not create hiding places and uncontrolled, unprotected "no man's land" areas with the landscaping design.
      ii. Incorporate traffic patterns of pedestrians and vehicle into landscaping design. Plan landscaping design to avoid high-speed entry into the site (see site access issues, below).
      iii. Use secure concrete barriers, no less than 4 feet apart and near curbing, to prevent access to site grounds.
      iv. Utilize aesthetic barriers and landscaping materials as barriers to restricted entrance and parking areas. Consider water basins, fountains, ponds, concrete floral bollards, trees, hedges, etc.
      v.   Check planned location/placement of trash bin facilities on the site. Arrange them in a visible, isolated location.
3. Building Design Security Measures

Relevant resources:

- *Building Security Through Design,* http://www.aia.org/security/default.asp.
- U.S. General Services Administration, *Facilities Standards for the Public Buildings Service, PBS-P100,* at http://hydra.gsa.gov/pbs/p100/ (for very detailed site design specifications).

- Atlas, http://www.cpted-security.com.
- Bambi Tran, *Balancing Security/Safety & Sustainability Objectives*, Whole Building Design Guide (Nov. 18, 2002), http://www.wbdg.org/design/resource.php?cn=0&cx=0&rp=28.
  The Whole Building Design Guide (http://www.wbdg.org) contains numerous site plan analyses, as well as effective case studies implementing the National Institute of Building Sciences' security recommendations.

Consider building design/retrofit standards for sensitive facilities, to include the following:
  a. *Identification stations and facility entry checkpoints*
      i.   Minimize the number of vehicle and pedestrian access points. Design the site perimeter to implement limitations on access.
      ii. Install lighting, fencing, etc. to define entryways for visitors clearly. Consider the use of horizontally maintained foot-candles to light entrances.
      iii. Channel visitors through controlled access points and include easily identifiable visitor entry booths.
      iv. Design clearly recognizable, controlled security space for building superintendents and check-in officials.
  b. *Inspection facilities*
      Investigate particularly sensitive carrying "vehicles," such as:
      i.   Undersides, under hoods, and trunks of vehicles;
      ii. Incoming package and freight deliveries; and
      iii. Briefcases and purses.
      Utilize effective inspection techniques:
      iv. Canine detection teams;
      v.   Radiation detectors; and
      vi. Explosives detectors.
      Realize that stopping vehicles and the use of inspection techniques will not provide a secure defense against pedestrian or moped-riding suicide bombers. Consider additional security measures to protect against these threats, such as armed-guard stations and general site perimeter design—for example, fences, walls, etc.—where appropriate.
  c. *Surveillance measures*
      i.   Uninterrupted lines of sight for security personnel;
      ii. Visible closed circuit television and infra-red cameras; and
      iii. Visible motion and heat detectors.
  d. *Access controls*
      i.   Parking facility protection (see 4. Vehicle Access and Parking, below);
      ii. Locks on manhole covers and any other outdoor-to-indoor or above-ground-to-underground entry routes;
      iii. Controlled access to windows, doors, skylights, storm sewers, rooftops, fire escapes, ledges, and tunnels in and around the site;

iv. Security features, including separate ventilation systems, for lobbies, mail rooms, and delivery docks and bays (see details below);

v. Unique, traceable "smart cards,"[8] with access restrictions;

vi. Advance notification of sensitive deliveries (for example, chemicals), including driver's name, truck number;

vii. Use of ID badges and access controls at sensitive locations (for example, power/heat plants, gas mains, water supplies, and electrical and telephone system hubs);

viii. Personnel background reviews (to include landscaping, custodial, and delivery personnel) at sensitive locations;

ix. Burglar alarms, to include adoption of an alarm ordinance; and

x. Entry phones to prevent unauthorized site access.

Many of the above access measures should be considered in the initial site planning stages to allow for sufficient wiring and technical space requirements.

e. *Architectural Site Design Protections*

i. Design new buildings in simple, geometric, rectangular layouts to minimize "defraction" effect from blast waves. Traditional "U" and "L" shaped buildings facilitate blast wave "bouncing" after an explosion and cause extra damage.

ii. Avoid building designs that are vulnerable to progressive collapsing. Ask designers to show in their plans how the risk that the building will collapse due to the loss of single support structures is reduced or eliminated.

iii. Plan limited external cladding, avoiding unnecessary sun control shading devices. Construct external cladding from lightweight materials to minimize damage from detached, flying pieces after an explosion.

iv. Consider placement of offices of vulnerable or important personnel and facilities to face internally into the site (onto an internal courtyard, for example) or to face controlled areas.

v. Provide separate, identifiable entranceways and harden shared partitions for retail stores, restaurants, cafes, etc. in mixed-use buildings (for example, office buildings that contain restaurants or gift shops in lobbies).

f. *Internal Site Design Protections*

i. Elevator lobby and stairway: Design as open and as lit as possible under building code allowances. Design spaces where security personnel easily can see people using these spaces. Close off potential hiding places below indoor and outdoor stairs.

ii. Public facilities: Place public restrooms, telephone booths, ATM machines, etc., in easily observable, secure areas.

iii. Emergency stairs: Design emergency staircases to discharge into places other than lobbies, loading areas or parking garages. Design emergency stairs with appropriate width for evacuation.

iv. Mailroom design: Locate mailroom facility to have a clear, un-obstructed line to delivery area. Secure mailroom with an access control mechanism and locate mailroom in an isolated area on the perimeter of the building with the outside wall or window designed for pressure relief in event of an explosion.

v. Loading and storage areas: Locate loading, receiving, and storage areas in isolated places within the site. These represent some of the most vulnerable entry points for chemical, biological, or radiological agents.

vi. Computer systems control rooms and mechanical rooms for centralized systems (ventilation, water, electric, elevator, etc.): Secure rooms with keycard or key-lock mechanisms for limited, controlled access. Provide for easy supervision of rooms through use of cameras, heat/motion detectors, etc.

vii. Windows: Design and locate windows with possible explosion detonation points in mind. Consider designing window systems to protect against broken glass. Consider use of thermally tempered, heat strengthened, or annealed glass with Mylar window-film coatings, blast curtains, and other blast and ballistic-resistant glazing materials.

viii. Exterior walls: Design walls to ensure that they can withstand the dynamic reactions from window explosions. Design exterior walls to resist actual blast loads from identifiable, possible threats.

ix. Ventilation/HVAC systems: Use mechanical ventilation systems with special internal and external air filters to protect against biological, chemical, or radiological attacks. Note that different filters apply to chemical attacks, as compared to filters for biological/radiological attacks. Use systems that can monitor internal pressures to prevent the introduction of biological, radiological, and chemical agents into the system.

Design a "tight" building plan to reduce infiltration cracks in the building envelope through doors and windows.

Locate fresh-air intake vents to avoid ground-level access outside the building. Prevent access to outdoor air intakes by locating them in publicly inaccessible locations, such as secure roofs or high side walls. If that is not possible, construct intake extensions to elevate access at least twelve feet from ground level.

Cover the entrances to vents with forty-five degree sloped metal mesh to reduce the threat of objects being thrown into vents and becoming lodged atop the openings.

Use secure grilles for HVAC return air filters, to cover and limit access.

Use low-leakage dampers that close tightly upon HVAC system shutdown.

Identify and protect against significant airflow pathways in the site, such as utility chases, elevator shafts, and fire stairs.

Install HVAC systems with energy management and control systems that can regulate airflow and building pressures on an emergency response basis. Install HVAC systems that respond to fire detection systems.

RELATED RESOURCE:

James Glanz, *Report Sees Lower Towers That Can Empty Faster*, N.Y. TIMES, Mar. 28, 2002, at A15 (citing the chairman of a mechanical, electrical, and plumbing firm in Manhattan, and explaining that it can cost millions of dollars "to fully rework an existing building to filter out all biological and chemical agents, move and monitor intake vents, and keep internal air pressure just high enough to prevent terror agents from being sucked in through the small cracks around windows and doors"). Glanz's article references a study by the Construction Institute of the American Society of Civil Engineers that addresses the effect of 9/11 on building designs and discusses the importance of controlling access to intake vents in a building's HVAC system. The article illustrates the need for site planners to address HVAC requirements in their *initial* building designs.

    x.   Fire protection system: Implement active features, including sprinklers, fire alarms, smoke control, etc. Implement passive features such as fire resistant barriers. Implement operational features, including system maintenance and employee training.

  g. *Indoor environments*
Consider requiring applicants for development or redevelopment permits for sensitive facilities to submit evidence of consideration of, and—as appropriate—review for, conformity with the recommendations in the NIOSH GUIDANCE document, cited below.

RELATED RESOURCE:

CENTERS FOR DISEASE CONTROL AND PREVENTION & NATIONAL INSTITUTE FOR OCCUPATIONAL SAFETY AND HEALTH, DEPARTMENT OF HEALTH AND HUMAN SERVICES, GUIDANCE FOR PROTECTING BUILDING ENVIRONMENTS FROM AIRBORNE CHEMICAL, BIOLOGICAL, OR RADIOLOGICAL ATTACKS, DHHS (NIOSH) PUBLICATION No. 2002-139 (May 2002), http://www.cdc.gov/NIOSH/bldvent/2002-139.html.

  h. *Emergency generator fuel tanks*
Consider the least vulnerable location for emergency generator fuel tanks (away from loading docks, entrances and parking areas). Restrict access to storage areas. Hospitals and other facilities that rely on emergency backup in the event of power outages must consider this issue in their site plans. The inherent danger of on-site fuel tanks can implicate tort liability if site designers and reviewers do not protect against foreseeable harms.

RELATED RESOURCES:

- John M. Barkett, *Combating Terrorism in the Environmental Trenches: Terrorism and the Future of Torts: If Terror Reigns, Will Torts Follow?*, 9 WID.

L. Symp. J. 485 (2003) (providing a critical analysis of this issue). Barkett discusses the dangers posed by on-site fuel tanks, citing the case of 7 World Trade Center, which collapsed seven hours after fire ignited in the building. The fire ignited from flammable fuel that poured down from the Twin Towers. However, the fire intensified due to 7 World Trade's multiple fuel tanks, each holding up to 6,000 gallons of fuel. Investigators believe the ignited fuel caused a significant part of the building collapse.

- James Glanz, *Engineers Have a Culprit in the Strange Collapse of 7 World Trade Center: Diesel Fuel*, N.Y. Times, Nov. 29, 2001, at B9.
- James Glanz and Eric Lipton, *Burning Diesel is Cited in Fall of 3rd Tower*, N.Y. Times, Mar. 2, 2002, at A1.

    i. *Blast Deflection*
        Berms and other blast-deflecting measures to protect lobbies, underground parking and glass building facades.

Related resource:
Committee on Feasibility of Applying Blast-Mitigating Technologies and Design Methodologies from Military Facilities to Civilian Buildings, National Research Council, Protecting Buildings from Bomb Damage: Transfer of Blast-Effects Mitigation Technologies from Military to Civilian Applications (1995), http://www.nap.edu/books/0309053757/html/index.html.

    j. *Lighting*
        i.   Security review: Do plan reviews consider whether lighting is adequate for security purposes?
        ii. Dark skies policies: There is a "dark skies" concept supported and promoted by, among others, the Illuminating Engineering Society of North America (IESNA) to require reduced lighting levels and therefore sky glow. Reevaluate your jurisdiction's approach to this issue in light of security issues.

Related resource:
Alex Wilson, *Light Pollution: Efforts to Bring Back the Night Sky*, Environmental Building News (Sept. 1998) (article favoring a dark skies policy), http://www.buildinggreen.com/features/night/nightlight.cfm.

   4. Vehicle Access and Parking
      a. *Security Review*
         Does your jurisdiction consider whether on-site parking under high-rise buildings and other sensitive facilities is still a good idea?
      b. *Impose Security Conditions*
         Condition approval of on-site parking at sensitive facilities on inclusion of appropriate levels of access controls.
      c. *Threat Reduction*
        i.   Protect on-site parking to reduce the threat of truck bomb "gate-crasher" penetration by requiring the installation and use of barrier devices, such as those which require entering vehicles

to negotiate low speed "S" turns at the entries to underground parking garages. Use explosives detectors to reduce the threat posed by an attack using multiple vehicles, each parked adjacent to a critical support column.

ii.   Use bollards and moats to protect against truck bomb access to building lobbies and areas with high concentrations of people. NOTE: Design these barriers to ensure that they are not used as hiding places for criminals or others.

iii. Maximize distance between parking and building. Locate parking as far from buildings as possible—but consistent with Americans with Disabilities Act guidelines—and within view of site access supervisors.

iv.   Eliminate or strictly control underground parking beneath facilities.

v.   Design and control placement of bike racks and carpool parking lots on the site.

vi.   Design separate service routes for service deliveries and for visitors, site users, and employees.

RELATED RESOURCES:
ATF Explosives, Bomb Threat and Detection Resources publications are no longer available online. Send a written request to the following to receive a copy:

Bureau of Alcohol, Tobacco and Firearms
Arson and Explosives Programs Division 800
K Street, NW, Tech World Suite 710
Washington, DC 20001

d. *Alternatives*
   i.   Off-site parking in secure government facilities. Should off-site secure government parking facilities, with enhanced detection and inspection facilities, be the new norm?
   ii. Mass transit. Is mass transit a threat-reducing alternative to on-site parking under high-rise buildings and other sensitive facilities?

Land Uses Adjacent to Sensitive Facilities

1. Consider compatibility of land uses adjacent to sensitive facilities in light of homeland security concerns. Consider threat reduction through compatible, prudent threat-minimizing, adjacent land uses. (For example, are picnic areas on the banks of a reservoir a security-compatible land use?)
   a. What are the ideal, site-specific, buffer zone needs of facilities sensitive to terrorist attacks?
   b. Airports: Off-site check-in, baggage screening, and auto rentals?

   c. Off-site parking
2. Access Routes to Sensitive Facilities
   a. Are access routes easily controlled and readily defended?
   b. Should the site owner/developer negotiate for control of common rights of way affecting adjacent land?
   c. Are the needs for emergency response to the sensitive facility a factor in land use approvals and cost recovery?

Homeland Security Land Use Procedural Issues

Land Use Approvals and Plan Checks

1. Do your jurisdiction's land use approval review and plan check processes include identification of facilities sensitive to terrorist attack and analysis of homeland security concerns?
2. Does your jurisdiction's environmental analysis require consideration of "worst-case scenario" of accidents or terrorist attacks on sensitive facilities? Do those who prepare environmental analyses utilize vulnerability assessment protocols in "worst case scenario" analyses? What steps do you take to avoid having worst-case scenario analyses become "how-to" manuals for terrorists?
3. Do the land use review and plan check processes include police and fire department reviews for security issues?
4. Do local security reviews consider requirements of, and is development approval conditioned on compliance with, federal standards? For example, for transportation facilities, consider compliance with the Department of Transportation Hazardous Materials Regulations, 49 C.F.R. Parts 171-180, 68 Fed. Reg. 23,831 (May 5, 2003), http://hazmat.dot.gov/rules/68fr-23831.htm.
5. Are federal preemption issues analyzed?
6. Does your jurisdiction have ordinances that require consideration and adoption of protective measures for sensitive facilities?
7. Do your land use application reviews for sensitive facilities address and condition approval on the facility's impacts on increased patrolling and coordination among law enforcement agencies? Do governing laws provide for the creation of a special benefit assessment district for the recovery of increased costs for additional police services for terrorist-sensitive facilities?
8. Does your approval process provide for imposition of fees and cost recovery for increased security impacts of the sensitive facility?

Is "Smart Growth" Inconsistent with Homeland Security?

Development reviews should consider carefully the compatibility of infill development and the concentration of facilities in the light of vulnerability assessments.

General Plan Elements for Homeland Security

Should your jurisdiction's general plan be amended to add a new "homeland security" element? Or should homeland security considerations be added to other general plan elements?

Are Building and Mechanical Code Revisions Needed?

1. Reduction of Vulnerability
   Consider building and mechanical code revisions to address the issues raised in the section on Internal Site Design Protections, above.[9] Consider how indoor environments in buildings, especially sensitive facilities, might be designed and built to reduce chemical, biological and radiological threats (for example, PCBs in smoke from on-site fires, or anthrax, spread by the HVAC system?)

RELATED RESOURCE:
CENTERS FOR DISEASE CONTROL AND PREVENTION & NATIONAL INSTITUTE FOR OCCUPATIONAL SAFETY AND HEALTH, DEPARTMENT OF HEALTH AND HUMAN SERVICES, GUIDANCE FOR PROTECTING BUILDING ENVIRONMENTS FROM AIRBORNE CHEMICAL, BIOLOGICAL, OR RADIOLOGICAL ATTACKS, DHHS (NIOSH) PUBLICATION NO. 2002-139 (May 2002), http://www.cdc.gov/NIOSH/bldvent/2002-139.html.

2. Accommodation of Security Facilities in Sensitive Facilities
   Design review of sensitive facilities might include accommodation of new security equipment, package, and freight inspection stations, delivery vehicle inspection sites, etc.
3. Alarm Ordinances
   Consider adoption of an alarm ordinance, setting standards for alarm systems.

Access to Public Records

Are revisions to your state and local public records access policies required to limit public access to information about sensitive facilities in light of homeland security concerns? Do the statutes and ordinances that govern your agency make HVAC plans, public water system vulnerability assessments, and other security-sensitive materials available to the public, including terrorists?

The new Section 1433(a)(3) of the Safe Drinking Water Act (SDWA) exempts drinking water system vulnerability assessments from disclosure under the Freedom of Information Act (FOIA), 5 U.S.C. § 552. The Bioterrorism Act did not create "FOIA events" at the state and local level. It provides that the requirement for a community water system to submit a vulnerability assessment to the Environmental Protection Agency insulates the community water system from any obligation under state and local law to submit a copy of the assessment to any other governmental authority. SDWA § 1433(a)(4) provides:

(4) No community water system shall be required under State or local law to provide an assessment described in this section to any State, regional of local gov-

ernmental entity by reason of the requirement set forth in paragraph (2) that the system submit such assessment to the Administrator.

Moreover, under the Homeland Security Act of 2002,[10] state and local procedures which require disclosure of a record that the Department of Homeland Security considers to be "critical infrastructure information"[11] are preempted.

RELATED RESOURCES:
- The American Institute of Architects and the National Society of Professional Engineers have developed a form for reporting unusual requests, due to the structures identified or type of information solicited, to the FBI. It is available at http://www.aia.org/letter/buildingplanform.pdf. Clean Air Act § 112(r)(7)(H)(xii)(II), 42 U.S.C. § 7412(r)(7)(H)(xii)(II), added to limit release of sensitive sections 2 through 5 of RMPs.
- 40 C.F.R. Part 1400, 65 Fed. Reg. 48,108-133 (Aug. 4, 2000).

Vulnerability Assessment Coordination

Are land use decisions regarding sensitive facilities coordinated with EPA-initiated preparedness measures?

RELATED RESOURCES:
- Public Health Security and Bioterrorism Preparedness and Response Act of 2002, Pub. L. No. 107-188; http://www.ncsl.org/statefed/health/PL107-188overview.htm.
- http://www.epa.gov/safewater/security/community.html.

Audit Compliance

Are land use approvals of sensitive facilities conditioned on compliance with security audit requirements?

RELATED RESOURCE:
For port security measures, *see* 33 C.F.R. Parts 125, 126; 67 Fed. Reg. 51,082, http://www.marinecompliance.org/downloads/Aug2002/67_FR_51082_8-7-02_USCG_Credentials.PDF.

Homeland Security and Environmental Liabilities

Terrorist attacks could result in releases of hazardous substances into the environment. Does your jurisdiction consider the use of Conditional Use Permits, or other development approval conditions, to impose cleanup responsibility on the property owner or operator in the event a terrorist attack results in the release of hazardous substances at the facility, notwithstanding §§ 107(b)(2) and (3) of the Comprehensive Environmental Response, Compensation, and Liability Act (CERCLA), 42 U.S.C. § 107(b)(2) and (3)? But be prepared for claims of federal preemption.

Homeland Security and Tort Liability

Can tort liability be imposed for a building owner's failure to provide proper and fast ways to escape a building? Or for failure to take steps to protect the HVAC system? Consider the hotel and shopping center cases, holding building owners and operators liable for foreseeable assaults.

See *In Re September 11 Litigation*, Opinion and Order Denying Defendants' Motions to Dismiss, No. 21-MC-97-AKH, 2003 WL 22077747, 2003 US DIST LEXIS 15522 (S.D.N.Y. Sept. 9, 2003) (denying building owner's and other defendants' motions to dismiss based on argument that the terrorist attack was a supervening cause relieving them of tort liability).

Pursuant to the Terrorism Risk Insurance Act of 2002, if the secretary of the treasury makes a determination that an act of international terrorism has occurred, a federal cause of action will exist, and state law causes of action are preempted.

RELATED RESOURCE:
John M. Barkett, *Combating Terrorism in the Environmental Trenches: Terrorism and the Future of Torts: If Terror Reigns, Will Torts Follow?*, 9 Wid. L. Symp. J. 485 (2003).

Constitutional Limitations on Access Restriction

1. *Vlasak v. Superior Ct.*, 329 F.3d 683 (9th Cir. 2003) (prohibition on carrying "demonstration equipment" [elephant bull hook] upheld).
2. *Virginia v. Hicks*, 539 U.S. 113 (2003) (exclusion from public housing project upheld).

Force Majeure *Clauses*

Construction, and many other, contracts typically include *force majeure* clauses, which excuse a party from contract obligations if certain events outside the party's control occur. A typical *force majeure* provision is to excuse performance in the event of "Acts of War." But are acts of terrorism within the meaning of "Acts of War?" In the post-9/11 and anthrax attack era, obviously it is advisable to make explicit whether "acts of terrorism" are to excuse performance.

In *Pan American World Airways, Inc. v. Aetna Casualty & Surety Co.*, 505 F.2d 989 (2d Cir. 1974), the court held that the skyjacking and subsequent destruction of a Pan American 747 by PLO terrorists was not an "act of war." The *Pan American* court noted that the PLO terrorists were not in uniforms, and were not on a battlefield. While the *Pan American* case involved insurance coverage, and not a *force majeure* clause, the court's holding provides an obstacle in arguing that "act of war" in a *force majeure* clause includes acts of terrorism.

Recommendation: In future contracts, or amendments, specify that "acts of terrorism" are included, or excluded, from the definition of *force majeure*, depending on how and to whom this risk is to be assigned. Recall also that risks include not only the direct impact from a terrorist attack, but also impacts caused by responses to such attacks. For example, projects in Manhattan were impacted not only by the attacks on the World Trade Center, but also by government restrictions preventing trucks from freely crossing into Manhattan after the attack

Notice Provisions

In the homeland security era, standard notice provisions calling for delivery by mail or personal delivery, or both, to a designated address, may no longer be adequate. Not only was delivery to the World Trade center rendered impossible, the Hart Senate Office Building was closed for 95 days due to an anthrax (*bacillus anthracis*) attack. A portion of the Morgan Processing and Distribution Center, the central mail processing center in New York City, a two million square foot facility occupying two city blocks, was closed for the same reason. The Brentwood Road mail-handling facility in Washington, D.C., remained closed for more than a year after the anthrax attacks.The Postal Service closed 11 post offices in the Washington, D.C. area on November 6, 2003, following the discovery of anthrax in an air sample at a site that handles mail for federal agencies.

It is entirely possible and foreseeable that mailed notice could be "marooned" in a closed post office, and not delivered, or that the delivery address could cease to exist, or that the building to which notice has been delivered is inaccessible due to anthrax or other terrorist attack. Recall that e-mail can be received by the intended recipient just about anywhere.

Recommendations: Standard notice provisions should be redrafted in light of homeland security considerations. Routinely include provision for delivery by both mail *and* overnight service to the recipient at a specific address *and to a second address*. Provide for additional notice to be sent by e-mail to more than one e-mail address. Notice provisions should address whether terrorist attacks are to excuse failure to deliver notices.

Conclusion

Local government officials, land use planners, architects, developers, and building owners who fail to take proactive homeland security steps—such as reviewing building design, lighting, and landscaping plans and providing for the protection of heating, ventilating, and air conditioning systems, mail rooms, delivery docks and parking facilities—do so at considerable risk. The full extent of the liability risk is unknown, but after the decision in *In Re September 11 Litigation,* the concern is that the risk could increase and past actions and inactions will form the basis for liability. This seems to be a case of better to be safe than sorry.

The authors recommend that local governments undertake comprehensive reviews of their land development review and permitting processes. Homeland security considerations should be incorporated. Checklists and processing steps will require revisions to incorporate homeland security concepts.

Ordinances and codes may have to be revised. Local governments might also consider audits or inspections by law enforcement personnel and building inspectors for compliance with homeland security defensive steps.

Land use planners, architects, developers, and building owners also must take homeland security measures into consideration in the planning phase. Due diligence in the acquisition of existing structures also requires consideration of these homeland security factors. Homeland security considerations must also be a factor in retrofit and remodeling decisions.

Such steps cannot be ignored. While the measures suggested in this chapter and the references might be particularly appropriate for terrorist-sensitive facilities in an effort to make them less attractive and vulnerable to terrorist attacks, they also should be helpful in reducing the threats posed by common criminals and vandals.

Citations and Resources

Articles and Publications

Randall Atlas, *Designing Against Terror: Site Security Planning and Design Criteria*, (from ARCHITECTURAL GRAPHICS STANDARDS 1999 rev.), http://www.cpted-security.com/cpted4.htm.

Randall Atlas, *Environmental Design That Prevents Crime*, (from THE CONSTRUCTION SPECIFIER Apr. 1999), http://www.cpted-security.com/cpted11.htm.

Randall Atlas, *Coping with Threats, From Bombs to Break-Ins*, (from ARCHITECTURAL RECORD Mar. 1996), http://www.cpted-security.com/cpted2.htm.

Randall Atlas, *Building Design Can Provide Defensible Space*, (from ACCESS CONTROL Sept. 1989), http://www.cpted-security.com/cpted3.htm.

John M. Barkett, *Combating Terrorism in the Environmental Trenches: Terrorism and the Future of Torts: If Terror Reigns, Will Torts Follow?*, 9 WID. L. SYMP. J. 485 (2003).

Barbara Basler, *Protecting the Home Front*, AARP BULLETIN, May 2003, at 20, http://www.aarp.org/bulletin/yourlife/Articles/a2003-06-26-protecting.html.

James Glanz, *Engineers Have A Culprit in the Strange Collapse of 7 World Trade Center: Diesel Fuel*, N.Y. TIMES, Nov. 29, 2001, at B9.

James Glanz and Eric Lipton, *Burning Diesel is Cited in Fall of 3rd Tower*, N.Y. TIMES, Mar. 2, 2002, at A1.

Barbara Nadel, *Better Safe: Planning Secure Environments*, AREA DEVELOPMENT: SITE AND FACILITY PLANNING (May 2001) http://www.areadevelopment.com/past/0501/features/better.html.

Jennifer Oldham, *Project for LAX Security Faulted*, LOS ANGELES TIMES, May 15, 2003, B-1, col. 1.

Bambi Tran, *Balancing Security/Safety & Sustainability Objectives*, Whole Building Design Guide (*updated* Nov. 18, 2002), http://www.wbdg.org/design/resource.php?cn=0&cx=0&rp=28.

Alex Wilson, *Light Pollution: Efforts to Bring Back the Night Sky*, ENVIRONMENTAL BUILDING NEWS (September 1998), http://www.buildinggreen.com/features/night/nightlight.cfm.

CENTERS FOR DISEASE CONTROL AND PREVENTION & NATIONAL INSTITUTE FOR OCCU-
PATIONAL SAFETY AND HEALTH, DEPARTMENT OF HEALTH AND HUMAN SERVICES,
GUIDANCE FOR PROTECTING BUILDING ENVIRONMENTS FROM AIRBORNE CHEMI-
CAL, BIOLOGICAL, OR RADIOLOGICAL ATTACKS, DHHS (NIOSH) PUBLICATION
No. 2002-139, May, 2002, http://www.cdc.gov/NIOSH/bldvent/2002-
139.html, or order by e-mail to pubstaft@cdc.gov.

COMMITTEE ON FEASIBILITY OF APPLYING BLAST-MITIGATING TECHNOLOGIES AND DESIGN
METHODOLOGIES FROM MILITARY FACILITIES TO CIVILIAN BUILDINGS, NATIONAL
RESEARCH COUNCIL, PROTECTING BUILDINGS FROM BOMB DAMAGE: TRANSFER OF
BLAST-EFFECTS MITIGATION TECHNOLOGIES FROM MILITARY TO CIVILIAN APPLICA-
TIONS (1995), http://www.nap.edu/books/0309053757/html/index.html.

Eugene Sevin & Richard G. Little, *Mitigating Terrorist Hazards*, THE BRIDGE, Volume 28, Number 3 (Fall 1998), http://www.nae.edu/nae/naehome.nsf/
weblinks/NAEW-4NHMEP?opendocument.

Patti Gallagher and Alex Krieger, *Security with Dignity*, URBAN LAND (March
2003), at 73, http://www.chankrieger.com/frames/aboutus/principals/
security.htm.

Eric V. Larson and John E. Peters, PREPARING THE U.S. ARMY FOR HOMELAND
SECURITY: CONCEPTS, ISSUES, AND OPTIONS (2001), http://www.rand.org/
publications/MR/MR1251/.

*National Preparedness: Technologies to Secure Federal Buildings, Testimony Before
the Subcommittee on Technology and Procurement Policy, H. Committee on
Government Reform*, GAO-02-687T (April 25, 2002) (testimony of Keith A.
Rhodes), http://www.gao.gov/new.items/d02687t.pdf.

THE NATIONAL STRATEGY FOR THE PHYSICAL PROTECTION OF CRITICAL INFRASTRUC-
TURES AND KEY ASSETS (February 2003), http://www.dhs.gov/interweb/
assetlibrary/Physical_Strategy.pdf.

Citations

Ports and Waterways Safety Act, 33 U.S.C. §§ 1221-1250 (2005).

Safe Explosives Act, Title XI, Subtitle C of Pub. L. No. 107-296, (Homeland Security Act of 2002); and regulations, 27 C.F.R. Part 555, 68 Fed. Reg. 13,768-
93 (March 20, 2003) (interim rule).

Maritime Transportation and Security Act of 2003, Pub. L. No. 108-136, 117
Stat. 1392.

Uniting and Strengthening America by Providing Appropriate Tools Required
to Intercept and Obstruct Terrorism Act, (USA PATRIOT Act), Pub. L. No.
107-56, 115 Stat. 272 (2001).

Department of Transportation Hazardous Materials Regulations, 49 C.F.R.
Parts 171-180, 68 Fed. Reg. 23,831 (May 5, 2003).

Public Health Security and Bioterrorism Preparedness and Response Act of
2002, Pub. L. No. 107-188.

Clean Air Act § 112(r), 42 U.S.C. § 7412(r) (regulates facilities handling extremely hazardous materials. Requires preparation and implementation
of risk management plan and off-site consequences analysis. Amended to

limit release of information; and regulations, 65 Fed. Reg. 48,107-133 (Aug. 4, 2000).

Emergency Planning and Community Right-to-Know Act of 1986, (EPCRTKA), 42 U.S.C. §§ 11001-11050. Requires emergency planning at facilities at which the quantity of extremely hazardous materials exceed the threshold planning quantity, notifications of emergency releases, reporting and toxic chemical release inventory. EPCRTKA also requires the establishment of state commissions, planning districts and local committees to prepare emergency plans to address releases of extremely hazardous chemicals.

The Homeland Security Act of 2002, Pub. L. No. 197-296. *See* Procedures for Handling Critical Infrastructure Information, 68 Fed. Reg. 18,253 (proposed Apr. 15, 2003).

THE NATIONAL STRATEGY FOR THE PHYSICAL PROTECTION OF CRITICAL INFRASTRUCTURES AND KEY ASSETS (February 2003), http://www.dhs.gov/interweb/assetlibrary/Physical_Strategy.pdf.

Links

http://www.epa.gov/safewater/security/community.html

http://www.awwa.org

http://www.fema.gov/fima/antiterrorism/links.shtm

Building Security Through Design: http://www.aia.org/security/default.asp

http://www.whitehouse.gov/homeland/

For additional information, see the following table, downloaded from http://www.epa.gov/iaq/ohs.html:

Several organizations have developed guidance to assist building owners and operators in addressing issues related to building security and CBR terrorist attacks. Many other organizations have guidance that addresses security needs and disaster response plans for events such as fire, natural disasters, and bomb threats. While this latter guidance may not specifically address a terrorist threat to heating, ventilation, and air conditioning (HVAC) systems, readers may find portions of the information below beneficial in establishing their own building's emergency response plans.

The following list is not all-inclusive. Available guidance is updated regularly as additional organizations and evolving technologies identify new protective recommendations. An Adobe Acrobat PDF version of this table is also available: http://www.epa.gov/iaq/images/ohs_table.pdf (last checked October 31, 2003).

Organization	Reference or Link	Description
National Institute for Occupational Safety and Health (NIOSH)	http://www.cdc.gov/NIOSH/homepage.html	Health and safety guidance, publications, and training information.
Centers for Disease Control and Prevention (CDC)	http://www.cdc.gov/	Health guidance for CBR agents.
U.S. Army Corps of Engineers (USACE)	http://buildingprotection.sbccom.army.mil/basic/ *Protecting Buildings and Their Occupants from Airborne Hazards*	Document presents a variety of ways to protect building occupants from airborne hazards.
U.S. Environmental Protection Agency (EPA) http://www.epa.gov	http://www.epa.gov/iaq/largebldgs/baqtoc.html *Building Air Quality: A Guide for Building Owners and Facility Managers*	Provides procedures and checklists for developing a building profile and performing preventative maintenance in commercial buildings.
	http://www.epa.gov/iaq/schools/*Indoor Air Quality (IAQ) Tools for Schools Kit*	Provides procedures and checklists for developing a building profile and performing preventative maintenance in schools.
U.S. General Services Administration (GSA) http://www.gsa.gov	http://hydra.gsa.gov/pbs/p100/*Facility Standards for the Public Building Service (PBS-P100)*	Establishes design standards and criteria for new buildings, major and minor alterations, and work in historic structures for the Public Building Service. Also provides information on conducting building security assessments.

Organization	Reference or Link	Description
Central Intelligence Agency (CIA) http://www.cia.gov	http://www.cia.gov/cia/reports/cbr_handbook/cbrbook.htm *Chemical Biological, Radiological Incident Handbook*	Unclassified document describing potential CBR events, recognizing potential CBR events, differences between agents, common symptoms, and information for making preliminary assessments when a CBR release is suspected.
Lawrence Berkeley National Laboratory	http://securebuildings.lbl.gov	Web site with advice for safeguarding buildings against chemical or biological attack.
Federal Facilities Council (FFC)	http://www7.nationalacademies.org/ffc/FFC_Chemical_Biological_Threats.html	Online notes and presentations from FFC seminar on chemical and biological threats to buildings.
American Institute of Architects (AIA)	http://www.aia.org/security/default.asp *Building Security Through Design*	An AIA resource center offers architects and others, up-to-date, in-depth material on building security issues.
American Society of Heating and Refrigerating and Air Conditioning Engineers (ASHRAE) http://www.ashrae.org	http://xp20.ashrae.org/about/extraordinary.pdf *Risk Management Guidance for Health and Safety under Extraordinary Incidents*	Draft report provides recommendations for owners and managers of existing buildings.
American Society for Industrial Security	http://www.asisonline.org/	Locates security specialists and provides the *Crises Response Resources* link to find information related to terrorism and building security.
Building Owners and Managers Association http://www.boma.org	http://www.boma.org/ProductsAndResearch/SafetyAndEmergencyPlanning	Information on emergency planning and security assessment.
International Facility Management Association (IFMA)	http://www.ifma.org/	Information on security-related training courses.
National Institute of Building Sciences (NIBS)	http://www.wbdg.org *Whole Building Design Guide*	Internet site featuring security-related design information.

The views expressed in this article do not necessarily reflect the views of the authors' firms, or any of their respective current or former clients. The authors acknowledge the foresight and encouragement of Frank Schnidman, planning chair of the ALI-ABA Land Use Institute and senior fellow at the Center for Urban & Environmental Solutions at Florida Atlantic University, for suggesting this topic and encouraging the authors to develop this aspect of homeland security law. (Our planning chair knew that as a retired Marine Corps Colonel and Navy Reserve Captain, respectively, we would follow orders!)

NOTES

1. *See generally,* THE NATIONAL STRATEGY FOR THE PHYSICAL PROTECTION OF CRITICAL INFRASTRUCTURES AND KEY ASSETS (February 2003), at vii (NATIONAL STRATEGY), http://www.dhs.gov/interweb/assetlibrary/Physical_Strategy.pdf.

2. As an excellent starting point, the authors recommend CENTERS FOR DISEASE CONTROL AND PREVENTION & NATIONAL INSTITUTE FOR OCCUPATIONAL SAFETY AND HEALTH, DEPARTMENT OF HEALTH AND HUMAN SERVICES, GUIDANCE FOR PROTECTING BUILDING ENVIRONMENTS FROM AIRBORNE CHEMICAL, BIOLOGICAL, OR RADIOLOGICAL ATTACKS, DHHS (NIOSH) PUBLICATION NO. 2002-139 (May 2002), http://www.cdc.gov/NIOSH/bldvent/2002-139.html.

3. NATIONAL STRATEGY, at 8.

4. *Giuliani Goes Private—for Now,* MONEY MAGAZINE, October 2003, at 88.

5. NATIONAL STRATEGY, at 78.

6. *See generally,* NATIONAL STRATEGY.

7. *See* the section on Homeland Security and Tort Liability, *infra,* for a brief discussion of potential tort liability of property owners and operators for failure to take steps adequate to protect persons on the premises from terrorist attacks.

8. A "smart card" is a plastic device about the size of a credit card that contains an embedded integrated circuit chip capable of both storing and processing data. By securely exchanging data, a smart card can help authenticate the identity of the individual possessing the card in a far more rigorous way than is possible than with a traditional identification card.

9. "Additionally, providing support and input to organizations that develop standards and guidance for building construction and facility heating, ventilating and air conditioning (HVAC) systems constitutes an important federal government activity." NATIONAL STRATEGY, at 78.

10. Pub. L. No. 107-296.

11. HSA § 213(3) defines "critical infrastructure information" as information related to the security of critical infrastructure or protected systems, 6 U.S.C.S. § 131. *See also,* Procedures for Handling Critical Infrastructure Information, 68 Fed. Reg. 18,253, (proposed April 15, 2003).

CHAPTER 6

Preparedness Funding

by Alan Cohn

Introduction

Since the attacks of September 11, 2001, the federal government has provided billions of dollars to state and local governments for terrorism and first responder preparedness.[1] This chapter describes the primary Department of Homeland Security (DHS) terrorism preparedness grant programs as of fiscal year 2004, as well as a number of other DHS and non-DHS programs that provide funding to state and local governments for first responder preparedness. This chapter also describes how some of the overarching questions concerning first responder funding colored the debate over first responder funding authorization in the 108th Congress. These debates will likely continue for the foreseeable future.

Grant Funding Programs

Set forth herein is a summary of the main federal preparedness programs for state and local government entities that were available in fiscal year 2004, with additional information available from the fiscal year 2005 homeland security appropriations bill.[2] This list is not exclusive, and other preparedness programs exist across the federal government. Moreover, the information set forth in likely to change, perhaps in each subsequent year, so current grant guidance from the DHS Office of State and Local Government Coordination and Preparedness (OSLGCP), as well as the most recent version of the Catalog of Federal Domestic Assistance (CFDA), should always be consulted.[3]

As a general note, Homeland Security Presidential Directive 5 (HSPD 5) requires adoption of the National Incident Management System (NIMS) as a condition of federal grant assistance from DHS's Office for Domestic Preparedness (ODP)—part of OSLGCP—beginning in fiscal year 2005.[4] In a letter to the nation's governors dated September 8, 2004, Secretary of Homeland Security Tom Ridge explained the steps that state, local, and tribal governments should take during fiscal year 2005 to become compliant with the NIMS.[5] Since "HSPD 5 established ambitious deadlines for NIMS adoption and implementation," and "[fiscal year] 2005 is a start up year for NIMS implementation," "full compliance with the NIMS is not required" for states to receive fiscal year 2005 grant funds.[6] However, "[t]o the maximum extent possible, States, territories, tribes, and local entities are encouraged to achieve full NIMS implementation and institutionalization across the entire response system during [fiscal year] 2005."[7]

Minimum fiscal year 2005 NIMS compliance includes, at a minimum, the following:

- "Incorporating NIMS into existing training programs and exercises";
- "Ensuring that Federal preparedness funding (including DHS Homeland Security Grant Program [and] Urban Area Security Initiative funds) support NIMS implementation at the State and local levels (in accordance with the eligibility and allowable uses of the grants)";
- "Incorporating NIMS into Emergency Operations Plans";
- "Promoti[ng] intrastate mutual aid agreements";
- "Coordinating and providing technical assistance to local entities regarding NIMS"; and
- "Institutionalizing the use of the Incident Command System (ICS)."[8]

Applicants for DHS grant funds "will be required to certify as part of their [fiscal year] 2006 grant applications that they have met the [fiscal year] 2005 NIMS requirements."[9]

Terrorism Preparedness Grant Funding Programs

In fiscal year 2004, there were two major terrorism preparedness grant funding programs for state and local governments administered by ODP[10]: the Homeland Security Grant Program (HSGP)—a formula-based program—and the Urban Areas Security Initiative (UASI)—a discretionary risk-based program. Another DHS terrorism preparedness grant program for which certain state and local government entities were eligible in fiscal year 2004 was the Port Security Grant Program (PSGP). Described below are the HSGP, UASI, and PSGP as they existed in fiscal year 2004. Because the HSGP and UASI programs have no formal authorizing provisions in law, program design for fiscal year 2005 and beyond may differ significantly, slightly, or not at all from fiscal year 2004.[11]

HOMELAND SECURITY GRANT PROGRAM. The fiscal year HSGP is an agglomeration of three existing terrorism preparedness grant programs: the State Homeland Security Program (SHSP); the Law Enforcement Terrorism Prevention Program (LETPP); and the Citizen Corps Program (CCP).[12] The programs remain separate, although states make application for these funds through a single application kit. This was done "to streamline the grant application process and better coordinate federal, State and local grant funding distribution and operations."[13] Funding provided under the HSGP is to be "applied against critical resource gaps identified through the assessments and prioritized in the State strategies."[14]

General Provisions. Fiscal year 2004 state funding under the HSGP grant programs was determined using base formula amounts set forth in the USA PATRIOT Act of 2001: Three-quarters of a percent of the total allocation for the states (including the District of Columbia and Puerto Rico), and one-quarter of one percent of the total allocation for the U.S. territories (American Samoa, the Commonwealth of the Northern Mariana Islands, Guam, and the U.S. Virgin Islands).[15] The balance of the total funds allocated were distributed on a population-share basis.[16]

All three programs are governed by the same general requirements for distribution of funds. The governor of each state designates a State Administrative Agency (SAA) to apply for and administer HSGP funds.[17] Each state is obligated to pass along not less than 80 percent of the total amount of the grant provided to the state for the three programs to local units of government—which include cities, counties, towns, and other traditional units of local government, as well as Indian tribes, which are defined in the Homeland Security Act as "local governments"—within sixty days after the grant award.[18] The state may use the remaining 20 percent of the funds for other statewide homeland security efforts.[19] The state and each local unit of government must allocate their funding in support of goals and objectives identified in the State Homeland Security Strategy (SHSS).[20] No more than 3 percent of the total amount allocated to each state may be used statewide for management and administrative purposes.[21]

The period of performance for fiscal year 2004 HSGP grants is two years.[22] The Office for State and Local Government Cooperation and Preparedness (OSLGCP) will not provide grant funding to the SAA until the state submits its SHSS, and the SHSS is reviewed and approved by OSLGCP.[23] States may not transfer funds between the HSGP programs.[24] States are required to apply for HSGP funding through the online Grant Management System (GMS).[25] There is no matching requirement for HSGP funds in fiscal year 2004.[26] Based on complaints about the speed with which money was reaching first responder agencies, for fiscal year 2004, OSLGCP provided that "no budget information or program narrative is required to apply for the grant"; however, states were "expected to maintain complete and accurate accounting records" and to "make those records available to DHS upon request."[27]

State Homeland Security Program (SHSP). The fiscal year 2004 SHSP "provides funds to enhance the capability of State and local units of government to prevent, deter, respond to, and recover from incidents of terrorism involving the use of chemical, biological, radiological, nuclear, and explosive (CBRNE) weapons and cyber attacks."[28] This includes the following general categories:

- Planning, including homeland security and emergency operations planning activities;

- Equipment, including the purchase of specialized equipment;
- Training, including "the design, development, and conduct of a State CBRNE and cyber security training program and attendance at ODP-sponsored courses";
- Exercises, including "the design, development, conduct, and evaluation of CBRNE and cyber security exercises"; and
- Management and administrative, subject to the 3 percent cap.[29]

In addition, SHSP funds may be used for agricultural homeland security issues in those states that address agriculture in their homeland security strategies.[30]

OSLGCP grant guidance for the SHSP describes the allowable costs in each of the five categories listed above, as well as with respect to agricultural homeland security issues.[31] Only equipment listed on the fiscal year SHSP "authorized equipment list" (AEL) is eligible for purchase with SHSP funds.[32] There are sixteen types of eligible planning activities, and eighteen categories of eligible equipment costs.[33] With respect to interoperable communications equipment, all new or upgraded radio systems and new radio equipment "should be compatible with [the] suite of standards called ANSI/TIA/EIAA-102 Phase I (Project 25)."[34] Both overtime and backfill costs associated with attendance at ODP-sponsored or approved classes, as well as costs associated with the establishment of CBRNE and cyber security training program, are allowable.[35] Exercises conducted with SHSP funds must be conducted in accordance with the Homeland Security Exercise and Evaluation Program (HSEEP).[36]

Law Enforcement Terrorism Preparedness Program (LETPP). The LETPP "seeks to provide law enforcement communities with enhanced capabilities for detecting, deterring, disrupting, and preventing acts of terrorism."[37] The LETPP provides funds for the following categories of expenditures:

- Information sharing to prevent terrorist attacks;
- Target hardening to reduce vulnerability;
- Threat recognition;
- Intervention activities; and
- Interoperable communications.[38]

As noted above, each state's SAA applies for and administers LETPP grants, but must coordinate the implementation of the LETPP with the state's Lead Law Enforcement Agency (LLEA).[39] State and local units of government may expend LETPP funds on planning, organizational activities, equipment, training, exercises, and management and administrative costs.[40]

Under the LETPP, there are twelve types of eligible planning activities, including the development of information- and intelligence-sharing groups, point vulnerability analyses and assessments, soft target security planning, and cyber risk and vulnerability assessments.[41] Allowable organizational activities include the formation of antiterrorism task forces, Joint Terrorism Task Forces, Area Maritime Security Committees, and Terrorism Early Warning Groups.[42] No more than 20 percent of LETPP funds may be used for overtime costs associated with these organizational activities without approval from ODP.[43]

There are twelve categories of eligible equipment costs under the LETPP.[44] As with the SHSP, new or upgraded radio systems and new radio equipment should be Project 25 compliant.[45] There are fourteen categories of eligible training costs, including "joint training with other homeland security entities" at other levels of government.[46] ODP encourages LETPP grant recipients to focus such multiple-level training "on a regional model."[47] As with the SHSP, overtime and backfill costs associated with attendance at ODP-sponsored or approved classes are allowable, as are costs associated with planning and conducting training workshops and conferences.[48] Exercises conducted with SHSP funds must be conducted in accordance with the HSEEP.[49] Allowable costs include exercises involving "facility and/or vessel security protection," "threat recognition capabilities," and "'Red Team' (force on force) exercises."[50]

Citizen Corps Program (CCP). CCP funds are used "to support Citizen Corps Councils with planning, outreach, and management of Citizen Corps programs and activities."[51] The funds can be used to:

- "Bring together the appropriate leadership to form and sustain a Citizen Corps Council";
- "Develop and implement a plan for the community to engage all citizens in homeland security, community preparedness, and family safety";
- "Conduct public education and outreach in order to inform the public about their role in crime prevention, mitigation, emergency preparedness for all hazards, and public health measures, including bioterrorism, and to encourage personal responsibility and action";
- "Develop and implement Citizen Corps programs offering training and volunteer opportunities to support first responders, disaster relief groups, and community safety efforts, to include the four charter federal programs: Community Emergency Response Teams (CERT), Neighborhood Watch, Volunteers in Police Service (VIPS), and Medical Reserve Corps (MRC)"; and
- "Coordinate Citizen Corps activities with other DHS funded programs and initiatives."[52]

Local units of government receiving CCP funding are instructed to "develop a plan for implementing the Citizen Corps mission—to have every American participate in homeland security through public education, training and volunteer service opportunities."[53] The SAA is also instructed to coordinate Citizen Corps program activities with the state agencies that administer those programs.[54]

There are five categories of allowable costs for CCP funds: planning; public education and outreach; training, exercises, and equipment; volunteer program costs; and management and administrative costs.[55] Each of these categories is discussed more extensively in the CCP program guidance.[56]

URBAN AREAS SECURITY INITIATIVE. The Urban Areas Security Initiative (UASI) is the other major DHS terrorism preparedness grant program for state and local governments. The UASI program is intended "to create a sustainable national model program to enhance security and overall preparedness to prevent, respond to, and recover from acts of terrorism."[57] The fiscal year 2004 Department of Homeland Security Appropriations Act provided $725 million to the secretary of homeland security "for discretionary grants for use in high-threat, high-density urban areas."[58] DHS chose to allocate $675 million toward urban area security, and $50 million "for the protection of critical mass transit systems with heavy rail and commuter components," both administered under the rubric of the UASI program.[59] Fifty urban areas received grants from the urban area security funding, and twenty-five mass transit systems received grants from the mass transit security funding.[60]

The urban area grants and mass transit system grants are both governed by the UASI program guidance, which is very similar to the HSGP program guidance. As with the HSGP, the SAA applies for and administers UASI program funding.[61] The period of performance for the fiscal year 2004 UASI program is up to two years.[62] Like the HSGP, the state is obligated to pass along not less than 80 percent of the total amount of the UASI grant to the urban area within sixty days after the grant award.[63] Unlike the HSGP, the SAA may not retain any funds for management and administration costs; local jurisdictions may use no more than 3 percent of their UASI funds for management and administration costs.[64] States include UASI program information in their Biannual Strategy Implementation Reports, which must be submitted under the requirements of the HSGP.[65] There is no matching requirement for fiscal year 2004 UASI program grants.[66]

Like the HSGP, for fiscal year 2004, OSLGCP provided that "no budget information or program narrative is required to apply for the grant"; however, the Urban Area Working Group (UAWG) and the mass transit authority are "expected to maintain complete and accurate accounting records" and to "make those records available to DHS upon request."[67] As noted above, adoption of the minimum NIMS implementation requirements will become a condition for receiving UASI funds in fiscal year 2005.[68]

As with the HSGP, the UASI program guidance permits expenditures in five general categories: planning; equipment; training; exercises; and management and administrative costs. Like the HSGP, the UASI program guidance describes the allowable costs in each of these five categories.[69] Similar to the HSGP, there are sixteen types of eligible UASI planning activities, and eighteen categories of eligible equipment costs.[70] Similar guidelines exist with respect to interoperable communications, training, and exercises.[71] Recipients of UASI grants are required to submit the same reports as HSGP funding recipients.[72]

Differences between the two programs are discussed more fully below.

Urban Areas Funding. The urban areas funding element is intended to "significantly enhance the ability of urban areas to prevent, deter, respond to, and recover from threats and incidents of terrorism."[73] As noted above, the SAA applies for and administers UASI program funding.[74] The state is then responsible for ensuring that the urban area selected for funding "take[s] a regional metropolitan area approach to the development and implementation of the FY 2004 UASI Program and involve core cities, core counties, contiguous jurisdictions, mutual aid partners, and State agencies."[75] That is, the urban areas are "encouraged to employ regional approaches to planning and preparedness and to adopt regional response structures whenever appropriate."[76] The urban area is required to develop an Urban Area Homeland Security Strategy (UAHSS), and all funding received under the UASI program must be spent in support of the goals and objectives set forth in the UAHSS and the SHSS.[77]

DHS allocated UASI funding in fiscal year 2004 to urban areas according to "a formula using a combination of current threat estimates, critical assets within the urban area, and population density."[78] The New York City urban area (New York City; Nassau, Suffolk, and Westchester Counties; and the Port Authority of New York and New Jersey) received the most amount of money under the UASI program—more than $47 million.[79] The San Antonio urban area (the City of San Antonio, and Bexar and Comal Counties) received the least—about $6.3 million.[80]

Some urban areas, such as Jersey City, Minneapolis, Las Vegas, and Anaheim, consisted only of the city and its surrounding county.[81] Other areas included a wider variety of governmental entities. As noted above, the New York City urban area included the Port Authority of New York and New Jersey.[82] The Phoenix urban area included the Gila River Indian Community, Salt River-Pima Indian Community, and Fort McDowell Indian Tribe, with respect to portions of their lands that fell within Maricopa County.[83] The Memphis urban area included the city as well as counties in both Tennessee and Mississippi.[84] The National Capitol Region, incorporating the District of Columbia and portions of suburban Maryland and Virginia, received the third-highest UASI program grant—around $29.3 million.[85]

A subset of fiscal year 2004 urban areas participated in previous UASI funding programs. Those urban areas already participating in the UASI program were obligated to "utilize their existing [UAHSS] as the basis for allocating funds to the prioritized needs outlines in their goals and objectives in enhancing and refining their preparedness efforts."[86] DHS requires that there be a "clear correlation between the issues identified in the [UAHSS] and FY 2004 UASI activities."[87] Although UASI funding is distributed to the SAA, "the core city and core county/counties, as members of the UAWG, must provide written concurrence on the allocation of funds provided through the FY 2004 UASI."[88]

For urban areas participating in the UASI program for the first time in fiscal year 2004, the SAA is required to designate a specific point of contact for the urban area, and then work with the chief executive of each core city and core county to identify a point of contact for each unit of government.[89] The SAA point of contact is also responsible, in coordination with the core city and core counties, for "fully defining" the urban area, including the specific geographical borders and all of the participating jurisdictions.[90]

New urban area participants in the UASI program are required to establish an Urban Area Working Group (UAWG), conduct an Urban Area Assessment, and develop a UAHSS.[91] The UAWG, representing the jurisdictions within the defined urban area, is "responsible for coordinating development and implementation of all initiative elements, including the urban area strategy development, the methodology for the allocation of funds (in coordination with the SAA), and any direct services that are delivered by ODP."[92] The Urban Area Assessment is compiled using data from the 2003 State Homeland Security Assessment and Strategy Program, and in turn guides the development of the UAHSS.[93]

Mass Transit System Funding. The mass transit funding element of the UASI "is intended to address security needs at these high risk critical infrastructure facilities and to promote comprehensive regional planning and coordination."[94] The state in which the mass transit authority is located is the grantee for mass transit authority's UASI mass transit funds.[95] The SAA, in conjunction with the mass transit system, is responsible for the administration of the mass transit system funding.[96] The state must pass through at least 80 percent of the funding awarded, and may use up to 20 percent of the award "to complement state assets that will provide direct assistance to that mass transit system in order to prevent, respond to, and recover from any terrorist attack."[97]

The mass transit agency is responsible for designating a point of contact and providing a description of its operating system, including "the location, infrastructure, miles of track, number of vehicles, types of service, ridership, and other important features."[98] The mass transit agency also is responsible for conducting a threat and vulnerability assessment (TVA), if it has not already done so, consistent with the requirements set forth in *The Public Transportation System Security and Emergency Guide*.[99] This review is used "to identify and prioritize mass transit agency needs, according to risk, security, and response capability," and involves three primary components: risk assessment; response capabilities assessment; and needs assessment.[100] This leads to the development of two "products": "prioritization of security countermeasures and emergency response capability needs based on terrorist threat and risk"; and "development of a roadmap for future transit agency funding allocations for terrorist attack risk reduction."[101] From these products, the mass transit agency develops a Transit Security and Emergency Preparedness Plan (TSEPP).[102] This plan "must demonstrate that the security program is an integrated one, and has been coordinated with other agencies, including the UAWG (for those transit systems located in urban areas that were recipients of UASI funds)."[103] Funding received by mass transit authorities must be allocated according to the TSEPP.[104]

DHS identified the twenty-five mass transit systems eligible for funding "using a formula based upon ridership and total route miles."[105] Only heavy rail and commuter rail systems were considered eligible.[106] The New York City Metropolitan Transit Authority received the most amount of money, $10 million, for the heavy rail NYC Transit system, and $6.2 million divided among the commuter rail Long Island Railroad, Metro North Commuter Railroad, and Staten Island Railway.[107] The Port Authority of New York and New Jersey received an additional $1.2 million.[108] The Dallas Trinity Railway Express, a commuter rail system, received the least, $800,000.[109]

PORT SECURITY GRANT PROGRAM. The purpose of the Port Security Grant Program (PSGP) is to "support efforts of critical national seaports/terminals to enhance port security through enhanced facility and operational security including but not limited to access control, physical security, cargo security, and passenger security."[110] The PSGP is administered by the Transportation Security Administration (TSA) in conjunction with OSLGCP.[111] The fiscal year PSGP awarded total funding of $49.5 million.[112]

Eligible applicants for PSGP funding include "federally regulated public and private ports, terminals, U.S. inspected passenger vessels, or ferries," and "consortia composed of local stakeholder groups (i.e., river groups, ports, and terminal associations) representing federally regulated ports, terminals, U.S. inspected passenger vessels, or ferries."[113] Applicants "must have completed a security assessment and tie the security enhancements to that assessment in order to be eligible."[114] In addition, applicants must be a "critical national seaport/terminal."[115] To be considered such a seaport or terminal, an applicant must meet one or more of the following criteria:

- The applicant must be "a nationally important economic port or terminal responsible for a large volume of cargo movement or movement of products that are vital to U.S. economic interests as required for national security";
- The applicant must be "responsible for movement of a high number of passengers";
- The applicant must be "responsible for the movement of hazardous cargo";
- The applicant must be a Strategic Port "as designated by a Maritime Administration port planning order"; or
- The applicant must be a Controlled Port, which is a port which has "access controls for vessels from certain countries due to national security issues."[116]

Eligible projects in fiscal year 2004 were limited to Enhanced Facility and Operational Security Projects.[117] These projects included "access controls," "physical security," "surveillance," "communications," "cargo security," "passenger security," "radiological detection equipment," "local physical access control or identification/credentialing systems," and "terminal-based common operational picture systems (hardware only)."[118] Preference was given to the following types of projects:

- "Projects that impact a port system [versus] a single terminal or facility."
- "Projects that address prevention, deterrence and detection systems [versus] consequence (response) management."
- "New installation [versus] replacing or enhancing existing infrastructure (fences, etc.)."
- "Projects that enhance intermodal transportation security within the footprint of the port, including pipelines within the terminal."

- "Eligible applicants that have made prior security enhancements/ investments, at their own expense (eligible applicants must document cost and enhancements completed)."
- "Projects that address access, command, control, coordination, and communication, and physical security (such as lighting, fencing, cameras, etc.)."[119]

The period of performance for fiscal year 2004 PSGP grants was one year.[120] While TSA "encourages grantees to cost share project costs," there was no cost share requirement.[121] Applications were required to be completed and submitted via the Internet.[122]

Discipline-Specific and All-Hazards Preparedness Grant Funding Programs

In addition to terrorism preparedness funding programs, there are a number of additional discipline-specific and all-hazards preparedness funding programs, some administered by DHS, others by other federal agencies. Funding from these programs can be leveraged by state and local government entities to improve all-hazards preparedness, including preparedness for acts of terrorism. A number of these programs are described below. However, this list is not exclusive. Moreover, the information set forth is likely to change, perhaps in each subsequent year, so current grant guidance, as well as the most recent version of the CFDA, should always be consulted.

ASSISTANCE TO FIREFIGHTERS GRANT PROGRAM. The Assistance to Firefighters Grant Program (AFGP) is authorized under the Federal Fire Prevention and Control Act of 1974.[123] The purpose of the AFGP is to "provide funding directly to fire departments of a State for the purpose of enhancing departments' abilities to protect the health and safety of the public, as well as that of firefighting personnel, facing fire and fire-related hazards."[124] The primary goal of the AFGP is to "provide assistance to meet fire departments' firefighting and emergency response needs."[125] The program was previously administered by the U.S. Fire Administration—an entity of the Federal Emergency Management Agency—but for fiscal year 2004, Congress transferred authority for the program to ODP.[126]

The Federal Fire Prevention and Control Act lists fourteen activities eligible for funding under the AFGP.[127] However, not all activities are eligible for funding in a given year. The specific activities that are eligible for funding in a given year are set forth in the "notice of funds availability" published by DHS.[128]

Eligible applicants are limited to "fire departments of a State."[129] A "fire department of a State" is defined for purposes of the AFGP as "an agency or organization that has a formally recognized arrangement with a State, local or tribal authority (city, county, parish, fire district, township, town or other governing body) to provide fire suppression to a population within a fixed geographical area."[130] Therefore, state, local, and tribal fire departments are eligible to apply for funding. Not eligible are federal fire departments, "departments that are contracted by the Federal government and . . . solely responsible for suppression of fires on Federal installations," and for-profit fire departments.[131] Also not eligible are independent ambulance services, rescue squads, auxiliaries, dive teams, urban search and rescue teams, fire service organizations, and "State/local agencies such as a forest service, fire marshal, hospitals, and/or training offices."[132] Nonfederal airport and port authority fire departments are eligible, but "only if they have a formally recognized arrangement with the local jurisdiction to provide fire suppression, on a first-due basis, outside the confines of the airport or port facilities."[133]

DHS is obligated to ensure that AFGP grants are made to a variety of departments, including career, volunteer, and combination fire departments,[134] fire departments located in communities of varying sizes, and fire departments located in urban, suburban, and rural communities.[135] Moreover, DHS is obligated to ensure that volunteer and combination departments "receive a proportion of the total grant funding that is not less than the proportion of the United States population that those fire departments protect."[136]

Grants are limited to $750,000 in any fiscal year, and not more than 25 percent of funds appropriated in a given year may be used for vehicle acquisition.[137] There is also a matching requirement for AFGP grants. Fire departments serving jurisdictions of more than 50,000 residents are required to make a 30 percent match,[138] while fire departments serving jurisdictions of 50,000 or fewer residents are required to make only a 10 percent match.[139] Fire departments also are required to maintain expenditures for grant-related purposes at or above the average level of those expenditures in the two fiscal years preceding the fiscal year for which the assistance will be received.[140] DHS will not provide AFGP funds for "activities for which another Federal agency has more specific or primary authority to provide assistance for the same purpose."[141]

Applications can be filed both online and in paper format, although DHS encourages the use of the online application.[142] Applicants may file only one application per year.[143] Fire departments that have received AFGP grants in previous years can apply in subsequent years. However, since DHS is obligated to ensure adequate distribution of awards among career, volunteer, and combination departments, and among geographic areas, DHS reserves the right to not fund those departments that have received prior grants, even if their grant applications score higher than other applications.[144]

Fire departments must include in their applications, among other things, a statement of financial need, a cost-benefit analysis, and an agreement to provide information to the National Fire Incident Reporting System for the period covered by the grant.[145] Cost-benefit can be demonstrated by describing how a grant award will: "fit in with a regional approach"; "promote interoperability of equipment/technology with other fire departments and local, State, and Federal first responders"; and/or "allow the fire department to respond to all hazards."[146] Fire departments have one year to incur obligations and complete the work for which the grant was awarded.[147]

The fiscal year 2004 AFGP contained similar provisions to previous years' programs.[148] For fiscal year 2004 there were three programs for which grant funding was available: the Operations and Firefighter Safety Program; the Fire Prevention Program; and the Firefighting Vehicle Acquisition Program.[149] The Operations and Firefighter Safety Program included five different eligible activities: training; equipment acquisition; personal protective equipment acquisition; wellness and fitness activities; and modifications to fire stations and facilities.[150] DHS states that "equipment requests in this program should have the intent and/or goal of solving applicable interoperability or compatibility problems."[151] DHS explains its methodology for ranking requests concerning each of these different eligible activities depending on different variables, including the type of community served.[152]

Applications were ranked based on "the substance of [the fire department's] application relative to the established program priorities for the type of community served."[153] Funding priorities differed between program and activity areas, as well as among urban, suburban, and rural communities.[154] For CBRNE equipment and training requests, the applications were judged on the merits of the request "relative to the critical infrastructure that the applicant protects."[155] The state's homeland security office also is given the opportunity to contribute to the technical review of any application that is seeking CBRNE equipment or training, in order to "attest to and certify that any CBRNE-related requests are consistent with the State's homeland security plan and . . . do not duplicate assistance already provided or about to be provided."[156]

EMERGENCY MANAGEMENT PERFORMANCE GRANTS. The purpose of the Emergency Management Performance Grant (EMPG) program is to "assist the development, maintenance, and improvement of State and local emergency management capabilities."[157] EMPG funds are "used for a variety of emergency management related expenses, but predominantly for personnel who plan, train, coordinate, and conduct exercises and other functions essential to effective preparedness, mitigation, response, and recovery efforts."[158] The EMPG program has been characterized as "the backbone of our nation's emergency management system."[159]

EMPG awards are designed to support state and local government efforts to improve the following "key functional areas of emergency management":

- Laws and authorities;
- Hazard identification and risk assessment;
- Hazard management;
- Resource management;
- Planning;
- Direction, control, and coordination;
- Communications and warning;
- Operations and procedures;
- Logistics and facilities;
- Training;
- Exercises;
- Public education and information; and
- Finance and administration.[160]

EMPG funds are provided to each state, as well as the District of Columbia and U.S. territories.[161] Local governments are not eligible to apply directly for EMPG funds, but rather must obtain these funds through the state.[162] A "target allocation" is derived for each eligible state and territory by dividing the appropriated amount in the same proportion as the previous year's allocation.[163] Recipients are required to match grant funds in an amount up to 50 percent.[164] Because sub-grants are made by the states themselves, eligibility requirements vary from state to state. California, for instance, has designated fifty-eight "operational areas" as eligible EMPG recipients,[165] whereas Oklahoma makes EMPG funds available to local governments generally.[166] States are provided annual guidance on EMPG application procedures by the federal agency responsible for administering the EMPG in that fiscal year.[167]

HAZARDOUS MATERIALS EMERGENCY PREPAREDNESS GRANT PROGRAM. The Hazardous Materials Emergency Preparedness (HMEP) Grant Program was established under the Federal Hazardous Materials Transportation Act.[168] The purpose of the HMEP Grant Program is to "increase State, local, territorial, and Native American tribal effectiveness to safely and efficiently handle hazardous materials accidents and incidents . . . and encourage a comprehensive approach to emergency planning and training by incorporating response to transportation standards."[169] States, U.S. territories, and Indian tribes are eligible to receive HMEP Grant Program funds.[170] The HMEP Grant Program is administered by the U.S. Department of Transportation, Research and Special Projects Administration (RSPA).[171]

The HMEP Grant Program has two components: planning grants and training grants. HMEP Grant Program planning grants are intended to provide funding for the following activities, as well as any additional activities deemed appropriate by RSPA:

- "Development, improvement, and implementation of emergency right to know plans under [EPCRA]," as well as "exercises which test the emergency plan," "enhancement of emergency plans to include hazard analysis," and "response procedures for emergencies involving transportation of hazardous materials";
- "An assessment to determine flow patterns of hazardous materials . . . and development and maintenance of a system to keep such information current";
- "An assessment of the need for regional hazardous materials emergency response teams";[172]
- "An assessment of local response capabilities";
- "Conduct of emergency response drills and exercises associated with emergency preparedness plans"; and
- "Provision of technical staff to support the planning effort."[173]

Recipients of planning grants must ensure that "planning under the grant is coordinated with emergency planning conducted by adjacent States and Indian tribes."[174]

HMEP training grant funds can be used for the following activities:

- "An assessment to determine the number of public sector employees employed or used by a political subdivision who need the proposed training," and to select appropriate courses;
- "Delivery of comprehensive preparedness and response training to public sector employees," including training "to meet specialized needs," as well as "financial assistance" for trainers and trainees, including tuition, travel expenses, and room and board;
- "Emergency response drills and exercises";
- "Expenses associated with training" and "activities necessary to monitor such training"; and
- "Provision of staff to manage the training effort."[175]

Recipients of HMEP training grants must agree to utilize courses developed, identified, or approved by RSPA.[176]

The Federal Hazardous Materials Transportation Act authorizes $5 million in HMEP planning grants and $7.8 million in training grants per year.[177] Recipients of HMEP grants must certify that they will not replace their own annual funding for planning and training with HMEP funds, but instead they will supplement their ongoing funding, and state recipients must agree to make 75 percent of grant funds available to local emergency planning committees established under EPCRA.[178] HMEP grants are subject to a 20 percent cost share.[179] In fiscal year 2004, California received the largest amount of HMEP funds ($964,316), followed by Illinois ($612,982).[180] Indian tribes also received funding. The Inter-Tribal Council of Arizona received $160,000 in HMEP funds in fiscal year 2004, and eight tribes received grants of approximately $25,000 each.[181]

EDWARD BYRNE MEMORIAL STATE AND LOCAL LAW ENFORCEMENT ASSISTANCE PROGRAM. The Edward Byrne Memorial State and Local Law Enforcement Assistance Program (Byrne Formula Grant Program or BFGP) was established under the Anti-Drug Abuse Act of 1988.[182] The purpose of the BFGP is "to assist States and units of local government in carrying out specific programs which offer a high probability of improving the functioning of the criminal justice system, with special emphasis on a nationwide and multilevel drug control strategy."[183] The BFGP seeks to accomplish this "by developing programs and projects to assist multijurisdictional and multi-State organizations in the drug control problem and to support national drug control priorities."[184] The BFGP is administered by the U.S. Department of Justice (DOJ), Bureau of Justice Assistance (BJA).[185]

Under the BFGP, grants are made to states and U.S. territories for "additional personnel, equipment, training, technical assistance, and information systems for the more widespread apprehension, prosecution, adjudication, and detention and rehabilitation of persons" who violated state and local drug laws.[186] There are twenty-nine categories of assistance under the BFGP.[187] These include:

- "[M]ultijurisdictional task force programs that integrate Federal, State, and local drug law enforcement agencies and prosecutors for the purpose of enhancing interagency coordination, intelligence, and facilitating multijurisdictional investigations";[188]
- "[P]roviding community and neighborhood programs that assist citizens in preventing and controlling crime, including special programs that address the problems of crimes committed against the elderly and special programs for rural jurisdictions";[189]
- "[D]eveloping and implementing antiterrorism plans for deep draft ports, international airports, and other important facilities";[190]
- "[F]inancial investigative programs that target the identification of money laundering operations and assets obtained through illegal drug trafficking, including the development of proposed model legislation, financial investigative training, and financial information sharing systems";[191]
- "[C]riminal justice information systems to assist law enforcement, prosecution, courts, and corrections organizations (including automated fingerprint identification systems)";[192] and
- "[D]evelop[ing] and implement[ing] antiterrorism training programs and . . . procur[ing] equipment for use by local law enforcement authorities."[193]

States also may use BFGP funds to support participation in state and local narcotics task forces established by the Drug Enforcement Administration, and for evaluating programs established under the BFGP program.[194]

States apply for BFGP funds on an annual basis.[195] Grant applications must be submitted online.[196] Each state designates an administering office for the grant.[197] Each state is allocated $500,000 or one-quarter of one percent of the appropriated amount, whichever is greater, and the remaining money appropriated in a given year is allocated to the states based on population.[198] States are instructed to distribute BFGP funds to units of local government in accordance with a formula based on state and local government spending on criminal justice in the previous year.[199] However, "[i]n distributing funds received under this subchapter among urban, rural, and suburban units of local government and combinations thereof, the State shall give priority to those jurisdictions with the greatest need."[200] After making such distributions, the state may spend any remaining grant funds.[201] States must develop a statewide strategy for drug and violent crime control programs, under which BFGP funds are spent.[202]

BFGP funds may not be used to supplant state and local criminal justice funds, but rather must be used "to increase the amounts of such funds that would, in the absence of Federal funds, be made available for law enforcement activities."[203] There is a 25 percent hard (cash) matching requirement for BFGP funds, except for grants to U.S. territories and sub-grants to Indian tribes, for which the matching requirement is waived.[204] The state may use no more than 10 percent of its BFGP funds for administering BFGP funding.[205] Five percent of each state's annual grant funds must be used for "the improvement of criminal justice records."[206] Other programs may be funded under the BFGP only once every four years.[207] Awards under the BFGP are for four years.[208]

STATE AND COMMUNITY HIGHWAY SAFETY GRANT PROGRAM. The Highway Safety Act of 1966 authorizes block grants to states "to reduce traffic accidents and deaths, injuries, and property damage resulting therefrom."[209] These State and Community Highway Safety Grant Program (SCHSGP) grants are administered by the U.S. Department of Transportation, National Highway Transportation Safety Administration (NHTSA).[210]

NHTSA has identified nine "National Priority Program Areas" eligible for funding under the SCHSGP, including traffic records and emergency medical services (EMS).[211] NHTSA also has issued Highway Safety Program Guidelines concerning these areas, including guidelines concerning driver licensing, traffic records, and EMS.[212] These guidelines overlap in many respects with what are now considered homeland security-related functions. For example, the Driver Licensing Guideline recommends that state programs provide that each driver hold only one license, that each driver "submits acceptable proof of date and place of birth" in applying for a driver's license, and that a record is maintained for each driver "which includes positive identification, current address, and driving history."[213] The Traffic Records Guideline recommends that states maintain a database that includes the driver history record of licensed drivers in the state, as well as "provisions for file linkage through common data elements."[214] The EMS Guideline recommends that each state maintain an EMS program that ensures adequate training for EMS personnel, safe and reliable ambulance transportation, an effective communications system, a fully functional statewide trauma system, and public information and education.[215]

SCHSGP grants are administered through a state highway safety agency designated by the governor of each state.[216] A minimum of 40 percent of highway safety grant funds provided to each state must be passed along to local governments and Indian tribes within the state for "carrying out local highway safety programs."[217] SCHSGP funds are apportioned 75 percent on population and 25 percent on total public road mileage, with at least one-half a percent allocated per state, one-quarter of one percent allocated per U.S. territory, and three-quarters a percent allocated to the U.S. Department of the Interior (DOI) for use by Indian tribes.[218] States apply for funds on an annual basis, specifying "objective and measurable performance goals within the National Priority Program Areas."[219]

RURAL HOUSING SERVICE COMMUNITY FACILITIES GRANTS. The Consolidated Farms and Rural Development Act authorizes the U.S. Department of Agriculture (USDA) to make grants to "associations, units of general local government, nonprofit corporations, Indian tribes, and federally recognized Indian tribes" for "developing specific essential community facilities in rural areas."[220] This program, known as the Community Facilities Grant Program (CFGP), is administered by USDA's Rural Housing Service (RHS).[221] Grants may not exceed $10 million total in any year.[222]

CFGP grants can be leveraged for homeland security-related functions. Although not less than 10 percent of the amount appropriated each year for CFGP grants must be used for developing and constructing day care facilities for children in rural areas,[223] the remainder is available for other "essential community facilities," which are defined as "those public improvements requisite to the beneficial and orderly development of a community that is operated on a nonprofit basis."[224] A "facility" is defined as "[t]he physical structure financed by [CFGP funds] or the resulting service provide to rural residents."[225] CFGP funds may be used to "construct, enlarge, extend, or otherwise improve essential community facilities."[226] "Essential community facilities" include "fire, rescue, and public safety," "health services," and "telecommunications equipment as it relates to medical and educational telecommunications links."[227] "Otherwise improve" includes the purchasing of vehicles and other equipment "which will in themselves provide an essential service to rural residents."[228] Eligible grant uses for fire, rescue, and public safety include fire trucks, fire department buildings, public safety communications centers, mobile communications centers, and rescue equipment.[229]

Prospective applicants file a preapplication with their local RHS field office, and if the applicant is eligible for CFGP funding, RHS will provide the forms and instructions necessary to complete an application.[230] There is no match requirement *per se*. Instead, CFGP funds may be used for up to 75 percent of the "cost of developing the facility"; other federal funds may be used to fund the remaining costs.[231] RHS maintains a priority system for projects serving rural communities with the lowest populations and household median income, as well as for projects addressing, among other things, health care and public safety.[232] Moreover, CFGP assistance is provided "on a graduated scale with smaller communities with the lowest median household income being eligible for projects with a higher proportion of grant funds."[233] There are limitations on the use of CFGP funds, including a prohibition on using such funds for "initial operating expenses or annual recurring costs," refinancing or interest costs, or for "costs to construct facilities to be used for commercial rental unless it is a minor part of the total facility."[234]

SAFER ACT GRANTS. The fiscal year 2004 defense authorization bill[235] created a new grant program for firefighter staffing.[236] This new program, modeled on the never-enacted Staffing for Adequate Fire and Emergency Response (SAFER) Act,[237] is intended to "increas[e] the number of firefighters to help communities meet industry minimum standards and attain 24-hour staffing to provide adequate protection from fire and fire-related hazards, and to fulfill traditional missions of fire departments that antedate the creation of [DHS]."[238] The grant program is an amendment to the Federal Fire Prevention and Control Act of 1974.[239] Congress appropriated $65 million for these new grants in fiscal year 2005.[240]

Because fiscal year 2005 is the first year for SAFER Act grants, DHS has not yet published guidance for these grants. However, the authorizing language for the grants is relatively specific. Like the AFGP, SAFER Act grants are awarded on a competitive basis directly to career, volunteer, and combination fire departments of states, local governments, and Indian tribes.[241] SAFER Act grants are for four years, and are to be used "for programs to hire new, additional firefighters."[242] In the first year, the grant covers up to 90 percent of the cost of hiring firefighters; this goes down to 80 percent in the second year, 50 percent in the third year, and 30 percent in the fourth year.[243] Grant recipients are required "to commit to retaining for at least 1 year beyond the termination of their grants those firefighters hired" under the grant program.[244] Ten percent of funding available for SAFER Act grants is reserved for grants to "departments with majority volunteer or all volunteer personnel."[245] Another 10 percent of available funds are reserved for grants for the recruitment and retention of volunteer firefighters.[246]

Applications for SAFER Act funding must include, at a minimum: an explanation of "the applicant's inability to address the need without Federal assistance"; an explanation of "how the applicant plans to meet" the requirement that firefighters hired under SAFER Act grants will be retained for at least one year beyond the termination of the grant, and will be permitted to volunteer in their off-duty hours; the department's "long-term plans for retaining firefighters following the conclusion of Federal support"; and assurances that "the applicant will, to the extent practicable, seek, recruit, and hire members of racial and ethnic minority groups and women in order to increase their ranks within firefighting."[247] Funds may not be used to supplant state or local funds, or Bureau of Indian Affairs (BIA) funds in the case of Indian tribes, but rather must "be used to increase the amount of funds that would, in the absence of Federal funds . . . be made available from State and local sources, or in the case of Indian tribal governments, from funds supplied by the [BIA]."[248] Total funding provided under a SAFER Act grant cannot exceed $100,000 per firefighter.[249] Departments whose annual budgets for fire-related programs and emergency response have been reduced at the time of application to a level below 80 percent of the average funding level over the previous three years are not eligible for SAFER Act grants.[250]

The Future of Preparedness Funding

During its 108th session, in 2003 and 2004, Congress struggled to change the distribution formulas for preparedness funding. A number of bills were introduced in both houses, but by the end of the term a primary bill had emerged in each house. Republican Congressman Christopher Cox of California, the Chairman of the House Select Committee on Homeland Security, introduced the Faster and Smarter Funding for First Responders Act.[251] A subcommittee of the Select Committee marked up the bill on November 20, 2003, and the full committee marked up the bill and reported it out on March 18, 2004.[252] Meanwhile, Republican Senator Susan Collins of Maine, the chair of the Senate's Governmental Affairs Committee, introduced the Homeland Security Grant Enhancement Act of 2003.[253] The Governmental Affairs Committee marked up the bill and reported it out on June 17, 2003.[254]

While each of these bills, in their final forms, were included in each chamber's intelligence reform bill,[255] Congress ultimately dropped these provisions from the conference on the bills, and therefore, efforts to authorize new first responder funding allocations were ultimately unsuccessful. But the course of discussions gives a good indication of the primary issues under consideration and the likely course of future efforts to revamp first responder funding.

Leaving aside the question of which disciplines (*e.g.*, law enforcement, fire and rescue, emergency medical services) receive grant funding, and in what amounts, the questions most often asked cut across all disciplines:

- Should federal first responder preparedness money be distributed just for terrorism preparedness, or to prepare for all types of events regardless of cause?
- Should federal preparedness money be distributed on the basis of risk, or should it be divided equally among the states, or proportionately based on population?
- Should federal preparedness money be distributed to the states, which then distribute funding generally as they wish to local governments, or should some or all local governments be able to access federal preparedness money directly?

These questions are discussed briefly below.

Terrorism Preparedness vs. All-Hazards Preparedness

The debate between terrorism preparedness and all-hazards preparedness was a significant issue of disagreement with respect to first responder preparedness funding in the 108th Congress. The most marked dispute over terrorism preparedness versus all-hazards preparedness took place in relation to the House bill. The Select Committee listed among its findings, in its reported version of the bill, that "[i]n order to achieve its objective of minimizing the damage, and assisting in the recovery, from terrorism attacks, [DHS] must play a leading role in assisting communities to reach the level of preparedness they need to respond to a terrorist attack," and that "an essential prerequisite to achieving the Nation's homeland security objectives for first responders is the establishment of well-defined national goals for terrorism preparedness."[256] According to the Select Committee, the bill "would reform the manner in which [DHS] issues grants to enhance the ability of States, local governments, and first responders to prevent, prepare for, mitigate, and respond to acts of terrorism."[257] The Select Committee stated that "[a]rming our first responders with the best technologies, equipment, and training to react in the event of a catastrophic terrorist attack is vital for protection of the nation."[258]

By contrast, the House Transportation and Infrastructure Committee, which also marked up that bill, had a different view of the purpose of preparedness funding. According to the Transportation and Infrastructure Committee, the purpose of first responder funding legislation should be "to better prepare the nation to respond to major disasters and other emergencies, including those caused by acts of terrorism by providing for the coordinated delivery of first responder funds to State, tribal, regional and local governments in order to achieve essential capabilities developed in the context of a national preparedness goal."[259] The Transportation and Infrastructure Committee over-hauled the bill to require that "grant funds be spent according to a comprehensive all-hazards preparedness strategy . . ."[260] Ultimately, the focus remained on terrorism, and much of the Transportation and Infrastructure Committee's all-hazards language was not included in the final version of the bill.[261]

Congressional appropriators struck a middle ground. They acknowledged "state and local jurisdictions' ability to detect, prevent and respond to a terrorist attack as a high priority."[262] However, appropriators balked at DHS's plan to reprogram the AFGP and EMPG to focus on terrorism preparedness. With respect to the AFGP, appropriators stated that they were "concerned by the Department's proposed shift in grant focus from all-hazards to placing priority on terrorism . . . [t]he Department should continue the present practice of funding applications according to local priorities and those established by the United States Fire Administration . . ."[263] Similarly, the appropriators stated that the EMPG grants "are vital to state and local emergency management systems, and therefore do not agree to shift from an all-hazards to a terrorism-specific focus . . ."[264]

Ultimately, the debate may be more semantic than substantive. As can be seen from a review of the grant criteria for terrorism preparedness grants such as the HSGP, the UASI, and the PSGP, and for nonterrorism focused grants such as the AFGP, the EMPG, and the BFGP, many of the assistance categories are the same or similar, and many of the grant recipients are the same. Ultimately, state and local governments are tasked with preparing for all potential hazards; they also are on notice that a primary hazard—at least in destructive potential, if not in frequency—is terrorism. Consequently, state and local governments will be well served by maximizing their federal preparedness funding to ensure preparedness for all hazards that they might face, including the hazards of terrorism.

Equal Distribution vs. Distribution Based on Risk

As noted above, HSGP funds are distributed according to a formula that allocates a base amount of funding to each state. By contrast, UASI funds are distributed to high-threat urban areas on the basis of risk. Debate continues as to which is the better method of distribution.

The debate over the Senate bill is particularly instructive in this respect. According to the Senate's Governmental Affairs Committee, the bill was intended to create three funding streams. First, 10 percent of funds appropriated would be "allocated through direct discretionary grants to local governments in high threat areas."[265] Those risk criteria were: large population and high population density; high degree of threat, risk and vulnerability because of "critical infrastructure or key national assets"; an international border or coastline bordering international waters; or "other threat factors specified in writing by [DHS]."[266] Another 40 percent of grant funds, under the title "Maintaining a Baseline Level of Security," would be allocated based on the USA PATRIOT Act formula of three-quarters of a percent to each state, and one-quarter of one percent to each U.S. territory.[267] Finally, the remaining funds were to be allocated to the states on the basis of a "risk-based formula to be developed by the DHS Secretary."[268] That formula would be based on similar factors as for the funding distributed directly to local governments.[269]

In the words of the committee, the state minimums "should ensure that every State would be able to achieve a minimum baseline of capability."[270] The committee explained:

> The Committee has attempted to strike a balance between those who support the current formula and those who would like less populous states to receive fewer homeland security dollars. To ensure that States with high risks and vulnerabilities receive sufficient homeland security funding, the Secretary would provide a baseline level of homeland security dollars to each State, but then distribute the remaining 60 percent of funding based on threat, risk, and vulnerability.[271]

The committee clarified that because of the 90/10 split, the formula set forth in the bill "is similar to the existing ODP formula program, but with a revision to specify more risk factors than population in awarding some of the funds."[272]

The committee view on this question was not unanimous. Republican Senator Arlen Specter of Pennsylvania, in "additional views" included with the report, noted that "setting aside only 10 percent of funds for 'high threat, high density' programs would undermine needed efforts to increase funding for the [UASI program]."[273] Two Democratic senators, Carl Levin of Michigan and Frank Lautenberg of New Jersey, were even more blunt, stating that "S. 1245 is seriously flawed."[274] The senators stated:

> [S. 1245] imposes a minimum state funding formula ("small state provision") which requires a disproportionately large portion of the grant funds to go to small states, regardless of need. The small state formula arbitrarily benefits approximately 30 so-called small population states and uses a state minimum that was nearly unprecedented when first established in the USA PATRIOT Act two years ago.
>
> *   *   *
>
> It is one thing to say that all states should receive a minimum amount of funding to support their homeland security goals, but the issue is how to balance per state funding with grants that will protect all Americans by targeting funds to address the greatest terrorist threats. S. 1245 fails to strike the right balance.[275]

The senators noted, "[a]llocating scarce federal dollars disproportionately to states with the fewest persons, and often less risk, is not an effective or fair use of federal homeland security grant programs."[276]

The appropriations committees again sought a middle ground. House appropriators recognized that "no community is immune from terrorism" and approved of the "balance between basic formula grants, used by States and localities to achieve a minimum level of preparedness, and funds for high-risk urban areas."[277] The committees divided funding approximately 50/50 between state grants and high-threat urban areas.[278] Both committees directed DHS to distribute UASI funds on the basis of risk criteria, the Senate listing "credible threat, vulnerability, population, cooperation of multiple jurisdictions in preparing domestic preparedness plans, and identified needs of public agencies,"[279] and the House adding critical infrastructure to this list.[280]

State vs. Local

A question related to the debate over risk versus population is whether first responder funding should be allocated in the form of state block grants, or instead should be awarded directly to local governments by DHS.

The major terrorism preparedness grant funding programs, such as the HSGP and the UASI program, distribute funds to the states even if most of the money must ultimately be passed on to units of local government.[281] However, other grant programs, most notably the AFGP and SAFER Act programs, allow local governments to apply to DHS directly, on a competitive basis, for grant funding.[282]

The Senate Governmental Affairs Committee noted that there was "disagreement . . . as to whether a new formula program should distribute funds initially to States or directly to local entities."[283] The committee pointed out that "a number of State and local organizations, including the National Conference of State Legislatures, the National Governors Association, the National League of Cities, the National Association of Counties, the Council of State Governments, and the International City/County Management Association have supported State coordination of the first responder grant program . . ."[284] However, the National League of Cities (NLC), along with the U.S. Conference of Mayors (USCM), also both advocated for direct funding to local governments.[285] NLC advocated specifically for direct funding for "cities and regions with populations of 100,000 or more."[286]

One of the issues involved in state funding were complaints that funding was not being "passed through" to local governments quickly enough. The House Select Committee on Homeland Security pointed out that, at the time of its report in April 2004, "roughly $11 billion has been, or will be, appropriated to DHS for distribution to state and local governments. Of this amount, almost $9 billion either remains in, or has yet to be put into, the terrorism preparedness grant program pipeline."[287] The Governmental Affairs Committee noted that "state-wide coordination in homeland security planning is needed," but also sought to "ensure that funding reaches the local level in a timely manner."

In formulating its bill, the Select Committee chose to depart from the idea of formula grants to states, choosing instead to make both states and "regions" eligible for competitive grants based on risk.[288] The Select Committee defined a "region" as follows:

> (A) any geographic area consisting of all or parts of 2 or more contiguous States, counties, municipalities, or other local governments that have a combined population of at least 1,650,000 or have an area of not less than 20,000 square miles, and that, for purposes of an application for a covered grant, is represented by 1 or more governments or governmental agencies within such geographic area, and that is established by law or by agreement of 2 or more such governments or governmental agencies in a mutual aid agreement; or
>
> (B) any other combination of contiguous local government units (including such a combination established by law or agreement of two or more governments or

governmental agencies in a mutual aid agreement) that is formally certified by the Secretary [of DHS] as a region for purposes of this Act with the consent of—

(i) the State or States in which they are located, including a multi-State entity established by a compact between two or more States; and

(ii) the incorporated municipalities, counties, and parishes which they encompass.[289]

States awarded grants under the program would be required to pass along at least 80 percent of funds to local governments.[290] This approach deemphasized the states' role as the exclusive funding vehicle, while preserving their preparedness coordination role.

The Senate Governmental Affairs Committee took an approach more similar to that of current programs. As noted above, the Senate bill allocated 10 percent of funds for direct grants to local governments based on risk, with the remaining 90 percent of funds distributed as grants to the states (40 percent based on an equal distribution formula and the remaining 50 percent based on risk).[291] As with the House bill, states receiving grant funds under the Senate bill would have been responsible for passing along at least 80 percent of funds to local governments.[292] Unlike its House counterpart, therefore, the Senate bill would have ensured that at least 10 percent of grant funds were passed directly from DHS to local governments; however, unlike the House bill, no more than 10 percent of funds could pass in this way.

While arrangements can be made to accommodate both terrorism preparedness and all-hazards preparedness, as well as risk-based distribution versus formula-based distribution, it is more difficult to find a middle ground with respect to the question of state "pass through" grants versus direct local government grants. Ultimately, funds must be passed one way or the other, although dividing the money between the different types of programs, as the Senate Governmental Affairs Committee did, is a possible accommodation. It remains to be seen whether the House Select Committee's competitive grants, or the Senate Governmental Affairs Committee's local government set aside, or some third accommodation, will ultimately control grant funding.

NOTES

1. The federal government also has provided billions of dollars for hospital and health system preparedness. This funding is discussed separately in Chapter 4.

2. While some federal first responder preparedness funding programs have remained relatively stable over time, some programs, especially those created or greatly expanded in the wake of Sept. 11, 2001, appear to change annually, with different sums of money, different distributing agencies, and sometimes even different names. For example, the main Office for State and Local Government Cooperation and Preparedness (OSLGCP) terrorism preparedness program finds its genesis in the Nunn-Lugar-Dominici Domestic Preparedness Equipment Program, which was authorized in the Department of Defense Authorization Act, Pub. L. No. 104-201 (1996). *See* U.S. DEPARTMENT OF JUSTICE, OFFICE OF JUSTICE PROGRAMS, OFFICE FOR STATE AND LOCAL DOMESTIC PREPAREDNESS SUPPORT, FISCAL YEAR 2001 NUNN-LUGAR-DOMINICI DOMESTIC PREPAREDNESS EQUIPMENT PROGRAM, PROGRAM GUIDELINES AND

APPLICATION KIT, at 1. This program was originally administered by the U.S. Department of Defense (DoD), but was transferred in fiscal year 2000 to DOJ. *Id.*

3. OSLGCP grant guidance can be found at http://www.ojp.usdoj.gov/odp/grants_programs.htm. The Catalog of Federal Domestic Assistance can be found online at http://www.cfda.gov.

4. *Homeland Security Presidential Directive No. 5*, 39 WEEKLY COMP. PRES. DOC. 263, 280 § 20 (Mar. 7, 2003) (hereinafter HSPD-5).

5. Letter from Tom Ridge, Secretary of Homeland Security to Governors (Sept. 8, 2004) (hereinafter NIMS Letter), *available at* http://www.fema.gov/nims/nims_news.shtm.

6. NIMS Letter, *supra* note 5 at 2.

7. NIMS Letter, *supra* note 5 at 2.

8. NIMS Letter, *supra* note 5 at 2-3. DHS also recommends that states, territories, tribes, and local entities take the following additional steps: (1) complete the NIMS Awareness Course, "National Incident Management System (NIMS): An Introduction," IS-700; (2) formally recognize the NIMS and adopt the NIMS principles and policies through legislation, executive orders, resolutions, or ordinances; (3) establish a "NIMS baseline" by determining which NIMS requirements entities already meet; and (4) establish a timeframe and a strategy for fully implementing the NIMS. *Id.* at 3-4.

9. NIMS Letter, *supra* note 5 at 4.

10. In 2004, the Office for Domestic Preparedness (ODP) was consolidated into the OS-LGCP, in the immediate office of the secretary at DHS. OSLGCP is intended to function as the "one-stop shop" for DHS first responder preparedness grants. *See* H. Rep. No. 108-774, at 62 (Oct. 9, 2004) (hereinafter FY05 Conference Report).

11. In the fiscal year 2004 Congress appropriated $2.3 billion for the Homeland Security Grant Program (HSGP) and $725 million for the Urban Areas Security Initiative (UASI) program. *See* Department of Homeland Security Appropriations Act, Pub. L. No. 108-90, Title III, Office for Domestic Preparedness, State and Local Programs (2004). Congress also separately appropriated $125 million for the Port Security Grant Program (PSGP). *Id.* at Title II, Transportation Security Administration, Maritime and Land Security. DHS based the fiscal year 2004 HSGP and UASI programs, as well as the PSGP, on these appropriations. For fiscal year 2005, Congress appropriated $1.5 billion for HSGP-type formula grants and $1.2 billion for discretionary grants, which includes $885 million for a UASI urban areas-type program, $150 million for a PSGP-type program, and $150 million for "intercity passenger rail transportation, freight rail, and transit security grants." *See* Department of Homeland Security Appropriations Act, Pub. L. No. 108-334, Title III, Office of State and Local Government Coordination and Preparedness, State and Local Programs (2005).

12. *See* DEP'T OF HOMELAND SECURITY, FISCAL YEAR 2004 HOMELAND SECURITY GRANT PROGRAM GUIDELINES AND APPLICATION KIT 2, 5 (2004), *available at* http://www.ojp.usdoj.gov/odp/docs/fy04hsgp_appkit.pdf (hereinafter HSGP Program Guide).

13. HSGP Program Guide, *supra* note 12 at 5. Consolidation of the programs also will "provide the opportunity to enhance regional preparedness efforts. States are encouraged to employ regional approaches to planning and preparedness and to adopt regional response structures whenever appropriate to meet the need identified through the assessments and in the State's Strategy." *Id.* Regional approaches to planning and preparedness, and regional response structures, are discussed more fully in Chapter 11.

14. HSGP Program Guide, *supra* note 12 at 5.

15. USA PATRIOT Act of 2001, Pub. L. No. 107-56, § 1014(c)(3) (2001); HSGP Program Guide, *supra* note 12 at 2.

16. HSGP Program Guide, *supra* note 12 at 2.

17. HSGP Program Guide, *supra* note 12 at 2. A list of SAAs is http://www.ojp.usdoj.gov/odp/contact_state.htm.

18. HSGP Program Guide, *supra* note 12 at 2, 7, 11-12, 15, 38, 55. As stated by DHS, "[i]n accordance with Congressional Conference language addressing ODP programs, to meet eligibility requirements for FY 2004 HSGP funds where applicable, a local unit of government will be defined as 'any county, city, village, town, district, borough, port authority, transit authority, water district, regional planning commission, council of government, Indian tribe, authorized tribal organization, Alaska Native village, or other political subdivision of any State." *Id.* at 7.

19. HSGP Program Guide, *supra* note 12 at 2, 7, 11-12, 15, 38, 55. A local unit of government may request, in writing, that the state retain some or all of the local unit of government's allocation of grant funds for central purchasing by the state on behalf of the local unit of government. *Id.* However, states holding grant funds for local units of government must enter into a written memorandum of understanding with the local unit of government specifying the amount of funds the state may retain. *Id.*

20. HSGP Program Guide, *supra* note 12 at 2, 6. Special rules exist for the use of funds for the development of and attendance at non-ODP training courses. *See id.* at 7 and app. D.

21. HSGP Program Guide, *supra* note 12 at 7.

22. HSGP Program Guide, *supra* note 12 at 6.

23. HSGP Program Guide, *supra* note 12 at 6.

24. HSGP Program Guide, *supra* note 12 at 7.

25. HSGP Program Guide, *supra* note 12 at 11, app. A, at 1.

26. HSGP Program Guide, *supra* note 12, app. A, at 1.

27. HSGP Program Guide, *supra* note 12 at 7-8. The HSGP program guidance describes the grant program's reporting requirements. HSGP Program Guide, app. A, at 3-5, apps. C, F. The program guide also includes guidance for developing an interoperable communications plan. *Id.* app. E.

28. HSGP Program Guide, *supra* note 12 at 15.

29. HSGP Program Guide, *supra* note 12 at 15, 16.

30. HSGP Program Guide, *supra* note 12 at 15.

31. HSGP Program Guide, *supra* note 12 at 16 (Planning), 16-31 (Equipment), 31-33 (Training), 33-35 (Exercises), 35 (Management and Administrative).

32. HSGP Program Guide, *supra* note 12 at 16. The authorized equipment list (AEL) is based on the standardized equipment list (SEL) developed by the Interagency Board for Equipment Standardization and Interoperability (IAB). *Id.*

33. HSGP Program Guide, *supra* note 12 at 16, 17. The eighteen categories of eligible equipment costs are described in detail in pages 17-31 of the HSGP Program Guide.

34. HSGP Program Guide, *supra* note 12 at 21.

35. HSGP Program Guide, *supra* note 12 at 31.

36. HSGP Program Guide, *supra* note 12 at 33. According to OSLGCP, the Homeland Security Exercise and Evaluation Program (HSEEP) "is a threat- and performance-based exercise program that includes a cycle, mix and range of exercise activities of varying degrees of complexity and interaction." *See* Dep't of Homeland Security, Office of Domestic Preparedness, Exercise Planning & Support, *at* http://www.ojp.usdoj.gov/odp/exercises.htm. HSEEP "is both doctrine and policy for designing, developing, conducting and evaluating exercises." *Id.* HSEEP includes a series of four reference manuals, which are available at the ODP Exercise Planning and Support Web site. *Id.*

37. HSGP Program Guide, *supra* note 12 at 38.

38. HSGP Program Guide, *supra* note 12 at 38.

39. HSGP Program Guide, *supra* note 12 at 38.

40. HSGP Program Guide, *supra* note 12 at 39-52.

41. HSGP Program Guide, *supra* note 12 at 39.

42. HSGP Program Guide, *supra* note 12 at 39.

43. HSPG Program Guide, *supra* note 12 at 39.

44. HSGP Program Guide, *supra* note 12 at 40. The twelve categories of eligible equipment costs are described in detail in pages 40-48 of the HSGP Program Guide.

45. HSGP Program Guide, *supra* note 12 at 43-44.

46. HSGP Program Guide, *supra* note 12 at 48-49.

47. HSGP Program Guide, *supra* note 12 at 49.

48. HSGP Program Guide, *supra* note 12 at 49-50.

49. HSGP Program Guide, *supra* note 12 at 50-51

50. HSGP Program Guide, *supra* note 12 at 50.

51. HSGP Program Guide, *supra* note 12 at 55.

52. HSGP Program Guide, *supra* note 12 at 55. Program guidance on the four charter programs is available at the Citizen Corps Web site, http://www.citizencorps.gov. Citizen Corps programs are discussed more fully in Chapter 10.

53. HSGP Program Guide, *supra* note 12 at 55.

54. HSGP Program Guide, *supra* note 12 at 56. A list of state Citizen Corps points of contact can be found at http://www.citizencorps.gov/councils. *Id.*

55. HSGP Program Guide, *supra* note 12 at 56-59.

56. HSGP Program Guide, *supra* note 12 at 56-59.

57. Dep't of Homeland Security, Fiscal Year 2004 Urban Areas Security Initiative Grant Program, Program Guidelines and Application Kit, 9, *available at* http://www.ojp.usdoj.gov/odp/grants_programs.htm (hereinafter UASI Program Guidelines). The UASI program is grant program number 97.008 in the Catalog of Domestic Federal Assistance. *See* UASI Program Guidelines, at 18.

58. Department of Homeland Security Appropriations Act, Pub. L. No. 108-90, Title III, Office for Domestic Preparedness, State and Local Programs (2004); UASI Program Guidelines, *supra* note 57 at 2.

59. UASI Program Guidelines, *supra* note 57 at 2.

60. UASI Program Guidelines, *supra* note 57 at 3-7.

61. UASI Program Guidelines, *supra* note 57 at 2, 18.

62. UASI Program Guidelines, *supra* note 57 at 10, 18.

63. UASI Program Guidelines, *supra* note 57 at 10, 19-20. This includes Indian tribes that participate in the urban area. *Id.* As with the HSGP, a local unit of government may request, in writing, that the state retain some or all of the local unit of government's allocation of grant funds for central purchasing by the state on behalf of the local unit of government. *Id.* However, states holding grant funds for local units of government must enter into a written memorandum of understanding with the local unit of government specifying the amount of funds the state may retain. *Id.*

64. UASI Program Guidelines, *supra* note 57 at 10.

65. UASI Program Guidelines, *supra* note 57 at 20.

66. UASI Program Guidelines, *supra* note 57 at 20.

67. UASI Program Guidelines, *supra* note 57 at 10-11.

68. UASI Program Guidelines, *supra* note 57 at 11; HSPD-5, *supra* note 4, ¶ 20; NIMS Letter, *supra* note 5 at 4.

69. UASI Program Guidelines, *supra* note 57, app. A.

70. UASI Program Guide, *supra* note 57, app. A. The sixteen eligible planning activities are found on page one of Appendix A, and the eighteen categories of eligible equipment costs are described in detail in pages 2-18 of Appendix A. Like the HSGP, only equipment listed on the AEL is eligible for purchase with SHSP funds. *Id.* app. A, at 1-2.

71. For example, with respect to interoperable communications equipment, all new or upgraded radio systems and new radio equipment should be APCO 25 compliant.

UASI Program Guidelines, *supra* note 57, app. A, at 6-7. Both overtime and backfill costs associated with attendance at ODP-sponsored or approved classes, as well as costs associated with the establishment of chemical, biological, radiological, nuclear, and explosive (CBRNE) weapons and cyber-security training programs, are allowable. *Id.* app. A, at 17-19. Exercises conducted with UASI funds must be conducted in accordance with the HSEEP. *Id.* app. A, at 19-21.

72. UASI Program Guidelines, *supra* note 57 at 23-25. Each of these reports is described in more detail in the program guidance.

73. UASI Program Guidelines, *supra* note 57 at 2.

74. UASI Program Guidelines, *supra* note 57 at 2.

75. UASI Program Guidelines, *supra* note 57 at 9.

76. UASI Program Guidelines, *supra* note 57 at 9.

77. UASI Program Guidelines, *supra* note 57 at 2, 9. DHS's UASI ADMINISTRATOR HANDBOOK, which provides guidance in developing the UAHSS, can be found at http://www.shsasresources.com.

78. UASI Program Guidelines, *supra* note 57 at 2.

79. UASI Program Guidelines, *supra* note 57 at 3.

80. UASI Program Guidelines, *supra* note 57 at 6.

81. UASI Program Guidelines, *supra* note 57 at 3-4.

82. UASI Program Guidelines, *supra* note 57 at 3.

83. UASI Program Guidelines, *supra* note 57 at 4.

84. UASI Program Guidelines, *supra* note 57 at 5.

85. UASI Program Guidelines, *supra* note 57 at 3.

86. UASI Program Guidelines, *supra* note 57 at 14.

87. UASI Program Guidelines, *supra* note 57 at 14.

88. UASI Program Guidelines, *supra* note 57 at 14, 15-16.

89. UASI Program Guidelines, *supra* note 57 at 14.

90. UASI Program Guidelines, *supra* note 57 at 14-15. The urban area is "limited to jurisdictions contiguous to the core city and county/counties, or with which the core city or county/counties have established formal mutual aid agreements," although states may request waivers for this limitation for "regions previously established by Executive Order, law, or compact." *Id.* at 15.

91. UASI Program Guidelines, *supra* note 57 at 15.

92. UASI Program Guidelines, *supra* note 57 at 15. DHS "strongly encourages that, wherever possible, previously established local working groups are leveraged for this purpose." *Id.*

93. UASI Program Guidelines, *supra* note 57 at 15.

94. UASI Program Guidelines, at *supra* note 57 2, 9.

95. UASI Program Guidelines, at *supra* note 57 10, 17.

96. UASI Program Guidelines, at *supra* note 57 16.

97. UASI Program Guidelines, at *supra* note 57 17.

98. UASI Program Guidelines, at *supra* note 57 16.

99. U.S. DEPARTMENT OF TRANSPORTATION, FEDERAL TRANSIT ADMINISTRATION, THE PUBLIC TRANSPORTATION SYSTEM SECURITY AND EMERGENCY GUIDE, *available at* http://transit-safety.volpe.dot.gov/publications/security/planningguide.pdf; *see* UASI Program Guidelines, *supra* note 57 at 16. The mass transit agency can substitute an FTA Security Readiness Assessment for the TVA.

100. UASI Program Guidelines, *supra* note 57 at 16-17.

101. UASI Program Guidelines, *supra* note 57 at 17.

102. UASI Program Guidelines, *supra* note 57 at 17.

103. UASI Program Guidelines, *supra* note 57 at 17.

104. UASI Program Guidelines, *supra* note 57 at 2, 17.

105. UASI Program Guidelines, *supra* note 57 at 2.

106. UASI Program Guidelines, *supra* note 57 at 2.

107. UASI Program Guidelines, *supra* note 57 at 7.

108. UASI Program Guidelines, *supra* note 57 at 7.

109. UASI Program Guidelines, *supra* note 57 at 7.

110. DEP'T OF HOMELAND SECURITY, PORT SECURITY FY 2004 FUNDING OPPORTUNITY ANNOUNCE-MENT, 2, *available at* http://www.portsecuritygrants.dottsa.net/TSAdotnet/default.aspx (hereinafter PSGP Announcement). The PSGP is grant program 97.056 in the Catalog of Domestic Federal Assistance.

111. PSGP Announcement, *supra* note 110 at 2.

112. PSGP Announcement, *supra* note 110 at 2.

113. PSGP Announcement, *supra* note 110 at 3, 4.

114. PSGP Announcement, *supra* note 110 at 3-4.

115. PSGP Announcement, *supra* note 110 at 4.

116. PSGP Announcement, *supra* note 110 at 4. In fiscal year 2004, the Controlled Ports were: "New London/Groton, CT; Portsmouth, NH (including Kittery, ME and Dover, NH on the Piscataqua River); Hampton Roads, VA (including Norfolk, Newport News, Jamestown, Yorktown, and Portsmouth, VA); Charleston, SC; Kings Bay, GA; Port Canaveral, FL; Panama City, FL; Pensacola, FL; Port St. Joe, FL; Port Hueneme, CA; San Diego, CA; [and] Honolulu, HI." *Id.*

117. PSGP Announcement, *supra* note 110 at 5.

118. PSGP Announcement, *supra* note 110 at 5.

119. PSGP Announcement, *supra* note 110 at 2-3.

120. PSGP Announcement, *supra* note 110 at 3.

121. PSGP Announcement, *supra* note 110 at 6.

122. PSGP Announcement, *supra* note 110 at 7.

123. 15 U.S.C. §§ 2201-2232 (2003).

124. 15 U.S.C. § 2229(b) (2003). The act also directs that not less than 5 percent of appropriated funds be used for grants to fund fire prevention programs, with priority given to the prevention of injuries to children from fire. *Id.* at § 2229(b)(4). DHS provides these funds through the Fire Prevention and Safety Grants (FPSG) program. DEP'T OF HOMELAND SECURITY, OFFICE FOR STATE & LOCAL GOVERNMENT COORDINATION & PREPAREDNESS, 2004 GUIDANCE FOR THE FIRE PREVENTION & SAFETY GRANTS, *available at* http://www.firegrantsupport.com/ fp_guidance.aspx.

125. DEP'T OF HOMELAND SECURITY, 2004 PROGRAM GUIDANCE FOR THE ASSISTANCE TO FIREFIGHTERS GRANT PROGRAM, at 2 (2004), *available at* http://www.firegrantsupport.com/ guidance.aspx (hereinafter AFGP Program Guidance).

126. AFGP Program Guidance, *supra* note 125 at 2.

127. 15 U.S.C. § 2229(b)(3) (2003). Those fourteen activities are as follows: "(A) to hire additional firefighting personnel; (B) to train firefighting personnel in firefighting, emergency response (including response to a terrorism incident or use of a weapon of mass destruction), arson prevention and detection, or the handling of hazardous materials, or to train firefighting personnel to provide any of the training described in this subparagraph; (C) to fund the creation of rapid intervention teams to protect firefighting personnel at the scenes of fires and other emergencies; (D) to certify fire inspectors; (E) to establish wellness and fitness programs for firefighting personnel to ensure that the firefighting personnel can carry out their duties; (F) to fund emergency medical services provided by fire departments; (G) to acquire additional firefighting vehicles, including fire trucks; (H) to acquire additional firefighting equipment, including equipment for communications, monitoring, and response to a terrorism incident or use of a weapon of mass destruction; (I) to acquire

personal protective equipment required for firefighting personnel by the Occupational Safety and Health Administration, and other personal protective equipment for firefighting personnel, including protective equipment to respond to a terrorism incident or the use of a weapon of mass destruction; (J) to modify fire stations, fire training facilities, and other facilities to protect the health and safety of firefighting personnel; (K) to enforce fire codes; (L) to fund fire prevention programs; (M) to educate the public about arson prevention and detection; and (N) to provide incentives for the recruitment and retention of volunteer firefighting personnel for volunteer firefighting departments and other firefighting departments that utilize volunteers." *Id.*

128. 44 C.F.R. § 152.1(d) (2004).

129. 15 U.S.C. § 2229(b)(1)(A) (2003); AFGP Program Guidance, *supra* note 125 at 2.

130. 44 C.F.R. § 152.1(b) (2004); AFGP Program Guidance, *supra* note 125 at 2.

131. 44 C.F.R. § 152.1(b) (2004); AFGP Program Guidance, *supra* note 125 at 3.

132. 44 C.F.R. § 152.1(b) (2004); AFGP Program Guidance, *supra* note 125 at 3.

133. 44 C.F.R. § 152.1(b) (2004); AFGP Program Guidance, *supra* note 125 at 3.

134. A career fire department is "a fire suppression agency or organization in which all active firefighters are considered full-time employees, are assigned regular duty shifts, and receive financial compensation for their services rendered on behalf of the department." 44 C.F.R. § 152.2 (2004). A volunteer fire department is "a fire suppression agency or organization in which no active firefighters are considered full-time employees, and in which no members receive financial compensation for their services rendered on behalf of the department other than life/health insurance, workers' compensation insurance, length of service awards, pay per-call or per-hour, or similar token compensation." *Id.* A combination fire department is "a fire suppression agency or organization in which at least one active firefighter receives financial compensation for his/her services rendered on behalf of the department and at least one active firefighter does not receive financial compensation for his/her services rendered on behalf of the department other than life/health insurance, workers' compensation insurance, length of service awards, pay per-call or per-hour, or similar token compensation." *Id.*

135. 15 U.S.C. § 2229(b)(9) (2003).

136. 15 U.S.C. § 2229(b)(11) (2003).

137. 15 U.S.C. § 2229(b)(10) (2003); 44 C.F.R. §§ 152.3(b), (d) (2004).

138. 15 U.S.C. § 2229(b)(6)(A) (2003); 44 C.F.R. § 152.4(b)(1) (2004).

139. 15 U.S.C. § 2229(b)(6)(B) (2003); 44 C.F.R. § 152.4(b)(1) (2004). There is no provision for waiver of these cost-share requirements "except for fire departments of Insular Areas as provided for in 48 U.S.C. § 1469a (2002)." 44 C.F.R. § 152.4(b)(1) (2004).

140. 15 U.S.C. § 2229(b)(7) (2003); 44 C.F.R. § 152.4(b)(2) (2004).

141. 44 C.F.R. § 152.3(e) (2004).

142. 68 Fed. Reg. 12,544 (2003); AFGP Program Guidance, *supra* note 125 at 3, 4.

143. 44 C.F.R. §§ 152.1(b), 152.3(c) (2004); AFGP Program Guidance, *supra* note 125 at 2.

144. 44 C.F.R. § 152.3 (2004).

145. 15 U.S.C. § 2229(b)(5)(B) (2003); 44 C.F.R. §§ 152.4(b)(8), 152.7(g).

146. AFGP Program Guidance, *supra* note 125 at 9.

147. 44 C.F.R. § 152.7(a) (2004).

148. AFGP Program Guidance, *supra* note 125 at 3.

149. AFGP Program Guidance, *supra* note 125 at 5.

150. AFGP Program Guidance, *supra* note 125 at 10-18.

151. AFGP Program Guidance, *supra* note 125 at 10.

152. AFGP Program Guidance, *supra* note 125 at 10-18. For example, for departments serving rural communities, DHS believes that "funding basic, operational-level . . . train-

ing . . . has greater benefit than funding officer training, safety officer training, or incident-command training . . . [c]onversely, for departments that are serving urban or suburban communities . . . there is a higher benefit to be gained by funding specialized training . . ." *Id.* at 11.

153. AFGP Program Guidance, *supra* note 125 at 7.

154. AFGP Program Guidance, *supra* note 125 at 7.

155. AFGP Program Guidance, *supra* note 125 at 8. Critical infrastructure is defined as "any system or asset that if attacked would result in catastrophic loss of life or catastrophic economic loss." *Id.* The program guidance also lists thirteen specific types of critical infrastructure. *Id.*

156. AFGP Program Guidance, *supra* note 125 at 9.

157. General Services Administration, Catalog of Federal Domestic Assistance, No. 97.042, Emergency Management Performance Grants, 1, *available at* http://www.cfda.gov (hereinafter EMPG Summary).

158. H.R. Rep. 108-541, 71 (2004) hereinafter FY05 House Report).

159. FY05 House Report, *supra* note 158 at 71.

160. EMPG Summary, *supra* note 157 at 1.

161. EMPG Summary, *supra* note 157 at 2.

162. EMPG Summary, *supra* note 157 at 2.

163. EMPG Summary, *supra* note 157 at 2.

164. EMPG Summary, *supra* note 157 at 2.

165. Cal. Governor's Office of Emergency Serv., FY 04 Emergency Management Performance Grant Program, Grant Guide for Local Governments (2004).

166. Okla. Dep't of Emergency Mgmt., Federal Fiscal Year 2004 Emergency Management Performance Grant Sub-Grant Guidance (2004).

167. EMPG Summary, *supra* note 157 at 2.

168. 49 U.S.C. §§ 5105-5127 (2002).

169. General Services Administration, Catalog of Federal Domestic Assistance, No. 20.703, Hazardous Materials Emergency Preparedness Training & Planning (HMEP) Grants, 1, *available at* http://www.cfda.gov. The HMEP Grant Program "was designed to support the framework and working relationships established within the National Response System and the Emergency Planning and Community Right-to-Know Act of 1986 (EPCRA)." 42 U.S.C. §§ 11001-11005 (2002). Office of Hazardous Materials Safety, Hazardous Materials Emergency Preparedness (HMEP) Grants Program Fact Sheet: Concentration on Transportation Hazmat Planning/Training, 2, *available at* http://hazmat.dot.gov/training/state/hmep/hmepfact.htm (hereinafter HMEP Fact Sheet); *see also* 49 C.F.R. § 110.1.

170. 49 U.S.C. § 5116 (2002); 49 C.F.R. § 110.10 (2004).

171. However, the secretaries of transportation, labor, and energy, directors of the Federal Emergency Management Agency and National Institute of Environmental Health Sciences, chairman of the Nuclear Regulatory Commission, and administrator of the Environmental Protection Agency are to periodically review "all emergency response and preparedness training programs" of their agencies in order "to minimize duplication of effort and expense." 49 U.S.C. § 5116(h) (2002).

172. Legal issues concerning regional response teams are discussed in Chapter 11.

173. 49 C.F.R. § 110.40(a) (2004); 49 U.S.C. § 5116(a)(1) (2002).

174. 49 U.S.C. § 5116(a)(3) (2002).

175. 49 C.F.R. § 110.40(b) (2004).

176. 49 U.S.C. § 5116(b)(2)(B) (2002). HMEP training grant allocations are determined based on: "(A) the number of hazardous materials facilities in the State or on land under the jurisdiction of the tribe; (B) the types and amounts of hazardous material transported in the

State or on that land; (C) whether the State or tribe imposes and collects a fee on transporting hazardous material; (D) whether the fee is used only to carry out a purpose related to transporting hazardous materials; and (E) other factors the Secretary decides are appropriate to carry out this subsection." *Id.* at § 5116(b)(4).

177. HMEP Fact Sheet, *supra* note 169 at 2.

178. 49 U.S.C. §§ 5116(a)(2), (b)(2)(A), (C) (2002). Local emergency planning committees are committees appointed by State Emergency Response Commissions under Section 301(c) of EPCRA, 42 U.S.C. § 11001(c) (2002). *See* 49 C.F.R. § 110.20 (2004).

179. 49 U.S.C. § 5116(e) (2002); 49 C.F.R. § 110.60 (2004).

180. Office of Hazardous Materials Safety, Hazardous Materials Emergency Preparedness Grants Made for Use in Fiscal Year 2004, *available at* http://hazmat.dot.gov/training/state/hmep/hmepgrants.fy2004.pdf.

181. *Id.*

182. Drug-Free Workplace Act, Pub. L. No. 100-690 (1988); 42 U.S.C. §§ 3750-3764 (2002). The BMGP is CFDA grant number 16.579.

183. 42 U.S.C. § 3751(a) (2002).

184. 42 U.S.C. § 3751(a) (2002).

185. 42 U.S.C. § 3751(b) (2002).

186. 42 U.S.C. § 3751(b) (2002). Funding is allocated only to these entities. U.S. Department of Justice, Bureau of Justice Assistance, Edward Byrne Memorial State and Local Law Enforcement Assistance Program: Formula Grant Program Guidance, FY 2004, 1, *available at* http://www.ojp.usdoj.gov/BJA/grant/byrneguide_04/printer_fr.html (hereinafter BFGP Program Guidance).

187. 42 U.S.C. §§ 3751(b)(1)-(29) (2002).

188. 42 U.S.C. § 3751(b)(2) (2002).

189. 42 U.S.C. § 3751(b)(4) (2002).

190. 42 U.S.C. § 3751(b)(7)(B) (2002).

191. 42 U.S.C. § 3751(b)(9) (2002).

192. 42 U.S.C. § 3751(b)(15)(B) (2002).

193. 42 U.S.C. § 3751(b)(26) (2002).

194. 42 U.S.C. §§ 3754(c), (d) (2002).

195. 42 U.S.C. § 3753 (2002).

196. BFGP Program Guidance, *supra* note 186 at 3-4.

197. 42 U.S.C. § 3757(a) (2002); BFGP Program Guidance, *supra* note 186 at 2. This may be the same SAA used for other DOJ grants, and for the HSGP and UASI programs, which are DOJ legacy programs.

198. 42 U.S.C. § 3756(a) (2002); BFGP Program Guidance, *supra* note 186 at 2.

199. 42 U.S.C. § 3756(b)(1) (2002); BFGP Program Guidance, *supra* note 186 at 1-2. State government agencies, local units of government, and Indian tribes with law enforcement functions recognized by the federal government are eligible for subgrants. BFGP Program Guidance, *supra* note 186 at 12.

200. 42 U.S.C. § 3756(b)(2) (2002).

201. 42 U.S.C. § 3756(b)(3) (2002). Alternately, if BJA determines that the state will be unable to qualify for or receive funds, or the state chooses not to participate in the BMGP, then BJA may award funds to local units of government within the state directly, "giving priority to those jurisdictions with the greatest need." *Id.* at § 3756(e).

202. BFGP Program Guidance, *supra* note 186 at 9. Required elements of the strategy are set forth on pages 9-11 of the BFGP Program Guidance. The SAA must make the grant application and the strategy available for review by the state legislature and the public. *Id.* at 7.

203. 42 U.S.C. § 3753(a)(2) (2002); BFGP Program Guidance, *supra* note 186 at 3.

204. 42 U.S.C. §§ 3754(a), (e) (2002); BFGP Program Guidance, *supra* note 186 at 2. "The SAA may impose this matching requirement on a project-by-project basis"; however, "[t]he SAA must commit to this matching requirement to receive funds," and "matching funds cannot supplant other funds." BFGP Program Guidance, *supra* note 186 at 2-3.

205. 42 U.S.C. § 3754(b) (2002); BFGP Program Guidance, *supra* note 186 at 1-2.

206. 42 U.S.C. § 3759(a) (2002); BFGP Program Guidance, *supra* note 186 at 3. Program funds must be spent in support of four goals: (1) "Completion of criminal histories to include the final disposition of all arrests for felony offenses;" (2) "Full automation of all criminal justice histories;" (3) "Improvement of state records systems and the sharing of all records described above with the Attorney General;" and (4) "Improvement of state records systems and the sharing of all the records described above and the child abuse crime records required under the National Child Protection Act of 1993 (42 U.S.C. §§ 5119 *et seq.*) among state criminal justice agencies." BFGP Program Guidance, *supra* note 186 at 3.

207. 42 U.S.C. § 3754(f) (2002).

208. BFGP Program Guidance, *supra* note 186 at 8. Another BJA grant program, the Local Law Enforcement Block Grants (LLEBG) program, also distributes block grants to states and local governments for seven specified law enforcement program areas. *See* GENERAL SERVICES ADMINISTRATION, CATALOG OF FEDERAL DOMESTIC ASSISTANCE NO. 16.592, LOCAL LAW ENFORCEMENT BLOCK GRANTS PROGRAM, *available at* http://www.cfda.gov; U.S. DEPARTMENT OF JUSTICE, BUREAU OF JUSTICE ASSISTANCE, FY 2004 LLEBG GUIDELINES, *available at* http://www.ojp.usdoj.gov/BJA/grant/llebg_toc.html. However, Congress has reduced funding for LLEBG funds over the past five years, appropriating only $115 million for the program in fiscal year 2004. *Id.*

209. 23 U.S.C. § 402(c) (2002).

210. 23 C.F.R. § 1200.1 (2004).

211. 23 C.F.R. § 1205.3 (2004). SCHSGP funds also may be used for other highway safety program areas identified in a State's Highway Safety Plan. *Id.* at § 1205.4(b).

212. NATIONAL HIGHWAY TRANSPORTATION SAFETY ADMINISTRATION, UNIFORM GUIDELINES FOR STATE HIGHWAY SAFETY PROGRAMS, *available at* http://www.nhtsa.dot.gov/nhtsa/whatsup/tea21/tea21programs/402Guide.html (hereinafter UGSHSP).

213. UGSHSP, *supra* note 212, Highway Safety Program Guideline No. 5: Driver Licensing, §§ I, II, IV.

214. UGSHSP, *supra* note 212, Highway Safety Program Guideline No. 10: Traffic Records, §§ I(B), (H).

215. UGSHSP, *supra* note 212, Highway Safety Program Guideline No. 11: Emergency Medical Services, §§ III, IV, VI, VII, VIII.

216. 23 U.S.C. § 402(b)(1)(A) (2002).

217. 23 U.S.C. § 402(b)(1)(C) (2002). NHTSA has established guidelines for determining whether states are in compliance with this requirement. *See* 23 C.F.R. § 1250.1-1250.5 (2004).

218. 23 U.S.C. § 402(c) (2002). With respect to the allocation to DOI, 95 percent of those funds must be "expended by Indian tribes to carry out highway safety programs within their jurisdictions." *Id.* at § 402(i)(2).

219. 23 C.F.R. § 1200.10 (2004).

220. 7 U.S.C. § 1926(a)(19)(A) (2003); 7 C.F.R. §§ 3750.52, .61(a) (2004). After federal fiscal year 1999, the terms "rural" and "rural areas" include "a city, town, or unincorporated area that has a population of 50,000 inhabitants or less, other than an urbanized area immediately adjacent to a city, town, or unincorporated area that has a population in excess of 50,000 inhabitants." 7 C.F.R. § 3750.53 (2004).

221. 7 C.F.R. § 3750.51(a) (2004). The CFGP is CFDA program number 10.766.

222. 7 U.S.C. § 1926(a)(19)(A) (2003).

223. 7 U.S.C. § 1926(a)(19)(C) (2003).

224. 7 C.F.R. § 3750.53 (2004). In order to qualify as an "essential community facility," a facility must "(1) Serve a function customarily provided by a local unit of government; (2) Be a public improvement needed for the orderly development of a rural community; (3) Not include private affairs or commercial or business undertakings (except for limited authority for industrial parks) unless it is a minor part of the total facility; (4) Be within the area of jurisdiction or operation for the public bodies eligible to receive assistance or a similar local rural service area of a not-for-profit corporation; and (5) Be located in a rural area." *Id.* The essential community facility also must serve a population whose median household income is "below the higher of the poverty line or the eligible percentage (60, 70, 80, or 90) of the State nonmetropolitan median household income." 7 C.F.R. § 3750.61 (2004).

225. 7 C.F.R. § 3750.53 (2004).

226. 7 C.F.R. § 3750.62(a) (2004).

227. 7 C.F.R. § 3750.62(a)(1) (2004).

228. 7 C.F.R. § 3750.62(a)(2)(i) (2004).

229. USDA Rural Development, Housing Program, Essential Community Facilities, 2, *at* http://www.rurdev.usda.gov/rhs/cf/essent_facil.htm.

230. 7 C.F.R. § 3750.65 (2004).

231. 7 U.S.C. § 1926(a)(19)(B) (2003); 7 C.F.R. §§ 3750.51(i), 3750.52 (2004).

232. 7 C.F.R. § 3750.67 (2004).

233. 7 C.F.R. § 3750.62(b) (2004). Grant assistance runs from a maximum of 75 percent of eligible project costs for communities with a population of 5,000 or less and a median household income below the higher of the poverty line or 60 percent of the state nonmetropolitan median household income, to 15 percent for communities with a population of 20,001 to 50,000 and a median household income below the higher of the poverty line and 90 percent of the state nonmetropolitan median household income. *Id.*

234. 7 C.F.R. § 3750.63(a) (2004).

235. National Defense Authorization Act for Fiscal Year 2004, Pub. L. No. 108-136, 117 Stat. 1391 (2003) (codified at 15 U.S.C. § 2229a).

236. *Id.* at § 1057.

237. H.R. 1118, 108th Cong. (2003).

238. 15 U.S.C. § 2229a(a)(1)(A) (2003). This program is modeled on the Community Oriented Policing Services or "COPS ON THE BEAT" program, which provided grants "to expand and improve cooperative efforts between law enforcement agencies and members of the community to address crime and disorder problems." 42 U.S.C. § 3796dd(a) (2002). This included a program specifically for hiring additional police officers. *Id.* at § 3796dd(b). This part of the COPS ON THE BEAT program was not funded for fiscal year 2005.

239. *See* 15 U.S.C. § 2229a (2003).

240. Dep't. of Homeland Security Appropriations Act, 2005, Pub. L. No. 108-334, Title III, Office of State and Local Government Coordination and Preparedness, Firefighter Assistance Grants (2004).

241. 15 U.S.C. §§ 2229a(a)(1)(A), (D), (G) (2003).

242. 15 U.S.C. § 2229a(a)(1)(B)(i) (2003).

243. 15 U.S.C. § 2229a (a)(1)(E) (2003). Applicants willing to pay a greater share of the cost of hiring the firefighters may be given preferential consideration for grants. *Id.* at § 2229a(a)(1)(C).

244. 15 U.S.C. § 2229a(a)(1)(B)(ii) (2003). Grant recipients also are required to permit firefighters hired under SAFER Act grants to volunteer in other jurisdictions during their off-duty hours. *Id.* at § 2229a(a)(1)(F). This has been a bone of contention between firefighting unions and volunteer fire departments.

245. 15 U.S.C. § 2229a(a)(1)(H) (2003).

246. 15 U.S.C. § 2229a(a)(2) (2003).

247. 15 U.S.C. § 2229a(b)(3) (2003).

248. 15 U.S.C. § 2229a(c)(1) (2003). However, BIA funds may be used to cover the non-federal share of costs under the SAFER Act program. *Id.* at § 2229a(c)(3).

249. 15 U.S.C. § 2229a(c)(4)(A) (2003). This cap will be adjusted annually for inflation. *Id.* at § 2229a(c)(4)(B).

250. 15 U.S.C. § 2229a(c)(2) (2003).

251. H.R. 3266, 108th Cong. (2003).

252. H. Rep. No. 108-460, pt. 1, at 17 (Apr. 2, 2004) (hereinafter Select Committee Report). The bill was then referred to the House Judiciary Committee, Transportation and Infrastructure Committee, Energy and Commerce Committee, and Science Committee, each of which had concurrent jurisdiction over the bill. The Science Committee chose not to exercise its jurisdiction; the other three committees reported separate versions to the full House. *See Id.* at pts. 2, 3, and 4. The final version of the bill, which was included in the House's intelligence reform bill, represented a compromise among all four committees. *See* H.R. 10, 108th Cong. § 5003 (2004).

253. S. 1245, 108th Cong. (2003).

254. S. Rep. No. 108-225, at 14-15 (2004) (hereinafter Governmental Affairs Committee Report).

255. *See* H.R 10, 108th Cong. § 5003 (2004); S. 1245, 108th Cong. (2003).

256. H.R. 3266, 108th Cong. §§ 2(1), (7) (2003) (as reported to the House); Select Committee Report, *supra* note 252 at 2.

257. Select Committee Report, *supra* note 252 at 15.

258. Select Committee Report, *supra* note 252 at 16.

259. H. Rep. No. 108-460, pt. 3, at 11 (2004) (hereinafter Transportation and Infrastructure Report).

260. Transportation and Infrastructure Report, *supra* note 259 at 13.

261. *See* H.R. 10, 108th Cong. § 5003 (2004).

262. FY05 Conference Report, *supra* note 10 at 63.

263. FY05 Conference Report, *supra* note 10 at 68.

264. FY05 Conference Report, *supra* note 10 at 69. The final version of the House's first responder funding bill, included in the House's intelligence reform bill, retained its terrorism focus. *See* H.R. 10, 108th Cong. § 5003 (2004).

265. Governmental Affairs Committee Report, *supra* note 254 at 3. Indian tribes also would be eligible for these grants "if they otherwise met the criteria set forth for high threat areas." *Id.* at 9.

266. S. 1245 (as reported to the Senate), 108th Cong. § 4(f)(2) (2003).

267. Governmental Affairs Committee Report, *supra* note 254 at 3, 10-11; S. 1245 (as reported to the Senate), 108th Cong. § 4(g)(2) (2003).

268. Governmental Affairs Committee Report, *supra* note 254 at 3.

269. Governmental Affairs Committee Report, *supra* note 254 at 3; S. 1245 (as reported to the Senate), 108th Cong. § 4(g)(3) (2003). The House Select Committee on Homeland Security struck out the furthest from the existing formula grants, with H.R. 3266 distributing funds on a competitive basis solely based on risk. *See* H.R. 3266 (as reported to the House), 108th Cong. at § 1804 (2003); Select Committee Report, *supra* note 252 at 28. However, the final version of the House legislation included state minimums. *See* H.R. 10, 108th Cong. at § 5003 (2004).

270. Governmental Affairs Committee Report, *supra* note 254 at 11, 26.

271. Governmental Affairs Committee Report, *supra* note 254 at 11.

272. Governmental Affairs Committee Report, *supra* note 254 at 25.

273. Governmental Affairs Committee Report, *supra* note 254 at 46.

274. Governmental Affairs Committee Report, *supra* note 254 at 47.

275. Governmental Affairs Committee Report, *supra* note 254 at 48.

276. Governmental Affairs Committee Report, *supra* note 254 at 48. With respect to H.R. 3266, the House Select Committee on Homeland Security favored distribution based solely on risk, but the other three committees that had jurisdiction favored state minimums. The final version of the bill included state minimums. *See* H.R. 10, 108th Cong. § 5003 (2004).

277. FY05 House Report, *supra* note 158 at 67.

278. See H.R. 10, 108th Cong. (2004); S. 1245, 108th Cong. (2003)

279. S. REP. No. 108-280, at 56 (2004).

280. FY05 House Report, *supra* note 158 at 69-70.

281. *See* sections of chapter on Homeland Security Grants Program and Urban Areas Security Initiative, *supra*.

282. *See* sections of chapter on Assistance to Firefighters Grant Progam and SAFER Act Grants, *supra*.

283. Governmental Affairs Committee Report, *supra* note 254 at 8.

284. Governmental Affairs Committee Report, *supra* note 254 at 8.

285. Alice Lipowicz, *Tired of Waiting, Cities Launch Push for Direct Homeland Security Funding*, CQ HOMELAND SECURITY (Mar. 4, 2004); Chris Strohm, *Mayors Want More Direct Homeland Security Funding*, GOVEXEC.COM (Feb. 11, 2004).

286. *See*, Lipowicz, *supra* note 285.

287. Select Committee Report, *supra* note 252 at 15.

288. Select Committee Report, *supra* note 252 at 15.

289. H.R. 3266 (as reported to the House), 108th Cong. at § 1807(5) (2003).

290. H.R. 3266 (as reported to the House), 108th Cong. at § 1805(e) (2003).

291. S. 1245 (as reported to the Senate), 108th Cong. §§ 4(f), (g) (2003).

292. *Id.* § 4(g)(4).

CHAPTER 7

Experiencing the 2004 Florida Hurricanes: A Lawyer's Perspective

by Alfred O. Bragg III

Introduction

This chapter shares the experience of providing legal services in the context of an actual disaster, in this case, a series of them. The writer had the privilege of acting as legal counsel to the Florida State Emergency Response Team during the unprecedented series of hurricanes that ravaged the state over the course of almost seven weeks, beginning on August 10, 2004. This is a reflective look at what a lawyer in that situation is likely to be called upon to do, and it is being provided to help other lawyers anticipate some of the problems that may arise. While emergency situations are rare, it may be useful when they do occur to have had the opportunity to understand and anticipate what lawyers may be called upon to provide their governmental clients. This chapter presents a chronicle of some of the problems that government counsel may be called upon to deal with in such emergency situations.

The Legal Context

In the United States, it has never been quite true that the measures needed to meet emergencies are outside the strictures of the law;[1] it is more accurate to say that, in the past, the law and its normal processes have been too slow to keep up with the pace of emergencies. This is probably even more accurate given the potential of new threats of terrorist acts and other situations that have not been encountered previously.

The ability of lawyers to function in such pressure situations is changing with the development of ever-faster microprocessors. This evolution of information and its processing, in less than a generation, has vastly improved the lawyer's ability to function in emergencies. While the rise of the Internet and the refinements in the microprocessor have transformed the practice of law, it is not as well known that these developments have created whole new legal specialties. The role of legal counsel in representing emergency managers while responding to disasters is one of these, and their ability to perform has been improved greatly as a result of these developments.

As an emergency situation unfolds, a lawyer must make many legal decisions in rapid-fire sequence. If properly prepared, and with access to relevant legal materials, it is now possible to render legal advice and guidance to clients in the real-time environment of a cascade of events that arise from a single, albeit many faceted, cumulative disaster. In the past—and even now, unless advance thought is given to the situation confronting the lawyer—it was not possible to give the client for consideration all the applicable legal variables that would allow a better informed set of decisions.

The improvements in information processing, and the speed of access to information, has changed all this. Clients can be given a better grounding in the law that is relevant to the operational decisions that need to be made while options are still open. This differs from decision making during disaster response only a few decades ago, when the only variables considered were operational ones; the actions taken rested solely on operational needs, and only after those needs were met were the legal consequences of the actions considered. Whether actions complied with legal requirements (and therefore triggered liability or other legal exposures) remained largely up to chance.

In performing as legal counsel, a lawyer now has the opportunity to provide timely advice from a position of advantage in several respects. First, the lawyer has the use of up-to-date computer hardware and software unknown to most members of the legal profession even fifteen years ago. Second, in responding to events during the recent spate of Florida hurricanes, the lawyers operating from a workstation in the State Emergency Operations Center had immediate access both to the State Coordinating Officer and to the personnel staffing all of the state's Emergency Support Functions. Third, because these lawyers had been involved beforehand in every exercise the Division of Emergency Management had staged for five years, a close working relationship had evolved that resulted in the lawyers being able to interact successfully with the operational personnel.

This provided an opportunity for the lawyers to play an integral role and to take advantage of the relationships built from the earlier training opportunities on the operational side. Each of these advantages made its own contribution and allowed the lawyers to play a significant role in an evolving process in which the state coordinating officer, in effect, had to rewrite the law of the state to enable it to meet an unprecedented series of disasters.

The Florida Legal Environment

Under the Florida Constitution, as in many states, the power of the state to act in emergencies is vested in the governor as its chief executive authority. The governor is the "commander-in-chief of all military forces of the state not in active service of the United States . . . . [and] the chief administrative officer of the state responsible for the planning and budgeting for the state."[2] The state constitution further provides that the governor "shall have power to call out the militia to preserve the public peace, execute the laws of the state, suppress insurrection, or repel invasion."[3]

Much of the Florida governor's authority to meet emergencies comes from the state's constitution. Nevertheless, the legislature also has allowed for the exercise of that authority in the Florida Emergency Management Act, which creates the Division of Emergency Management, and spells out specific operational roles for the governor and his or her subordinates in responding to disasters.[4]

Upon being notified of a disaster in the state that is beyond the response capability of the local government, the State Emergency Response Team is likely to advise the governor to declare a state of emergency. The declaration or proclamation of an emergency, usually in an executive order, has a life of only sixty days, unless renewed.[5] Unless the event is a "minor" disaster within the meaning of the act,[6] the governor also is likely to request the president of the United States to declare it a major disaster in accordance with the Stafford Act.[7] This is one purpose of the proclamation or declaration. Another is to designate a "state coordinating officer" for the disaster, not only to delegate the operational powers of the governor to that official,[8] but also to give the state coordinating officer the power to act for the state as the governor's "authorized representative" in dealing with the Federal Emergency Management Agency (FEMA).[9]

The declaration or proclamation of a state of emergency opens with a recital of the event or series of events that constitutes the disaster and classifies it as a minor, major, or catastrophic disaster.[10] The proclamation declares the existence of a state of emergency and defines its territorial scope,[11] which may be statewide. Depending on the complexity of the response demanded by the disaster, the declaration or proclamation may not only designate a State Coordinating Officer and Authorized Representative,[12] but may activate the Florida National Guard.[13]

In recent years, declarations of emergency issued by the governor have delegated the following powers to the state coordinating officer, all of which are vested in the governor in the first instance by the Emergency Management Act: the authority to suspend the effect of any statute, rule, ordinance, or order of any state, regional, or local governmental entity as needed to cope with the disaster;[14] to direct all state, regional, and local governmental agencies, including law enforcement agencies;[15] to confiscate any private property needed to meet the disaster;[16] to order the evacuation of all persons from any part of the state and regulate the movement of persons and traffic within the state;[17] and to redelegate his powers to subordinates by the designation of one or more "deputy state coordinating officers" and "alternate authorized representatives" to act in his absence.[18] As it turned out, this redelegation proved critical in the 2004 hurricanes, because senior officials were scattered in different locations as the disasters passed from one phase to the next; the state was well into the process of trying to recover from Hurricane Charley while Hurricane Jeanne was on its way to making landfall.

The declaration of a state of emergency has yet other effects that arise by operation of law, regardless of whether the executive order mentions them. Agencies are relieved of budgetary restrictions as needed and are allowed to exceed these restrictions in meeting the emergency.[19] Under the Florida Mutual Aid Act, the director of the Department of Law Enforcement takes direct command of all the state law enforcement agencies, regardless of whether they are statewide or local.[20] One immediate effect of the declaration of emergency is to freeze the prices of essential services and commodities, and any increase in prices following the declaration gives rise to a rebuttable presumption of price gouging that may subject the offender to judicial penalties.[21] The state of emergency also gives all executive and administrative agencies independent legal authority under the Florida Administrative Procedure Act to promulgate emergency rules and orders to the extent that the latter are needed to meet the emergency.[22]

The Florida Operational Environment

The activities that comprise emergency management in its broadest sense have been clustered into four classes of activities: preparedness, response, recovery, and mitigation. The first and last are preventive in character.[23] The response and recovery phases are remedial in the purest sense. Unlike response, the recovery phase may take years, depending on the scale of the disaster. The response phase may be the one best known to the general public, because the response activities take place just as the disaster qualifies as "breaking news" and attention from the press is at its height.

The response to a disaster is different from the other three phases of emergency management in the salient respect that, in the response phase, everything happens much faster. The other three are "planned" processes in the sense that disaster planners have some time to engage in operational planning. The response to a disaster can be planned only insofar as preparedness measures ensure that needed resources are staged and in place and that vulnerable elements of the population are ordered to evacuate those areas in immediate danger. Beyond that, the only "planning" function is performed by the disaster itself, which dictates the response needs as it moves in and has its way.[24] In the end, the disaster determines its own response.

Another fundamental characteristic of the response phase follows from the first: its unpredictability. While some response needs are foreseeable (generators, water, shelter), not all of them are. Construction cranes may be needed to remove wreckage from highways before anything else can be done. Even the resources known to be needed cannot be delivered to the scene until conditions allow. Without knowing what obstacles lay in their way, responders can only estimate their time of arrival at the scene. Information concerning physical conditions at the scene may be conflicting or nonexistent. In many large disasters, the first mission may be the removal of wreckage from highways, airport runways, or other components of the transportation infrastructure.

Humane assistance from the outside may not be possible until at least some part of that infrastructure is up and running.[25]

This, then, is the operational environment in which legal counsel must function; to most lawyers it is an alien setting. Lawyers are accustomed to bringing order out of chaotic situations after the fact, not while the chaotic events themselves are occurring.[26] With the onset of the disaster, a communications blackout may ensue. During this interlude, no information from the scene is forthcoming at all. This is likely to be followed by a cascade of information, much of it conflicting, and only some of it reliable. Once communications with responders at the scene are established, reports and requests for missions flow in torrents; the operational environment that at first was made chaotic by too little information is now made chaotic by too much.

With the director of the Division of Emergency Management now acting as state coordinating officer, and a state of emergency in place arming him with the authority to rewrite the law as needed to meet the disaster, the question becomes what legal actions are needed. The state coordinating officer and his subordinates take these actions in one of two ways. The first, and far more common, is the assignment of missions that cannot be performed without infringing on some legal requirement, such as the statutory requirement for competitive bidding in the procurement of services and supplies. To the extent that the statutes and rules setting up the procurement procedures may impede the timely performance of the mission, the mission assignment or other order by the state coordinating officer is deemed *pro tanto* to have overridden any competing statutory or regulatory requirement.[27]

The second is at once more formal and less commonplace. In accordance with his delegation of authority from the governor, the state coordinating officer may issue his own formal written orders to override legal requirements that threaten to delay or otherwise impede the response to a disaster. Through gradual experimentation, lawyers have devised approaches for use of such orders in Florida,[28] although this device almost surely exists in other jurisdictions. Drafting such orders to meet a fluid situation is a chronic challenge. During the recent hurricanes, the challenge differed in degree, but not in kind, from those posed by lesser disasters.

Like other disasters, hurricanes generate so many different kinds of crises that it is impossible to foresee even a substantial fraction of the situations calling for legal intervention. Anyone can foresee that evacuations have to be ordered, turnpike tolls lifted, highways reconfigured for one-way traffic, and utility equipment sent in from other jurisdictions to restore electrical power; all these measures require the state coordinating officer to supersede one or more statutes, rules, or other legal requirements.

Less apparent is the need to override other statutes and rules whose requirements may have become impossible to meet due to the disaster or that have to be modified in order to enable government and regulated businesses to function under disaster conditions. Like the potential universe of smaller emergencies bred by one large disaster, the potential universe of legal issues awaiting emergency management counsel has no boundaries; counsel may expect almost anything.[29]

The Police Power

It is also vital for emergency management counsel to stake out in advance the known boundaries of the police power as it relates to general emergencies in their jurisdiction, regardless of whether the application of that power has been codified in legislation or exists only in decisional law. Such information is the *sine qua non* of the law governing disaster response; without it emergency managers cannot undertake any response operation with adequate assurance that it passes legal muster.

While to a large extent the Florida Emergency Management Act codifies many of the specific acts that constitute the exercise of the police power as it applies to emergencies, it should be recalled that the police power is an attribute inherent in the powers of the state as sovereign, and that the existence of legislation allowing for its exercise within a specified organizational structure should not be construed as a limitation on the power to take the measures needed in emergencies.[30] Even after the legislature has invoked its constitutional powers by the creation of a comprehensive statutory and regulatory scheme through which the governor can meet emergencies, an untapped residue of constitutional authority still may be present. If legal counsel for emergency management are allowed to participate in crafting the proclamation or other document by which the governor declares a state of emergency, they should frame the document so that, in it, the governor invokes this residual authority as well.[31]

Counsel may not always find the boundaries of the police power easy to locate, especially as applied to general emergencies in their jurisdiction. The precedential boundaries established by statutes that were passed to regulate such day-to-day matters as building, zoning, and sanitation do not measure the scope of the police power in emergencies, because in emergencies the stakes are higher. During Hurricane Frances, counsel advised a local government that it had legal authority to bulldoze a system of drainage pipes on private property. The local government had tried to find the owner to procure his consent, but had not been able to. The water in the system was backing up so that some sixty nearby homes were in danger of flooding. Venerable precedent was available to apply the police power to allow the destruction of property in order to protect the community as a whole.[32] The essential lesson for legal counsel is to identify such applicable precedents in advance and have them at hand concerning the limitations of the police power, favorable and unfavorable alike, so that emergency managers and responders can be advised at least as to what extent legal grounds support their decisions.

The Balance Between Authority and Power

If every issue posed to emergency management counsel were a "legal" issue in its purest sense, the professional duties of counsel would be much easier to perform than they are in fact. In addition to the likelihood that, during the opening hours of the disaster, counsel may be asked to render legal advice and guidance based on information that is inaccurate or incomplete, ethical issues also are likely to arise. The pivotal question of how best to meet the state co-ordinating officer's operational objectives has a surface simplicity that belies some of the complexities of the operational environment. Difficult decisions are made more so when ethical issues are piled onto the legal ones. Such issues may beset lawyers even where their client has sufficient legal authority to act. Indeed, sometimes it is in the very environment where the operational side of disaster response has an abundance of legal authority that ethical questions may loom the largest.

The sweeping delegation of authority from the governor to the state coordinating officer relates to this in several ways. First, the delegation con-centrates formidable powers into the hands of the state coordinating officer. Second, these powers are not the exercise of executive powers only. While countenanced by authorizing legislation or based on constitutional powers relating to emergencies, the exercise of such authority may be used to counter-mand, at least for a time, other laws adopted by the legislature. Exercising that emergency authority intrudes upon the legislative function. This is something more than the exercise of executive power. Third, as a practical matter, the state coordinating officer is often too preoccupied with operational duties to select *ad interim* statewide policies from the wide array of options available, for better or worse. This may include such quasi-legislative determinations as choosing which features of the statute or rule should be suspended, for how many days, and for which cities or counties.

Often, these decisions are left to counsel. Therefore, counsel must take on the added role of policymaker. This should not come as a complete surprise. Beset on all sides by operational and logistical headaches of every description, it is natural for the state coordinating officer to defer to counsel in any legal matter, and, in so doing, counsel may even be asked to set the relevant param-eters of the policy. In such circumstances, lawyers should understand that they are assuming a multiple role that may compromise their independent profes-sional judgment, or pose yet other ethical issues.[33]

Even counsel who are able to function free of ethical distractions may find it a challenge to strike a proper balance in the preparation of emergency or-ders. On the one hand, counsel must frame the orders to ensure that agencies or other parties are relieved of literal compliance with a statute or rule whose requirements can no longer be met, or circumstances arise where adherence to those requirements cannot be justified in the face of an emergency. On the other hand, an important role and obligation of counsel is to limit the scope and duration of the order, so that it is no broader than necessary to achieve the intended purpose. By declaring a state of emergency, the governor has not only called up the formidable powers of that office to countermand what the legislature has done, but has in turn delegated that power to a state coordinat-ing officer, who has not been elected by anyone.[34]

It therefore falls to counsel to be aware of the need to strike the appropriate balance between what is needed to meet the disaster and the public interest in restoring the law to its *status quo ante* once the need has passed. This is not the only variable in the equation. The interests of various political constituencies do not go into hibernation when disaster strikes. Indeed, some of them see the disaster as a window of opportunity to achieve ends the law denies them in ordinary times. Counsel may need to anticipate these issues, and be aware of appropriate restrictions on setting limits on actions taken during emergencies.

Lawyers preparing for a role in emergency management must be prepared to assume their roles before an emergency exists, and they need to be familiar with the statutory and regulatory maze applicable to situations where they will be asked to make adjustments to existing policies when the emergency arises. Undertaking this role effectively would not have been possible a generation ago, but the current texts of relevant statutes, rules, and cases are now only keystrokes away. Regardless of the positions urged by other agencies and special pleading by outside constituencies, counsel for the state coordinating officer are answerable for the legal and factual integrity of the emergency order, so they must master the subject matter to which the order will apply, at least to ensure that it strikes a proper balance between the immediate object of getting the job done and the narrowness and specificity needed to prevent abuse, whether intended or unintended.

As can be seen from the discussion above, advance planning for the role of legal counsel in emergency situations is essential. Knowledge of the laws, statutory and regulatory, in which counsel will be asked to function is critical to counseling for clients who are likely to be overwhelmed by operational decisions and will be relying on legal counsel for support on the scope and soundness of governmental actions that will be undertaken. Hopefully, the recitation of only some of the issues encountered in Florida's recent hurricane emergencies may stimulate counsel in other jurisdictions to prepare themselves to take on similar roles.

NOTES

1. *See* Sterling v. Constantin, 287 U.S. 378 (1932).

2. Fla. Const. art. IV, § 1(a) (1968).

3. Fla. Const. art. IV, § 1(d) (1968). In addition, the constitution provides for the continuity of governmental operations: "Upon vacancy in the office of governor, the lieutenant governor shall become governor. Further succession to the office of governor shall be prescribed by law . . . ." Fla. Const. art. IV, § 3(a) (1968).

4. Fla. Stat. §§ 20.18(2)(a), 252.32(1)(a), 252.36(1)(a) (2004).

5. Fla. Stat. § 252.36(2) (2004). Proclamations and declarations of states of emergency have the force and effect of law. Fla. Stat. § 252.36(1)(b) (2004).

6. Fla. Stat. § 252.34(1)(c) (2004).

7. 42 U.S.C. § 5170 (2000).

8. *See* Fla. Stat. § 252.36(8) (2004).

9. 42 U.S.C. § 5143(c) (2000). During recent years, the division's director has performed the role of state coordinating officer. The designations of "State Coordinating Officer" and "Authorized Representative" have the same meanings assigned to them in the regulations that implement the Stafford Act. *See* 44 C.F.R. §§ 206.2(a)(13), 206.2(a)(23) (2004).

10. Fla. Stat. § 252.36(3)(c) (2004).

11. Fla. Stat. § 252.36(2) (2004).

12. *See,* Fla. Stat. § 252.36(8) (2004).

13. FLA. STAT. § 252.36(4) (2004). Depending on the type of expertise needed in responding to the disaster, the declaration also may designate one or more "incident commanders." *Id.*

14. FLA. STAT. §§ 252.36(5)(a), 252.46(2) (2004); *see* FLA. EXEC. ORDER NO. 04-192 (Sept. 1, 2004) (Hurricane Frances); FLA. EXEC. ORDER NO. 04-206 (Sept. 10, 2004) (Hurricane Ivan); FLA. EXEC. ORDER NO. 04-217 (Sept. 24, 2004) (Hurricane Jeanne). All the Executive Orders are on file with the author, as well as with the Florida Secretary of State.

15. FLA. STAT. §§ 252.36(5)(b), 252.36(6) (2004).

16. FLA. STAT. §§ 252.36(5)(d), 252.43(1), 252.43(3) (2004).

17. FLA. STAT. §§ 252.36(5)(e), 252.36(5)(f) (2004).

18. FLA. STAT. §§ 252.36(4), 252.36(8) (2004). In addition, the declaration directs the state coordinating officer to activate the Statewide Comprehensive Emergency Management Plan, to invoke the Statewide Mutual Aid Agreement and Emergency Management Assistance Compact, and to distribute all supplies stockpiled for emergencies. *See* FLA. STAT. §§ 252.36(3)(a), 252.36(3)(b) (2004).

19. FLA. STAT. § 252.37(2) (2004). When the governor declares a state of emergency, the act also gives the chief financial officer the authority to take over the operations of any financial institution in the state or to enter any other orders needed to ensure its financial soundness. *See,* FLA. STAT. § 252.62(2)(a) (2004). In disasters other than minor ones, the declaration also constitutes authority for medical practitioners licensed in other jurisdictions to practice in Florida, subject to such conditions as the declaration may prescribe. FLA. STAT. § 252.36(3)(c)(1) (2004).

20. FLA. STAT. § 23.1231(2)(d) (2004).

21. FLA. STAT. §§ 501.160(1)(b), 501.160(2) (2004).

22. FLA. STAT. §§ 120.54(4)(a), 252.46(1) (2004).

23. Mitigation is the coordination of planning, zoning, building and other land use policies to ensure that when a disaster strikes, its impact will be minimal; each state must submit its own state plan to be eligible for federal mitigation assistance. 42 U.S.C. § 5165(a) (2000); *see,* 44 C.F.R. § 201.4(a)(1) (2004). Mitigation strategies may include the placement of infrastructure away from zones prone to flooding, and the dedication of such lands for use as green space. Preparedness is a well-known aspect of emergency management; typical preparedness measures include the simulation of disasters in formal exercises whose "players" include elected officials, emergency managers, and responders at all levels of government.

24. The expression "disaster," as used here, is intended to cover not only the event itself (such as a fire, hurricane or explosion), but its primary effects (casualties and the destruction of infrastructure), as well as secondary consequences (looting, injuries to responders, congestion on highways resulting from evacuations), and tertiary ones (stalled vehicles on highways, stranded passengers running out of prescription medications, and altercations between drivers). Large disasters tend to breed smaller ones.

25. Response measures in Florida are aggressive rather than passive; resources are pushed to the scene regardless of whether local officials have requested them. The rationale for this is simple: It is better to have too many commodities and supplies on hand than too few, and, in any case, sooner is better than later.

26. Members of the legal profession are trained to intervene in situations that are in disarray and restore them to order. In many such cases, the lawyer at least finds the situation stable in the sense that it cannot get any worse. Emergency management counsel do not even have this meager consolation.

27. FLA. STAT. §§ 252.36(5)(a), 252.46(2) (2004).

28. FLA. STAT. §§ 252.35(2)(s), 252.36(4), 252.36(8) (2004). During the hurricanes, the state coordinating officer issued some sixty-one Supplemental Orders that overrode statu-

tory and regulatory requirements encompassing such varied subjects as property valuations for ad valorem taxes, the cancellation of homeowners' insurance policies, the staffing requirements for home care services, and the reconstruction of facilities for cattle auctions. All the Supplemental Orders are on file with the author and with the Division of Emergency Management.

29. As one instance, Hurricane Frances threatened to close the Gulf of Mexico to shipping at a time when Hurricane Charley had already depleted fuel supplies statewide; the further curtailment of fuel shipments from refineries could have caused a statewide shortage. To prevent such a shortage, the governor issued an Executive Order "to regulate the allocation and distribution of fuel supplies" during the emergency. FLA. EXEC. ORDER NO. 04-196 (Sept. 5, 2004). In order to protect fuel suppliers from potential antitrust liability, the Executive Order was framed to trigger the protection of state-action immunity for the suppliers. *See,* Parker v. Brown, 317 U.S. 341 (1942).

30. The text of the act itself implies that, in it, the legislature did not use all the constitutional power the state has. FLA. STAT. § 252.33(4) (2004). Moreover, the act obligates the state to compensate the owners of real and personal property that it confiscates in responding to a disaster. FLA. STAT. §§ 252.43(1), 252.43(3) (2004). Yet under the traditional use of the police power in responding to an imminent danger, the state would have no obligation to pay. *See,* Nordmann v. Dep't of Agric., 473 So. 2d 278 (Fla. Dist. Ct. App. 5th 1985).

31. Florida has shown some reluctance to exercise its police power to the fullest. As one application of that power, the state arguably has the authority to vaccinate persons to prevent communicable disease. *See* Jacobson v. Mass., 197 U.S. 11 (1905). Yet parents in Florida may elect to allow their children to go without vaccinations. FLA. STAT. § 381.003(1)(e)2 (2004).

32. *See* Dudley v. Orange County, 137 So. 2d 859 (Fla. Dist. Ct. App. 2d 1962), *appeal dismissed,* 146 So. 2d 379 (Fla. 1962), *cert. denied,* 372 U.S. 959 (1963).

33. Such issues may arise when political constituencies or public agencies with ties to them request the State Coordinating Officer to relieve them of statutory or regulatory requirements that not only can be met, but that should be met to prevent future disasters from being even worse. This writer was informed during Hurricane Frances that one such interest was seeking to reconstruct its public facilities without meeting the requirements of the Florida Building Code.

34. For the state coordinating officer to relieve agricultural officials of bidding requirements on cattle auction facilities for a few weeks to enable local cattle breeders to meet a seasonal market scarcely qualifies as a step down the slippery slope to totalitarian government, but, like all other powers, it is capable of abuse. As discussed, *supra,* the danger of abuse here is more likely to come from the very interests the statute or rule was intended to regulate.

CHAPTER 8

Coordinated Federal
Emergency Responses
within the National Response Plan

by David A. Trissell and Diane Donley[1]

Introduction

The Department of Homeland Security (DHS) receives, and must react to, emergency information of a widely varying nature, ranging in levels of urgency and scope. What emergencies will look like, what triggers them, and how major they will be cannot be predicted. What is clear is that multiple incidents are likely to arise within any given time period, and they all will need to be assessed so that the department can initiate appropriate coordinated responses.

For instance, on a warm summer day, the DHS Operations Center (HSOC) receives a call from the New Jersey Emergency Operations Center alerting it to the fact that the entire eastern part of that state has suddenly lost electric power. In late summer, the HSOC is alerted—through the Emergency Preparedness and Response Directorate's (EP&R) National Response Coordination Center (NRCC)—to the frequent warnings and updates that the National Hurricane Center in Miami issues to emergency management officials in hurricane-prone areas. And when an approaching "Category III" hurricane suddenly changes course, gains tremendous momentum and wind speed, and is predicted to strike land in two hours less time than predicted, the HSOC and NRCC must react in a compressed time period to mobilize and coordinate the response of a number of federal, state, and local responders.

The HSOC may field another call from an agent with DHS's Immigration and Customs Enforcement (ICE) bureau in Galveston, Texas, confirming the interdiction of ten men on what appears to be more than immigrant smuggling allegations, and perhaps relates to some missing radioactive nuclear materials.

All of these incidents—both natural and man made—require the capacity to coordinate the information and then formulate and carry out possible responses among federal, state, and local governments, regardless of which entity will have primary responsibility for the potential event. DHS' HSOC in Washington, D.C. (in coordination with other emergency operations centers within the federal, state and local governments), receives and processes this information to assess and inform the appropriate level of support required for each incident. For the hurricane expected to hit and overwhelm several Mid-Atlantic states, DHS's EP&R (also known as the Federal Emergency Management Agency, or FEMA), is the lead federal agency. FEMA will have primary responsibility, under the Robert T. Stafford Disaster Relief and Emergency Assistance Act (Stafford Act),[2] to coordinate and provide federal assistance to state and local government disaster-relief efforts.

In the absence of additional information, the New Jersey power failure appears to be a localized incident, well within the capabilities of state or local officials to respond, but deserves monitoring by federal interests in case the event expands and spreads on the Eastern power grid, which did occur in the summer of 2002. Federal action could be required if new information regarding an increase in the incident's scope, or regarding its cause, were to be discovered. The Texas immigrant-smuggling and nuclear materials incident is potentially an incident of primary federal interest requiring responses from DHS's Borders and Transportation Security and FEMA Directorates, and, potentially, there may be a need to call on the resources of the Departments of Energy, Defense, and Justice.

While each incident involves disparate causes, conditions, and political jurisdictions—and varying degrees of potential federal involvement—every incident of national significance (that is, excluding those purely local in nature) is likely to require coordination and involvement among multiple agencies and levels of government. These situations can best be addressed if all agencies operate under one consistent over-arching framework, and the National Response Plan provides that necessary framework.

The National Response Plan (NRP)[3] was created as the core plan for national incident management, and it provides direction and consistency for federal participation in emergency incidents. The NRP has combined traditional emergency plans or other incident-specific plans (i.e., National Oil and Hazardous Substances Pollution Contingency Plan, Federal Radiological Emergency Response Plan) under the concepts and broad framework outlined by the NRP. The NRP is designed to outline the federal government's responses to and coordination of all incidents, whatever their size. For "incidents of national significance," the NRP specifies DHS as *the* single coordinator of the federal government's role in the incident. Incidents of national significance include credible threats and incidents of terrorism, major disasters and emergencies, and catastrophic events where one or more federal entities must respond to an incident. For those incidents not rising to this level—such as a state power outage or other localized incident—the NRP enables DHS to monitor the situation and provide a scalable response as the incident requires.

Role of State and Local Governments

Regardless of the federal involvement identified within the NRP, state, local, and tribal authorities remain the most likely first responders for any incident, whether or not it subsequently develops into an incident of national significance. Under their own legal authority, these entities have primary responsibility for responding to the event and, if their efforts are not sufficient, they may request federal coordination and resources. As a state's chief executive officer, its governor is primarily responsible for protecting the public safety and welfare of the people of that state or territory. For the most part, that person has extraordinary powers available to carry out these roles under state constitutions and statutes.[4] These powers include establishing curfews, suspending existing state laws and regulations, directing evacuations, creating price embargoes, and ordering quarantines.

For example, several of these measures were implemented by the state of Florida during the unprecedented string of massive hurricanes that struck Florida and the East Coast beginning in August 2004. These efforts proved to be effective, and brought under control a variety of situations that did not require any federal intervention.

States can request and obtain assistance from other states through their Emergency Management Assistance Compact. In addition, to enable local jurisdictions to respond fully to an incident, municipalities are encouraged to participate in mutual aid agreements among jurisdictions to enable resource sharing and adequate coordination. This type of intrastate coordination and planning prior to an event eases uncertainty during the first critical moments of an incident, and potentially makes dependence on scarce federal response assets less critical. Of note in this area is the recent passage of the Intelligence Reform and Terrorism Prevention Act of 2004 (IRTP Act),[5] which included a mutual aid provision for the National Capital Region (NCR). Section 7302 of the IRTP Act provides federal authority for localities within the NCR not only to enter into intrastate mutual aid agreements, but also into interstate and inter-local mutual aid agreements, consistent with state laws. The IRTP Act defines these agreements as covering "emergencies" and "public service events," and outlines the responsibilities for liability among the parties to the agreements.

The Federal Response Under
the National Response Plan (NRP)

The NRP offers a single all-hazards, coordinated, and scalable plan that works effectively to coordinate actions at the federal, state, and local government levels. Not only does this approach make sense, the law requires it. The Homeland Security Act of 2002 (HSA)[6] charged the DHS, under the guidance of the under secretary for FEMA/EP&R, with "consolidating existing Federal Government emergency response plans into a single, coordinated national response plan." Consistent with Congress's direction, Homeland Security Presidential Directive No. 5 (HSPD 5)[7] tasked the secretary of DHS with developing a "National Response Plan." Hand-in-glove with the NRP, both the HSA and HSPD 5 also require the creation of a "comprehensive national incident management system with Federal, state and local government personnel, agencies and authorities, to respond to such attacks [terrorist attack] and disasters." The National Incident Management System (NIMS)[8] provides the necessary framework of common concepts, principles, and terminology for incident command and multiagency and multijurisdictional coordination.

The NRP[9] was not created in a vacuum, but was derived with input from various sources. Those sources included federal government Emergency Support Function (ESF) leaders, as well as representatives from state and local government and the private sector. DHS held national and regional level meetings to ensure that stakeholders were kept informed about its development and the process for interagency review. At the same time, the NRP derived substantial guidance and direction from information and analysis gleaned from field exercises and actual events, including the September 11 terrorist attacks, the Anthrax letter attacks, Operation Liberty Shield, Hurricane Isabel, and the most recent Top Officials (TOPOFF) II exercise.

To facilitate its role within the NRP as the federal coordinator of major events, DHS has implemented several new, and adapted existing, emergency management tools. In addition to the NIMS and the HSOC mentioned above, these new management tools include the Interagency Incident Management Group (IIMG), Principal Federal Official (PFO), and the Joint Field Office (JFO). Additionally, the NRP includes several incident-specific annexes,[10] separate ESF annexes,[11] and Support Annexes.[12]

The NRP establishes the secretary of DHS's authority over incidents of national significance. The NRP defines "incidents of national significance" as follows: (1) credible threats of a terrorist incident or an actual terrorist event; (2) major disasters or emergencies under the Stafford Act; (3) when another federal department or agency requests DHS assistance; (4) when the president directs the DHS secretary to assume control; (5) where events involve one or more federal departments or agencies; or (6) National Special Security Events (NSSE).[13] Once such an event triggers DHS involvement, the secretary carries out his responsibility by relying on the following tools:

The Homeland Security Operations Center (HSOC)

The HSOC is the primary national hub of communications and information sharing for DHS, providing situational awareness for all domestic incident management. It also coordinates operational activities across the federal government by linking up with the various other command centers throughout the Federal government to obtain and consolidate separate intelligence reports and information. State and local operations centers also link up to the HSOC and receive, as well as disseminate, necessary information to coordinate among federal, state and local jurisdictions, including changes in the threat level, warnings, and bulletins.

The HSOC provides situational awareness and coordination ability to the IIMG. Desk officers at the HSOC provide information 24/7, and have decision-making authority on behalf of the departments and agencies they represent.

More than thirty-five agencies participate in the HSOC, ranging from state and local law enforcement to federal intelligence agencies. Law enforcement and intelligence gathering and analysis functions are linked to provide situational briefings, and issue advisories and bulletins concerning homeland security threats, as appropriate. Partners communicate with one another utilizing the Homeland Security Information Network (HSIN) and its Internet-based counterterrorism communications tool.

This tool allows communication among more than 40,000 separate state and local law enforcement agencies across the country. Another critical part of the HSOC is HSIN-Critical Infrastructure (CI), which is used to send real-time threat information to critical infrastructure owners—more than 80 percent of which are private sector entities. Also included within the HSOC are mapping and imagery capabilities. These tools map vulnerabilities against threats and then allow dissemination of this information to the most appropriate parties for action or monitoring.

The Interagency Incident Management Group (IIMG)

The IIMG is a "task-organized," senior-level group within DHS—which includes senior-level representatives from other federal, state and local governments, as well as from nongovernmental entities—meant to facilitate strategic coordination of domestic incidents. This includes receiving and reviewing threat assessments, distilling information for recommendations to the secretary of DHS, recommending resource allocations among federal entities, and providing situational awareness of any incident. The IIMG acts as an advisory board to the secretary and relevant DHS under secretaries, and can facilitate resolution of conflicts over competing requests for resources.

The IIMG is made up of several components, including the "executive staff," "core group," and "scenario-based groups." The executive staff includes a director, deputy director, and operations deputy to facilitate decision making and recommendations from the IIMG. The core group is made up of predesignated key department and agency representatives. Scenario-based groups are formed from predesignated experts in their respective fields, based on initial information about the scenario.

The IIMG aims to pull together in one place all available information from the various existing federal department-level coordination groups, so that it can advise the DHS secretary and the president on the management of domestic incidents, consistent with HSPD 5. Additionally, the IIMG receives and assists in implementation of policy decisions made by the Homeland Security Council (HSC)[14] or National Security Council (NSC)[15] deputies' or principals' meetings for those decisions relevant to the DHS's responsibilities.

The National Incident Management System (NIMS)

The NIMS provides an underlying structure for all levels of government responses to domestic incidents by defining a common set of concepts, principles, and terminology for incident command structure and multiagency coordination. NIMS establishes common principles—based on the Incident Command Structure—that: establish one chain of command at the scene of significant incidents; define roles for local, state, and federal officials; and describe how these entities interact during responses to events. NIMS provides the foundation for, "One mission, one team, one fight."

HSPD 5 requires that all federal departments and agencies adopt the NIMS and provide support to DHS in developing and maintaining the NIMS. Federal departments and agencies must use the NIMS for all domestic incident management and emergency prevention, preparedness, response, recovery, and mitigation activities. Key components of the NIMS include sharing common information among responders, ensuring consistent communications and information management during an incident, and emphasizing interoperable communications.

While the benefits of using the NIMS protocols themselves should be persuasive enough to convince jurisdictions to use them, HSPD 5 conditions the receipt of federal preparedness grants (for preventing terrorism) by state and local authorities upon compliance with NIMS. Beginning with fiscal year 2005, all federal departments and agencies were required to make adoption of the NIMS a requirement—(consistent with the law—for providing federal preparedness assistance through grants, contracts, or other activities. DHS guidelines determine compliance with the NIMS requirements.

FEMA's Emergency Management Institute (EMI) already has begun offering NIMS training, and 35,000 people have registered and taken the Internet-based three-hour course.[16] The course allows first responders to begin integrating the concepts and principles of NIMS into their own planning and policies. The goal is to build on the unified command structure to ensure consistent communication and information management so that responders and emergency managers from all different levels of government have a common operating picture to enable a consistent and efficient response. Additionally, training courses soon will be offered by FEMA's National Fire Academy and the DHS-sponsored Center for Domestic Preparedness, and, eventually, by all federal training providers.

To facilitate the NIMS concept, DHS—through FEMA—has established the National Incident Management System Integration Center (NIC). Located at FEMA's headquarters in Washington, D.C., the center supports state and local response agencies—such as fire, police, emergency response, etc.—in their adoption of the NIMS model. This support includes training on the fundamental concepts and definitions of the NIMS, not only to state and local emergency responders, but to federal responders as well. The NIC will include a team of advisors from all areas of emergency response, including the fire service, emergency medical services, law enforcement, and emergency management communities.

The NIC is divided into several different branches, including the "standards and resources branch," "training and exercises branch," "system evaluation and compliance branch," "technology, research and development branch," and "publications management branch." The NIC is being created in two phases. The initial phase has been completed and includes establishing, coordinating, and monitoring work groups with cross-DHS, interagency, and multijurisdictional participation. The start-up work also includes coordinating and providing initial guidance and tools to federal, state, and local entities on understanding, implementing, and complying with the NIMS. Initial work also involves establishing a NIC Advisory Committee and developing and delivering NIMS awareness training, education, and publications.

The second phase of the NIC implementation will include increasing staffing, refining of processes, and integrating all NIC roles and responsibilities consistent with the NIMS. These types of activities include developing and publishing standardized templates to support the implementation and refinement of NIMS; establishing and maintaining a publications management system for NIMS supporting documents; promoting compatibility between national-level standards for NIMS and other standards developed by private, public, or other groups; and developing national standards and protocols for qualification and certification of emergency responders and incident management personnel, as necessary.

Principal Federal Official (PFO) and Joint Field Office (JFO)

HSPD 5 designates the secretary of DHS as the "principal federal official" (PFO) for domestic incident management during incidents of national significance. The PFO provides strategic-level information and guidance to federal entities, facilitates resolution of interagency jurisdictional disputes, and coordinates response resource needs as required by multiple events and multijurisdictional responses. The PFO does not, however, replace the existing primary coordinator of federal operational assets and resources—the "federal coordinating officer" (FCO)—who provides direction and coordination of federal assets during a presidentially declared disaster or emergency under the Stafford Act.

The Joint Field Office (JFO) is a temporary facility established to coordinate federal assistance to affected jurisdictions during incidents of national significance. The JFO replaces FEMA's Disaster Field Office (DFO) in instances of a declared disaster or emergency. It provides a flexible design that adapts to the particular size of the incident, consistent with the NIMS Incident Command Structure (ICS). For an incident involving potential terrorism activities, plus response and recovery efforts led by FEMA, the JFO also coordinates the Federal Bureau of Investigation's actions, managed through the Joint Operations Center.

Funding Mechanisms

An event declared a "major disaster or emergency" by the president under the Stafford Act becomes eligible to receive funding from the Disaster Relief

Fund administered by FEMA. FEMA traditionally assigns tasks directly to appropriate federal agencies or departments for disaster-related work, and then pays for the costs associated with the work from the federal Disaster Relief Fund.[17] In advance of an impending disaster or emergency, limited funds are available to pre-deploy federal resources so that they can respond as soon as the calamity strikes in an effort to minimize loss of life and property. Absent a Stafford Act declaration, funding for federal response or coordination efforts must be obtained through alternative means, including under the Economy Act,[18] under the authority of the responding agency or department, or through interagency agreements or memoranda of understanding.

A "financial management annex" is included within the NRP that will identify procedures and funds available to pay for federal, state, and local operations. Without legislative changes, however, most of the funding requirements—outside a Stafford Act declaration—will need to be met through memoranda of understanding, interagency agreements, or other traditional funding arrangements under the Economy Act.

Under the NRP, after a Stafford Act emergency or disaster declaration, the DHS secretary has been delegated the president's authority to task federal departments and agencies—with or without reimbursement—to perform certain functions in support of the federal government's response. Therefore, even without an available funding mechanism, DHS has authority to direct agencies to perform tasks to meet emergency needs.

Military Responses for Civil Incidents and Limitations

HSPD 5 and the NRP both recognize the special status of the secretary of defense, the attorney general, and the secretary of state, with respect to their roles in providing emergency responses at the federal level.[19] With respect to the Department of Defense (DoD) in particular, its authorities relative to assistance for civil situations are limited, and its authorities are contained within a variety of statutes. The outline below offers a general and cursory summary of some of the important DoD-related statutes, as well as general conclusions about their relationship to the HSA, the Stafford Act, and HSPD 5, including the Posse Comitatus Act,[20] which generally limits the DoD's involvement in law enforcement. Other authorities that reference the DoD provide specific exceptions to the Posse Comitatus Act.

The Posse Comitatus Act (PCA)

The Posse Comitatus Act (PCA) prohibits the use of the Army or the Air Force for law enforcement purposes, except as otherwise authorized by the Constitution or a statute. This prohibition also applies to Navy and Marine Corps personnel, as a matter of DoD policy. The PCA's primary prohibition is against direct involvement by active-duty military personnel (including reservists on active duty and National Guard personnel in federal service) in traditional law enforcement activities (including interdiction of vehicles, vessels, aircraft, or other similar activity; a search or seizure; or an arrest, apprehension, stop and frisk, or similar activity). Originally passed in 1878, the purpose of this section was to end the use of federal troops to police state elections in ex-Confederate states where civil power had been reestablished. However, case law regarding the PCA has established the following parameters regarding appropriate civil use of DoD assets:

- It does not violate the PCA to use Army equipment and material, as appropriate, to assist civilian authorities.[21]
- The omission of the Navy and Marine Corps does not constitute congressional approval for their involvement in enforcing civilian laws.[22]
- If involvement of the military is indirect, a civilian agency was in command of a drug surveillance and search operation, and if the civilian agency instructed other agents about the extent of their participation, no violation of PCA occurred.[23]
- The president's authority to use federal troops under 10 U.S.C. §§ 332-333 to enforce federal authority where judicial proceedings are impracticable, or where the president determines it is necessary to suppress domestic violence or insurrection, is not impaired by the PCA.[24]

DoD-Related Authorities

Independently, DoD has several additional authorities available for providing emergency-response support in civilian situations. For example:

The Economy Act[25] authorizes federal agencies to provide goods or services *on a reimbursable basis* to other federal agencies when more specific statutory authority to do so does not exist.

The National Emergencies Act of 1976[26] establishes procedures for presidential declaration and termination of national emergencies. The act requires the president to identify the specific provision of law under which he will act in dealing with a declared national emergency, and contains a sunset provision requiring the president to renew a declaration of national emergency to prevent its automatic expiration. The presidential declaration of a national emergency under the act is a prerequisite to exercising any statutory special or extraordinary powers in the event of a national emergency. *The Insurrection Statutes*[27] recognize that the primary responsibility for protecting life and property, and maintaining law and order in the civilian community, is vested in state and local governments. The Insurrection Statutes authorize the president to direct the armed forces to enforce the law to suppress insurrections and domestic violence. Military forces may be used to restore order, prevent looting, and engage in other law enforcement activities. When this specific statutory authority is activated, the Posse Comitatus Act does not apply to such civil disturbance missions.

The Defense Against Weapons of Mass Destruction (WMD) Act[28] is intended to enhance the federal government's capability to prevent and respond to terrorist incidents involving WMD. Congress has directed that DoD provide: certain expert advice to federal, state, and local agencies with regard to WMD; domestic terrorism rapid response teams; training in emergency response for the use or threat of use of WMD; and a program for testing and improving the response of civil agencies to biological and chemical emergencies. This authority is provided, however, only if such assistance will not adversely "affect military preparedness or adversely affect national security."[29]

Emergencies Involving Chemical or Biological Weapons. Pursuant to 10 U.S.C. § 382, in response to an emergency involving biological or chemical WMD that is beyond the capabilities of civilian authorities to handle, the attorney general may request DoD assistance directly. Assistance to be provided can include monitoring, containing, disabling, and disposing of the weapon, as well as direct law enforcement assistance that would otherwise violate the Posse Comitatus Act. Among other factors, such assistance must be considered necessary for the immediate protection of human life.

Emergencies Involving Nuclear Materials. 18 U.S.C. § 831(e) authorizes the attorney general to request DoD law enforcement assistance—including the authority to arrest and conduct searches—notwithstanding the prohibitions of the Posse Comitatus Act—when both the attorney general and the secretary of defense agree that an "emergency situation" exists, and the secretary of defense determines that the requested assistance will not impede military readiness. An emergency situation involving nuclear material is defined as a circumstance that poses a serious threat to the United States in which (1) enforcement of the law would be seriously impaired if the assistance were not provided, and (2) civilian law enforcement personnel are not capable of enforcing the law. In addition, the statute authorizes DoD personnel to engage in "such other activity as is incident to the enforcement of this section, or to the protection of persons or property from conduct that violates this section."

(a) Authorization for Use of Military Force. With respect to activities linked to al Qaeda, 50 U.S.C. § 1541 gives the president the authority to "use all necessary and appropriate force against those nations, organizations, or persons he determines planned, authorized, committed, or aided the terrorist attacks that occurred on September 11, 2001, or harbored such organizations or persons, in order to prevent any future acts of international terrorism against the United States by such nations, organizations, or persons."

Conclusion

The NRP has been signed by all participating entities. During the first 120 days of the implementation process (Phase I), the Initial National Response Plan, Federal Response Plan, U.S. Government Domestic Terrorism Concept of Operations Plan (CONPLAN), and the Federal Radiological Emergency Response Plan (FRERP) will remain in effect. Phase I (first 60 days) of the implementation will involve a transitional period for departments and agencies to modify training, designate staffing for NRP organizational elements, and become familiar with NRP concepts and processes. Phase II (60 to 120 days) of the implementation involves modification of existing federal interagency plans to make them consistent with the NRP and conduct necessary training and certification. Phase III (120 days to 1 year) allows for full implementation of the NRP, requiring assessments of NRP coordinating structures and procedures during exercises, incidents of national significance and National Special Security Events (NSSE). Following this initial phase-in period, DHS will conduct a one-year review to assess the implementation period and make recommendations to the secretary on necessary NRP revisions. Thereafter, the NRP will undergo review and reissuance every four years.

While the NRP is just beginning to be implemented, the benefits from this overarching plan for emergency response at the federal response level are just becoming evident. Already, through exercises and some real-life incidents, components of the NRP have successfully guided federal, state, and local responders and emergency managers in responding to events involving all levels of emergency response.

NOTES

1. The views and opinions expressed in this chapter are those of the authors alone, and do not reflect the official position of the Department of Homeland Security.

2. 42 U.S.C. §§ 5121-5206 (2005).

3. The National Response Plan—signed by all cabinet departments of the federal government and several other agencies and organizations—was released in final form on Nov. 16, 2004. *See,* http://www.dhs.gov/dhspublic/display?theme=14&content=4264.

4. For example, the governor of Florida has the following powers upon declaration of a state of emergency: the authority to suspend the effect of any statute, rule, ordinance, or order of any state, regional, or local governmental entity as needed to cope with the disaster; to direct all state, regional and local governmental agencies, including law enforcement agencies; to confiscate any private property needed to meet the disaster; and to order the evacuation of all persons from any part of the state and regulate the movement of persons and traffic within the state. FLA. STAT. § 252.36(5) (2004)

5. Pub. L. No. 108-458, 118 Stat. 3638 (2004).

6. Pub. L. No. 107-296, 116 Stat. 2229 (2002).

7. President Bush issued Homeland Security Presidential Directive 5 (HSPD 5) on Feb. 28, 2003. *See,* http://www.whitehouse.gov/news/releases/2003/02/20030228-9.html.

8. NIMS was issued in March 2004. *See,* http://www.dhs.gov/interweb/assetlibrary/NIMS-90-web.pdf.

9. NRP was issued on Nov. 16, 2004. *See,* http://www.dhs.gov/dhspublic/display?theme=14&content=4264.

10. The incident-specific annexes that have been established include: Biological Incident; Catastrophic Incident; Cyber Incident; Food and Agriculture Incident (pending); Nuclear/Radiological Incident; Oil and Hazardous Materials Incident; Terrorism Incident Law Enforcement and Investigation.

11. The ESF annexes are: ESF #1—Transportation; ESF #2—Communications; ESF #3—Public Works and Engineering; ESF #4—Firefighting; ESF #5—Emergency Management; ESF #6—Mass Care, Housing, and Human Services; ESF #7—Resource Support; ESF #8—Public Health and Medical Services; ESF #9—Urban Search and Rescue; ESF #10—Oil and Hazardous Materials Response; ESF #11—Agriculture and Natural Resources; ESF #12—Energy; ESF #13—Public Safety and Security; ESF #14—Long-term Community Recovery and Mitigation; ESF #15—External Affairs.

12. Support annexes have been established in the following areas: Financial Management; International Coordination; Logistics Management; Private-Sector Coordination; Public Affairs; Science and Technology; Tribal Relations; Volunteer and Donations Management; and Worker Safety and Health.

13. NSSEs are defined in NRP, *supra*, at 70. NRP provides further descriptions of federal roles and responsibilities at 8-21.

14. DHS has produced a fact sheet about HSC. *See*, http://www.dhs.gov/dhspublic/display?content=347.

15. A description of NSC is available online. *See*, http://www.whitehouse.gov/nsc.

16. The NIMS training site is http://training.fema.gov/EMIWEB/IS/is700.asp.

17. The Disaster Relief Fund contains no-year money appropriated by Congress to pay for response and recovery measures taken under authority of the Stafford Act.

18. 31 U.S.C.A. §§ 1535-1536.

19. *See*, HSPD 5, at ¶¶ 8, 9 & 10.

20. 18 U.S.C. § 1385.

21. U.S. v. Red Feather, 392 F. Supp. 916 (D.S.D. 1975).

22. U.S. v. Chon, 210 F.3d 990 (9th Cir. 2000).

23. U.S. v. Hitchcock, 103 F. Supp. 1226 (D. Hawaii 1999). *See also*, U.S. v. Red Feather, 392 F. Supp. 916 (D. S.D. 1975) (passive role of federal troops permitted).

24. 41 Op. Att'y Gen 331 (1957). *See also*, The Insurrection Statutes discussed *infra*.

25. 31 U.S.C. §§ 1535-1536.

26. 50 U.S.C. §§ 1601-1651 (2005).

27. 10 U.S.C. §§ 331-334.

28. 50 U.S.C. §§ 2301-2369 (2005).

29. 50 U.S.C. § 2312(d)(3).

CHAPTER 9

Marshalling Resources

by Alan Cohn

Introduction

Success in responding to a major incident depends on effective preincident marshalling of resources through mutual aid relationships and other intergovernmental agreements for emergency management and response. This chapter discusses various methods by which state and local governments can accomplish this goal. This chapter also discusses common legal pitfalls encountered in marshalling resources.[1]

Mutual Aid Issues Are Complicated

It is tempting to assume that when disaster strikes, the resources needed to respond effectively can be summoned and put to use relatively easily. However, prior preparation is essential in order effectively to access and deploy resources during a major incident. Specifically, mutual aid agreements, interstate compacts, and other types of intergovernmental agreements for emergency management and response are necessary. Each of these arrangements pose complicated issues of state and local government law and authority, as well as related issues such as municipal liability, indemnification, and employee benefits.

The basic intergovernmental agreement for emergency response is the mutual aid agreement. Mutual aid agreements can and should be scalable, able to address routine day-to-day requests for assistance as well as larger-scale response to major incidents. Legal issues relating to mutual aid agreements are discussed in this chapter, and attention to detail is essential in structuring mutual aid relationships. In addition to basic mutual aid agreements, there are a number of other arrangements for emergency management and response, including interstate compacts, statewide mutual aid legislation, and direct agreements among multiple layers of government. A number of these arrangements are discussed in this chapter as well. Jurisdictions are encouraged to review the benefits and pitfalls associated with each of these arrangements, and to structure intergovernmental agreements for emergency management and response that best meet the needs of the jurisdiction, facilitating operational effectiveness while minimizing legal and financial risk.

The Role of the State and Local Government Lawyer

The state or local government lawyer plays a crucial role in helping governmental agencies navigate the issues presented by emergency preparedness and response. The state or local government lawyer also can play a key role in creating functional models for intergovernmental coordination and cooperation before a major incident. This includes:

- Understanding the sources and limitations of state and local government authority to prepare for and respond to catastrophic incidents.
- Knowing federal, state, and local statutes, regulations, and ordinances governing emergency preparedness and response, including those involving intergovernmental cooperation, hazardous materials response, and terrorism.
- Assisting in the construction of lines of authority for emergency preparedness and response that are consistent with both applicable legal authorities and identified operational prerogatives.
- Mediating among competing factions, either within a single jurisdiction (police, fire and rescue, emergency medical services) or among different jurisdictions or different levels of government (federal, state, local, county, etc.).
- Understanding workers' compensation and tort liability issues, including the workers' compensation exclusive remedy provision, the boundaries and limits of sovereign immunity, and applicable tort claims statutes.
- Addressing interoperability issues—including interoperable communications and equipment issues—that require interpretation of legal standards and rulings.
- Making sure that legal issues do not hamstring emergency operations, while ensuring that arrangements for emergency operations minimize the legal risk to participating jurisdictions.[2]

Because all of these issues can come into play during the drafting and negotiation of mutual aid agreements and other intergovernmental arrangements for emergency preparedness and response, it is critical for state and local government lawyers to understand these issues and bring this understanding to the drafting and negotiating process. It is also critical for these same lawyers to be prepared to assist with the implementation of these agreements in the event of a catastrophic incident.

The Need for Intergovernmental Cooperation

The Imperatives for Intergovernmental Cooperation

No single governmental agency or entity is equipped to respond to all possible incidents—especially large-scale incidents—that might occur within its jurisdiction. Likewise, each jurisdiction must be prepared to contribute its resources to local, regional, and statewide response efforts. Mutual aid relationships and other intergovernmental arrangements for emergency preparedness and response are essential to fulfilling a governmental entity's preparedness obligations.

Intergovernmental and interdisciplinary cooperation is also becoming a legal requirement.[3] For example, the fiscal year 2004 guidance for the Office for Domestic Preparedness (ODP) Homeland Security Grant Program specifically explains that "[s]tates are encouraged to employ regional approaches to planning and preparedness and to adopt regional response structures whenever appropriate" to meet identified homeland security needs.[4] Moreover, states are required to report to ODP the establishment and maintenance of mutual aid agreements.[5] Indeed, legislation was introduced in the 108th Congress mandating intergovernmental and interdisciplinary cooperation, and encouraging regional cooperation and preparedness efforts.[6]

Incident Command Structures Encourage Intergovernmental Cooperation

In order to understand mutual aid arrangements, it is helpful to understand the concept of standardized incident management systems, which form the underpinning of multijurisdictional incident response. Standardized incident management systems were developed over the years for response to major incidents such as wildfires.

The primary example of a standardized incident management system is the Incident Command System (ICS), developed in the 1970's by firefighting and emergency management agencies in the state of California, and later transitioned to a national model called the National Interagency Incident Management System (NIIMS).[7] The ICS is "the combination of facilities, equipment, personnel, procedures, and communications operating within a common organizational structure, designed to aid in domestic incident management activities."[8] The ICS is organized around five functional areas: command, operations, planning, logistics, and finance.[9]

Homeland Security Presidential Directive 5 and the National Incident Management System

In February 2003, President George W. Bush issued Homeland Security Presidential Directive 5 (HSPD 5), which mandates intergovernmental cooperation for major incident response. A cornerstone of this national approach to domestic incident management outlined in HSPD 5 is the National Incident

Management System (NIMS). The NIMS is "a consistent nationwide approach for Federal, State, and local governments to work effectively and efficiently together to prepare for, respond to, and recover from domestic incidents, regardless of cause, size, or complexity."[10] The NIMS "uses a systems approach to integrate the best of existing processes and methods into a unified national framework for incident management . . . It does this through a core set of concepts, principles, procedures, organizational processes, terminology, and standards requirements applicable to a broad community of NIMS users."[11] The NIMS focuses on six elements: command and management; preparedness; resource management; communications and information management; supporting technologies; and ongoing management and maintenance.

With respect to the command and management element, the NIMS is grounded in three separate systems: the ICS; multiagency coordination systems; and public information systems.[12] The ICS is used for scalable, flexible command of discrete incidents.[13] Area command also is contemplated, which is a method for coordinating multiple site incidents, each with its own ICS structure.[14] Use of the ICS permits the authority having jurisdiction over the incident to retain command and control, while accessing the resources of local, state, and federal agencies through mutual aid agreements and other mechanisms. Multiagency coordination systems provide interjurisdictional and interdisciplinary support for incident operations.[15]

The NIMS recognizes that "[p]reparedness is the responsibility of individual jurisdictions; this responsibility includes coordinating various preparedness activities among all appropriate agencies within a jurisdiction, as well as across jurisdictions and with private organizations."[16] Successful adoption of the NIMS by every jurisdiction in the United States is essential to ensure that multijurisdictional incident response functions smoothly.

Under HSPD 5, all federal departments and agencies are directed to adopt the NIMS, and use it in their "domestic incident management and emergency prevention, preparedness, response, recovery, and mitigation activities, as well as those actions taken in support of State or local entities."[17] HSPD 5 also requires that "[b]eginning in Fiscal Year 2005, Federal departments and agencies shall make adoption of the NIMS a requirement, to the extent permitted by law, for providing Federal preparedness assistance through grants, contracts, or other activities," and directs the Secretary of Homeland Security to "develop standards and guidelines to determine whether a State or local entity has adopted the NIMS."[18] DHS already has explained that this requirement will apply to the receipt of ODP grant funds beginning in fiscal year 2005.[19] Therefore, state and local governments will be required to implement the NIMS as part of their all-hazards preparedness efforts, including their preparedness for acts of terrorism.[20]

Intergovernmental Agreements for Emergency Preparedness and Response

This section discusses several major legal issues that arise in the context of mutual aid arrangements, including authority, compensation for injuries, liability to responders, and liability to third parties. These issues are discussed in the context of various types of mutual aid arrangements.

Operational Mutual Aid Agreements

GENERALLY. Mutual aid agreements form the basis for public safety cooperation on a day-to-day basis. These agreements can be between neighboring jurisdictions, among all jurisdictions in a particular region, among all jurisdictions statewide, between jurisdictions in different states, and between various levels of government (local, state, federal, and tribal). Moreover, these agreements can be intended for both day-to-day and major incident response. The defining feature of what I characterize as an "operational" mutual aid agreement, however, is that the mutual aid arrangement is intended to function first and foremost on a day-to-day basis, and not just in response to declared disasters or emergencies.[21]

PITFALLS WITH OPERATIONAL MUTUAL AID AGREEMENTS. There are numerous legal issues that can arise with respect to operational mutual aid agreements. The most important issues involve authority, compensation for injuries, liability to responders, liability to third parties and governmental immunity, and indemnification and reimbursement.

Authority. State and local governments in virtually all instances possess sufficient authority to enter into intergovernmental agreements for emergency preparedness and response, either through state constitutions, local government home rule charters, general legislative grants of authority, or specific emergency management statutes. However, it is important to ensure that local jurisdictions have the authority not only to enter into agreements, but to agree to provide the specific types of assistance contemplated in the agreement under the conditions set forth. It is also important that an individual with authority to bind the local jurisdiction actually sign the agreement.

Many states specifically authorize operational mutual aid agreements. For example, the Alaska Disaster Act encourages local governments to enter into operational mutual aid agreements, and indeed grants the governor authority to compel local governments to enter into mutual aid agreements if necessary.[22] The Kansas Emergency Preparedness for Disasters Act permits the governor to require two or more counties "to participate and enter into an interjurisdictional agreement or arrangement" if the governor finds:

> (1) such counties, or the cities therein, have equipment, supplies and forces which are necessary to provide mutual aid on a regional basis; and

> (2) such counties have not made adequate provisions in their disaster emergency plans for the rendering and receipt of mutual aid for the emergency management needs of the entire region.[23]

Other states place requirements on jurisdictions entering into operational mutual aid agreements. For example, Maryland law requires that mutual aid agreements concerning law enforcement services contain a provision requiring the requesting jurisdiction to defend and indemnify officers from the responding jurisdiction.[24]

Certain states also authorize interstate operational mutual aid agreements. Rhode Island law authorizes the governor to enter into agreements with bordering states for law enforcement mutual aid.[25] Likewise, local police chiefs may enter into mutual aid agreements with local governments in other states that border Rhode Island.[26] Wyoming law provides similar authority for mutual aid agreements across state lines with respect to fire protection, emergency medical services, emergency management, and other emergency-response capabilities.[27]

Compensation for injuries. Public safety agencies are responsible for providing workers' compensation coverage to employees, including employees who take part in emergency responses across jurisdictional lines. A common issue in mutual aid arrangements is which jurisdiction ultimately will be responsible for workers' compensation claims brought as a result of injuries sustained on mutual aid responses. Questions may arise regarding which jurisdiction—responding or requesting—has primary responsibility for such claims, and whether a requesting jurisdiction may be obligated to indemnify a responding jurisdiction for the cost of any claims, either based on provisions of the mutual aid agreement or by operation of state law. Parties to mutual aid agreements carefully must consider issues relating to workers' compensation, and should structure such agreements accordingly.

Under a typical state workers' compensation statute, an employee is automatically entitled to certain benefits when the employee suffers an injury or illness arising out of and in the course of employment. In exchange for this automatic entitlement, the employee and his or her dependents give up their right to bring suit against the employer under common law for negligence or other cause of action; this is known as an "exclusive remedy" provision.[28] In some circumstances, more than one employer can become responsible for workers' compensation, such as when an employee of one employer is lent to, or borrowed by, another employer. In this situation, the lending employer is considered the "general employer" and the borrowing employer is considered a "special employer" (the employee sometimes being referred to as a "borrowed servant").[29] In several states, statutory provisions also identify categories of second employers who become "statutory employers" of another employer's employees.[30] In either case, the result is typically the same; the general employer and the special or statutory employer both become liable for workers' compensation claims filed by the employee.

Some states' mutual aid authorizing legislation may control the determination of whether the firefighter is an employee of the requesting jurisdiction. For example, in *Lauria v. Borough of Ridgefield*,[31] a responding jurisdiction sought reimbursement for a workers' compensation claim filed by one of its firefighters for an injury suffered while responding to a mutual aid call. The court noted that New Jersey law authorized local governments to enter into mutual aid agreements, which could, but were not required to, include provisions providing for reimbursement of payments lawfully made to a firefighter's dependents.[32] Because the mutual aid agreement in question included no such provision, the responding jurisdiction could not obtain reimbursement from the requesting jurisdiction.[33] By contrast, courts in other states have found that an injury suffered while responding to a mutual aid call is chargeable to the receiving jurisdiction even where the receiving jurisdiction refused the offered assistance from the responding jurisdiction.[34]

Liability to responders. As noted above, workers' compensation statutes generally include an "exclusive remedy" provision, barring tort suits by employees against their employers for negligence or other causes of action as the result of a workplace injury or illness; such protection typically extends to special and statutory employers as well as general employers. In the absence of a state statute specifically applying to mutual aid arrangements, local jurisdictions should structure mutual aid arrangements to clarify whether responders should be considered special employees or borrowed servants of a requesting jurisdiction, as appropriate, for both workers' compensation and tort liability purposes.

In the absence of provisions in the mutual aid agreement itself, there is division among the courts as to whether a firefighter responding to a mutual aid call in another jurisdiction is a "special employee" or "borrowed servant" for tort liability purposes. Some courts have pointed to the mutual aid agreement as evidence that the firefighter responding to a mutual aid call was acting solely as an employee of the responding jurisdiction in the fulfillment of its duties, and not as a special employee of the requesting jurisdiction.[35] Other courts, however, have found to the contrary.

For example, in *Enslow v. United States*,[36] a California Department of Forestry and Fire Protection (CDF) firefighter was killed on a U.S. Forest Service (USFS) fire in the Mendocino National Forest. The CDF firefighter's minor child brought suit against the USFS under the Federal Tort Claims Act (FTCA) for failing adequately to supervise and provide for the safety of the firefighters.[37] The district court granted summary judgment in favor of the USFS, concluding that the CDF firefighter was a "special employee" of the USFS because the mutual aid arrangement contemplated general supervision of CDF resources by the USFS, and therefore workers' compensation provided the sole remedy for injuries resulting from the accident.[38] However, the court of appeals reversed the district court's grant of summary judgment, holding that in order to be deemed a special employer, the USFS must have "actually exercised control over the *details* of the person's work."[39]

By contrast, in *Roma v. United States*,[40] a local volunteer firefighter who suffered injuries while fighting a fire at a U.S. Navy facility was found to be a "paradigmatic example of a special employee."[41] The volunteer fire department responded to a mutual aid call from a Naval Air Engineering Station (NAES) fire department pursuant to a mutual aid agreement. The naval facility's fire department, utilizing the ICS, placed the volunteer fire department's resources into the ICS under the general command of the NAES fire department incident commander.[42] The court found that, in those circumstances, the volunteer firefighter was a "special employee" of the NAES fire department during the fire, and therefore the volunteer firefighter's claim against the federal government for negligent instruction was barred by the exclusive remedy provision of New Jersey workers' compensation statute.[43]

Liability to third parties. Both requesting and responding jurisdictions may face liability concerns with respect to third parties as a result of mutual aid arrangements.[44] Governmental immunity will provide local governments with some degree of protection. This may be the same immunity that local governments generally possess, or specific immunity conferred by state emergency management statutes.[45] Local jurisdictions should take care to craft mutual aid arrangements to maximize the protection provided by governmental immunity.

A state may retain governmental immunity either in full or in part, or may waive governmental immunity. Where governmental immunity is retained in part, one of two different tests is typically used to determine whether the government is immune from suit: the "governmental function" test; and the "discretionary action" test.[46] Under the governmental function test, whole classes of activities are immunized from potential tort liability where they are "considered to be traditionally or inherently governmental in nature."[47] Under the discretionary function test, a particular act of a governmental official is immunized if it "involves an element of choice, and if the choice involves applying judgment of a sort deemed worthy of protection from suit."[48]

In jurisdictions applying the governmental function test, elements of emergency response—such as firefighting, public safety, and law enforcement—generally are considered exempt.[49] In jurisdictions applying discretionary function analysis, however, courts are more likely to entertain tort suits complaining of the methods by which emergency response activities are conducted.[50] Commentator Ken Lerner identifies four categories of governmental emergency preparedness and response activities to which tort liability might attach: planning (lack of plan or flawed plan); plan implementation (failure to follow plan); executive-level decision making (poor decision); and street-level operations (operational error).[51] Each of these is discussed briefly below.

- *Planning.* Lerner speculates that neither a jurisdiction's lack of an emergency plan, nor the drafting of a flawed plan, would be actionable as a nondiscretionary function.[52] However, recent developments call into question whether a jurisdiction's decision not to draft a homeland security or emergency management plan, especially a large jurisdiction with significant emergency response obligations, is in fact discretionary. Especially given that local jurisdictions must adopt the NIMS as a condition of receipt of federal funding, in the current environment courts may not protect a jurisdiction's decision not to adopt or properly promulgate an emergency plan, or to implement the NIMS and its elements, including ICS.
- *Plan implementation.* Lerner posits that the failure to follow a mandatory aspect of a disaster plan may be actionable as a nondiscretionary func-

tion, while the failure to follow advisory aspects of the plan would not.[53] Therefore, Lerner cautions that framers of disaster plans should consider whether specific elements of the plan should be mandatory or advisory.[54] In addition, drafters of emergency plans may consider advisory plans more advantageous for operational reasons. Since no plan can set out mandatory responses to every conceivable disaster or emergency, the best plan may place an emphasis on establishing a management structure capable of improvisational problem-solving in the face of unforeseen events.

- *Executive-level decision making.* Lerner concludes that executive-level decision making in response to a crisis is a paradigmatic example of discretionary decision making.[55] In support of this conclusion, Lerner points to two cases involving the evacuation of residents and building owners in anticipation of the eruption of Mount St. Helen in Washington State in 1980. One case addressed allegations that the governor was negligent in designating evacuation zones that were too small, and the other addressed allegations that the evacuation zones were too large.[56] In both cases, Washington state courts held that the governor's designation of the zones were exercises of discretion entitled to immunity.[57] This conclusion is likely to hold true today.

- *Street-level operations.* With respect to decision making by incident commanders and other management and supervisory personnel, the area of contention arises in situations where "personnel at the operational level are acting without specific mandatory instructions covering the action in question."[58] In this regard, Lerner points out that courts are split. Some courts have held that street-level decisions concerning emergency operations or firefighting methods are immune exercises in discretion.[59] However, as Lerner acknowledges, courts in other states have held the opposite. For example, in *Invest Cast, Inc. v. City of Blaine,*[60] the Minnesota Court of Appeals held that a suit could proceed based on various operational decisions made on the fire ground. The court stated:

> [T]he fire department's decision on how many firefighter personnel and trucks to send to a fire is a policy decision protected as a discretionary function. How the firefighter personnel actually fight the fire, however, is not within the discretionary function exception. The underlying purpose of the discretionary function exception to municipal liability would not be furthered by allowing immunity for negligent firefighting methods.[61]

Similarly, in *Commerce & Industry Ins. Co. v. Grinnell Corp.,*[62] the court rejected a local government's claim of discretionary function immunity, finding that firefighters had failed to follow specific regulations and fire department procedures.

In those jurisdictions where emergency response methods are subject to examination as nondiscretionary functions, perceived failure to properly implement the ICS or other standardized incident management systems can give rise to liability. For this reason, local governments should not conclude automatically that the implementation and operation of a standardized incident management system constitutes a function covered by traditional governmental immunity. For example, in *Buttram v. United States*,[63] two volunteer firefighters were killed fighting a wild land fire (referred to as the Point Fire) after their department, the Kuna Rural Fire District (Kuna RFD), offered their services to the U.S. Department of the Interior, Bureau of Land Management (BLM). The BLM implemented the ICS in fighting the Point Fire, and included the Kuna RFD personnel under this command structure.[64]

The court found that both BLM and the Kuna RFD owed duties to the deceased firefighters, which were breached and resulted in the firefighters' deaths. Based on the BLM's command of the Point Fire and utilization of the ICS, the court found that BLM owed the deceased firefighters the duty to ensure that the deceased firefighters were "assigned duties commensurate with their experience"; to "fully instruct" the volunteers concerning the nature of the fire, fuel and weather conditions, and safety conditions; to ensure that any warnings issued on the fire were received by all firefighters fighting the fire; and to ensure that all firefighters assigned to the fire acted in accordance with any warnings.[65] The court found that Kuna RFD owed the two firefighters the duty to exercise reasonable care to protect the two firefighters from foreseeable hazards in fighting the fire. The court specifically found that "[t]his duty continues even after [the BLM IC] assigned duties to [the two firefighters] and the two volunteers began working the fire line."[66] The court found both BLM and Kuna RFD liable for the deaths of the firefighters.

- *Contractual provisions intended to avoid liability to third parties.* Contractual provisions alone may not limit liability to third parties. For example, in *Heil v. United States*,[67] a landowner brought suit for damages after firefighters cut four miles of fire line on the landowner's property during firefighting efforts on a USFS fire in Colorado. The USFS contended that it was immune from liability pursuant to the terms of the federal-state-local wild land firefighting agreement, which stated that when federal personnel "are suppressing wildfires on lands for which the State is responsible, the United States shall not be liable to the State or any landowner for any damage in consequence of the performance of the work under this section of the agreement."[68] The court held that while the agreement may have apportioned responsibility among the federal, state, and local governments, this had no effect on the federal government's responsibility under the FTCA because the plaintiff was not a party to the agreement.[69]

Indemnification and Reimbursement. Local jurisdictions should be sure to specify whether the parties to a mutual aid agreement will indemnify one another for negligent acts committed by their own employees, or whether the requesting jurisdiction will reimburse the responding jurisdiction for its costs incurred in responding. Typically, jurisdictions hold one another harmless for negligent acts incurred during mutual aid responses, and do not seek reimbursement from requesting jurisdictions absent unusual circumstances. However, state or local law may govern whether local jurisdictions must include such provisions in their agreements.

Some mutual aid agreements include a clause that converts an ordinarily non-reimbursable response into a reimbursable one after a certain period of time, such as responses that last more than twelve hours. Such a conversion clause makes the mutual aid response non-reimbursable if it lasts fewer than twelve hours, but reimbursable (either in full or just for the part after the first twelve hours) once the response exceeds twelve hours.[70] Conversion clauses help jurisdictions distinguish between routine non-compensable assistance and extraordinary compensable costs.

A Sample Operational Mutual Aid Agreement. One example of a successful local-to-local mutual aid agreement involving multiple jurisdictions is the Northern Virginia Emergency Service Mutual Response Agreement (NOVA Agreement).[71] The NOVA Agreement is an agreement between Arlington County, the city of Alexandria, the city of Fairfax, Fairfax County, and the United States Army Base at Ft. Belvoir, for fire/rescue and related services.[72] Provisions of the agreement include the following:

- The parties agree to exchange fire suppression, emergency medical services, hazardous materials response, technical rescue, and/or "other disaster-related types of emergency services." The parties also agree to exchange other services pursuant to the agreement "if mutually agreed upon by the parties."
- The parties agree to participate in a mutual response system that "will automatically dispatch the most appropriate response resource(s) available, to an incident location, without regard to jurisdictional boundary lines." This is known as an "automatic aid" provision. To facilitate this and avoid confusion, apparatus from participating jurisdictions are given unique numerical identifiers that are common across jurisdictional boundaries. So, for example, Fairfax County Station 5's engine is Engine 405 (4 for Fairfax County, 05 for Station 5); Arlington County Station 5's engine is Engine 105.
- Each party to the agreement retains primary jurisdiction for "determining the most appropriate response resources to be utilized within its jurisdiction."
- Each party's dispatch center is to "maintain direct links to the other communications centers within the Northern Virginia region."
- All tactical units and personnel responding to mutual aid calls are required to "operate in accordance with the Incident Command System." Incidents are "under the command of the first arriving officer on scene, regardless of jurisdiction, until command is assumed by an officer of appropriate rank from the jurisdiction in which the incident is located."
- Each party agrees to "participate in the development of operational guidelines to be used during mutual response incidents," including

guidelines covering dispatch procedures, communications, apparatus response, tactical operations, medical control, EMS protocols, incident command, and incident reporting."[73]

The parties agree that they will not reimburse each other for the costs of any "usual or customary emergency services" rendered under the NOVA Agreement, unless the responsible jurisdiction recovers the costs of responding to the incident from "the party legally responsible for causing the incident."[74]

The parties structured the agreement to preserve all governmental immunities available under Virginia law, specifying that "[a]ll services performed and expenditures made under this agreement shall be deemed for public and governmental purposes and all immunities from liability enjoyed by federal, state and local governments, within its boundaries, shall extend to its participation in rendering emergency services, in accordance with this agreement, outside of its boundaries."[75] The parties also waive all claims against the other parties that might arise out of the provision of services under the agreement.[76] With respect to emergency medical services (EMS), the parties "agree[] to acknowledge and accept the use of the pre-hospital medical protocols, procedures, and standards of care regularly employed by another parties [*sic*] EMS agency for use by said agency when providing patient care during a mutual response incident."[77] The agreement also is intended to "work in concert with any other existing agreement(s) between parties, which address issues relating to cooperation of emergency service agencies."[78]

PRACTICE RECOMMENDATIONS. Based on the foregoing, state and local government lawyers should consider the following key recommendations when drafting or negotiating operational mutual aid agreements:

- Clarify the legal authorities under which the jurisdictions are entering into the agreement, taking into account any limitations those authorities impose on the jurisdiction;
- Set forth the procedures to be used for requesting and providing assistance;
- Clarify workers' compensation arrangements, including whether each jurisdiction will be responsible for providing workers' compensation coverage for its own employees or whether the requesting jurisdiction will provide such coverage, and whether employees of the responding jurisdiction are intended to become special employees of the requesting jurisdiction for the purposes of the response;
- Address liability and immunity issues, including how governmental immunities are intended to apply and whether the requesting jurisdiction will indemnify the responding jurisdiction;
- Identify whether reimbursement will be available for services provided, and if so, set forth procedures, authorities, and rules for payment, reimbursement, and allocation of costs;
- Require each jurisdiction to develop standard operating procedures describing how the mutual aid agreement will be implemented; and

- Require the use of a standardized incident command or management system such as the ICS.

Other recommendations include the following:

- Spell out notification procedures;
- Define relationships with other agreements among jurisdictions;
- Recognize qualifications and certifications (*e.g.*, emergency medical technician, paramedic) across jurisdictional lines;
- Encourage participation by a broad range of emergency responders;
- Mandate joint planning, training, and exercises, with liability provisions operating as if an actual emergency had occurred;
- Set up protocols for interoperable communications;
- Develop forms, manuals, and other job aids to facilitate requests for aid, recordkeeping regarding movement of equipment and personnel, and reimbursement;
- Include a provision requiring arbitration of disputes concerning reimbursement; and
- Keep agreements as short as possible, using appendices and standard operating procedures where possible.[79]

Other Emergency Preparedness and Response Arrangements

In addition to operational mutual aid agreements, there are other types of emergency preparedness and response arrangements. These include statewide and state-to-state disaster assistance compacts, and agreements between multiple levels of government. The same legal issues that arise in the context of operational mutual aid agreements can arise with these agreements as well; but each type of arrangement addresses these issues in somewhat different ways.

EMERGENCY MANAGEMENT ASSISTANCE COMPACT. The Emergency Management Assistance Compact (EMAC) is the basic state-to-state disaster assistance agreement. Forty-eight states are members of this interstate disaster assistance agreement, which a state joins by enacting legislation enabling it to operate within the EMAC system.[80] EMAC offers member states the ability to request and receive resources across state lines after declaring a disaster or emergency, with or without a federal disaster or emergency declaration. EMAC is administered by the National Emergency Management Association (NEMA).[81]

The EMAC has certain inherent limitations. For example, Article IV of the EMAC states that the terms and conditions of the EMAC apply only after the governor of the receiving state declares a state of emergency or disaster, or commences a mutual aid exercise, and last only as long as the state of emergency or disaster exists or the loaned resources remain in the state, "whichever is longer."[82] This makes the significant assistance contemplated in the EMAC available as soon as a disaster or emergency is declared. It also makes resources available for exercises. However, the restriction to declared disasters and emergencies limits the EMAC's usefulness with respect to operational mutual aid, since the vast majority of operational mutual aid takes place in the absence of a declared disaster or emergency. While the EMAC requires member states to craft mutual aid agreements implementing the EMAC, if the EMAC authorizing legislation is the sole authority for these agreements, the agreements' applicability will be limited accordingly.

Article IX of the EMAC requires that the requesting state reimburse the responding state for any loss or damage to, or expense incurred, in the operation of any equipment and the provision of any service in responding to a request for assistance. One of the reasons for this provision is to ensure that the requesting jurisdiction will receive reimbursement for these costs under the Federal Emergency Management Agency's (FEMA) Public Assistance Program. Under the Public Assistance Program, FEMA will reimburse requesting jurisdictions for mutual aid costs, provided that "the entity that received the aid was actually charged for that aid."[83] However, this type of reimbursement provision is not typically an element of operational mutual aid agreements, where each jurisdiction typically bears its own costs. Therefore, local jurisdictions should contemplate the ramifications of requesting aid under the EMAC if a source of reimbursement, such as the FEMA Public Assistance Program, is not assured.[84] Local jurisdictions also should exercise caution in constructing interstate mutual aid agreements based on the EMAC's authorities, because of the requirements of this provision.

Article VIII addresses workers' compensation and death benefits by requiring each party state to provide for the payment of compensation and benefits to members of their emergency services injured or killed while responding to a request for assistance "in the same manner and on the same terms as if the injury or death were sustained within their own state." The EMAC addresses liability questions—both with respect to responders and third parties—by stating as follows:

- Personnel remain under the command and control of the responding state, but fall under the "operational control" of the requesting state (Article IV);
- Personnel from a responding state are considered agents of the requesting state for tort liability and immunity purposes (Article VI);
- Neither the requesting state nor any responding states "shall be liable on account of any act or omission in good faith on the part of such forces while so engaged or on account of the maintenance or use of any equipment or supplies in connection therewith" (Article VI).

These provisions are intended to allocate responsibility for workers' compensation costs on behalf of responding states' personnel to the responding state, and to shield both the requesting state and the responding state from liability for actions taken by responders. However, the EMAC does not specify, for example, whether employees of a responding jurisdiction are intended to become special employees of the requesting jurisdiction. Instead, these provisions leave to the courts the job of harmonizing the workers' compensation programs (and tort claim preclusions) of the requesting and responding states.

In addition, while the EMAC speaks to the question of governmental immunity, the EMAC does not specifically address issues that arise when governmental immunity varies from state to state. This has been a significant issue in certain multistate regions.[85]

For example, conflicting governmental immunity standards have posed a problem for responders in the National Capital Region, where the three different jurisdictions—Virginia, Maryland, and the District of Columbia—have three very different governmental immunity standards.[86] Virginia has preserved complete sovereign immunity.[87] The District of Columbia has waived sovereign immunity for all tort claims, except those involving discretionary functions.[88] Maryland maintains a hybrid system, under which the state retains immunity for governmental functions,[89] recoveries are limited for accidents involving emergency vehicles responding to calls or pursuing suspects,[90] and local governments are required by statute to indemnify and defend their employees for allegations of misconduct that occur within the scope of their employment.[91]

The conflict between these governmental immunity standards came to light in a case involving police pursuit. In *Biscoe v. Arlington County*,[92] a police officer from the Arlington County, Virginia Police Department (ACPD) spotted a bank robbery suspect driving on a state road, and followed the car into the District of Columbia, where he stopped the vehicle. However, while the officer was otherwise engaged, the driver ran back into the vehicle and drove off. The ACPD officer gave chase, and in the ensuing pursuit, the suspected bank robber ran a red light and hit another vehicle, which in turn struck a pedestrian, severely injuring him.[93]

The pedestrian brought suit against the ACPD in the District of Columbia, and the county asserted governmental immunity under Virginia law.[94] The circuit court rejected this defense, stating that the issue of a non-forum state's immunity is controlled solely by the forum state's law. The court noted that the District of Columbia retained sovereign immunity only for discretionary functions, and that because the ACPD officer's actions were nondiscretionary acts, "[f]orced application of Virginia's law would . . . frustrate the policies that underlie the District's immunity rules."[95] The court also noted that while the district could extend immunity to neighboring states such as Virginia, it had expressly chosen not to in a previous case.[96] Therefore, the circuit court affirmed the trial court's ruling against Arlington County on the question of immunity.[97]

MODEL INTRASTATE MUTUAL AID LEGISLATION. Another model for mutual aid arrangements is the Model Intrastate Mutual Aid Legislation (Model Legislation), published by NEMA in March 2004.[98] The Model Legislation is intended to complement the recommendations for mutual aid agreements contained in the NIMS.[99] However, the Model Legislation is based largely on the EMAC. Therefore, there are several provisions, similar to those in the EMAC, that place significant limitations on the usefulness of the Model Legislation in fostering operational mutual aid agreements.

The Model Legislation includes several innovative provisions. For example, Article II of the Model Legislation defines "emergency responder" as "anyone with special skills, qualifications, training, knowledge and experience in the public or private sectors that would be beneficial to a participating subdivision in response to a locally declared emergency as defined in any applicable law or ordinance or authorized drill or exercise; and who is requested and/or authorized to respond." The services of a number of these individuals are not contemplated in many current mutual aid agreements. Likewise, Article III sets forth the responsibilities of "each participating political subdivision with jurisdiction over and responsibility for emergency management within that certain subdivision."[100] These are recommended steps for any local jurisdiction participating in a mutual aid arrangement.

However, by its terms, the Model Legislation is intended to create a statewide mutual aid system specifically intended to "provide for mutual assistance among the participating political subdivisions in the prevention of, response to, and recovery from, any disaster that results in a formal state of emergency in a participating political subdivision, subject to that participating political subdivision's criteria for declaration."[101] Under Article IV of the Model Legislation, a participating jurisdiction may request assistance "in preventing, mitigating, responding to and recovering from disasters that result in locally-declared emergencies" *or* "in concert with authorized drills or exercises" as allowed under the legislation. Likewise, under Article V, a requesting jurisdiction either must have declared a state of emergency or authorized a drill or exercise.[102] Each of these provisions necessarily limits the scope of the Model Legislation to mutual aid agreements intended to be used only during major incidents. These limitations prevent the Model Legislation from fostering networks of operational mutual aid agreements that can be used for both day-to-day operations and major incident response.

Article VII of the Model Legislation requires that "[a]ny requesting political subdivision shall reimburse the participating political subdivision rendering aid under this system." As noted with respect to the EMAC, this rarely is an element of operational mutual aid agreements, under which each jurisdiction typically bears its own costs.[103] A better approach may be the "conversion" language discussed above, or changing FEMA's administrative rules to make mutual aid costs reimbursable under the Public Assistance Program even if such costs are not normally incurred under day-to-day mutual aid.

Similar to the EMAC, the Model Legislation addresses liability to responders and third parties in several ways:

- By stating that personnel and equipment remain under the command and control of the responding state, but fall under the "operational control" of the requesting state (Article V);
- By stating that personnel are entitled to "all applicable benefits normally available to personnel while performing their duties for their employer," as well as "any additional state and federal benefits that may be available to them for line of duty deaths" (Article IX);

- By including activities under the Model Legislation under the category of governmental functions (Article X);
- By deeming responding personnel to be employees of the requesting jurisdiction for immunity purposes (Article X); and
- By relieving responders of liability except in the event of willful misconduct, gross negligence, and bad faith (Article X).

Like the EMAC, the Model Legislation's liability provisions do not specifically harmonize potentially conflicting governmental immunity doctrines where municipal areas have adopted different standards for government immunity than the rest of the state. This difference in governmental immunity standards is not as much of an issue for intrastate mutual aid as it is for interstate mutual aid, but it remains an issue that is left unaddressed by the Model Legislation. The Model Legislation should be modified by each state to take into consideration the individual state's particular governmental immunity scheme. If the Model Legislation is intended to apply a different governmental immunity scheme to mutual aid, this should be done deliberately and explicitly.

THE CALIFORNIA FIRE ASSISTANCE AGREEMENT. A different model for operational mutual aid arrangements between states or among different levels of government is the Agreement for Local Government Fire Suppression Assistance to Forest Agencies, referred to as the California Fire Assistance Agreement (CFAA), and known in previous iterations as the "Five-Party Agreement" or the "Four-Party Agreement."[104]

The CFAA is an agreement for wild land fire suppression entered into by the state of California, Office of Emergency Services (OES); CDF; USFS; the DOI Bureau of Land Management (BLM); the DOI National Park Service (NPS); and the DOI Fish and Wildlife Service (FWS). Together, USFS, BLM, NPS, and FWS are the federal agencies responsible for providing wild land fire protection for federal lands, and are referred to in the CFAA as the "Forest Agencies."[105]

The CFAA builds on existing mutual aid agreements within the state of California, as well as agreements between the Forest Agencies and other federal agencies. Each signatory is expected to fulfill its obligations either through its own resources or through mutual aid; the Forest Agencies do not directly access California local government resources (aside from those of local governments abutting federal lands with which the Forest Agencies have their own mutual aid agreements), and vice versa. The CFAA also builds upon use of the ICS and the NIIMS, in that all California equipment and personnel that might be assigned to fires under the CFAA, and all Forest Agency equipment and personnel, must meet ICS and NIIMS qualifications.[106]

The CFAA specifies that Forest Agency requests for apparatus and personnel are to be placed following the procedures set forth in the California Fire and Rescue Service Emergency Mutual Aid Plan (Mutual Aid Plan), and filled through the State Fire and Rescue Mutual Aid System (Mutual Aid System).[107]

The CFAA contemplates the assignment of an OES officer to the fire command structure to facilitate the use of state resources on Forest Agency fires.[108]

The CFAA requires that each jurisdiction sending emergency personnel to an incident provide such protective equipment and clothing to those personnel as required under California law.[109] The agreement also requires that fire engines assigned to the incident meet minimum ICS-type standards.[110]

The CFAA also addresses interoperable communications. The CFAA requires that each jurisdiction sending a "strike team" (a defined number of similar resources, such as fire engines, with a single leader) or "task force" (a grouping of different types of resources under a single leader) ensure that the leader has a VHF high-band radio with a minimum of thirty-two channels programmed as recommended in the Statewide Frequency Plans published in an appendix to guide number ICS 420-1.[111] Each jurisdiction sending apparatus is responsible for ensuring that the apparatus has common communications capability with the strike team or task force leader.[112]

Appendix A to the CFAA includes a conversion clause, clearly setting forth the reimbursement policy and procedures to be used under the CFAA.[113] Reimbursement for personnel, apparatus, and equipment begins after the twelfth hour of an incident. If an incident is less than twelve hours in duration, then there is no reimbursement by the Forest Agencies. However, if the duration of the incident exceeds twelve hours, then reimbursement for personnel, apparatus, and support equipment covers the *entire time* of commitment, including the initial twelve hours.[114] Appendix A also provides for the conversion of resources ordered under the California Mutual Aid Agreement to resources ordered under the CFAA in appropriate circumstances, thus triggering federal reimbursement.[115] This conversion language is a contrasting approach to that taken in the EMAC and the Model Legislation.

For reimbursement, the CFAA utilizes standard average rates, rather than actual rates, for administrative ease.[116] Reimbursement is "portal-to-portal"; that is, based on twenty-four hours per day from the time of dispatch.[117] Workers' compensation claims and payment of unemployment benefits remain the responsibility of the local jurisdiction providing resources.[118] Similar provisions govern reimbursement for apparatus use.[119] The CFAA also specifies that a Forest Agency may reimburse a local agency for the cost of apparatus or equipment loss or damage where that loss or damage is caused directly by the fire being suppressed, and where the local agency and its employees or operational failures are not a contributing factor to the damage or loss.[120]

The CFAA, therefore, establishes a structure where: regional and statewide mutual aid is built on local mutual aid; use of ICS, including standardized resource typing, is required; un-reimbursed local mutual aid can be converted to reimbursable mutual aid under the CFAA after the incident reaches a certain size or duration; reimbursement is based on standardized average rates for administrative simplicity; each responding local jurisdiction provides workers' compensation coverage for its own employees; and personal protective equipment and interoperable communications are mandatory. This arrangement facilitates reimbursement by the state or federal government, if appropriate, without interfering with operational mutual aid arrangements. Reimbursement processes are streamlined, workers' compensation coverage is well defined, and PPE and interoperable communications are required.

The issue of special employment and tort liability, however, is not specifically addressed in the CFAA, and this has led to some confusion. Courts have come to different conclusions as to whether the CFAA and similar arrangements extend the workers' compensation exclusive remedy to all parties to the agreement.

For example, in *Enslow v. United States*,[121] discussed above, a CDF firefighter was killed on a USFS fire in the Mendocino National Forest. The CDF firefighter was assisting the USFS under the CFAA.[122] The district court concluded that the CDF firefighter was a "special employee" of the USFS under the following terms and conditions of the work:

- Under the CFAA, USFS reimbursed CDF for salaries, overtime, employee benefit costs, travel, and subsistence directly related to the fire;
- The work performed by the CDF firefighter was part of the USFS's regular business;
- The CFAA specifies that the "protecting agency," in this case, USFS, "shall retain responsibility for command of all fire suppression action if a qualified employee of that agency is present at the fire"; and
- A USFS crew liaison officer supervised the CDF crew of which the decedent was a member during their activities fighting the USFS fire.[123]

However, the court of appeals reversed the district court's grant of summary judgment. The court held that USFS, in order to be deemed a special employer, must have "actually exercised control over the *details* of the person's work."[124] The court pointed to the following factors that indicated USFS retained only general supervision under the CFAA:

- "CDF commanders remained at the fire scene and directly supervised the decedent at the site";
- While USFS issued a safety warning, this did not in and of itself indicate that USFS controlled the CDF firefighters' work details;
- USFS had the power to remove a CDF firefighter from the worksite, but not to terminate his employment; and
- There was no evidence that the CDF firefighter consented "either impliedly or expressly" to become a USFS employee.[125]

Similarly, no special employment relationship was found (or apparently alleged) in *Buttram v. United States*,[126] which involved the deaths of two volunteer firefighters with the Kuna Rural Fire District (Kuna RFD) who died on a BLM fire in Idaho. In that case, the court entered a judgment against both the DOI and the local fire department. The court found that both BLM and the Kuna RFD owed duties to the deceased firefighters, which were breached and resulted in the firefighters' deaths.[127]

Thus, the appeals court in *Enslow* and the trial court in *Buttram* found that no employment relationship existed between the federal agency with authority over the fire and the local firefighters responding under mutual aid, while the trial court in *Enslow* (like the appeals court in *Roma*, discussed above) found a special employment relationship in virtually the same circumstances. Jurisdictions seeking to utilize the CFAA as a model for mutual aid arrangements should take care to add specificity regarding workers' compensation and employment status.

AGREEMENTS WITH TRIBAL GOVERNMENTS. Mutual aid arrangements between state and local governments and Indian tribes present a number of issues in addition to those normally encountered in operational mutual aid agreements and statewide disaster assistance arrangements. These issues include tribal sovereignty,[128] tribal sovereign immunity, the jurisdiction of tribal governments and various federal agencies with responsibility for Indian Country,[129] and the authority of each party to enter into the agreement.[130] For these reasons, in addition to the provisions recommended for other operational mutual aid agreements, mutual aid agreements with tribes should also include delineation of authorities, jurisdiction, and intergovernmental cooperation, and should address the issue of tribal sovereignty and tribal sovereign immunity. The CFAA, as an agreement between sovereigns, may present a better model for mutual aid agreements with tribes than local-to-local agreements.

Many states have enacted legislation concerning cooperation with tribal law enforcement, and the state or local powers, authorities, or qualifications tribal law enforcement officers can or should possess.[131] In addition, BIA recently published updated guidance concerning tribal law enforcement Memoranda of Agreement (MOA), Memoranda of Understanding (MOU), Cross-Deputization Agreements (CDA), and Special Law Enforcement Commission (SLEC) Deputation Agreements (which grant special law enforcement commissions to tribal and local law enforcement officers).[132] So, for example, a tribe can consent to having a state assume and exercise concurrent law enforcement jurisdiction over tribal lands through a mutual aid agreement.[133] Agreements can also grant tribal officers the right to enforce state law on tribal lands.[134]

Tribal nations will want to ensure that any mutual aid agreement involving tribal government agencies includes an express provision that no waiver of sovereign immunity has occurred by virtue of entering into a mutual aid agreement. In *Williams v. Bd. of County Comm'rs of San Juan County*,[135] the plaintiff, a non-Indian, brought suit after he was stopped for speeding by a Navajo Nation police officer on a state road located within the boundaries of the Nation. The police officer issued the plaintiff a speeding ticket under Navajo law, and when plaintiff refused to cooperate with the officer, he was arrested and taken to the San Juan County Detention Center pursuant to a mutual aid agreement between the Navajo Nation and San Juan County.[136] The plaintiff sued the Navajo Nation, San Juan County, and a number of individuals. The court dismissed the action against the Navajo Nation on the grounds of sovereign immunity, specifically noting that "the mutual aid agreement between the Navajo Nation and San Juan County states, '[N]othing in this Agreement . . . shall be construed as a waiver of sovereign immunity by the Nation. . . .' "[137]

Note that some state statutes require a limited waiver of sovereign immunity as a pre-condition for law enforcement activities under a cross-deputization agreement.[138] However, even where a tribe has waived sovereign immunity in a mutual aid agreement, a third party bringing an action against the tribe based on law enforcement actions may still be required to exhaust tribal remedies before bringing suit in federal court.[139] Courts also have held that simply entering into a mutual aid agreement does not constitute a waiver of tribal sovereign immunity.[140]

Interoperable Communications and Intergovernmental Cooperation

Interoperable communications plans and mutual aid agreements are mutually reinforcing. A robust interoperable communications plan is an essential part of an effective mutual aid agreement.[141] According to the NIMS, "[p]reparedness organizations must ensure that effective communications processes and systems exist to support a complete spectrum of incident management activities."[142] Each individual jurisdiction will be required to comply with national interoperable communications standards, and incident communications will follow ICS standards.[143]

Much has been made of the failure of the communications systems during the response to the attacks on the World Trade Center on September 11, 2001. By contrast, interoperable communications and intergovernmental cooperation at the Pentagon that day worked relatively well. The governments of the National Capital Region recognized after the 1982 crash of Air Florida flight 90 in Washington, D.C., that enhanced interoperable land mobile radio (LMR) communications were essential to effective regional emergency response.[144] In 1983, regional governments, through the Metropolitan Washington Council of Governments (MWCOG), negotiated and adopted regional mutual aid agreements.[145] However, these agreements did not establish true regional interoperable communications.[146] Therefore, in the late 1990s, Northern Virginia jurisdictions negotiated and implemented the Northern Virginia Trunked Mutual Aid Agreement (NVTMA), a mutual aid agreement designed to facilitate interoperable 800 MHz LMR communications among emergency response agencies.[147] The NVTMA complements the Northern Virginia Mutual Aid Agreement (NOVA Agreement), described above.[148]

Because of these efforts, by September 11, 2001, most jurisdictions that responded to the Pentagon were using compatible 800 MHz trunked LMR systems, with Arlington County's radio frequencies preprogrammed into their LMRs.[149] Thus, both law enforcement and fire-rescue responders were able to communicate from the first moments of the response.[150] Responding jurisdictions simply switched to predesignated frequencies and were able to communicate directly with Arlington County public safety dispatchers and the on-scene incident commander from the Arlington County Fire Department (ACFD).[151] It was only when responders from jurisdictions not part of the NVTMA began arriving that interoperability began to break down; as a result, additional communications equipment was supplied by the system's private vendor, Motorola, which immediately transported one hundred fifty additional compatible LMRs to the Pentagon for distribution to on-scene managers from these jurisdictions.[152]

The Public Safety Wireless Network (PSWN) credited a large degree of the incident response's success to the interlocking arrangements set forth in the MWCOG Mutual Aid Plan, the NOVA Agreement, and the NVTMA.[153] The PSWN, in its report on the Pentagon response, included specific recommendations for public safety agencies at the local, state, or federal level to enhance interoperable communications during day-to-day operations *and* major incident response. These include the following:

- Establishment of mutual aid agreements that include interoperability issues.
- Exercise of communications interoperability through mass casualty drills, operational drills and management (tabletop) exercises; these drills, combined with the use of interoperability procedures on a day-to-day basis, prepare responders for the challenge of large-scale multijurisdictional incident response. PSWN noted that with respect to NVTMA jurisdictions, "interoperability training takes form as a daily occurrence for public safety personnel when responding to routine incidents in other jurisdictions and using alternate radio systems to support these operations."
- Adherence to the ICS (and now, the NIMS and its three major elements). At the Pentagon, the incident commander immediately established, and all local government agencies strictly observed, the ICS.[154]
- Development of regional and/or statewide communications systems, which can provide the scalability necessary to accommodate the influx of responders due to a major incident.[155] PSWN noted in particular compatible LMR systems such as the NVTMA's trunked 800 MHz radio systems.
- Creation of inventories of assets that facilitate interoperability (*e.g.,* mobile command vehicles, mobile interoperability vehicles, fixed switches), as well as standard operating procedures for their activation and use.
- Adoption of common technological standards, such as the ANSI/TIA/EIA-102 standard (the P25 suite of communications standards).
- Caution in reliance on public commercial communications services, which were unreliable during the initial phases of the Pentagon response.[156]

Other Methods of Intergovernmental Cooperation

Interstate Regional Cooperation

Interstate regions also have begun exploring other ways to cooperate for homeland security and emergency management issues. These interstate regional relationships seek to leverage local capabilities and local-to-local mutual aid agreements effectively to manage disasters and emergencies that have regional impact.[157] By doing so, these interstate regional relationships can avoid some of the limitations identified with respect to the EMAC and the Model Legislation, while leveraging potentially beneficial aspects of these arrangements.

An example of this is the homeland security and emergency management coordination function of the Metropolitan Washington Council of Governments (MWCOG). As discussed above, prior to September 11, 2001, MWCOG had an effective regional response plan that included mutual aid agreements between and among jurisdictions in Virginia, Maryland, and the District of Columbia. As noted, these agreements functioned well in the response to the attack on the Pentagon.

After September 11, 2001, MWCOG developed an extensive Regional Emergency Coordination Plan (RECP).[158] The RECP contemplates three types of hazards: natural hazards; human-induced nonterrorism hazards; and terrorism.[159] The RECP includes a Baseline Plan, fifteen Regional Emergency Support Functions (R-ESF) that track the Emergency Support Functions set forth in the Federal Response Plan, eleven Support Annexes and six Appendices. The Support Annexes are "mini-plans" that address particular types of incidents; one of the six appendices covers terrorism. The RECP "concept of coordination" includes a recognition that "most emergencies are handled by individual jurisdictions using standard operational plans and procedures"; that regional resources can be engaged through the RECP and the EMAC if additional resources are needed; that state and local emergency operations plans should incorporate the ICS; and that "communication before, during, and after the incident facilitates effective relationships among member organizations and ensures that the exchange of accurate information occurs on a regular basis."[160]

The R-ESFs include communications infrastructure (R-ESF 2); fire, technical rescue, and hazardous materials operations (R-ESF 4/9/10); and law enforcement (R-ESF 13). R-ESF 13 is notable because it represents one of the first attempts to integrate law enforcement into an ICS-based multidisciplinary system as contemplated under the NIMS. In order to accomplish this, R-ESF 13 states that:

- "The continuity of police services must be sensitive and responsive to the national security-related law enforcement requirements."
- "There may be multiple command posts to handle the different aspects of the police services response to an event, such as an investigative command post and a response command post. There will be a need to coordinate information among these various posts."
- "For a regional incident or regional emergency resulting from criminal acts, command and control of the criminal investigation and dissemination of non-sensitive intelligence, as necessary, will need to have communication and coordination focus."
- "Existing regional mutual aid agreements will be invoked."
- "Due to the inherent nature of law enforcement, information flow must be sensitive to operational security."[161]

Thus, the RECP recognizes that fire and rescue and law enforcement, as well as other emergency response disciplines, may have different prominence and roles depending on the nature of the incident. Such a structure permits flexibility in the response to major incidents.

Intrastate Regional Response Teams

In addition to mutual aid relationships, state and local governments may choose to pool resources into regional response teams.[162] Regional teams provide the opportunity to build regional capacity, which is then available to all local jurisdictions within the region, without any one local jurisdiction having to bear the entire burden of creating and maintaining that capacity. Regional teams can be used for law enforcement (*e.g.*, special weapons and tactics teams, explosive ordnance disposal teams), fire and rescue (*e.g.*, technical rescue teams, hazardous materials teams), emergency medical services (*e.g.*, regional decontamination and mass triage teams), and other emergency response disciplines.

Regional teams can be loose alliances of specialists from various departments, or formally structured task forces with independent leadership, separate equipment caches, and specialized training. However, as with mutual aid agreements, certain key issues must be addressed with respect to these teams, namely the relationship between local governments and regional teams, the authority of regional teams to act, workers' compensation and tort liability issues with respect to team members, and liability issues with respect to third parties. The structure of these teams, their relationship with federal, state and local governments, the authority of the teams to act, and the arrangements for liability incurred by the teams should be specifically spelled out in implementing agreements, and should be consistent with applicable state law.[163]

RELATIONSHIPS BETWEEN LOCAL GOVERNMENTS AND REGIONAL TEAMS. *Hauber v. Yakima County*[164] points out the importance of formalizing arrangements between local jurisdictions and regional response teams. In *Hauber*, a career city firefighter who was also a member of a volunteer dive rescue team died in the course of an attempted dive rescue. In response to an emergency call, the county sheriff's department, which was responsible for the volunteer dive rescue team, summoned dive team members for an emergency response.[165] Included among those summoned was the career firefighter at issue, who was on duty that day at a city fire station. The firefighter received permission from his battalion chief to respond to the call, and died while engaged in the attempted rescue.[166]

The firefighter's estate brought a wrongful death action against the county. In Washington State, firefighters are permitted to collect workers' compensation *and* bring related negligence suits against their employers, while search and rescue volunteers are not.[167] Therefore, the court noted that if the firefighter had responded to the call as a city firefighter pursuant to a mutual aid agreement, his estate would be permitted to bring suit for negligence, but that if the firefighter responded as a search and rescue volunteer, his estate would not.[168] The court noted that search and rescue and dive rescue services were not included in the regional mutual aid agreement, nor did the responding fire department request mutual aid from the city fire department.[169] The court also rejected the contention that the regional Comprehensive Emergency Management Plan constituted a mutual aid agreement.[170] The court concluded that the firefighter was not responding pursuant to a mutual aid agreement, and was therefore a volunteer who was not entitled to maintain the negligence suit at issue.[171]

REGIONAL TEAM AUTHORITY. Because a regional team, by its definition, crosses jurisdictional lines to perform its tasks, the issue of the regional response team's authority to act should be addressed during the team's formation. In *State v. Knight*,[172] two defendants contested their felony drug convictions on the grounds that officers from a regional narcotics task force recorded certain narcotics transactions within a town that was not part of the task force, pursuant to an authorization issued by the county sheriff, who was the supervisor of the task force. The court held that the county sheriff, while acting as the supervisor of the task force, "had jurisdiction coextensive with the task force's jurisdiction."[173] The court continued that, therefore, the task force had jurisdiction within the incorporated municipality not because the municipality was a member of the task force and a signatory to the mutual aid agreement that formed the task force, but rather because under state law the county sheriff had jurisdiction over all areas within the county, including any incorporated municipalities.[174] Therefore, the task force officers were entitled to act according to the authorization within the incorporated municipality.[175]

The defendants also argued that the mutual aid agreement did not permit the county sheriff, as supervisor of the task force, to issue authorizations to officers not under the immediate supervision and control of the county sheriff's department, since the mutual aid agreement provided that each participating department supervised only its own employees.[176] The court, however, held that the paragraph at issue pertained only to the allocation of liability, not to the jurisdiction of officers participating in the task force.[177]

WORKERS' COMPENSATION ISSUES. Nothing better illustrates the need for clear provisions concerning workers' compensation and employee status than *Brassinga v. City of Mountain View*[178] and *Berger v. Mead*.[179] Each case arose after a police officer who was shot during a training exercise conducted by a regional response team brought suit against the jurisdictions participating in the regional response team for the negligence of their police officers. The courts reached exactly opposite results with respect to the liability of the jurisdictions participating in the regional response teams.

In *Brassinga*, the North County Regional SWAT Team (Regional Team), a composite of the SWAT teams of the Mountain View, Palo Alto, and Los Altos, California, police departments, conducted a day-long training exercise during which a Palo Alto reserve police officer participating as a role-player was shot and killed by a Mountain View police officer who was a member of the Regional Team.[180] The Regional Team had uniform standards for membership, and a "unified chain of command," meaning, in the words of the court, that "a Regional Team member from one department could supervise Regional Team members from another department."[181] The Regional Team paid no salaries and owned no equipment, although the team members "interchanged equipment all the time" and "wore identical team SWAT uniforms."[182]

The family of the deceased Palo Alto police officer brought suit against the Mountain View police officer and the city of Mountain View, among others. The parties did not dispute that Palo Alto was the deceased police officer's "general employer," but Mountain View argued that either Mountain View or the Regional Team itself was the "special employer" of both officers, and therefore the suit was precluded by the state workers' compensation statute.[183] The court found that the Regional Team was not an entity that could qualify as an "employer," special or otherwise, under the state statute.[184]

In *Berger v. Mead*, a Michigan court examined an almost indistinguishable situation. In that case, a Southfield City police officer who was a member of the South Oakland Tactical Support Unit (Tactical Unit) was shot during a training exercise by Royal Oak City police officer who was also a member of the Tactical Unit.[185] The cities whose officers participated in the Tactical Unit defended the suit on the grounds that the Tactical Unit was a joint venture between and among the participating police departments, and therefore the plaintiff's suit was barred by the exclusive remedy provision of the state workers' compensation statute.[186]

Although Michigan courts typically consider six elements when determining whether a joint venture exists, the court focused on the four applicable to nonprofit governmental ventures: an agreement indicating an intention to undertake a joint venture; a joint undertaking; contribution of skills or property by the parties; and community interest and control over the subject matter of the enterprise.[187] The court noted that "the key consideration is that the parties intended a joint relationship."[188]

The court found that the Tactical Unit was a joint venture, largely based on the South Oakland County Reciprocal Police Aid Agreement, which created the Tactical Unit.[189] The court noted that the agreement made obvious the community of interest among the parties; the agreement specified that each participant would contribute officers to the unit and pay its own officers' salaries; and the agreement "clearly shows a common responsibility among the municipalities in running the unit."[190]

The court also found that at the time of the accident, the injured police officer was an employee both of the Royal Oak City police department and the Tactical Unit.[191] The court found that the injured police officer was under the command of the Tactical Unit at the time of the accident, that Royal Oak City's payment of the injured police officer's wages was part of the city's contribution to the joint venture, that the Tactical Unit had the right to discipline the injured police officer at the time he was injured; and that the performance of the officer's duties at the time of his injury "constituted an integral part of the joint venture's business in accomplishing the goal of the unit: to provide mutual aid protection to each of the unit's municipalities."[192] Therefore, the injured police officer's tort action against the Southfield City Police Department and the other departments participating in the Tactical Unit was barred.

LIABILITY TO THIRD PARTIES. Each jurisdiction participating in regional response teams should be mindful of the possibility of direct liability for actions of the regional response team, even if the actions at issue were taken by employees of another jurisdiction. In *Timberlake v. Benton*,[193] two individuals subjected to strip searches by members of a regional narcotics task force brought suit against the director of the task force, among others, for civil rights violations. The court evaluated the suit against the director of the task force using the principle that a suit against a person in his or her official capacity is a suit against the entity for which the named official is an agent.[194]

Under Tennessee law, two or more public agencies may enter into agreements for joint cooperation that may, but are not required to, create separate legal entities.[195] The court therefore found it imperative to determine whether the jurisdictions participating in the task force had created a separate legal entity when they established the task force, and concluded that they did not.[196] The court cited the following factors:

- The lack of explicit language in the cooperation agreement indicating that the task force was an independent legal entity;
- The fact that police officers assigned to the task force remained employees of the city or county assigning them, and continued to be paid by those cities or counties;
- The fact that each participating city or county was required under the agreement to carry its own liability insurance; and
- The fact that upon a jurisdiction's termination of its participation, the equipment that jurisdiction contributed to the task force would be returned to the jurisdiction.[197]

The court found that the creation of a separate board of directors for the task force did not "in itself indicate the creation of a separate legal entity."[198] Because the participating jurisdictions did not create a separate legal entity when they formed the task force, the court interpreted the lawsuit against the director of the task force in his official capacity as a suit against *all* of the cities and counties comprising the task force, and analyzed the suit accordingly.[199]

Conclusion

Mutual aid agreements and other intergovernmental arrangements for emergency preparedness and response present interesting and somewhat complex issues of local government law. However, through examination of applicable state law and careful drafting, state and local government lawyers can address these issues and minimize the risk of liability for their clients.

Notes

1. There are several excellent articles addressing a number of issues attendant to emergency preparedness and response. *See, e.g.,* James T. O'Reilly, *Planning for the Unthinkable: Environmental Disaster Planning Issues in an Age of Terroristic Threats,* 9 Widener L. Symp. J. 261, 263-268 (2003); William C. Nicholson, *Legal Issues in Emergency Response to Terrorism Incidents Involving Hazardous Materials: The Hazardous Waste Operations and Emergency Response ("HAZWOPER") Standard, Standard Operating Procedures, Mutual Aid and the Incident Management System,* 9 Widener L. Symp. J. 295, 296 (2003); Howard D. Swanson, *The Delicate Art of Practicing Municipal Law Under Conditions of Hell and High Water,* 76 N.D. L. Rev. 487 (2000).

2. Similar lists with additional roles and responsibilities are included in O'Reilly, *Planning for the Unthinkable, supra* note 1, at 263-268, and Swanson, *The Delicate Art of Practicing Municipal Law, supra* note 1, at 487.

3. For example, the Emergency Planning and Community Right to Know Act (EPCRA), 42 U.S.C. §§ 11001-11005 (2000) requires intergovernmental and interdisciplinary cooperation in preparation for major hazardous materials response. EPCRA requires that each state appoint a state emergency response commission (SERC), which in turn appoints local emergency planning committees (LEPCs), and designates emergency planning districts for which emergency plans must be developed. EPCRA also sets forth the required elements of the emergency plan contemplated in the statute. Many state statutes also contemplate regional preparedness. *See, e.g.,* Alaska Stat. § 26.23.070(a); Kan. Stat. Ann. § 48-928(n); Ohio Rev. Code Ann. § 5502.7.

4. Dep't of Homeland Security, FY 2004 Homeland Security Grant Program 5 (2004) (FY04 Grant Guidance), *available at* http://www.ojp.usdoj.gov/odp/docs/fy04hsgp_appkit.pdf.

5. *Id.* app. C, at C-4.

6. H.R. 3266, 108th Cong. (2003); *see also* H.R. Rep. No. 108-460, pt. 1 (Apr. 2, 2004). *See also* U.S. Gov't Accountability Office, GAO-04-1009, Effective Regional Coordination Can Enhance Emergency Preparedness (2004). H.R. 3266 was included as part of the House of Representative's intelligence reform bill, *see* H.R. 10, 108th Cong., § 5003 (2004), but was removed in conference.

7. National Wildfire Coordinating Group, History of ICS 1-2 (1994), *available at* http://www.nwcg.gov/pms/forms/comapn/history.pdf (part of the Incident Command System (ICS) National Training Curriculum). The ICS was initially developed in California by a cooperative interagency and intergovernmental (federal, state and local) task force, Firefighting Resources of California Organized for Potential Emergencies (FIRESCOPE). *Id.* at 2. The NIIMS is administered by the National Wildfire Coordinating Group (NWCG), an intergovernmental cooperative group. *Id.*

8. Dep't of Homeland Security, National Incident Management System (2004) (NIMS), app. A, at 63, *available at* http://www.dhs.gov/interweb/assetlibrary/NIMS-90-web.pdf.

9. *Id.* The ICS or similar incident management systems were adopted as a standard by a number of governmental entities and response agencies at the federal, state, and local level prior to September 11, 2001. For example, the U.S. Occupational Safety and Health Administration's hazardous waste operations and emergency response (HAZWOPER) standard requires the use of an incident command system for emergency response to hazardous materials incidents. 29 C.F.R. § 1910.120. Subsection (q) of that standard applies to hazardous materials emergency response teams. Subsection (q)(1) requires the development and implementation of an emergency response plan, and subsection (q)(3) requires the use of the incident command system in emergency response operations. Subsection (q)(6) sets forth standardized levels of training for personnel involved in hazardous materi-

als emergency response operations. Appendix C, subsection (6) contains a more extensive discussion of the incident command system. Many state statutes also mandate the use of an incident command system. *See, e.g.,* ALASKA STAT. §§ 26.23.075(c), 26.23.077(b), (c); IND. CODE § 10-14-3-10.6(d); KAN. STAT. ANN. § 48-928(o).

10. Homeland Security Presidential Directive 5, at § 15, 39 WEEKLY COMP. PRES. DOC. 263, 280 (Mar. 7, 2003) (HSPD 5).

11. NIMS, at 2.

12. *Id.* at 3.

13. *Id.* at 7-8.

14. *Id.* at 7-8, 25-26.

15. *Id.* at 26-28.

16. *Id.* at 34.

17. HSPD 5, at § 18.

18. *Id.* at § 20. The 9/11 Commission also "strongly support[s] the decision that federal homeland security funding will be contingent, as of October 1, 2004, upon the adoption and regular use of ICS and unified command procedures." NAT'L COMMISSION ON TERRORIST ATTACKS UPON THE UNITED STATES, THE 9/11 COMMISSION REPORT: FINAL REPORT OF THE NATIONAL COMMISSION ON TERRORIST ATTACKS UPON THE UNITED STATES 397 (W.W. Norton & Co. 2004) (9/11 Commission Report).

19. FY04 Grant Guidance, at 8.

20. All-hazards preparedness is the announced policy of the federal government. *See* Homeland Security Presidential Directive 8, §§ 1, 3, 39 WEEKLY COMP. PRES. DOC. 1795, 1822 (2003).

21. Indeed, the Public Safety Wireless Network (PSWN), in its report on the emergency response at the Pentagon on September 11, 2001, concluded that part of the success of that major incident response was due to the fact not only that "local jurisdictions instituted plans and procedures for mutual-aid interoperability," but that "these plans are used on a daily basis by most local agencies." PUBLIC SAFETY WIRELESS NETWORK, ANSWERING THE CALL: COMMUNICATIONS LESSONS LEARNED FROM THE PENTAGON ATTACK 20 (2002) (PSWN 9/11 Pentagon Report), *available at* http://www.safecomprogram.gov/admin/librarydocs7/Answering_the_Call_Pentagon_Attack.pdf. By contrast, McKinsey & Co., in its report to the Fire Department of New York (FDNY), found that FDNY was unable to utilize mutual aid from other jurisdictions effectively on September 11, 2001, because "the FDNY had rarely requested mutual aid from departments outside of the city to support fire operations," and therefore had no processes or systems in place, nor any institutional knowledge, concerning the effective use of mutual aid resources. *See* MCKINSEY & CO., REPORT TO THE FIRE DEPARTMENT OF NEW YORK 36 (Aug. 15, 2002). The staff of the 9/11 Commission found much the same thing. *See* 9/11 COMMISSION, STAFF STATEMENT NO. 14, CRISIS MANAGEMENT (2004), *available at* http://www.9-11commission.gov/staff_statements/staff_statement_14.pdf.

22. ALASKA STAT. § 26.23.180.

23. KAN. STAT. ANN. § 48-930(b). Ohio law states that "[p]olitical subdivisions, in collaboration with other public and private agencies within this state, may develop mutual aid arrangements for emergency management aid and assistance in case of any hazard too great to be dealt with unassisted." OHIO REV. CODE ANN. § 5502.29.

24. MD. CODE ANN., CRIM. PROC. § 2-105(e)(2)(ii). Curiously, there is no parallel requirement for agreements concerning fire, rescue, and emergency medical services. *See* MD. CODE ANN., PUB. SAFETY § 7-103.

25. R.I. GEN. LAWS § 30-15.8-1(a).

26. *Id.* at § 30-15.8-3.

27. WYO. STAT. ANN. §§ 19-13-201 to -210 (Mitchie 2004).

28. *See* 6 LARSON'S WORKERS' COMPENSATION L. (MB) § 100.01 (Apr. 4, 1992).

29. *See* 3 LARSON'S WORKERS' COMPENSATION L. (MB) § 67.01[1] (Nov. 1, 1987). Generally, a second employer becomes a "special employer" if: (1) the employee has made a "contract of hire, express or implied," with the second employer; (2) the work being performed "is essentially that of the second employer"; and (3) the second employer has the "right to control" the work of the employee. *Id.*

30. *Id.* at § 67.04.

31. 291 A.2d 155 (Bergen County Ct. 1972), *aff'd*, 305 A.2d 78 (N.J. Super. Ct. App. Div. 1973).

32. *Id.* at 292 (citing N.J. STAT. ANN. §§ 40:47-68).

33. *Id.* at 293-294. Significantly, because of the existence of the statute, the court concluded that "the common law principles of special employer and co-employer are irrelevant and inapplicable." *Id.* at 295. Despite this, the court also noted that because of the mutual aid agreement, the firefighter was acting as an employee of the responding jurisdiction, rather than the reimbursing jurisdiction, at the time of the injury.

34. *See* Gilewski v. Mastic Beach Fire District No. 1, 241 N.Y.S.2d 874 (N.Y. App. Div. 1963) (mutual aid agreement triggered automatic response to fire in area along border between two jurisdictions). However, the same state's courts also have found there to be no "call for assistance" triggering reimbursement where a responding jurisdiction participated in a drill pursuant to a request by the receiving jurisdiction. Woodworth v. Village of Watkins Glen, 179 N.Y.S.2d 226 (N.Y. App. Div. 1958).

35. *See, e.g.,* Nelson v. Borough of Greenville, 124 A.2d 675 (Pa. Super. Ct. 1956) ("decedent's attendance at the West Salem fire was at the command of his own chief and was under a mutual aid arrangement between the fire companies"); Kuntzweiller v. City of West Lafayette, 29 N.E.2d 1007 (Ind. Ct. App. 1940) (firefighter responding to mutual aid call not special employee of requesting jurisdiction). *See also* Garcia v. City of South Tucson, 640 P.2d 1117 (Ariz. Ct. App. 1981) (police officer responding to mutual aid call not special employee of requesting jurisdiction; no joint venture where mutual aid agreement specified that each agency retained control over its employees, and "each party shall be responsible and liable for damages caused by its personnel during the course of rendering mutual law enforcement assistance . . .").

36. 811 F. Supp. 503 (C.D. Cal. 1992) (Enslow I), *reversed and remanded*, No. 93-55164, 1994 WL 649979 (9th Cir. Nov. 15, 1994) (unpublished opinion, table citation at 42 F.3d 1399) (Enslow II).

37. Enslow I, 811 F. Supp. at 506-507.

38. *Id.* Under the FTCA, the liability of the United States is determined "in accordance with the law of the place where the act or omission occurred." 28 U.S.C. § 1346(b)(1). Therefore, in an action under the FTCA, the court applies the law the state courts would apply in the analogous tort action.

39. Enslow II, 1994 WL 649979, at **1-**2 (emphasis in original).

40. 344 F.3d 352 (3d Cir. 2003).

41. *Id.* at 356, 364.

42. *Id.*

43. *Id.* at 364. Indeed, the court stated that "[t]here can be little doubt that the District Court correctly concluded that Roma's work fighting the November 24, 1997 fire for the NAES Fire Department rendered him a *paradigmatic example of a special employee . . .*" *Id.* (emphasis added).

44. Individual property owners or developers, and their insurers, generally are not considered third-party beneficiaries of mutual aid agreements. *See, e.g.,* New Hampshire Ins. Co. v. City of Madera, 192 Cal. Rptr. 548, 555 (Cal. Ct. App. 1983) ("a holding that the insureds in this case were third party beneficiaries of the contract between the County and the City would be contrary to public policy since it would discourage cities and counties

from entering into mutual aid agreements due to the possibility of creating a civil liability that otherwise would not exist"). *See generally* 1 Eugene McQuillan, The Law of Municipal Corporations, § 3A.11 (3d ed., rev. vol. 1999).

45. For example, the Alabama Emergency Management Act deems all functions performed under the statute to be governmental functions, and states that neither public agencies nor individual emergency management workers "shall be liable for the death of or injury to persons, or for damage to property, as a result of any such activity," except in cases of willful misconduct, gross negligence, or bad faith. *See* Ala. Code §§ 31-9-16(a), (b). Arizona's emergency management statute sets forth that the state and its political subdivisions are not liable for performing, or failing to perform, any discretionary function, and immunities available within the state also apply extraterritorially. *See* Ariz. Rev. Stat. §§ 26-314(A), (B). The Kansas Emergency Preparedness for Disasters Act preserves full immunity for states, political subdivisions, and individuals for all acts taken during a declared disaster emergency, except for individuals in the case of willful misconduct, gross negligence, or bad faith. *See* Kan. Stat. Ann. § 48-915(b). The Michigan Emergency Management Act preserves full immunity for states, political subdivisions, and individuals, without exception. *See* Mich. Comp. Laws Ann. § 30.411. Note that, with respect to interstate mutual aid agreements, governmental immunity may have been retained differently in neighboring states. This situation is discussed in the section of this chapter on the Emergency Management Assistance Compact, *infra*.

46. Ken Lerner, *Governmental Negligence Liability Exposure in Disaster Management*, 23 Urb. Law. 333, 335, 338 (Summer 1991). Governmental immunity is used to "prevent judicial 'second-guessing' of legislative and administrative decisions grounded in social, economic, and political policy through the medium of a tort action." *Id.* (citing United States v. Varig Airlines, 467 U.S. 797, 814 (1984)).

47. *Id.* at 338-339.

48. *Id.* at 339.

49. *Id.* at 340.

50. *Id.* at 341.

51. *Id.* at 341-351.

52. *Id.* at 341 (citing DFDS Seacruises (Bahamas) Ltd. v. United States, 676 F. Supp. 1193, 1205 (S.D. Fla. 1987) (finding that U.S. Coast Guard's decision not to have a contingency plan for shipboard firefighting was a "textbook discretionary function"); Freeman v. Alaska, 705 P.2d 918, 920 (Alaska 1985) (adopting discretionary function test for governmental immunity under Alaska law, and stating that "decisions that rise to the level of planning or policy formulation will be considered discretionary acts immune from tort liability, whereas decisions that are operational in nature, thereby implementing policy decisions, will not be considered discretionary and therefore will not be shielded from liability.")).

53. *Id.* at 345. Lerner points out that, under Berkovitz v. U.S., 486 U.S. 531 (1988), the execution of a mandatory procedure would not constitute a discretionary action. *Id.* at 344. Lerner further points to McMichael v. U.S., 856 F.2d 1026 (8th Cir. 1988), and Fortney v. U.S., 714 F. Supp. 207 (W.D. Va. 1989), cases involving explosions at U.S. Department of Defense munitions plants, as demonstrating that failure to comply with mandatory procedures is not a protected discretionary function, while the failure to adopt an advisory procedure was a discretionary decision entitled to immunity.

54. *Id.* at 345.

55. *Id.* at 345-346.

56. *Id.* at 346 (citing Karr v. State, 765 P.2d 316 (Wash. Ct. App. 1988); Cougar Business Owners Ass'n v. State, 647 P.2d 481 (Wash.), *cert. denied*, 459 U.S. 971 (1982)). Karr was brought by the survivors of individuals who perished in the wake of the eruption, some inside the designated zones, many outside of the zones. Cougar was brought by business

owners in a town that was kept inside the "red zone" for six months, although the eruption never impacted the town.

57. *Id.* at 346-347 (citing Karr, 765 P. 2d at 319; Cougar, 647 P.2d at 488).

58. *Id.* at 348-349 (citing Dahelite v. U.S., 346 U.S. 15 (1953)). This is because the "faithful execution of specific, discretionary decisions will not result in liability," *id.* at 349 (citing Berkovitz and McMichael, *supra* note 53), while "discretionary immunity will not apply when specific instructions are not faithfully carried out."

59. For example, in U. S. v. Fidelity & Guaranty Co., 837 F.2d 116 (3d Cir. 1988), *cert. denied*, 437 U.S. 1235 (1988), the circuit court found that the U.S. Environmental Protection Agency On-Scene Coordinator's decision to continue remediation operations despite a contractor's recommendation that it not be performed that day because of wind conditions was discretionary, since the coordinator "had to weigh the comparative risks, costs and advantages of delaying the operation or using another method to deal with the hazardous chemicals." Lerner, at 349 (citing Fidelity & Guaranty Co., 837 F.2d at 122). Likewise, in City of Daytona Beach v. Palmer, 469 So.2d 121 (Fla. 1985), the Florida Supreme Court held that "[t]he decisions of how to properly fight a particular fire, how to rescue victims in a fire, or what and how much equipment to send to a fire, are discretionary judgment decisions which are inherent in this public safety function of fire protection." Lerner, at 349 (quoting Palmer, 469 So.2d at 123); *see also* Ayres v. Indian Heights Volunteer Fire Dep't, 493 N.E.2d 1229, 1232 (Ind. 1986) (manner in which fire is fought is discretionary function; "all fires are different and require separate and distinct judgments as to the proper manner of combating."); Kroger v. City of Mount Vernon, 480 N.Y.S.2d 370 (N.Y. App. Div. 1984) (even if a fire chief's choice of firefighting method amounts to negligence, property owner's suit barred by immunity).

60. 471 N.W.2d 368 (Minn. Ct. App. 1991).

61. *Id.* at 371. Lerner cites to cases in which firefighters arguably suffered some dereliction of duty, but the principle remains the same. *See* Gordon v. City of Henderson, 766 S.W.2d 784, 785 (Tenn. 1989) (firefighters were "absent from their regular duty station, and had to be located by the Henderson Police Department," resulting in longer response times, and some of the firefighters had "the smell of liquor on their breath."); Williams v. Tuscumbia, 426 So.2d 824, 826 (Ala. 1983) (driver of fire truck was sick and not replaced; the court stated that "the fire department acted unskillfully by not having a back-up driver who could have immediately taken the place of the sick driver . . . In other words, the fire department lacked proficiency.").

62. 280 F.3d 566 (5th Cir. 2002).

63. No. 9609234-S-BLW (D. Idaho Feb. 19, 1999) (order granting judgment in favor of plaintiffs against the United States), *available at* http://www.idd.uscourts.gov/ECM/dc_images/_IDVOTEGLM10033070.pdf.

64. *Id.* slip op. at 1.

65. *Id.* slip op. at 21-24.

66. *Id.* slip op. at 27.

67. No. 91-A-59, 1991 WL 236851 (D. Colo. Nov. 6, 1991).

68. *Id.* at *1. Under the agreement, the local government (in that case the Boulder County Sheriff's Department) was responsible for all wildfire suppression activities on private land. *Id.*

69. *Id.* at 2. With respect to the plaintiff's substantive claims, the court noted that the plaintiff was challenging the choices and judgments made by the USFS Incident Commander, and found that a determination as to whether these were "discretionary functions" and therefore immune from suit was inappropriate for determination at the summary judgment stage. *Id.* at *2-*3.

70. Reimbursement issues are discussed more fully in the section of this chapter on the Emergency Management Assistance Compact, *infra.*

71. *Northern Virginia Memorandum of Agreement*, in Answering the Call: Communications Lessons Learned from the Pentagon Attack, app. B (PSWN 2002) (NOVA Agreement).

72. *Id.* at § III. The Virginia jurisdictions participate in the NOVA Agreement pursuant to Title 27, Chapter 1, Sections 27-1 to 27-4 of the Code of Virginia. *Id.* at § IV. The U.S. Army Base at Ft. Belvoir participates pursuant to 42 U.S.C. § 1856a, which permits federal government entities to enter into local mutual aid agreements. Because the agreement includes only Ft. Belvoir, rather than all U.S. Army or U.S. military facilities in Northern Virginia, the NOVA Agreement is best evaluated as a local-to-local agreement, rather than an agreement between multiple levels of government.

73. *Id.* at § V.

74. *Id.* at § VI.

75. *Id.* at § VII(A). Virginia has preserved full sovereign immunity for local government activities. *See* Mann v. Arlington County, 98 S.E.2d 515 (Va. 1957) (Virginia counties cannot be sued unless they consent to suit by statute); Fry v. County of Albemarle, 9 S.E. 1004 (Va. 1890).

76. NOVA Agreement, at § VII(B).

77. *Id.* at § VII(C).

78. *Id.* at § VII(D).

79. NIMS, at 39-40; Nat'l Emergency Management Association, Model Intrastate Mutual Aid Legislation 9 (2004) (a checklist of best practices) (Model Legislation).

80. Article I, § 10, of the U.S. Constitution permits states to enter into compacts with one another with the consent of Congress. The Supreme Court has held that the requirement of congressional consent is required only where the compact enhanced state power to a point where it encroached on the power of the federal government. *See* U.S. Steel Corp. v. Multistate Tax Comm'n, 434 U.S. 452 (1978). Congress consented to the EMAC in 1997. *See* Emergency Management Assistance Compact, Pub. L. No. 104-321, 110 Stat. 3877 (1996) (EMAC).

81. There are other interstate emergency response compacts. For example, several Northeastern states are members of the New England State Police Compact. *See, e.g.*, Vt. Stat. Ann. tit. 20, §§ 1951-1972.

82. EMAC, at art. IV. The announced purpose of the EMAC is "to provide for mutual assistance between the states entering into this compact in managing any emergency or disaster that is duly declared by the governor of the affected state(s), whether arising from natural disaster, technological hazard, man-made disaster, civil emergency aspects of resources shortages, community disorders, insurgency, or enemy attack." EMAC, at art. I.

83. Federal Emergency Management Agency, FEMA 322, Public Assistance Guide 25 (2004); *see also* FEMA Recovery Division Policy 9523.6 (2004). In order for a requesting jurisdiction to receive reimbursement, the Public Assistance Guide requires that: a written mutual aid agreement be in effect prior to the disaster; the entity that received the aid actually be charged for that aid; the agreement not contain a contingency clause that specifies payment only upon receipt of FEMA funds—that is, reimbursement must be a feature of *all mutual aid responses under the agreement, not just those for which federal reimbursement is available*; and the entity provide documentation of payment for services upon request. FEMA Public Assistance Guide, at 25.

84. The EMAC also provides that individuals who are licensed, certified, or permitted in the responding state are deemed to be licensed, certified, or permitted in the requesting state. However, care should be taken to ensure that the receiving state has completed any

other necessary procedural or regulatory steps, beyond adoption of EMAC implementing legislation, that would be required under its own rules and regulations to deem an individual licensed, certified, or permitted. EMAC, at art. V.

85. In addition, to the extent that the EMAC would address such issues, it addresses those issues only in the context of EMAC responses, which, as noted above, may occur only pursuant to a state disaster declaration.

86. *See* Alice Lipowicz, *National Capital Region Struggles to Strike Mutual Aid Agreements*, CQ Homeland Security (Aug. 23, 2004).

87. *See* Mann v. Arlington County, 98 S.E.2d 515 (Va. 1957) (Virginia counties cannot be sued unless they consent to suit by statute); Fry v. County of Albemarle, 9 S.E. 1004 (Va. 1890).

88. *See* Wade v. Dist. of Columbia, 310 A.2d 857 (D.C. 1973).

89. *See* Housing Auth. of Baltimore City v. Bennett, 754 A.2d 367 (Md. 2000); Tadjer v. Montgomery County, 479 A.2d 1321 (Md. 1984).

90. Md. Code Ann., Cts. & Jud. Proc. § 5-639; Md. Code Ann., Transp. § 19-103.

91. Md. Code Ann., Cts. & Jud. Proc. §§ 5-301 to 5-338 (2003).

92. 738 F.2d 1352 (D.C. Cir. 1984).

93. *Id.* at 1354-1355.

94. *Id.* at 1356.

95. *Id.* at 1357.

96. *Id.* at 1359 (citing Qasim v. Washington Metro. Area Transit Auth., 455 A.2d 904, 906 (D.C.), *cert. denied*, 461 U.S. 929 (1983)).

97. The 9/11 Commission recognized the difficulties posed by this decision, stating in its final report that "a serious obstacle to multi-jurisdictional response has been the lack of indemnification for mutual-aid responders in areas such as the National Capital Region." 9/11 Commission Report, at 397. Provisions to remedy this situation with respect to the National Capital Region were included in the intelligence reform bill signed into law by President Bush. *See* Pub. L. No. 108-796, § 7302. These provisions do not address similar situations that might arise in other multi-state regions. However, as the U.S. Supreme Court held in Nevada v. Hall, 440 U.S. 410 (1979), it is the forum state's decision whether or not to recognize the nonforum state's immunity doctrine in a suit brought in the forum state's court It remains to be seen how this issue will be addressed. Therefore, states can act to recognize each others' sovereign immunity rules for the purposes of mutual aid responses, and avoid the problem that arose in *Biscoe*.

98. Model Legislation, *supra* note 79. A number of states have enacted legislation codifying statewide mutual aid compacts for disaster response. *See, e.g.*, Ind. Code §§ 10-14-3-10.6, -10.7; Iowa Code § 29C.22; Ohio Rev. Code Ann. § 5502.41. In addition, several states have constructed statewide mutual aid compacts for use in response to declared disasters and emergencies. *See, e.g.*, Florida Statewide Mutual Aid Agreement, July 31, 2000; Georgia Emergency Management Agency Statewide Mutual Aid and Assistance Agreement; Commonwealth of Kentucky Statewide Emergency Management Mutual Aid and Assistance Agreement; Michigan Emergency Management Assistance Compact. FEMA recommends developing statewide mutual aid arrangements for major incident response. *See* FEMA, FA-282-May 2004, Responding to Incidents of National Consequence: Recommendations for America's Fire and Emergency Services Based on the Events of September 11, 2001, and Other Similar Events 30-31 (2004).

99. Article I clarifies that the Model Legislation is not intended to affect existing mutual aid agreements—or to prevent the execution of supplementary mutual aid agreements—among political subdivisions. Model Legislation, art. I. Article I also includes the creation of a State or Statewide Intrastate Mutual Aid Committee. The committee is to be "multidisciplinary" and "representative of emergency management and response disci-

plines as well as local government." The committee is to hold meetings to review the "prog-ress and status of statewide mutual aid, as well as to "assist in developing methods to track and evaluate activation of the system" and to "examine issues facing participating political subdivisions regarding the implementation" of the Model Legislation. *Id.*

100. Each such jurisdiction is required to: identify its own potential hazards using a common identification system; conduct joint planning, intelligence sharing, and threat as-sessment development, as well as joint training at least biennially; identify and inventory its currently available services, equipment, supplies, personnel and other resources; and adopt and put into practice the standardized incident management system approved by the state emergency management agency. *Id.* art. III.

101. *Id.* art. I.

102. *Id.* at art. IV. Under Article IV, requests for assistance are not required to go directly to the state emergency management agency, "but in all cases will be reported to the agency as soon as is practical." *Id.*

103. There may, however, be situations in which reimbursement is appropriate absent a federal source of reimbursement, such as where a jurisdiction is asked to provide a signifi-cant amount of assistance for a large-scale event that does not trigger a federal disaster or emergency declaration.

104. Agreement between OES, CDF, USFS, BLM, NPS, and F&WS, Agreement for Local Government Fire Suppression Assistance to Forest Agencies, Apr. 7, 2002 (CFAA), *available at* http://www.fs.fed.us/r5/fire/cooperators/rev03_ca_fire_assist_agrmt_2002-2006.pdf.

105. The Department of the Interior's Bureau of Indian Affairs (BIA) is responsible for wild land fire protection on tribal lands. However, BIA is party to separate agreements with CDF and the Forest Agencies.

106. The CFAA presumably will be harmonized with the NIMS when the CFAA is re-negotiated in 2006.

107. CFAA, at ¶ 18. As noted above, the agreement does not create a parallel federal-local mutual aid system that could be utilized when the Forest Agencies request state as-sistance.

108. CFAA, at ¶ 19.

109. CFAA, at ¶ 20.

110. *Id.*

111. CFAA, at ¶ 21.

112. CFAA, at ¶ 22.

113. Appendix A notes that OES agrees to the terms on behalf of participating local jurisdictions, and that local jurisdictions voluntarily provide personnel and equipment to the Forest Agencies under the CFAA and therefore by doing so accept the terms set forth in Appendix A. *See* CFAA, app. A, at A-1.

114. *Id.*

115. CFAA, app. A, at A-1 to A-2.

116. *Id.*

117. *Id.* at ¶ A-3.

118. *Id.* at ¶ A-2.

119. CFAA, app. A, at A-6 to A-7, ¶¶ A-16 to A-22. Appendix A makes note that DoD and tribal fire department resources may be accessed through the California Mutual Aid System, but that reimbursement for such resources will be reimbursed in accordance with CDF-U.S. Department of Defense and CDF-BIA agreements.

120. CFAA, at ¶ 23.

121. 811 F. Supp. 503 (C.D. Cal. 1992).

122. *Id.* at 504.

123. *Id.* at 506.

124. Enslow II, 1994 WL 649979, at **2 (*emphasis in original*). The appeals court rejected the district court's application of agency law principles, and instead required "more exacting proof" of an employment relationship between the CDF firefighter and USFS. *Id.* at **1-**2.

125. *Id.* at **2-**3.

126. No. 9609234-S-BLW (D. Idaho Feb. 19, 1999) (order granting judgment in favor of plaintiffs against the United States), *available at* http://www.idd.uscourts.gov/ECM/dc_images/_IDVOTEGLM10033070.pdf.

127. For further discussion of the *Buttram* decision, see the section of this chapter on Street-Level Operations, *supra.*

128. Federally recognized Indian tribes are sovereign governments that enjoy a direct government-to-government relationship with the federal government. Their sovereignty is akin to that of the states, limited in various ways by the Constitution. Their status as governmental entities, therefore, is different from that of a local government, which derives all of its powers and authorities from the state.

129. BIA has responsibility for law enforcement and firefighting on tribal lands, and the U.S. Department of Health and Human Services, Indian Health Service (IHS), has responsibility for emergency medical services. However, under the Indian Self-Determination and Assistance Act, 25 U.S.C. §§ 450-458 (2000), Indian tribes may enter into contracts with BIA and IHS to operate these services themselves.

130. Tribes are not prohibited by the federal government from entering into intergovernmental agreements with state and local governments. *See* State v. Manypenny, 662 N.W.2d 183 (Minn. Ct. App. 2003). However, a number of states have enacted legislation permitting mutual aid agreements with Indian tribes, limiting in certain ways the breadth or scope of such agreements. *See, e.g.,* MONT. CODE ANN. §§ 18-11-104, -110; NEB. REV. STAT. § 13-1508; Maxwell Carr-Howard, Comment, *Tribal-State Relations: Time for Constitutional Stature?*, 26 N.M. L. REV. 293, 316-317 (Spring 1996). Some states, including Minnesota and South Carolina, require such agreements. *See* MINN. STAT. § 471.59; S.C. CODE ANN. § 27-16-70. Tribal-local mutual aid agreements have been cited as a method of alleviating public safety concerns that accompany the opening of tribal gaming facilities, to the mutual benefit of both the tribe and surrounding local governments. Kevin Ryan, *Municipal and State Impact of Gaming*, 37 NEW ENG. L. REV. 553, 556 (2003).

131. *See, e.g.,* CAL. PENAL CODE §§ 830.1, 830.6, 832.6; FLA. STAT. ch. 285.18; MINN. STAT. § 626.93; MONT. CODE ANN. § 18-11-04; N.M. STAT. ANN. § 29-1-11; S.C. CODE ANN. § 27-16-70.

132. Internal Law Enforcement Services Policies, 69 Fed. Reg. 6321 (Bureau of Indian Affairs Feb. 10, 2004). As noted above, BIA is ultimately responsible for the provision of law enforcement in Indian country. *Id.* According to BIA, "[t]o increase the effectiveness of law enforcement in Indian country, the authority and status of law enforcement officers, relationships among and between law enforcement departments, as well as potential liability and liability coverage, must be clear." BIA enters into MOAs, MOUs, CDAs, and SLEC agreements in order to fulfill its law enforcement obligations in Indian country "and to make clear important policies and working relationships." *Id.* According to BIA, "[f]or SLEC officers to be used effectively" to fill law enforcement voids in Indian country, "it is important that all parties involved in Indian country law enforcement have a clear understanding of each of their roles and expectations." *Id.* at 6322. In addition, "the BIA encourages full and open coordination between and among relevant tribal, local, and Federal law enforcement, and any relevant task forces or other similar organizations. Whenever possible the BIA encourages the relevant parties to enter agreements governing these cooperative relationships." *Id.* These agreements should address tort liability, although BIA expects that officers carrying Federal SLECs will be covered by the FTCA. *Id.*

133. *See* County of Lewis v. State, 163 F.3d 509 (9th Cir. 1998).

134. *See, e.g.,* Dry v U.S., 235 F.3d 1249 (10th Cir. 2000); State v. Manypenny, 662 N.W.2d 183 (Minn. Ct. App. 2003); State v. LaRose, 673 N.W.2d 157 (Minn. Ct. App. 2003).

135. 963 P.2d 522 (N.M. Ct. App.), *cert. denied,* 964 P.2d 818 (N.M. 1998).

136. *Id.* at 524. Navajo Nation police officers are cross-deputized as San Juan County Sheriff's deputies and BIA Special Deputy Police Officers, and certified by the New Mexico State Police. *Id.*

137. *Id.* The court dismissed the action against the Navajo Nation police officers in their official capacity on the same grounds. *Id.* The court also dismissed § 1983 actions against the officers in their individual capacities, but not before assuming, without deciding, based on the mutual aid agreement and cross-deputization, that even though tribes do not as a matter of course act under the color of state law within the meaning of § 1983, the officers were in fact acting under color of state law. *Id.* at 527. The court concluded that the plaintiff failed to explain how the Navajo Nation police officers violated any federal law or constitutional provision while acting under the color of state law. *Id.* at 527-528. Note, however, that courts have resolved this question differently in different situations. *Compare, e.g.,* Armstrong v. Mille Lacs County Sheriffs Dep't, 112 F. Supp.2d 840 (tribal officers not acting under color of state law despite cross-deputization agreement) *with* Evans v. McKay, 869 F.2d 1341 (9th Cir. 1989) (cross-deputized BIA officers may have been acting as municipal police officers rather than tribal officers in performing law enforcement functions at issue).

138. *See, e.g.,* MINN. STAT. § 626.90(2).

139. *See* Armstrong, 112 F. Supp.2d at 840.

140. *See* Evans, 869 F.2d at 1341.

141. FY04 Grant Guidance, app. E, at E-1.

142. NIMS, at 50.

143. NIMS, at 50. According to the NIMS, "[s]ystems must be able to work together and should not interfere with one another if the multiple jurisdictions, organizations, and functions that come together under the NIMS are to be effective in domestic incident management." NIMS, at 55. This is because "[i]nteroperability and compatibility are achieved through the use of such tools as common communications and data standards, digital data formats, equipment standards, and design standards." *Id.*

144. PSWN 9/11 Pentagon Report, at 3-4.

145. *Id.* at 4.

146. *Id.*

147. *Id.* at 4, Appendix.

148. *See* the section of this chapter titled, A Sample Operational Mutual Aid Agreement, *supra.*

149. PSWN 9/11 Pentagon Report, at 9.

150. *Id.* at 9-10. In the words of Captain Blaine Corle, Alexandria Police Department, "Communications were seamless when using Arlington preprogrammed channels." *Id.* at 9.

151. *Id.* at 9-10. The ACFD had on-scene command of fire ground operations, including search and rescue, until the fire was extinguished and the area was deemed safe to enter without protective clothing, despite the site's status as a crime scene. *Id.* at 13.

152. *Id.* at 10. The PSWN reported that other interoperable communications tools, such as the Federal Bureau of Investigation's Transportable Public Safety Radio Interoperability Unit, the Alexandria Police Department's ACU-1000 switch, and various commercial services were not nearly as effective in facilitating interoperable communications. *Id.* at 10-12.

153. *Id.* at 13-17. The 9/11 Commission staff found much the same thing, stating that emergency response at the Pentagon "overcame the inherent complications of a response

across jurisdictions because the Incident Command System—a formalized management structure for emergency response—was in place in the National Capital Region on 9/11." *See* 9/11 COMMISSION, STAFF STATEMENT NO. 14, *supra* note 21, at 8.

154. The 9/11 Commission staff also commented on the mutually reinforcing nature of interoperable communications and the incident command system, stating that "a fully integrated Incident Command System will assure that evolving situation awareness is shared among responding agencies and will assist first responders in sizing up the situation at hand." *See id.* at 8.

155. As newer technologies, including wireless voice/data networks, come into use, these can be incorporated into such arrangements as well.

156. An exception was the Nextel Direct Connect system, which continued to function through all phases of the incident, and which was used by certain responding jurisdictions. PSWN 9/11 Pentagon Report, at 20-23. However, as dedicated wireless services are developed, either by the federal government or state and local governments, or in cooperation with commercial carriers, the use of such services should be reevaluated.

157. Many states also permit the establishment of mutual aid relationships with governmental units of other states. *See, e.g.,* R.I. GEN. LAWS §§ 30-15.8-1(a) to .8-3 (2004); WYO. STAT. ANN. §§ 19-13-201 to -210 (Mitchie 2004). Such relationships also can be incorporated into regional cooperation arrangements.

158. The RECP is a good example of an all-hazards response plan. The RECP applies to the National Capital Region, which the MWCOG defines as the District of Columbia; Montgomery, Prince George's, and Frederick counties in Maryland; Arlington, Fairfax, Loudoun, and Prince William counties in Virginia; and "all cities existing in Maryland or Virginia within the geographic area designated by the outer boundaries of the combined counties listed in [40 U.S.C. § 71(b)]," plus those cities within Frederick County, Maryland. METRO. WASH. COUNCIL OF GOV'TS, REGIONAL EMERGENCY COORDINATION PLAN 2 (2002) (Baseline Plan), *available at* http://www.mwcog.org/security/security/plan.asp.

159. *Id.* at 5.

160. *Id.* at 7-8. The RECP specifically "does not supercede existing policies, authorities, plans, or procedures that member and stakeholder organizations currently have in place," including mutual aid agreements and other operational documents. *Id.* at 4. The RECP does not "usurp or infringe on the authorities, plans, procedures, or prerogatives of any participating jurisdiction, agency, or organization," and it assumes that "[a]ll necessary decisions affecting response, recovery, protective actions, public health and safety advisories, etc., will be made by responsible officials under their existing authorities, policies, plans, and procedures." *Id.* at 6. The RECP also assumes that "[e]stablishing common terminology and structuring the plan for compatibility with accepted local, state, and federal emergency plans improve efficiency and effectiveness in regional communications and coordination." *Id.*

161. *Id.,* R-ESF 13, at 4-5.

162. Some state statutes authorize the formation of such teams, or the utilization of response teams from neighboring jurisdictions. *See, e.g.,* MONT. CODE ANN. § 10-3-701.

163. Although the teams at issue in the cases discussed below focus on a specific discipline, such as law enforcement or search and rescue, the principles are equally applicable to regional response teams of various disciplines.

164. 56 P.3d 559 (Wash. 2002).

165. *Id.* at 560.

166. *Id.*

167. *Id.* at 561 (citing WASH. REV. CODE §§ 38.52.260, 38.52.010(4) (search and rescue volunteers entitled to workers compensation), 38.52.190 (search and rescue volunteers barred from bringing suit for injury or death arising out of activities as an emergency responder),

51.04.010, 41.26.281 (firefighters and police officers permitted to both collect workers' compensation benefits and bring related negligence suits against their employers)).

168. *Id.* at 661.

169. *Id.* at 562-563.

170. *Id.* at 563. Contrast this with the approach taken by the Arizona legislature, which enacted a statute providing that "[a]ny emergency plans duly adopted and approved satisfy the requirement for mutual aid agreements." *See* Ariz. Rev. Stat. § 26-309(A).

171. *Id.*

172. 904 P.2d 1159 (Wash. Ct. App. 1995), *review denied*, 914 P.2d 65 (Wash. 1996).

173. *Id.* at 1165.

174. *Id.*

175. *See also* State v. Gabbard, No. CA98-06-124, 1999 WL 270308 (Ohio Ct. App. May 3, 1999) (police officers responding pursuant to regional "Joint Task Force Mutual Aid Agreement" conducted lawful inventory search within requesting jurisdiction's territory, since officers followed responding jurisdiction's inventory search policy, and officer from requesting jurisdiction aided in inventory search).

176. Knight, 904 P.2d at 1165. Paragraph 4 of the mutual aid agreement stated, "Personnel assigned to the task force shall be deemed to be continuing under the employment of the assigning jurisdiction. As among the participating agencies, liability shall be governed by the mutual aid agreement separately entered into by and among them." *Id.* at 1166.

177. *Id.*

178. 66 Cal.App.4th 195 (Cal. Ct. App. 1988).

179. 338 N.W.2d 919 (Mich. Ct. App. 1983).

180. Brassinga, 66 Cal.App.4th at 202-203.

181. *Id.* at 205.

182. *Id.*

183. *Id.* at 208-209.

184. *Id.* at 210-211. The court noted that the regional team was not a "joint powers agency" with independent existence, but rather a "joint enterprise arising out of a mutual aid agreement," as contemplated by state law. *Id.* at 211. The court found that such a cooperative enterprise did not rise to the level of an "employer" for the purposes of the workers' compensation law. *Id.* at 212-213. The court next considered whether Mountain View was the "special employer" of the deceased police officer. The court found that while there was no evidence that Palo Alto had ceded control over the deceased police officer to Mountain View, it was possible that Palo Alto and Mountain View had shared responsibility over the deceased police officer so as to create a special employment relationship between the officer and Mountain View. *Id.* at 215-216. The case was settled before this issue was brought to trial.

185. 338 N.W.2d at 922.

186. *Id.*

187. *Id.* (citations omitted).

188. *Id.* (citations omitted).

189. *Id.* at 923.

190. *Id.*

191. *Id.* at 924.

192. *Id.*

193. 786 F. Supp. 676 (M.D. Tenn. 1992).

194. *Id.* at 682.

195. *Id.* (*citing* Tenn. Code Ann. § 12-9-104, *as extended by* Tenn. Code Ann. § 6-54-307).

196. *Id.* at 682-683.

197. *Id.*

198. *Id.* at 683.

199. *Id.* at 683-684. By contrast, in Allis-Chalmers Corp. v. Emmet County Council of Gov'ts, 355 N.W.2d 586 (Iowa 1984), the Iowa Supreme Court found that jurisdictions participating in the Emmet County Council of Governments (ECCOG) pursuant to an Intergovernmental Cooperation Agreement had created a joint powers agency under Iowa law, and therefore a suit against member governments of the ECCOG for breach of a contract between ECCOG and a supplier was improper.

CHAPTER 10

Managing Donated Resources Following Catastrophic Events

by Jean Cox[1]

Introduction

In the immediate aftermath of the September 11, 2001, attacks on the World Trade Center, volunteers, offers of assistance, and unsolicited donated goods poured in from across New York State, the nation, and the world. This generosity is inspirational and quite typical. A similar outpouring of support occurred relative to the Pentagon attack. A wide variety of solicited and unsolicited donations of goods and services can be expected after virtually every catastrophic event.

Volunteers and donated goods can be of great assistance to emergency response efforts and to the families whose lives have been disrupted. But if the jurisdiction has not prepared for the influx of volunteers and donated materials by making a donations management plan part of its comprehensive emergency management plan, volunteers and donations can create transportation—and other logistical—bottlenecks, additional public health and safety risks, potential liability, and media and public relations disasters of their own.

This chapter describes the donations challenges that New York faced after the September 11, 2001, attacks. It also outlines a number of the different donations and volunteer management issues, both legal and practical, that should be addressed in a jurisdiction's donations management plan.

Donations Issues Arising Out of September 11 Events

On September 11, in accordance with the Donations Management Annex to New York's Comprehensive Emergency Management Plan, Governor George

E. Pataki quickly established a donations hotline at the state Department of Taxation and Finance in Albany to coordinate the large volume of calls offering assistance and donated goods. This resulted in a registry of goods that the state could use to support New York City operations. The governor also asked medical professionals to call two newly established hotlines, and urged New Yorkers to give blood at their local centers. Within 12 hours, the state received more than 9,400 offers of assistance from medical professionals. The governor also established a hotline at the state Department of Taxation and Finance to receive cash donations on behalf of the victims' families.

On September 13, Governor Pataki opened the Jacob Javits Center to serve as a staging and registration area for all those wishing to volunteer their services. This volunteer coordination center allowed people to register their names for a broad spectrum of necessary activities ranging from emergency medical response to cleanup and debris-removal activities. With the registry thus created, authorities could identify volunteers based on their skills and deploy them as effectively as possible. After 9/11, the response was so tremendous that the governor quickly announced the registry was full and people were asked not to report to the center until further notice.

Even with the donations hotline in place, there was a concern about unsolicited goods that were already en route to New York City from points scattered across the nation and the world. City and state officials realized that trucks bearing unsolicited goods would jeopardize an already burdened transportation network in the city. Items such as food and medical supplies needed special handling to avoid public health problems. (For example, medical syringes of unknown origin were included among the donated items.) Warehouse space was needed to accommodate a large amount of goods since it was uncertain what quantity of material would arrive in New York.

The responsibility for managing the donations efforts rested with the New York State Emergency Management Office (NYSEMO). Assisted by several state agencies, the Federal Emergency Management Agency (FEMA), Governor Pataki's office, and private companies, NYSEMO's donations management team identified and secured five locations with a total capacity of more than two million square feet to receive donated materials. Two sites were upstate, one was on Long Island, and one each was in New Jersey and Connecticut. The sites were located near interstate highways where the New York City-bound trucks easily could be diverted, minimizing congestion. The New York State Department of Transportation and the Thruway Authority coordinated traffic flow, along with the state police, by working with the neighboring states. This included use of variable message signs to provide route information to truckers. As time progressed, the warehouse inventories were consolidated, with the two upstate centers closing first.

Working with volunteer organizations, such as the Seventh Day Adventists and the Salvation Army, as well as the National Guard, the offloaded goods were sorted and inventoried. Unsolicited perishable goods were distributed quickly within existing public and voluntary social service networks. As requests for items came in from Ground Zero, they were matched up with donated goods from the inventory and then sent to staging areas within the city.

Donations Management Plan: Donated Goods

A donations management plan must serve a number of objectives. Its primary purpose is to assist disaster victims—this is the primary objective of the entire response. The plan meets this objective by providing an effective channel for offers of goods and services from the public—and to ensure that these goods and services support the local response effort.

The plan also has two critical public relations/public information objectives. Donations management activities must assure the public that their donations are appreciated and will be directed to the disaster victims in the most efficient manner. And the donations management team must use communications tools to influence the kinds and locations of donations that will be of most use to the response and recovery effort: It must educate the media and the public about the types of donations that will benefit the disaster victims most, including the benefit of cash donations.

A key management objective of New York State's plan is to minimize disruption from logistical and transportation bottlenecks. New York does this by utilizing the "pull" approach, directing donations away from the disaster area, and creating staging areas away from the disaster area where goods can be sorted, organized, and sent into the disaster area based upon specific criteria as prioritized by the first responders. Finally, the plan must recognize that the jurisdiction's efforts to "manage" the gifts provided by generous people and organizations must be a part of the overall coordination of the response actions of all levels of government, the private sector, and the volunteer community.

A donations management plan should include actions that will be performed before (preparedness), during (response), and after (assessment) a catastrophic event. These are the action checklists in New York's plan:

Preparing for Donations Management

1. Annually update the donations management plan by canvassing all human service agencies that address human services needs before and after a disaster.
2. Develop and maintain an inventory of warehouse facilities.
3. Develop a toll-free number to handle inquiries.
4. Establish procedures to accept cash.
5. Develop and maintain a database for recording offers of donated monies, goods and services.
6. Establish a policy for distributing the goods remaining after the relief effort ends.
7. Exercise the donations plan.
8. Designate and train staff on the donations management team.

Responding to a Disaster with a Donations Management Plan

1. Activate the donations management plan.
2. Alert local, state, and federal governments.

3. Notify the volunteer network.
4. Place the donations management team on stand-by, and determine staffing and support needs based on the incident.
5. Identify warehouse space and staging areas and secure agreements for their use, if necessary.
6. Search the database to identify goods or previous offers that may be useful in this event.
7. Coordinate with the public information officer to encourage the media to request that goods and services be held locally until needed.
8. Initiate a toll-free line and phone bank for donated goods and services.
9. Maintain continuous contact with involved agencies through the donations management team, to ensure a smooth flow of goods and services to the disaster area.
10. Monitor news accounts, to the extent practicable, to anticipate the number and type of goods that may arrive and try to divert them to the appropriate staging or warehouse areas.
11. Prepare daily status reports that document any issues and track the goods going into and out of the warehouses or staging areas.
12. Maintain all records of purchases, rentals, loans, and agreements to facilitate potential reimbursement.

Post-Emergency

1. Assess the continuing needs of the agencies involved in the recovery effort.
2. Determine if the scale of the donations management team is still appropriate to the effort.
3. Scale back the team if needed.
4. Ensure the database has been updated.
5. Assist with thank you letters.
6. Conduct a post-event evaluation.

Successful donations management plans must be an integral part of a disaster operation. In order to accomplish this, the donations management team should be well trained in the National Incident Management System (NIMS).[2] The NIMS includes a standardized incident management system that most states and local governments use to respond to an emergency or disaster. While most think of donations management in large scale disasters, for example, the World Trade Center disaster, lesser events can also trigger the need for the activation of the donations management plan, as well a need to coordinate donations activities of the state (and its donations management team), the volunteer agencies, and federal donations management staff.

Responsibilities of the State Donations Management Team

1. Utilize the volunteer organizations that are the primary receivers, managers, and distributors of donated goods and services.

2. Remember that the ultimate responsibility for donations management lies with the local government where the disaster occurred.
3. Ensure that transportation routes to the disaster area are accessible.
4. Ensure that volunteer agencies receive the support they need so they are not overwhelmed.
5. Ensure that useful donated goods and materials are matched with those in need, and are not wasted.
6. Support the affected community in the short term, and delegate the donations function to the community when it is capable of accepting it.
7. Determine the goods and donations most needed by the citizens in the disaster area.
8. Work with the public information officer to communicate clearly to the public that unsolicited goods can overwhelm an already stressed infrastructure and create more problems.
9. Publicize the items needed, and provide a hotline for those who wish to donate.
10. Facilitate a prompt response to donors and the prompt allocation of donated equipment, goods, services, and cash to the victims of the disaster.
11. Train the affected local government or volunteer organization to take over the donations management responsibilities.

Responsibilities of Volunteer Agencies

Volunteer agencies that assist in a disaster area must take responsibility for bringing and accepting donated goods into the disaster area. It is essential that these volunteer agencies do the following, at a minimum:

1. Accept only donations needed or for which there is an identified use.
2. Secure warehouses and distribution centers.
3. Off-load, sort, repackage, store, and distribute any donations accepted by the volunteer organization.
4. Inform the state and local government of any needs and unexpected shortfalls.

Responsibilities of FEMA

The federal government's role in donations management is to assist the state with additional federal resources, to facilitate coordination among the state and the volunteer organizations, and to discourage in-kind donations while urging cash donations. Specifically, FEMA's role is to support the state, as requested and required, in:

1. Assessing existing/proposed warehouses and other operational facilities, helping to establish a donations management system after disaster strikes, and supporting the disaster field office donations coordination team.

2. Providing technical assistance, managerial support, enhanced voluntary agency coordination, donations intelligence, facility support, and international donations.

3. Communicating and reinforcing to the public through the media the donations policy of state government, FEMA, and the volunteer agencies to avoid unwanted appeals for goods and services.

The FEMA donations program maintains many valuable contacts in the nonprofit and disaster-related voluntary agency communities, in business, labor, and industry, and with past donors and experienced disaster donors. All of this information is available to the donation management team and is part of the FEMA donations coordinator's contribution.

The network can provide possible assistance, such as road and rail transportation, guidance (the U.S. Conference of Mayors, Sister Cities International), and volunteer support (*e.g.*, Points of Light Foundation, Boy Scouts, Girl Scouts, National Jaycees, and Rotary International).

Donations Management Plan: Volunteer Management

Volunteers come to offer their services not just from the surrounding community, but also from all parts of the United States. Volunteers can fill sandbags to try to protect structures from flooding. They can staff emergency shelters, provide crisis counseling, and activate and provide pro bono legal services. They can disseminate significant funds raised from donors to help meet needs for food, furniture, clothing, school supplies, and other needs created by a catastrophic event. They can provide medical services or just provide manpower for physical tasks. Volunteers, trained and untrained, can be crucial to effective major incident response and must be treated with dignity and respect.

There are four primary volunteer groups that need to be approached and managed in different ways:

Professional volunteers. "Professional" volunteers can be obtained from emergency organizations in jurisdictions outside the disaster area. These include volunteer fire and rescue departments, volunteer rescue squads and ambulance services, and volunteer search and rescue teams. Volunteers for these organizations are "professionals." That is, they often have the same or similar training to their counterparts in paid or career public safety departments. Professional personnel are certified or licensed, and include physicians, EMTs, nurses, and fire fighters, among others. Often regulatory agencies within the affected area may waive or relax certification requirements when there is a need for these professionals.

Volunteers With Traditional Affiliations. These volunteers are attached to a recognized voluntary agency. They are pretrained for disaster response and form the core of the cadre for the nonprofessional volunteers.

Spontaneous Volunteers from Within the Affected Area. These volunteers are motivated by community ownership. They have no affiliation with any volunteer organizations and may have no formal training or relevant skills.

Spontaneous Volunteers from Outside the Affected Area. These volunteers do not have a prior affiliation with a recognized volunteer agency, and they may or may not have relevant skills.

It is essential that state and local governments have plans in place to marshal all these resources through remote staging areas, credential verification processes, and disaster assignment procedures. "Professional" and "traditional affiliated" volunteers can be effectively marshaled prior to a major incident through mutual aid agreements and inclusion of volunteer organizations in regional and statewide disaster response plans. Indeed, such agreements are critical in order to formalize the relationship between state and local governments and professional volunteer organizations.

By contrast, "spontaneous" volunteers will arrive unsummoned at the site of a disaster with various levels of training, expertise, tools, and equipment, as well as different understandings of and commitment to the affected community. Collection of spontaneous volunteers at a remote staging area permits the authority that has jurisdiction over the incident to assign volunteers to tasks and roles where they can be most effective, and to ensure that spontaneous volunteers have appropriate tools and personal protective equipment. Collection of volunteers in a "remote" location also allows registration and documentation, which is vital for personnel accountability and will help ensure tort liability and workers' compensation coverage for volunteers to the greatest extent possible.[3] Some state legislation permits the appointment of disaster volunteers;[4] it may be possible to use these statutes for this purpose.

Media Considerations in Donations Management

During any disaster, managing information is critical to success. It is essential to develop a relationship with the media prior to a disaster event and provide information on points of contact ahead of time. The media can help by broadcasting useful information in public service announcements, public affairs shows, and specials.

Frequently, the news media report live from disaster areas, interviewing disaster victims who have needs and are in distress. This motivates compassion and concern, and prompts actions that are intended to help disaster victims. Often, unfortunately, these actions are wasteful or of little assistance to victims. The reason is that the public may assume that certain items are needed when, in fact, they are not.

Donations spokespersons are essential to correcting misperceptions and providing accurate information. Public and nonprofit relief agencies should be specific and coordinated in their initial reports to best shape and temper the immediate public response. The most important message that public spokespersons can relate is that donating cash to a qualified organization is the best way to assist disaster victims. A major disaster is treated as fast-breaking news, so spokespersons should plan to answer questions quickly. While printed news releases are good for background, situation reports, updates, and live interviews are preferred, and it is best if the person interviewed is an official and informed source. Because the same questions and areas of interest generally are repeated by the media in every disaster, public information officers (PIOs) can plan some responses and be available with candid answers prior to the various media deadlines.

Messages to the media need to be coordinated by the appropriate personnel at each level before they are released to the press. It is best if the story is consistent at local, state, and federal levels. An effective method for dealing with the media is to establish a "joint information center" (JIC), where representatives of the various voluntary and government agencies meet to coordinate media relations. Although each voluntary agency remains responsible for its own media relations, the JIC makes it possible to have accurate and consistent information for the public.

The donations team leader should maintain contact with the JIC coordinator to monitor donations-related news and to correct misperceptions. The team leader also should work with the JIC to maintain a regular schedule of information releases to state and local governments, to the volunteer agencies, and to local, state and federal elected officials, with the understanding that the frequency of these releases will depend on the location, type, and scale of the event. Provisions for the multilingual and hearing impaired should also be addressed. Helping the media meet their deadlines is important and will assure more effective use of the media to present your message. TV, radio, local press, national press, and wire service requirements are all different. For large events, also expect requests from foreign media for interviews.

Liability and Workers' Compensation Issues

The donations team should be in compliance with state and local laws, and understand how flexibility in these laws can be used to support the operations. Subjects such as insurance, medical coverage, bonding of workers handling cash, worker safety, workers' compensation, and other liability issues are important. Similarly, consider local or state laws applicable to disposal of waste, and on-site sanitation, feeding facilities, storage of food, and hazardous materials, and child labor practices. The most effective method of monitoring these factors is to coordinate with the appropriate state government official who has authority to provide quick answers and waive requirements, if possible.

Certain steps can be taken before a major incident to address liability and workers' compensation issues. Liability issues for "professional" and "traditional affiliated" volunteers are generally handled in a mutual aid agreement that specifies who is considered the "employer" for purposes of workers' compensation, and which organization retains or accepts responsibility for civil liability for actions by, or injuries to, the volunteers. When these issues are ignored, litigation frequently ensues.[5]

Several new citizen corps initiatives give state and local governments additional tools to gather individuals who might be "spontaneous" volunteers, and make them "professional" volunteers prior to a disaster. Community Emergency Response Teams (CERT) are formed to prepare citizens to assist in response and recovery activities within their own communities.[6] The Medical Reserve Corps (MRC) provides a means for organizing medical and public health volunteers for service during emergencies.[7] In addition, some state statutes contemplate the creation and maintenance of lists of volunteers, or formation of volunteer corps, for use during disasters.[8] By forming CERTs and MRC teams, and assembling corps of state disaster service teams, state and local governments can marshal teams with various capabilities prior to major incident response through mutual aid agreements and incorporation into regional and statewide disaster response plans.[9] These volunteer teams also can be trained to manage the large numbers of "spontaneous" volunteers who typically arrive at disaster sites.

With respect to liability coverage, the CERT and MRC programs themselves do not shield from liability volunteers who participate on teams, or jurisdictions that utilize their services, nor do they provide for compensation for volunteers injured or killed while performing services. However, legislation at the federal level shields individual volunteers from liability. Moreover, many state statutes provide liability protection for disaster service volunteers.

Workers' Compensation. Disaster sites are inherently dangerous places. Hazards exist even for the most highly trained emergency responders. Neither spontaneous volunteers nor the jurisdictions that choose to utilize their services may have considered the implications of an injury to a spontaneous volunteer at a disaster site. Jurisdictions intending to utilize the services of spontaneous volunteers should consider the degree to which they intend that such volunteers be covered—or not covered—under applicable workers' compensation laws. State laws may include language broad enough to require coverage of individuals who serve, even in a volunteer capacity, under the direction and control of a political subdivision of the state. If the jurisdiction does not want to extend coverage to spontaneous volunteers, waivers executed at the time the volunteer enters service, or amendments to existing legislation, may be necessary in order to ensure this result.

Conversely, jurisdictions may choose to provide workers' compensation coverage to spontaneous volunteers. Doing so encourages volunteerism during times of disaster, and secure perimeters and remote staging areas allow jurisdictions to control the number and type of spontaneous volunteers eligible for coverage. Developing mechanisms to extend workers' compensation coverage to spontaneous volunteers prior to a disaster will obviate the need to do so during a disaster, should an event occur in which large numbers of spontaneous volunteers are injured and political pressure mounts to extend workers' compensation coverage to the injured. Finally, extending workers' compensation coverage to spontaneous volunteers may prevent lawsuits by those volunteers against the jurisdiction in the event of an injury, since such suits likely would be barred by the exclusive remedy provision of most workers' compensation statutes.

Several steps may be taken prior to a disaster to permit coverage of spontaneous volunteers under existing workers' compensation statutes. Simply assigning volunteers under the jurisdiction's standardized incident management system may be sufficient to bring spontaneous volunteers under the jurisdiction's workers' compensation responsibilities. If not, remote staging permits an opportunity for spontaneous volunteers to complete any necessary paperwork. State laws also may provide mechanisms for covering spontaneous volunteers as state disaster volunteers. Likewise, on a disaster involving federal assistance, it may be possible to designate certain functions involving volunteers as federal responsibilities, and place spontaneous volunteers under federal authority to provide coverage under the Federal Employees Compensation Act[10] Standard operating procedures (SOPs) establishing these procedures and the intended result should be developed in advance. If state or federal agencies are necessary to accomplish coverage, these agencies should be included in that process.

Liability to Third Parties. Tort liability is another concern for jurisdictions using both skilled and unskilled spontaneous volunteers. Unskilled spontaneous volunteers may damage property and injure rescuers and victims in the course of their activities. Skilled volunteers add the element of professional liability (malpractice) to their rescue activities. However, governmental immunity and various defenses based on the fact that volunteers may not become agents of the governmental unit having authority over the incident should serve to control jurisdictions' exposure to tort liability based on the actions of spontaneous volunteers.

In addition, at the local level, Good Samaritan acts should shield the individual volunteers from liability. In the great majority of states, Good Samaritan acts shield trained individuals from negligence associated with rendering care in an emergency (as long as the individual's actions were taken in good faith), except in cases of gross negligence or wanton misconduct.[11] Remote staging and registration procedures should be designed in such a way as to ensure that spontaneous volunteers remain within the scope of applicable Good Samaritan laws. Likewise, remote staging and spontaneous volunteer registration and control likely can be used to bring the volunteer under the protection of the federal Volunteer Protection Act (VPA).[12] Note, however, that the VPA does not provide any protection for the governmental entity utilizing the volunteer's service.[13]

Licensure. Licensure and certification issues are significant concerns attendant to the use of spontaneous volunteers. Often, individuals trained in firefighting, emergency medical services, search and rescue, law enforcement, engineering, construction trades, and other skills for which they are licensed or certified will arrive at the site of a major disaster ready to assist. These individuals can provide essential services in support of the jurisdiction's incident command system. However, use of licensed or certified spontaneous volunteers needs to be controlled in order to avoid unwanted results.

For example, without adequate scene control and remote staging for spontaneous volunteers, individuals dressed in first responder attire or wearing patches signifying licensure or certification may be let onto the disaster site and assigned to tasks for which they may not be trained. Of their own volition, some of these individuals may undertake tasks for which they are not qualified. Others may not be licensed or certified at all. Finally, the assignment of licensed or certified volunteers may be entirely dependent on the incident manager or supervisor with whom the volunteer first makes contact, rather than based on the actual needs of the authority having jurisdiction over the incident.

Instead, a special desk or section should be established in the remote staging area for licensed or certified spontaneous volunteers. Volunteers should be requested to provide documentation of their licensure or certification, and this should be verified to the greatest extent possible. The authority having jurisdiction should be mindful of provisions for intrastate and interstate transfer of licensure. Volunteers whose licenses and certificates are deemed valid and appropriate should be credentialed as such, and then they can be assigned to the incident, under the supervision of the authority having jurisdiction in support of the established incident command system.

Some considerations for preparing to marshal licensed and certified spontaneous volunteers:

- Determine in advance whether to accept the services of licensed and certified spontaneous volunteers, or to restrict skilled service during disaster response to members of the emergency response community and disaster response organizations.
- If you intend to accept the services of licensed or certified spontaneous volunteers, develop SOPs detailing how their licenses and certifications will be verified, and how spontaneous volunteers will be utilized. Make sure the entities that will be called upon to supervise these volunteers— hospitals and emergency medical services for medically trained volunteers, public works officials for engineering and construction trades volunteers—have a voice in designing these SOPs. Take advantage of the provisions in your state's Emergency Management Assistance Compact (EMAC) implementing legislation relating to licensed and certified responders to develop interlocking SOPs for recognition and verification of out-of-state licenses and certifications.

Licenses and certifications apply to many different disciplines and come in a variety of forms. Plan to utilize the services of professional responders, members of CERTs or MRC units, or other skilled personnel to staff the licensed and certified volunteers' section of the remote staging area to verify licenses and certifications. Include this in your emergency response plan.

Other Donations Management Issues

While others in the organization may have primary responsibility for the items below, the donations management team leader should be cognizant of them, understand their importance, and be prepared to assist others with collecting information or maintaining records relating to them.

Security Issues. Prepare for security of all personnel, and at each donations management facility. Each facility is likely to be a 24-hour operation and will require commensurate security. Special security for certain incoming goods, such as medicines and syringes, hazardous materials, and firearms, may be necessary.

Recycling/redistribution. There will be an abundance of goods that simply cannot be used in the immediate disaster situation, and arrangements must be made for managing these items. Recycling or redistribution to other needs is the first option to be considered.

Awareness of the Affected Community. Representation on the response team should reflect the ethnic and cultural diversity of the affected community. To reach each segment of the community, use appropriate communication mechanisms, such as through churches, synagogues, mosques, established community programs, and leaders. Material translated into local languages should be available for all steps—recruitment, training, maintenance, and follow through—in using volunteers. Sensitize volunteers to respect local customs, sensitivities, and religious traditions.

Local Economy Issues. One goal of disaster relief and rehabilitation is the restoration of the local economy. Care must be taken to ensure relief contributions do not impede recovery. For instance, large quantities of donated goods could have a negative impact on local businesses working to reestablish their predisaster vitality.

Environmental Impacts. Disposal of donated goods, and related environmental issues, are very much matters of public concern that must be taken into account in establishing a donations center. Know local laws that apply. Disposal of some items may require a contract with a hazardous material company. In isolated situations, a request for waiver of a particular law may be necessary. Center managers must remain aware of environmental cleanup work that remains after a disaster has passed.

Accountability. Accountability is critical. While a record of goods dispatched on a daily basis to the disaster area should be maintained, it is understood that perfect accountability may not be possible in situations where there is high volume flow in and out: The top priority is always to deliver critically needed items to the disaster area immediately.

Demobilization. Demobilization is the downsizing of the government's role in the donated goods and services operation. This allows appropriate voluntary agencies to take over completely. Demobilization involves the federal and state governments stepping back in terms of facilities, coordination, and other activities that can be transitioned to the affected local government or a particular voluntary agency group. Demobilization should be planned for soon after the operation is underway and implemented when there are signs of donor fatigue—that is, when the flow of goods starts to ebb. Close consultation with the voluntary agencies will help to determine this critical point in time.

Generally, transitioning control of a major donations operation back to the voluntary agencies should be straightforward. Voluntary agencies are very familiar with all aspects of donated goods and services, and typically should need assistance only when the event is unusually large. If the flow of goods continues, the government may consider requesting and supporting a single (or partnership) organization to handle a certain product. Certain organizations have a traditional interest and much experience in managing any given good (e.g., Goodwill Industries or Adventist Community Services for clothes), and the government can take advantage of their expertise and in-place systems.

Notes

1. The author acknowledges the contributions of Alan Cohn with respect to the legal and liability aspects of managing spontaneous volunteers.

2. Dep't of Homeland Security, National Incident Management System (2004) (NIMS), http://www.dhs.gov/interweb/assetlibrary/NIMS-90-web.pdf. In Homeland Security Presidential Directive 5 (HSPD 5), President Bush mandated federal agency adoption of the NIMS, and directed all federal agencies to provide federal preparedness grants only to jurisdictions found to be "NIMS compliant" by Sept. 30, 2005. HSPD 5, at ¶ 20, 39 Weekly Comp. Pres. Doc. 263, 280 (Mar. 7, 2003).

3. For another example of this approach, *see* David A. McEntire, *Coordinating Multi-Organisational Responses to Disaster: Lessons from the March 28, 2000, Fort Worth Tornado*, 11 Disaster Prevention and Mgmt. 369, 375 (2002); *see also* Federal Emergency Management Agency, FA-282-May 2004, Responding to Incidents of National Consequence: Recommendations for America's Fire and Emergency Services Based on the Events of September 11, 2001, and Other Similar Events, at 47 (2004) (discussing the Pentagon response).

4. *See, e.g.,* Ala. Code §§ 31-9-10(b)(2), 31-9-16(d); Ariz. Rev. Stat. § 26-314(C); Mich. Comp. Laws Ann. § 30.410(f).

5. *See, e.g.,* Hauber v. Yakima County, 56 P.3d 559 (Wash. 2002) (firefighter killed while on mission for volunteer dive-rescue unit); Buttram v. U.S., No. 9609234-S-BLW (D. Idaho Feb. 19, 1999) (order granting judgment in favor of plaintiffs against the United States), http://www.idd.uscourts.gov/ECM/dc_images/_IDVOTEGLM10033070.pdf (volunteer firefighters killed fighting a fire for U.S. Department of Interior, Bureau of Land Management).

6. For more information on CERTs, visit the CERT Web site, http://www.citizencorps.gov/programs/cert.shtm.

7. For more information on the MRC, visit the MRC Web site, http://www.medicalreservecorps.gov.

8. *See, e.g.,* Alaska Stat. § 26.23.045(a); Ariz. Rev. Stat. § 26-308(E); Kan. Stat. Ann. §§ 48-911, 48.922, 48.928(h), (i).

9. FEMA recommends forming CERTs and other teams of local civilian volunteers prior to a disaster. *See* Responding to Incidents of National Consequence, *supra* note 3, at 33-34.

10. 5 U.S.C. §§ 8101-8152 (2005). Section 8101(1)(B) defines the term "employee" to include "an individual rendering personal service to the United States similar to the service

of a civil officer or employee of the United States, without pay or for nominal pay, when a statute authorizes the acceptance or use of the service."

11.   W. Page Keeton, Prosser & Keeton on Torts § 56 (5th ed. 1984).

12.   *See* 42 U.S.C. § 14503(a) (extending protection to volunteers "of a nonprofit organization or governmental entity").

13.   *Id.*, at § 14503(c). For additional discussion of issues arising from the use of volunteer resources, *see* William C. Nicholson, Emergency Response and Emergency Management Law 159 (Charles Thomas 2003).

CHAPTER 11

Representing Local Governments in Catastrophic Events: DHS/FEMA Response and Recovery Issues

by Ernest B. Abbott

Introduction

It is a rare community that has never experienced a local disaster event. Storms wash out roads and flood low-lying areas. Heavy thunderstorms or ice storms drop power lines. Chemical tank trucks overturn. Radical ideologues mail—or claim to have mailed—envelopes filled with anthrax. Bombs are detonated at a clinic or a church. Whenever these mini-disasters occur, the affected community mobilizes. Police and firemen rescue stranded motorists and homeowners, and close off and reroute traffic. Red Cross and other volunteers open shelters and provide food and drink from mobile canteens. Insurance and contingency funds are tapped to pay for emergency overtime costs, and charities chip in to help those uprooted by the events. Communities are generally prepared and have adequate resources to respond to these events.

Some fifty times a year, however, in communities across the country, a natural disaster will be so widespread, and cause so much damage, that not only are many local communities overwhelmed, but the state's governor finds the situation to be beyond the state's capability and asks the president for help. Governors also request federal assistance in responding to the impact of terrorist attacks using biological, chemical, or nuclear devices. If the president declares a major disaster or emergency under the Robert T. Stafford Disaster Relief and Emergency Assistance Act of 1988[1] (the Stafford Act), then the community becomes eligible for significant federal assistance under programs of the Department of Homeland Security's Federal Emergency Management Agency (FEMA).[2]

Lawyers face a number of new and critical issues when representing communities receiving FEMA assistance. Federal response teams arrive immediately after a catastrophic event to assess damage and identify and meet imminent threats to life, property, and health. Depending on the nature and scope of damage, they remain in a community for months, and even years, to provide financial assistance covering most of the cost of necessary emergency measures and of eligible reconstruction activities. FEMA is generally proud of the speed and simplicity with which it delivers assistance under catastrophic conditions. The agency has a "can do" culture—particularly in the emergency environment of the initial, response phase of the disaster. That is the phase when the disaster occurs and satellite trucks transmit to the world overwhelming pictures of grief, of neighborhoods transformed into debris piles, and of vast resources deployed by the relevant federal agencies to clear roads and restore essential services. It is when out-of-town politicians arrive in droves to face the cameras and promise help.

In a few weeks' time, however, the satellite trucks and the out-of-town politicians are gone. The federal focus changes from restoring essential services at almost any cost to repairing the damage at the lowest cost and in accordance with applicable laws, regulations, and written and unwritten FEMA interpretations and policies. And because FEMA programs are reimbursement programs—where FEMA provides grant funding of expenditures already made by a community—it becomes particularly important for a community to understand what is eligible for federal assistance. The community needs to get confirmation of eligibility in writing from FEMA officials, and do so before many of those expenditures are made.

FEMA eligibility rules can be complex. In fact, two aspects of FEMA's mission conflict with each other. On the one hand, a significant part of FEMA's mission is to encourage predisaster mitigation and preparedness, because reducing the risk of damage from disaster, and preparing to deal with damage, has the biggest impact in reducing injuries, loss of life, loss of property, and reduced economic activity resulting from a disaster. FEMA is tasked with creating and enforcing incentives for communities and individuals so they will do more to prepare for and reduce the physical and financial consequences of disasters.

Local governments and their citizens face significant financial consequences, for example, if they do not restrict construction in a flood plain.[3] Local governments should also adopt and enforce building codes so that homes and businesses will withstand earthquakes in seismic zones[4] and hurricane-force winds in hurricane alley. Local governments, nonprofit organizations, and individuals should protect their facilities with insurance rather than rely on federal disaster assistance.[5] While FEMA provides several positive incentives,[6] Congress has in many cases instructed FEMA to deny disaster relief to those who fail to follow its rules.[7]

On the other hand, FEMA must deal with the reality that a great many institutions and individuals fail to prepare and are devastated when disaster strikes. They may have been intentionally profligate, they may have lacked the knowledge, or perhaps they simply did not have the resources to prepare. Or, the disaster event simply may have been of unimaginable proportions. When attention is focused on those most unprepared for the disaster, and often the most affected, the media and politicians ask FEMA to provide assistance to the destitute.

Thus, when the federal emergency response teams arrive, they commit to providing all the assistance they can—consistent with existing law and policy—to meet emergency needs and to help communities and individuals recover. But this assistance can only be as generous as is authorized by statute and regulation. Laws and rules prohibit the agency from providing assistance where some physical or financial mitigation rules have been violated, and all grants are subject to audit after the fact. Lawyers have a critical role in protecting their client communities from the financial disaster that will surely come after a physical disaster if federal rules are not understood and followed.

Legal Background

The principal legal authority providing assistance to state and local government in response to catastrophic events is the Stafford Act.[8] The text of FEMA's regulations and principal policies can be found on FEMA's Web site,[9] although it usually requires some effort to find the kind of technical information that lawyers need.

Emergency and Major Disaster Declarations

Disaster relief and emergency assistance is provided to state and local governments under the Stafford Act only if the president declares either a "major disaster" or an "emergency." While the president has delegated his authority under the Stafford Act to DHS/FEMA and a few other agencies,[10] the president has not delegated to anyone the authority to declare a major disaster or emergency. This remains a presidential prerogative only. The Stafford Act defines the two types of declarations and specifies the assistance programs that are triggered by each.

A "major disaster" is:

> any natural catastrophe (including any hurricane, tornado, storm, high water, winddriven water, tidal wave, tsunami, earthquake, volcanic eruption, landslide, mudslide, snowstorm, or drought), or, regardless of cause, any fire, flood, or explosion, in any part of the United States, which in the determination of the President causes damage of sufficient severity and magnitude to warrant major disaster assistance under this Act to supplement the efforts and available resources of States, local governments, and disaster relief organizations in alleviating the damage, loss, hardship, or suffering caused thereby.[11]

A disaster is an event that causes damage; it is an event that is happening or has already happened. By contrast, the statutory definition of an "emergency" does not require that any damage occur. Declaration of an emergency allows assistance to save lives, protect property and the public health and safety, and to help *prevent* a catastrophe from occurring:

> "Emergency" means any occasion or instance for which, in the determination of the President, Federal assistance is needed to supplement State and local efforts and capabilities to save lives and to protect property and public health and safety, or to lessen or avert the threat of a catastrophe in any part of the United States.

Several distinctions between major disaster and emergency declarations are critical. Major disaster declarations cannot apply to certain nonnatural events. By statute, a nonnatural event can be a "major disaster" only if caused by a fire, flood, or explosion. A computer virus or a Y2K programming glitch cannot be a major disaster—although any explosion caused by computer failure could. An engineered biological agent released by terrorists could not give rise to a "major disaster" unless arguably the resulting disease could be construed as a "natural catastrophe."[12]

Further, the president is not authorized to declare a major disaster unless the governor of an affected state requests the declaration after activating the state's emergency plan, and advising the president that the situation is beyond the capability of state and local government resources.[13] By contrast, the president is authorized to declare an "emergency" without a request from a governor, if the president "determines that an emergency exists for which the primary responsibility for response rests with the United States because the emergency involves a subject area for which, under the Constitution or laws of the United States, the United States exercises exclusive or preeminent responsibility and authority."[14] The president made a unilateral declaration of Stafford Act emergency after the Oklahoma City bombing because the event involved a federal building. Unilateral declarations also are likely in events involving weapons of mass destruction.[15]

Finally, declarations of a major disaster trigger the potential availability of more assistance programs than do declarations of emergency. Both declarations authorize assistance for "emergency measures" required to address "immediate threats" to life, property, and the public health and safety; to remove debris; and to provide individual assistance. These emergency measures may well authorize most of the programs appropriate to deal with emergency conditions in the absence of the damage to infrastructure and other property that might be caused by natural disasters (hurricanes, earthquakes, and the like) or by fire, flood, or explosion.

But a major disaster declaration authorizes a number of additional programs—including the public assistance program, hazard mitigation,[16] crisis counseling,[17] disaster unemployment assistance,[18] food stamps,[19] emergency public transportation,[20] and community disaster loans[21]—that are not available if only an emergency is declared.

The president's declaration notice includes an initial designation of the counties within the state that are covered by the declaration, the specific programs that are being activated for this declaration, and whether the federal cost share for emergency measures and other public assistance activities is the "normal" level of 75 percent or whether it is more. This "county designation" is absolutely critical to eligibility under the Stafford Act. If a county is included in the declaration for purposes of the public assistance program, then all public entities in that county, and certain nonprofit ones, that have incurred damage from the disaster event are eligible for federal disaster grants. If a county is not included, or a particular assistance program is not activated for that county, then no federal assistance is available, without regard to the scope of damage suffered by any particular entity.

Although the president has not delegated the authority to declare disasters or emergencies, gubernatorial requests for declarations are processed through FEMA, and FEMA's regulations specify the information that must be presented to justify a declaration.[22] FEMA transmits a recommendation to the president.

The largest two Stafford Act assistance programs are examined below: the public assistance program and the Federal Assistance to Individuals and Households Program (IHP). The former reimburses emergency and repair costs incurred by state and local governments as a result of a declared major disaster or emergency; the latter provides limited support to individuals for "necessary expenses and serious needs," including temporary housing.

Public Assistance Program

The public assistance program primarily is a grant program that funds eligible costs incurred by state and local governments, and by some nonprofit entities providing "government-type" services. In general, under the Stafford Act, the federal government pays "not less than 75%" of the cost of "emergency measures"—such as police overtime and debris removal—incurred by state or local governments and some nonprofit organizations in either a declared major disaster or emergency, and also pays the cost of repairing, restoring, reconstructing, or replacing virtually any public facility damaged or destroyed by a major disaster.

A number of critical legal issues are hidden within this simple summary of the public assistance program, and failure to understand them can jeopardize eligibility. Lawyers representing applicant local governments and nonprofits must become familiar with the basic FEMA publications explaining its public assistance policies: the *Public Assistance Applicant's Handbook*, the *Public Assistance Guide*, the *Public Assistance Digest*, and the *Debris Management Guide*.[23] While the statute, the regulations, and FEMA's published policies set forth relatively clear criteria for awarding disaster assistance grants, FEMA views all grants made under the public assistance to be discretionary. As a result, any applicant disappointed or "aggrieved" by a denial of assistance will have extreme difficulty in obtaining judicial review of this determination. The Stafford Act precludes federal government liability "for any claim based upon the exercise or performance of, or the failure to exercise or perform, any discretionary function or duty" of a federal agency or federal employee carrying out the Stafford Act's provisions.[24] This language has been construed to deny Administrative Procedure Act review of discretionary Stafford Act assistance grants in the absence of constitutional violations.[25]

Determining eligibility. FEMA uses a three-part analysis to determine what projects are eligible for assistance and what amount of assistance should be awarded. First, FEMA determines whether the particular legal entity applying for assistance is eligible for assistance under the Stafford Act. Next, FEMA reviews whether particular work performed is eligible. Finally, FEMA reviews whether the costs incurred in performing the eligible work are reasonable and should be allowed. Since grants are provided only to those who apply for them, the importance of starting the process cannot be overstressed.

How to apply. A prospective applicant initiates the process of obtaining public assistance funds by filing a simple one-page "Request for Assistance" within thirty days after the area has been designated as part of a major disaster. This form is simple and straightforward, and does not require any detailed estimate of the work or funding requested. Indeed, information on the form primarily allows FEMA to establish a file for the applicant and to record contact information for the applicant. Although FEMA individually reviews and approves all projects, state governments administer all grants, and communications are routed through the state. FEMA and the state establish a Joint Field Office[26] after most disasters to facilitate coordination and processing of applications.

Eligibility of state and local governments. State and local governments, including public authorities, are eligible to receive grants under the public assistance program. Federal assistance under the Stafford Act is provided "to assist state and local governments" in their response to a disaster. If a facility is a government facility, it is eligible even if it is supported primarily by attendance fees; an example would be a stadium or a theater.

Eligibility of nonprofit organizations "open to the general public." The Stafford Act also authorizes FEMA to provide assistance to nonprofit institutions providing what FEMA determines are "essential government-type services to the general public," including schools, utilities, and emergency services such as volunteer fire companies, medical facilities, and custodial care facilities.[27] Thus, a nonprofit organization that operates a hospital, emergency care, or nursing facility "open to the public generally" can be eligible for FEMA assistance.

FEMA looks closely at the identity of the nonprofit applicant to be sure it qualifies. To be eligible for assistance, that applicant must not only own or operate a facility providing essential government-type services, but that facility must be open to the general public.

FEMA construes these terms quite strictly. For example, when Tropical Storm Allison flooded most of the Texas Medical Center, the plant providing electricity and chilled water to most of the nonprofit hospitals in the center suffered damage. This plant previously had been owned by one of the nonprofit hospitals in the center, and the hospital would have been eligible for assistance related to the plant if it had retained ownership. However, to allow this plant to serve other nonprofit hospitals, and to allow joint financing of expansion projects, the hospital had transferred the plant into a separate nonprofit entity owned by a number of nonprofit hospitals. All power from the plant was provided to the member hospitals, all of which were "open to the general public"—but the nonprofit organization that owned the plant did not sell power to the general public.

FEMA concluded that damage to the plant was ineligible for assistance: the applicant was providing utility services, but the plant did not provide services "open to the general public." FEMA decided it was irrelevant that the member hospitals to which the plant provided services were open to the general public, or that by structuring ownership in this manner, the hospitals had assured that power would be available at a lower cost than had each separately incorporated a power and chilled water facility into its hospital facility.[28]

Ineligibility of for-profit organizations. For-profit businesses are ineligible for any assistance under the Stafford Act. A for-profit institution may well provide resources, equipment, and personnel in response to a federal disaster, but it is ineligible for reimbursement of its costs under the public assistance program. On the other hand, if the for-profit business was providing services or equipment for an eligible government or nonprofit applicant under a contract to provide these services, it will receive payment for services rendered in accordance with the contract—and the eligible applicant can receive reimbursement of the federal share of these contract costs under the public assistance program.

A good example of the issues raised by the ineligibility of for-profit entities for disaster assistance arose out of the terrorist attacks on the World Trade Center in New York City on September 11, 2001. On that day, casualties were high and were feared to be far higher. A call went out from the Port Authority of New York and New Jersey for all available ambulances to come to triage centers being established for the wounded. The ambulances responding included public ambulances, nonprofit ambulances, contract ambulances normally operating under contract with nonprofit hospitals (which may have had no other connection with the disaster), and for-profit ambulances working with for-profit hospitals or nursing homes. In this situation, FEMA exercised its discretion broadly and determined that the Port Authority had essentially contracted with all of these ambulance services and become liable for payment for services rendered—thus making it eligible for FEMA reimbursement of these costs.

The ineligibility of for-profit entities can be significant to communities where there has been substantial privatization of traditionally public functions. Communities that outsource requirements, or that develop the "public-private partnerships" that now have become increasingly frequent, may find that emergency services are no longer eligible for federal assistance.[29] Lawyers should be aware of the implications that the structure of potential arrangements may have on the availability of federal disaster assistance, and consider whether the costs of private-sector partners who provide governmental services in a municipality can be structured as contract costs of eligible entities that can be reimbursed under federal disaster programs.

Legal responsibility doctrine. By regulation, FEMA has established that, when eligible public applicants have contracted with ineligible applicants to transfer control of a structure—for example, by lease or in a construction contract—assistance is available to the eligible applicants only to the extent that they are "legally responsible" for performing the work.[30] This occurs most frequently in connection with construction or remodeling projects. During project construction, the contract documents frequently transfer control over a structure to the contractor, who is required to purchase insurance covering the structure during the period of construction. As a result, if a facility is destroyed by a natural disaster during project construction, the facility is not eligible for federal disaster assistance. A city's efforts to stimulate economic development also can lead to mixed ownership or responsibility for structures, and this can result in legal disputes over whether a structure is eligible for federal disaster assistance.

Eligible work: emergency measures. Under the Stafford Act, "emergency measures"—activities determined to address imminent threats of harm to life, property, and the public health and safety—and the "repair, restoration, reconstruction, or replacement" of damaged facilities are eligible for federal assistance.

Emergency measures include providing medicine, food, and other consumables, and:

> Performing on public or private lands or waters any work or services essential to saving lives and protecting and preserving property or public health and safety, including—
>
> (A) debris removal;
> (B) search and rescue, emergency medical care, emergency mass care, emergency shelter, and provision of food, water, medicine, and other essential needs, including movement of supplies or persons;
> (C) clearance of roads and construction of temporary bridges necessary to the performance of emergency tasks and essential community services;
> (D) provision of temporary facilities for schools and other essential community services;
> (E) demolition of unsafe structures which endanger the public;
> (F) warning of further risks and hazards;
> (G) dissemination of public information and assistance regarding health and safety measures;
> (H) provision of technical advice to State and local governments on disaster management and control; and
> (I) reduction of immediate threats to life, property, and public health and safety.[31]

To qualify for assistance, an emergency cost must be incurred because of the declared disaster event. The "causation" requirement is strictly interpreted for emergency costs. For example, even without a disaster, an applicant would have paid its workforce regular-time pay and benefits, so these costs do not result from the disaster and are not eligible for FEMA assistance. FEMA calls this "force account labor." Overtime paid to force account labor working on emergency measures in response to a declared emergency or major disaster is eligible. Both regular pay and overtime pay for *temporary* employees hired as a result of the disaster are eligible costs. The cost of performing "nonemergency" work—such as the normal day-to-day activities that continue during emergencies—is not eligible for assistance.[32] The primary rule used in evaluating eligibility of emergency costs is whether they were to address immediate threats to life, property, or the public health and safety.

The eligibility of broad categories of emergency costs for reimbursement will by no means cover all related losses and other economic impacts. Under the Stafford Act, FEMA reimburses "costs" suffered as a result of a disaster. The meaning of the word "costs" may appear obvious, but a cost is incurred only when someone pays for something. As interpreted by FEMA, a cost is not created when a disaster event keeps money from coming in. Thus, loss of revenue is not an eligible cost.

Repair, restoration, reconstruction, replacement, and improvements. In addition to the costs of "emergency protective measures" described above, eligible applicants can receive grants covering the federal share—which ranges from 75 to 100 percent—of the cost of bringing damaged facilities back into predisaster condition. "Facilities" include both real property—buildings, roads, sewer and utility systems, and the like—and personal property such as motor vehicles, medical equipment, and medical supplies.

By statute FEMA must give a generous interpretation of what it takes to restore a structure to predisaster condition; this can be significant, particularly for older structures. Thus, the Stafford Act provides that the eligible cost estimate for public assistance grants should be developed:

> (i) on the basis of the design of the facility as the facility existed immediately prior to the major disaster and (ii) in conformity with codes, specifications, and standards (including floodplain management and hazard mitigation criteria required by the President or under the Coastal Barrier Resources Act) applicable at the time the disaster occurred.[33]

What this means is that damaged hospital and building systems must be repaired in accordance with the building codes and specifications in the community that were in effect as of the date of the disaster.

FEMA regulations[34] specify which "codes and standards" trigger federal funding of improvements over the preexisting condition of a structure. The objective of the regulation is to fund code upgrades where the community requires that all new construction meet these standards, and not to fund upgrades where it appears that the code applies only, or principally, when federal funding is available.[35]

In addition, FEMA may be persuaded in its discretion to fund "cost-effective" upgrades to a structure that will have the effect of reducing future disaster damage.[36] Here the theory is that it does not make sense to spend federal funds to reconstruct a facility to be just as susceptible to collapse as it was before the disaster.

FEMA also has grappled with situations in which the community really did not want to rebuild the damaged structure, even with code upgrades thrown in. The community may want to replace a washed-out two-lane bridge with a three-lane bridge. Such an "improved project" can be eligible for assistance, but only in the amount that would have been received had only the original facility been replaced or repaired. Given the pattern of growth in the community, perhaps the community's hospital should be rebuilt in a different location more accessible to more neighborhoods. Perhaps the community really does not want to rebuild its public bathhouse and would rather use the money to build a community center or concert hall. "Alternate Facilities" of this type remain eligible for federal grants from the public assistance program, but the amount of funding is reduced. Essentially, FEMA first determines what the eligible cost would have been to repair, restore, reconstruct, or replace a damaged facility; computes what the federal share of this amount would have been; and then awards an "in-lieu-of" grant of 75 percent of this amount.[37]

Mutual aid. A community overwhelmed by disaster usually can count on receiving help from surrounding communities, building on a "neighbor helping neighbor" tradition that dates from the earliest days of our history. Even in the midst of the War of 1812, when the United States was at war with Britain and therefore with Canada, communities on the border between Maine and Canada would cross the border to help each other put fires out. Mutual aid has continued to be a significant part of the nation's emergency response system through the present day.

Most of these early mutual aid arrangements were handled informally, without paperwork and without expectation of payment. Each community recognized that if it helped a neighbor when in need, that neighbor would be there for it when needed. But as the dollars involved in overtime costs and in potential liabilities rose, more and more communities began to formalize these arrangements in mutual aid agreements. DHS and FEMA policies make the formalization of mutual aid even more important.

FEMA will not reimburse expenses incurred under informal, unwritten mutual aid agreements, or under agreements entered into after the expenses have been incurred. Further, in an effort to encourage predisaster execution of mutual aid agreements, FEMA will deny reimbursement for expenses incurred in the first eight hours of work at the incident site unless a mutual aid agreement was in effect before the disaster event.[38] As the nation implements the new National Incident Management System[39] and National Response Plan,[40] the Department of Homeland Security is adopting ever more stringent incentives for communities to participate in mutual aid arrangements. DHS has declared that no community will be eligible for federal preparedness funding unless it has adopted NIMS by fiscal year 2005,[41] and mutual aid agreements are an important component of mutual aid under NIMS.[42]

Donated resources. Even if FEMA determines that a cost is not incurred by a public entity due to the disaster, because they were in essence donated by citizens or by neighboring towns, it can remain quite important for communities and states to keep track of these and any other donated resources. FEMA public assistance grants in almost all disasters are cost-shared, requiring a "nonfederal" contribution—normally from the coffers of state or local government—of from 10 to 25 percent of eligible costs. Under FEMA's donated resources policy, the value of resources donated to the city can count toward the nonfederal matching requirement, thereby reducing the city's obligation to match a federal grant with cash.[43] Donated resources under this policy can be quite significant, and can include, for example, all the efforts of residents to do work that would be deemed FEMA-eligible emergency work if it were performed by the local government.

Debris removal complications. The debris generated by virtually every major disaster frequently leads to the most difficult emergency management issues. Debris removal frequently complicates lines of authority because many different governmental and private organizations have physical or financial responsibilities for debris removal. Contracting is frequently done in haste with debris removal firms previously unknown to the buyer's procurement staff, using emergency procurements that bypass or at least expedite normal competitive processes. Further, the debris itself may consist of a dangerous pile of the collapsed and intermingled property of multiple owners. It covers both public and private property, and often needs to be removed immediately because it blocks access to streets and utilities that are critical to the recovery effort. And in a disaster caused by a terrorist attack—as in the case of the Oklahoma City bombings and the attacks on the World Trade Center—the site of the debris is a crime scene, and therefore access to it is restricted.

To deal with potential liabilities from handling debris, the Stafford Act requires that a state or local government arrange an unconditional authorization for the removal of public and private property and indemnify the federal government before FEMA can provide any assistance in removing debris.[44] This required indemnity is placed in the FEMA-State Agreement signed by FEMA and the state at the onset of every major disaster.

The Stafford Act authorizes FEMA to assist in the removal of debris from both public and private lands if the removal of debris is found "in the public interest."[45] By regulation, FEMA has determined that it is in the public interest to remove debris from public and private property when public health and safety, or significant damage to improved property, or the economic recovery of the community, is threatened.[46] But FEMA has strictly limited who can obtain assistance for removal of debris on private property. Debris removal is eligible for federal assistance *only* if it is performed, or contracted for, by an eligible entity. FEMA will not provide assistance directly to an individual or private organization, nor to an eligible entity that chooses to reimburse private individuals or organizations for their costs of debris removal.[47]

Further, FEMA policy is that "[d]ebris removal from private property is generally not eligible because it is the responsibility of the individual property owner."[48] Debris removal from private property is considered "the responsibility of the individual property owner aided by insurance settlements and assistance from volunteer agencies."[49] FEMA policy is that debris removal on private property will be funded only if it causes a public health and safety hazard to the general public, the work is preapproved by FEMA, and coverage under the property owners' insurance is deducted from the federal assistance.[50] If residents move debris from their properties onto public property—such as the side of the street—the removal of this debris is generally eligible for FEMA funding.

Lawyers must review debris removal procedures and contract documents carefully. A good portion of the disputes between FEMA and communities arises from disallowance of debris removal costs. FEMA staff is perpetually on the lookout for ineligible debris removal costs. In fact, the inspector general has prosecuted fraud by unscrupulous debris removal contractors. A grant for debris removal may have arisen in emergency conditions, but it is still a federal grant. Management risk is on the community that contracts to remove the debris. The financial risk is on the local government if FEMA disallows costs. Where possible, it is advisable to obtain advance written confirmation from FEMA's federal coordinating officer of the eligibility of your community's debris removal program, including contracting/competition, eligibility of commingled private property, monitoring, and recordkeeping. FEMA's debris management guide includes a sample community debris management plan that helps avoid a number of debris management potholes.

Duplication of benefits. All assistance under the Stafford Act, including the public assistance program, is subject to a general statutory prohibition against making federal disaster payments that duplicate benefits.

> The President . . . in consultation with the head of each Federal agency administering any program providing financial assistance to persons, business concerns, or other entities suffering financial losses as a result of a major disaster or emergency, shall assure that no such person, business concern, or other entity will receive such assistance with respect to any part of such loss as to which he has received financial assistance under any other program or from insurance or any other source.[51]

This prohibition is not limited to duplicated assistance that a community in fact receives; it also extends to assistance that FEMA believes to be *available to* the community.[52] These provisions can lead to disputes over how much assistance, usually in the form of insurance, is in fact "available to" a local government and therefore how much is deducted from the "eligible cost" for federal disaster grants. These disputes usually arise when there is substantial coverage, and aggregate deductibles, available for both FEMA-eligible and FEMA-ineligible losses.

As part of the process of applying for public assistance, applicants must advise FEMA of all potential insurance proceeds. Applicants should document their efforts to recover under their insurance policies, carefully track insurance proceeds for FEMA-eligible losses, and avoid insurance checks that commingle eligible and ineligible losses. If there is a dispute over coverage, and an applicant contemplates settling for less than the policy amount, it should advise FEMA staff in an effort to gain their concurrence in the settlement.

Federal grant requirements. The public assistance program is a federal grant program and therefore subject to the Common Rule, which specifies uniform administrative requirements for grants to states and local governments.[53] All public assistance grants are made to the state government, which then serves as an administrative conduit for subgrants to the eligible local government and nonprofit entities. The subgrants reimburse eligible costs incurred. Failure to make sure contracts comply with federal grant requirements runs the risk of a FEMA determination that the costs are not eligible for federal assistance.

Probably the most important arena for conflict is the requirement that contracts be competitively bid unless "the public exigency or emergency for the requirement will not permit a delay resulting from competitive solicitation."[54] Beware this emergency exception! Applicants cannot safely ignore competitive procurements just because the president has found the situation to be of such severity that it is "beyond the capability of local resources" to respond, or just because it is seeking assistance for what FEMA regulations call Category A and B "emergency work." FEMA will not necessarily agree that sole source procurement is appropriate.

A mayor's recent unsuccessful appeal from a denial of assistance based on the city's failure to competitively bid a debris removal contract amply illustrates this point:

> The citizens of the County had no electricity, no heat, no water, and no telephone service. The County's 800 miles of paved roads were impassable. Emergency vehicles could not serve the County's citizens. The thaw compounded the problem by creating road washouts over 14 inches deep in some places and leading to severe rutting of the County's paved roads. The body of one deceased resident remained uncollected for over two days because no emergency vehicle could reach him. The weather forecast included more subfreezing temperatures. The County faced the possibility of more deaths due to lack of heat, food, running water and other necessities of life unless it could quickly reopen its roads.[55]

This appeal was denied on the ground that the county's sole source contract covered not just the emergency clearing of one lane of road for emergency vehicles, but the entire debris removal operation. FEMA's position in this case, which was sustained in litigation, was that the county could have conducted a competition—presumably after power and phone service had been restored—for the larger work of transporting and reducing the debris and placing it in a landfill.

In short, to protect the eligibility of debris removal costs for reimbursement, lawyers should ensure that at least an informal competition is conducted to obtain bids from multiple sources, to demonstrate that the client attempted the best competition possible under the circumstances—and to demonstrate what other bidders were willing to charge for similar work. When some work must be done before any competition can take place, communities should limit the scope of the work occurring in the first seventy hours after the disaster to allow for competition in later phases. The same contractor, whose resources already will be mobilized for the community, may well prevail in this competition, but separately procuring the follow-up work may well prevent denial of reimbursement for the frequently more substantial emergency costs that are incurred after the initial seventy-hour window.

Communities also can design and conduct a competitive procurement for predisaster contracts with reputable firms that will be triggered by a catastrophic event. This competition occurs in the predisaster environment, when procurement staff has working telephones and office systems, and time to evaluate the capabilities of the various firms with experience in the major disaster environment. The contract prices under contingent contracts like this, because they are the product of open competition, are generally presumed reasonable by FEMA.[56]

Federal Assistance to Individuals and Households Program (IHP)

The Stafford Act authorizes limited assistance to individuals and households in their efforts to recover from a major disaster. In contrast to the public assistance program, most aspects of IHP are now administered directly by the federal government and do not involve local governments. Indeed, to a large extent, applications for assistance are initiated through calls directly from individuals to FEMA's toll-free telephone number.[57] There are two areas described below, however, that frequently cause significant complications that could embroil local government lawyers in disputes.

Under IHP, a household is eligible for up to $25,000 in financial or, if necessary, direct assistance, covering "necessary expenses and serious needs" when individuals otherwise are unable to meet them.[58] A maximum of $5,000 of this total is available for repairs to make damaged housing habitable. IHP assistance programs are not designed to reimburse victims for disaster losses, but merely to cover "necessary expenses" stemming from a disaster. As a result, many individuals and households will suffer losses far greater than what FEMA's IHP assistance provides.

Under the Stafford Act's duplication of benefit provisions discussed earlier, no assistance is provided, other than for temporary housing or rental assistance, if the household is insured or has the financial ability to qualify for a disaster loan from the Small Business Administration.[59] Thus, this program primarily assists low-income households.

Duplication of benefits: multiple assistance programs. After many disasters, local government, business, and other community leaders often identify additional governmental funds, or organize charitable donation programs, to assist individuals and households also eligible for the limited assistance provided by IHP. Recall the duplication of benefits rules discussed above: federal assistance is available only if it does not duplicate assistance available from insurance or other federal programs ... *"or any other source."*[60] When community leaders decide to provide a supplemental assistance program, it is critical that they design it so that it is not deemed to duplicate federal assistance and result in dollar-for-dollar reduction of federal benefits. This is an area in which a local government lawyer should get involved and contact FEMA staff for advice. FEMA generally has been eager to help communities design supplemental assistance programs that do not run afoul of duplication-of-benefit restrictions. No one wants to invite the political and media fallout of trying to recover federal benefits already paid. And no one will want to hear that this recovery debacle is made necessary because the supplemental assistance program was not artfully drafted. The problem is not as simple as it appears, since the most obvious solution—sharing of information to permit identification of unmet needs and coordination of benefits—probably will not work. The Privacy Act restricts FEMA from giving access to information about the benefits it awards individuals. The solution normally will require careful specification of the need (distinct from that funded by IHP) or systems to obtain information from aid recipients (rather than from FEMA) about their FEMA assistance.

Temporary housing/mobile home parks. Local government lawyers also may become embroiled in local issues that can emerge from FEMA construction of temporary housing. Disasters that damage or destroy a sizable percentage of a community's housing stock create an immediate demand for temporary replacement housing. Although mobile home parks are the least favored form of housing assistance—FEMA much prefers rental assistance if rental units are available, or funding of repairs to make damaged housing habitable—the scale of destruction can make it necessary to provide manufactured temporary housing units in temporary mobile home parks. By statute, this program is one in which the federal government is in charge,[61] but the state or local government is asked to identify and supply a suitable site—preferably with utilities—on which to place the mobile homes.[62] And while these areas may be called "FEMA-villes," there is usually a strong desire on the part of both federal and state officials to move to local government or local public housing authorities the responsibility for managing what is, in essence, a large housing project. These mobile home parks, although intended for a life of only eighteen months, can generate substantial community opposition, litigation over siting issues, requirements for security and protection of residents, and eviction of tenants violating rules established for the community. Local communities may want to manage the land-use and housing challenges these projects represent. In doing so, however, community lawyers are strongly advised to identify the financial burdens that these responsibilities may impose on the community, and carefully craft policies, programs, and documents to ensure federal recognition and reimbursement of those costs.

Conclusion

This chapter highlights some of the most significant issues that lawyers representing local government are likely to grapple with in federally declared disasters. The key messages are quite simple.

Communities require capable and constructive legal work in order to minimize the costs and impact of catastrophic events. This work should begin before a catastrophic event looms on the horizon, by giving attention to the community's building and zoning codes. Failure to adopt and enforce codes to reduce the susceptibility of physical structures to damage almost certainly will increase the human and economic loss suffered when disaster strikes. Failure to properly follow and document the procedures required by FEMA rules can jeopardize the FEMA funding for which a community may be eligible, and that would allow recovery and rebuilding to occur.

Lawyers for communities will be effective in representing their clients in response and recovery issues only if they prepare in advance. They should review their community's mutual aid agreements, make sure insurance is adequate, develop contracting strategies that can be used in the disaster environment, and compare their community's debris plan with FEMA's debris removal guidance. It is also critical to anticipate mitigation and prevention actions—programs that will help the community identify and address its vulnerability to disaster events—and minimize the likelihood that failure to address known risks will trigger a reduction in federal assistance.

Finally, lawyers need to know who to call for help on legal issues peculiar to the disaster environment. Developing in each office a legal specialist in disaster law and issues will provide a knowledgeable source of guidance. Developing a working relationship with counsel to your state's emergency management agency is equally important. The state's disaster lawyer usually will have dealt with FEMA issues with some frequency, and therefore is usually a good resource for general—and free—information about FEMA programs.

NOTES

1. Robert T. Stafford Disaster Relief and Emergency Assistance Act (Stafford Act) 42 U.S.C. § 5121-5206 (2005).

2. The Homeland Security Act of 2002, Pub. L. No. 107-296; 116 Stat. 2229 (2002), transferred to the Secretary of the Department of Homeland Security (DHS) all functions previously delegated or entrusted by statute to the Director of the Federal Emergency Management Agency (FEMA). DHS has chosen to continue FEMA as a distinct unit; DHS' Under Secretary for Emergency Preparedness and Response also serves as Director of FEMA.

3. Stafford Act §§ 406(c)(1)(D), 406(c)(2)(C), 42 U.S.C. §§ 5172(c)(1)(D), 5172(c)(2)(C), *as amended by the* Disaster Mitigation Act of 2000, Pub. L. No. 106-390, 114 Stat. 1552 (2000).

4. Stafford Act §§ 323, 406(e)(1)(A), 42 U.S.C. §§ 5166, 5172(e)(1)(A), *as amended by the* Disaster Mitigation Act of 2000.

5. Stafford Act §§ 311-312.

6. The predisaster mitigation programs are of modest size—totaling less than $50 million annually. *See, e.g.,* FEMA's 2002 appropriation, Pub. L. No. 107-73 (2001). The National Flood Insurance Act of 1968, 42 U.S.C. §§ 4001-4129 as amended, provides federal subsidies for flood insurance in communities which adopt and enforce floodplain management regulations consistent with federal standards. The federal government also now provides annually billions of dollars to state and local governments to help prepare for potential terrorist attacks. *See, e.g.,* Pub. L. No. 108-334, 118 Stat. 1298 (2004) (FY 2005 Appropriations to the Department of Homeland Security, Office of State and Local Government Coordination and Preparedness.)

7. *See, e.g.,* the sanctions in the Stafford Act § 406(d), which reduce disaster assistance for public facilities damaged by flood in the floodplain by the maximum amount of flood insurance proceeds that would have been available had the facility been covered by flood insurance.

8. The statute was significantly amended in late 2000 by the Disaster Mitigation Act of 2000, Pub. L. No. 106-390, 114 Stat. 1552 (2000). FEMA also administers the National Flood Insurance Program, which provides most of the flood insurance available in the

United States today. This program is governed by the National Flood Insurance Act of 1968, as amended and the Flood Disaster Prevention Act of 1973, 42 U.S.C. 4001-4129 (2005). These programs are beyond the scope of this chapter.

9. *Available at* http://www.fema.gov.

10. A few provisions of the Stafford Act are delegated to other agencies (for example, the administration of unemployment assistance is delegated to the Secretary of Labor). Except as otherwise noted, all authority discussed in this paper was delegated to FEMA by Exec. Order No. 12,148. Upon creation of the Department of Homeland Security, these authorities were transferred to the Secretary of Homeland Security, who has redelegated them to the Under Secretary of DHS for Emergency Preparedness and Response—who also carries the title of Director of FEMA.

11. 42 U.S.C. § 5122(2).

12. At present, the federal government appears reluctant to interpret a release of a disease such as smallpox or anthrax by terrorists as a "natural catastrophe."

13. 42 U.S.C. § 5170.

14. 42 U.S.C. § 5191(b).

15. *See*, Atomic Energy Act, 42 U.S.C. Chapter 23.

16. 42 U.S.C. § 5170c.

17. 42 U.S.C. § 5183.

18. 42 U.S.C. § 5177.

19. 42 U.S.C. § 5179.

20. 42 U.S.C. § 5186.

21. 42 U.S.C. § 5184.

22. 44 C.F.R. §§ 206.35-.37, 206.48. For online access to FEMA's Regulations, *see* www.gpo.access.gov/cfr/index.html.

23. These policy and guidance documents are available for download at FEMA's web site, http://www.fema.gov/rrr/pa/padocs.shtm.

24. 42 U.S.C. § 5148.

25. *See, e.g.,* Graham v. FEMA, 149 F.3d 997 (9th Cir.1998); City of San Bruno v. FEMA, 181 F. Supp. 2d 1010 (N.D. Cal. 2001); United Power Association v. FEMA, No. AZ-99-180, 2000 WL 33339635, at *2-4 (D.N.D. Sept. 13, 2000); California-Nevada Methodist Homes v. FEMA, 152 F. Supp. 2d 1202 (N.D. Cal. 2001).

26. Called a "Disaster Field Office" before adoption of the National Response Plan (NRP), "The JFO fully replaces the DHS/EPR/FEMA Disaster Field Office (DFO), and accommodates all entities (or their designated representatives) essential to incident management, information-sharing, and the delivery of disaster assistance and other support." NRP, at page 28(December 2004), http://www.dhs.gov/dhspublic/display?theme=14&content =4264.

27. 44 C.F.R. § 206.221.

28. FEMA Second Appeal Decision; 1379-DR-TX; PA ID # 201-U917N-00; Thermal Energy Cooperative PW # N/A; Applicant Eligibility Determination (Aug. 6, 2002).

29. In addition to public assistance grants after a disaster, this issue also may be important to the eligibility of costs incurred to ensure that, for example, for-profit hospitals in a community have adequate equipment, training, and exercises to assure preparedness for terrorism attacks.

30. 44 C.F.R. § 206.223(a)(3).

31. 42 U.S.C. § 5170b(a)(3). For a more detailed description of "Emergency Measures," *see* FEMA Public Assistance Guide, at 47-53, http://www.fema.gov/pdf/rrr/pa/ pagdoc.pdf.

32. If existing employees are transferred to perform emergency work, and if temporary or contract workers are hired to handle the nonemergency work previously performed

by the transferred employees, then neither the regular pay of the transferred employees (because they are "force account labor") nor the cost of the temporary or contract workers (who are not performing emergency work) is eligible.

33. Stafford Act § 406(e)(1)(A), *as amended by the* Disaster Mitigation Act of 2000. The amendment to the portion of § 406(e) quoted here did not materially change the prior law as it had been interpreted by FEMA. Accordingly, although this amendment is not yet effective, the new version has been included here.

34. 44 C.F.R. § 206.226(c).

35. *See* FEMA Response and Recovery Policy 9527.2 (Interim Policy on Construction Codes and Standards for the Nisqually Earthquake Disaster) (6/8/01); FEMA Response and Recovery Policy 9527.3 (Interim Policy on Construction Codes and Standards for the San Simeon Earthquake) (6/25/04). *See also,* Second Appeal Analysis, FEMA-1008-DR-CA, PA ID # 000-92040;University of California, Los Angeles, DSR # 02623;Royce Hall (UC Seismic Safety Policy) (March 10, 1998).

36. 44 C.F.R. § 206.226(d) governs the "§406 Mitigation."

37. 42 U.S.C. § 5170c(c). If the reason a damaged facility is not replaced is that soil instability in the disaster area makes repair/replacement infeasible, the amount of the grant is 90 percent of the federal share of the eligible cost. *See* FEMA Response and Recovery Policy 9525.13 (Alternate Projects) (July 31, 2001).

38. FEMA Public Assistance Policy 9523.6 (Mutual Aid Agreements for Public Assistance) (September 22, 2004).

39. Issued in March 2004, and referred to herein as "NIMS," http://www.dhs.gov/interweb/assetlibrary/NIMS-90-web.pdf.

40. The NRP was signed by most federal agencies and several voluntary organizations, and was issued November 16, 2004.

41. Homeland Security Presidential Directive 5, ¶20 (Feb. 28, 2003), http://www.whitehouse.gov/news/releases/2003/02/20030228-9.html.

42. *See* NIMS, at 39.

43. FEMA Response and Recovery Policy 9525.2 (Donated Resources) (Aug. 17, 1999).

44. Stafford Act § 407(b), 42 U.S.C. § 5173(b).

45. Stafford Act § 407(a), 42 U.S.C. § 5173(a).

46. 44 C.F.R. § 206.224(a) (2000); see FEMA Publication 322, at 45, www.fema.gov/r-n-r/pa/paguided.htm.

47. 44 C.F.R. § 206.224(c) (2000).

48. Federal Emergency Management Agency, FEMA Pol'y Dig., FEMA Publication 321, Debris Removal (October 2001) (interactive ver.).

49. FEMA Public Assistance Guide, *supra*.

50. FEMA Fact Sheet on Insurance Considerations for Applicants, Response and Recovery Directorate Policy No. 9580.3 (Aug. 23, 2000) (Question 11).

51. Stafford Act § 312(a).

52. *See* Stafford Act § 312(c). (A person receiving federal assistance is "liable to the United States to the extent that such assistance duplicates benefits *available to* the person for the same purpose from another source." (emphasis added.))

53. FEMA's version of the Common Rule is at 44 C.F.R. Part 13. These regulations further incorporate by reference requirements in several Office of Management and Budget (OMB) circulars applicable to particular types of grantees. In particular, OMB Circular A-87 applies to the costs of state or local governments, http://www.whitehouse.gov/omb/grants/index.html.

54. 44 C.F.R. § 13.36(d)(4)(i).

55. First Appeal filed by Scott County, Arkansas, FEMA-1354-DR-AR, PA ID#127-99127-00, PW 124 (Mar. 9, 2001).

56. FEMA Public Assistance Policy 9580.1 (Debris Management Job Aid), at app. D-2 (Aug. 2000), http://www.fema.gov/pdf/rrr/pa/9580_1.pdf. ("Utilize pre-negotiated contracts if available.")

57. FEMA's regulations implementing the Disaster Mitigation Act's changes to the Individual and Household Assistance Program are published in the Federal Register at 67 Fed. Reg. 3412 (Jan. 23, 2002).

58. IHP assistance is in addition to the "emergency measures" funded by the public assistance program, and is oriented toward the emergency needs of individuals and households ("emergency medical care, emergency mass care, emergency shelter, provision of food, water, medicine, and other essential needs, including movement of supplies and persons").

59. Disaster loans provided by the Small Business Administration are not restricted to immediate needs, but can be awarded for all losses caused by the disaster up to a maximum loan amount.

60. Stafford Act § 312(a).

61. Stafford Act §§ 408(c), (d), *as amended by the* Disaster Mitigation Act of 2000.

62. *See* 44 C.F.R. § 206.117(b)(1)(ii)(C) (any "site must comply with State and local codes and ordinances," including zoning codes); 44 C.F.R. § 206.117(b)(1)(ii)(E) (indicating that site may by provided by state or local government).

CHAPTER 12

The Defense Production Act of 1950 and Homeland Security

by H. Crane Miller[1]

Introduction

Though little known—and some would even say arcane—the Defense Production Act of 1950 (DPA)[2] is one of the nation's primary authorities for ensuring the timely availability of resources needed for national defense,[3] including civil emergency preparedness and response, as well as critical infrastructure protection and restoration. It provides a number of important authorities to expedite production and delivery of supplies and services essential to national defense, including: preferential acceptance and performance of contracts or orders, as well as allocation of materials, services, and facilities to promote approved programs (Title I); financial assistance to the private sector to expedite production or services (Title III); protection against civil and criminal liability for private-sector participants in government-sponsored voluntary agreements to promote national defense (Title VII); and employment of private persons in government service to carry out the provisions of the DPA (also Title VII). The DPA's "declaration of policy" also serves as a foundation for federal emergency planning activities to mobilize civil economic resources.

Many defense contractors are familiar with the contract provisions relating to the DPA, which appear in an estimated 300,000 defense-related contracts annually. Relatively new and important to federal civil departments and agencies, state, local and tribal governments, and most recently, the private sector, is the expansion of DPA authority beyond military use to civil emergency preparedness and critical infrastructure protection and restoration.

This chapter explores the authority under each of the DPA's titles, and suggests how the DPA could be implemented under its existing provisions. As this chapter goes to press, directives and guidance for implementing the nonmilitary portions of the DPA are in process and not fully adopted. This chapter will discuss only the existing authority under the DPA itself, and will not deal with its implementing Executive Order 12,919, as amended,[4] which currently does not reflect the changes that Congress made to the DPA in 1994 and 2003.

A Brief Summary of the DPA

The DPA consists of three titles: Title I—Priorities and Allocations, Title III—Expansion of Productive Capacity and Supply, and Title VII—General Provisions.[5]

Title I authorizes the president to require priority performance under contracts or orders—other than contracts of employment—which he deems necessary or appropriate to promote the national defense under any other contract or order, and to allocate materials, services, and facilities the president deems necessary or appropriate to promote the national defense.[6] Control of general distribution of critical and strategic materials in the civilian market requires additional presidential findings that the materials are scarce and essential to national defense, and that national defense requirements cannot be met without dislocating normal distribution of the materials in the civilian market.[7] The president may require the allocation or priority performance of contracts or orders for domestic energy supplies under DPA § 101(c).[8] Although "energy production or construction" is included in the definition of "national defense", the president's authority under § 101(c) does not require a "national defense" nexus as a precondition to action under the subsection. In order to deal with the provisions of Title I principally affected by the 1994 and 2003 amendments to the DPA, this chapter will not cover sections 102 through 108, which are invoked infrequently.

Title III authorizes the president to provide financial incentives for emergency preparedness to ensure the availability of materials, services, and technologies for "national defense" requirements. The financial incentives include loan guarantees to public or private financial institutions,[9] or loans to private business enterprises to establish, maintain, modernize, or expand domestic production capacity for essential technology items, components, and industrial resources.[10] One limitation under existing law is that both § 301(a)(1)[11] and § 302(a)[12] of the DPA restrict loan guarantees and loans to private business enterprises operating or performing under "Government contracts." Accordingly, the government contracts restrictions must be removed from the DPA if Congress wants to extend the loan guarantee and loan authorities to protect and restore privately owned critical infrastructures that are not performing or operating under government contracts. Under § 303 of the DPA, the president may provide for purchases of industrial resource or critical technology items and encourage the exploration, development, and mining of critical and strategic materials.[13] Other provisions of Title III include establishment of a separate Defense Production Act Fund,[14] synthetic fuel production,[15] and annual reports on offset impacts.[16]

With respect to Title VII, which contains the DPA's general provisions, this chapter will address only certain of that title's definitions,[17] and some aspects of voluntary agreements and plans of action for preparedness programs and expansion of production capacity and supply, which include limited antitrust immunities.[18] Other provisions of Title VII include: appointment and use of an executive reserve;[19] provisions for the appointment of civilian personnel;[20] and nonliability for compliance with invalid regulations and nondiscrimination against orders or contracts assigned priority under Title I of the DPA,[21] among others.

Background

A key to understanding the DPA is that it gives authority to promote "national defense." Whether DPA authorities apply to military or homeland security requirements, including emergency preparedness and critical infrastructure protection and restoration, depends on the extent to which such programs and activities pertain to "national defense". Section 702(14) of the DPA states:

> The term 'national defense' means programs for military and energy production or construction, military assistance to any foreign nation, stockpiling, space, and any directly related activity. Such term includes emergency preparedness activities conducted pursuant to title VI of the Robert T. Stafford Disaster Relief and Emergency Assistance Act (42 U.S.C. 5195 et seq.) and critical infrastructure protection and restoration.[22]

Until 1994, the definition of "national defense" included only the first sentence of the current definition, thus limiting DPA application to programs for military and energy production or construction, foreign military assistance, stockpiling, space, and other directly related activities. With the October 1994 enactment of Public Law 103-337, Congress amended the definition of "national defense" to add "emergency preparedness activities conducted pursuant to title VI of the Robert T. Stafford Disaster Relief and Emergency Assistance Act" (Stafford Act),[23] authorizing use of DPA authority for emergency preparedness activities related to national defense. In that same law, Congress repealed the Federal Civil Defense Act of 1950, as amended,[24] reenacted most of its provisions as Title VI of the Stafford Act, and cross-referenced the DPA to the Stafford Act.[25]

Substituting "emergency preparedness" for the term "civil defense," which is the term that had been used in the Federal Civil Defense Act, Congress defined "emergency preparedness" in Title VI of the Stafford Act to cover planning, preparedness training and exercises, mitigation, response, and recovery activities related to all natural- and man-caused hazards.[26] The purpose of Title VI of the Stafford Act is to administer and carry out duties to provide a comprehensive system of emergency preparedness for the protection of life and property in the United States from all hazards, and to vest responsibility for emergency preparedness jointly in the federal government and the several states and their political subdivisions.[27]

In 2003, concerned whether the DPA's provisions DPA could be used to protect and restore critical infrastructures, and believing it important to make such authority explicit, Congress added "critical infrastructure protection and restoration" to the definition of "national defense."[28] Inclusion of "emergency preparedness activities" and "critical infrastructure protection and restoration" in the definition of "national defense" extends the DPA to broad new areas that it never previously and explicitly covered. Since this expansion in coverage, questions remain about the new scope of the DPA, such as how to determine the scope of "emergency preparedness" and "critical infrastructure protection and restoration," and how state, local and tribal governments and the private sector can benefit from use of DPA authorities.

Emergency Preparedness and the DPA

Title VI of the Stafford Act defines "emergency preparedness" as:

> EMERGENCY PREPAREDNESS. The term 'emergency preparedness' means all those activities and measures designed or undertaken to minimize the effects of a hazard upon the civilian population, to deal with the immediate emergency conditions which would be created by the hazard, and to effectuate emergency repairs to, or the emergency restoration of, vital utilities and facilities destroyed or damaged by the hazard.[29]

The DPA's definition of "national defense"[30] covers three categories of activities related to emergency preparedness. First, the definition of "national defense" expressly includes emergency preparedness activities involving the programs for military and energy production or construction, military assistance to any foreign nation, stockpiling, and space, and other activities directly related to these programs. Second, this definition specifically includes "emergency preparedness activities conducted pursuant to title VI of the Robert T. Stafford Disaster Relief and Emergency Assistance Act (42 U.S.C. 5195 et seq.)." Such activities include: preparation of federal response plans and programs; provision for emergency preparedness communications and warnings; study and development of emergency preparedness measures; development and conduct of training programs; public dissemination of emergency preparedness information; assistance to the states with respect to mutual aid pacts between states and neighboring countries (Mexico and Canada); acquisition, transportation, storage, maintenance, renovation or distribution of materials and facilities for emergency preparedness; provision of financial contributions to states for emergency preparedness personnel and administrative expenses; and sale or disposal of certain materials and facilities unnecessary or unsuitable for emergency preparedness purposes.[31]

Third, the definition of "national defense" includes activities related to emergency preparedness that overlap or fall within the term "critical infrastructure protection and restoration".

Although Title VI of the Stafford Act does specify certain state and local emergency preparedness activities,[32] many of Title VI's provisions do not distinguish among federal, state, and local programs and activities. No provision of Title VI would limit its coverage to state and local programs. There is nothing in Title VI that distinguishes among federal, state, and local programs and activities; nor is there anything that would limit exercise of other federal departments' and agencies' emergency preparedness responsibilities to a delegation under 42 U.S.C. § 5196(c).[33]

So, can Titles I, III and VII of the DPA apply to emergency preparedness activities? An appropriate response is that emergency preparedness activities apply to those provisions of Titles I (priorities and allocations), III (expansion of domestic production capacity) and VII (voluntary agreements, executive reserves, etc.) of the DPA that fit within the DPA's definition of "national defense". Under Title I, the president's priority and allocations authority can be used for emergency preparedness for national defense-related purposes, implemented by executive order (for example, Executive Order 12919), by regulation,[34] by Homeland Security Presidential Directive, or by other presidential means. The Department of Homeland Security/FEMA interprets these authorities to permit it to determine the need for priorities or allocations under DPA Title I for other federal departments and agencies. The department, through FEMA, has already done so for the Federal Bureau of Investigation, the Transportation Security Administration, Customs and Border Patrol, and the White House.

As noted earlier, federal departments and agencies, and state, tribal and local governments may use this authority where they establish the links between their proposed activities and "emergency preparedness" for "national defense" purposes. The procedures and guidance to implement use of Title I authority by or for state, tribal and local governments have not yet been established at this writing. One can anticipate that a federal interagency process will develop these procedures and guidance.

Title III authorities meant to provide financial incentives for civil emergency preparedness purposes—to ensure the availability of materials, services, and technologies for "national defense" requirements—have not been used to date. Title III might be used to establish, maintain, modernize, or expand domestic production capacity for essential technology items, components, and industrial resources, for which a viable capacity does not exist or is insufficient to meet demand. However, as mentioned earlier in this paper, sections 301(a)(1) and 302(a)(1) of the DPA must be amended if Congress wants to extend loan guarantee and loan authorities to private sector businesses, such as private utilities, that are not operating or performing under government contracts.

Title VII authorizes the president to consult with representatives of industry, business, financing, agriculture, labor, and other interests, in order that those persons, with the president's approval, can make voluntary agreements and plans of action to develop preparedness programs for the expansion of productive capacity and supply beyond levels needed to meet essential civilian demand in the United States.[35] They could include voluntary agreements and plans of action to expedite production related to emergency preparedness, by allowing exchange of information on production processes, new technological breakthroughs, and other information needed to enhance preparedness and to increase production capacity. The DPA confers limited antitrust immunity on participants in voluntary agreements or plans of action, as long as the participants abide by the DPA's requirements.[36]

Voluntary agreements under Title VII as it presently exists are best used as an advance-planning tool. If they are not already in effect before a major disaster or other emergency event occurs, they are not effective as a response tool. For example, it would not have helped to prepare plans of action for meeting acute gasoline, housing, roofing, or construction material shortages in Florida and elsewhere *after* Hurricanes Charley, Frances, Ivan and Jeanne. The DPA currently requires a substantial amount of time before a voluntary agreement can go into force, and voluntary agreements are simply not an effective last-minute response to resource needs after a major disaster.

Critical Infrastructure

When Congress took up reauthorization of the DPA in 2003, members had before them the concerns arising out of the tragedies of September 11, 2001 and the implications of that disaster for protection of the health, safety and welfare of the people and resources of the United States. Among the concerns were questions about protection and restoration of critical infrastructures raised in the 1997 report the President's Commission on Critical Infrastructure Protection (Commission).[37] Congress also had before it the recommendations of the President's Report to Congress on Modernization of the Authorities of the Defense Production Act, written in 1997, which urged further amendments to the DPA to conform to evolving national defense policies. Despite statements at congressional hearings from FEMA, the Department of Defense, and the Department of Commerce that DPA authorities would protect critical infrastructures, Senator Bennett of Utah pressed for explicit critical infrastructure provisions in the DPA. The Senate Committee on Banking, Housing, and Urban Affairs reported out in its bill a definition of "critical infrastructure," and redefined "national defense" to include "critical infrastructure protection and restoration."[38] Congress enacted both definitions.[39]

Congress defined "critical infrastructures" as "any systems and assets, whether physical or cyber-based, so vital to the United States that the degradation or destruction of such systems and assets would have a debilitating impact on national security, including, but not limited to, national economic security and national public health or safety."[40] Congress did not, however, express in the Defense Production Reauthorization Act of 2003 which systems and assets are included within this definition.

The president has authority to further define "critical infrastructure" by regulation or orders.[41]

Some guidance for further defining the term can be found in the Commission's 1997 report.[42] The Senate Committee on Banking, Housing, and Urban Affairs cited that Report as one of several factors influencing its decision to include "critical infrastructure protection and restoration" in the DPA.[43] Noting that most infrastructure is privately owned and operated, the Commission addressed and defined eight infrastructure sectors: information and communications; electric energy; gas/oil production and storage; banking and finance; transportation (all sub-sectors); water supply; emergency services; and government services. A presidential directive[44] expanded the list of critical infrastructure and key resources sectors to include:

- Agriculture and food
- Public health and health care
- Drinking water and water treatment systems
- Energy
- Banking and finance
- National monuments and icons
- Defense industrial base
- Information technology
- Telecommunications
- Chemical
- Transportation (including mass transit, aviation, maritime, ground/ surface, and rail and pipeline systems)
- Emergency services
- Postal and shipping
- Government facilities
- Commercial facilities
- Dams
- Nuclear reactors, materials, and waste

As noted, the term "critical infrastructure" lies expressly within the definition of "national defense," and so, accordingly:

Title I of the DPA allows the president to protect or restore critical infrastructures by requiring priority performance of contracts or orders (other than contracts of employment); and allocating materials, services, and facilities to promote national defense.

Title III of the DPA gives the president authority to provide financial incentives for the owners and operators of critical infrastructure to ensure the availability of materials, services and technologies. Title III can be used to establish, maintain, modernize, or expand domestic production capacity for essential technology items, components, and industrial resources, for which a viable capacity does not exist or is insufficient to meet demand. However, as noted earlier, sections 301(a)(1) and 302(a)(1) should be amended if Congress wants to extend loan guarantee and loan authorities to private owners of critical infrastructure that are not operating or performing under government contracts.

Title VII of the DPA gives the president authority to use voluntary agreements for such purposes as achieving agreement on common measures to reduce vulnerabilities, or for developing critical infrastructure sector response plans. He also may use voluntary agreements to develop action plans for allocation of resources to help restore critical infrastructure or to expedite production related to critical infrastructures through several means. These may include allowing exchange of information regarding production processes or new technological breakthroughs, as well as other information needed to enhance preparedness and to increase production capacity. As noted earlier, however, to accelerate the process for creating a voluntary agreement, Congress must amend section 708 of the DPA.

Enhanced Authority for the Private Sector

Enactment of the Defense Production Reauthorization Act of 2003, with its insertion of "critical infrastructure protection and restoration" in the definition of "national defense," immediately raised the question of whether Congress extended DPA authorities to the private sector. Congress noted, as had the Commission's 1997 report, that most critical infrastructure in the United States is owned and operated by the private sector. The simple answer to the question is that, under Title I, the president has discretionary authority to direct a private entity to give priority to contracts or orders that it has with another private entity, but the president may not delegate his authority to make this determination to a private party.

Before the 2003 amendments, the Department of Commerce and other agencies charged with administering this section interpreted § 101(a) of the DPA to require a federal contract or order under which a prime contractor and all of its subcontractors or suppliers could be required to perform on a priority basis. As a result of the Defense Production Reauthorization Act's amendment of the term "national defense," the president has discretionary authority to grant priorities directly to private sector companies, reinforced by the legislative history accompanying reauthorization of the DPA.

The legislative history of the Defense Production Reauthorization Act of 2003 supports this interpretation of the statute. For example, in a colloquy on the floor of the House of Representatives on October 15, 2003, between Chairman Peter T. King and Ranking Member Carolyn B. Maloney of the House Subcommittee on Domestic and International Monetary Policy, Trade, and Technology, Mr. King said:

> "[I]t is the intent of the House that the DPA be interpreted to allow the administration to exercise the authorities provided under Section 101 of the DPA to directly assist a private sector critical infrastructure owner or operator in furtherance of critical infrastructure protection or restoration."

In her response, Mrs. Maloney stated:

> "[I]t is the intent of the House of Representatives that the administration refrain from interpreting the Defense Production Act as limiting the administration's ability to provide direct assistance to critical infrastructure owners and operators under Section 101 of the Defense Production Act."[45]

The plain language of § 101 of the DPA does not distinguish between private and public contracts and orders. Under § 101(a), if the president deems performance under a contract or order "necessary or appropriate to promote the national defense," he may then require performance of that contract or order to "take priority over performance under any other contract or order, and, for the purpose of assuring such priority, to require acceptance and performance of such contracts or orders in preference to other contracts or orders by any person he finds to be capable of their performance."

But may the president delegate to a private entity his authority to direct a private entity to perform a contract or order that it has with another private entity? The answer to that is no. The president has discretionary authority to *direct* a private entity to perform a contract or order that it has with another private entity, but he may not *delegate* his authority to make this determination to a private party. Any person "exercising significant government authority pursuant to the laws of the United States is an 'Officer of the United States,' and must, therefore, be appointed in the manner prescribed by the Appointments Clause of the Constitution."[46] Under section 101(a) of the DPA, an individual who requires performance of a contract or order is exercising significant government authority. Accordingly, this person must be appointed in accordance with the Appointments Clause, and cannot be a private individual.[47]

Implementation of the private sector authority. The issue of private sector use of DPA authority appears to be less one of legal interpretation than one of policy and practical implementation. With unknown thousands of privately and publicly owned critical infrastructures in the United States, chaos would result if priority authority were granted to private sector companies—as well as to state, local and tribal governments—without clear, specific, limited application and some central federal guidance. Standards, guidelines, and regulations are needed. Many issues must be resolved, including whether the departments and agencies that currently have roles and responsibilities under Executive Order 12,919 have the primary roles of oversight, or whether those roles and responsibilities should be assigned to the sector-specific federal Agencies listed in HSPD-7. These and many other practical administrative questions and policies must be resolved before this expanded authority can be implemented.

Governmental services. Turning from the private sector, another question is whether the DPA can apply to critical federal, state, tribal and local governmental services such as law enforcement, fire, and emergency medical services. The definition of "critical infrastructure" includes vital systems and physical or cyber-based assets, the degradation or destruction of which would have debilitating effects on national security, including national public health and safety. Law enforcement, fire, emergency medical and government services clearly fall within the scope of public health and safety, regardless of which level of government provides them. In drafting the legislation, Congress relied on the Commission's 1997 report, which expressly included government services and medical, police, fire and rescue services as critical infrastructures. In his critical infrastructure protection mandate to the secretary of homeland security, the president expressly included emergency services.[48] This approach is consistent with the DPA. The authorities of the DPA may be used to support governmental services provided by all levels of government—federal, state, local and tribal.

Next Steps

Congress has enacted and granted powerful authority to the president to ensure the availability of materials, services, facilities and other resources needed for national defense. Authority that before 1994 was available only to the military now also is available to the civilian sectors for emergency preparedness and critical infrastructure protection and restoration. The next steps are basically implementation of the existing authority and further updating of the DPA itself.

Implementation of existing authority. The president implemented DPA authority through Executive Order 12,919, just months before Congress enacted its 1994 amendments. The executive order has not been updated since 1994, and one of the important first next steps would be to incorporate changes authorized by the 1994 and 2003 amendments. There are a number of issues regarding the policy and operational roles of several different federal departments and agencies, including: the roles of the National Security Council (NSC) and the new Homeland Security Council (HSC) regarding resource preparedness policy and their roles in DPA implementing guidance and procedures; clarification of the nonoperational role of the assistant to the president for national security affairs; the role of the secretary of homeland security as an advisor to the NSC and the HSC in coordination with other departments and agencies; authorizing the secretary of homeland security to determine the applicability of homeland security programs to promote national defense; expansion of the role of the secretary of agriculture; dispute resolution among competing claimants for resources; changes to Executive Order 12,919 to use voluntary agreements more effectively; clarify use of an "executive reserve" for national defense purposes; and adding or amending certain definitions to reflect the changes made in the DPA, among others. The other questions related to the roles and responsibilities of various departments and agencies under Executive Order 12,919, noted above, need to be answered, as well.

In addition to changes in Executive Order 12,919, it will be imperative to adopt standards and guidance for use of the expanded DPA authority, not only for the federal government, but also for and by state, tribal and local governments. Standards, guidelines, and regulations will be essential for applying Title I priority performance authority to private sector companies, and almost certainly will require central federal guidance, if not control. Assigning resources and appropriating funds to implement the DPA within the federal civilian departments and agencies, and providing training and exercises in the proper use of the authority, will be critical to effective use of the authority. These issues only scratch the surface of the work remaining to implement the existing authority.

Updating the DPA. The DPA needs relatively few changes; its authorities are sufficient overall to address homeland security resource requirements. The needed changes principally would eliminate defects and clarify DPA authorities to promote homeland security. Proposed changes are discussed below.

Title I needs no changes. Under Title III, the linkage of the loan and loan guarantee authority to procurement under federal contracts limits use of loans and loan guarantees to critical infrastructure businesses that contract directly with government departments and agencies for national defense purposes. Modifications to §§ 301 and 302 of the DPA would rectify that limitation. Under Title VII, DPA authorities are generally available for homeland security purposes. The DPA could be enhanced by changes to certain definitions, notably to the definition of "national defense," to include "homeland security" and "critical infrastructure assistance to any foreign nation," and to add a new definition of "homeland security." The current definition of "national defense" includes "military assistance to any foreign nation". If Congress amended the definition to read "military or critical infrastructure assistance to any foreign nation" it would explicitly authorize the military and civilian sectors to use DPA Title I authority to support foreign nation critical infrastructure procurement in the United States.

To reduce the time needed to establish a voluntary agreement or plan of action, an amendment to § 708(c) should permit the president to waive the time constraints that the DPA requires in terms of: consultation with the attorney general and the Federal Trade Commission (10 days); the effective date after publication of a rule (30 days); and the notice requirements before any meeting to develop a voluntary agreement (7 days).

The DPA currently provides certain exemptions from the Federal Advisory Committee Act after a voluntary agreement or plan of action is created. Extending this exemption to consultations to create a voluntary agreement or plan of action would provide additional protection and incentives to use this authority.

Individuals who serve the government without compensation or in the executive reserve may retain some ties with their former private employers, and both the individual and the employer would be subject to the antitrust laws. The executive reserve authorized under § 710 of the DPA would be greatly enhanced if Congress amended the DPA to give antitrust protection both to the individual and to his or her employer for actions taken within the scope of the individual's employment in the executive reserve.

There remains considerable work to be done to implement the DPA using existing authority. Any amendments that Congress might make to eliminate defects and clarify authority under the DPA would increase the effectiveness of this important legal tool.

NOTES

1. This paper contains contributions of attorneys and colleagues from several departments and agencies, who were invaluable to the underlying analysis of the Defense Production Act. I particularly acknowledge with thanks and appreciation the experience, insights and advice of Larry Hall of the Federal Emergency Management Agency (FEMA), FEMA consultants John Starns and Paul Winslow, and Rosemary Hart and John Demers of the Office of Legal Counsel, Department of Justice. The views, conclusions, and any mistakes in this paper are mine and do not necessarily represent the policies and views of the Depart-

ment of Homeland Security, the Department of Justice, or any other department or agency of the federal government.

2. 50 U.S.C. app. §§ 2061-2170.

3. Defense Production Act (DPA) § 702(14), 50 U.S.C. app 2152(14), defines "national defense," as follows: "The term 'national defense' means programs for military and energy production or construction, military assistance to any foreign nation, stockpiling, space, and any directly related activity. Such term includes emergency preparedness activities conducted pursuant to title VI of the Robert T. Stafford Disaster Relief and Emergency Assistance Act (42 U.S.C. 5195 et seq.) and critical infrastructure protection and restoration."

4. National Defense Industrial Resources Preparedness, Exec. Order No. 12,919, 59 Fed. Reg. 29,525 (June 7, 1994), *as amended by* Amendment of Executive Orders and Other Actions, in Connection With the Transfer of Certain Functions to the Secretary of Homeland Security, Exec. Order No. 13,286, 68 Fed. Reg. 10,619-10633 (March 5, 2003).

5. Congress allowed several titles from the law's original enactment to expire on April 30, 1953. Those were, Title II—Authority to Requisition and Condemn; Title IV—Price and Wage Stabilization; Title V—Settlement of Labor Disputes; and Title VI—Control of Consumer Credit and Real Estate Credit.

6. DPA § 101(a), 50 U.S.C. app. § 2071(a).

7. DPA § 101(b), 50 U.S.C. app. § 2071(b).

8. DPA § 101(c), 50 U.S.C. app. § 2071(c).

9. DPA § 301(a), 50 U.S.C. app. § 2091(a).

10. DPA §§ 302(a), (b), 50 U.S.C. app. §§ 2092(a), (b).

11. 50 U.S.C. app. § 2091(a)(1).

12. 50 U.S.C. app. § 2092(a).

13. DPA § 303(a), 50 U.S.C. app. § 2093(a).

14. DPA § 304, 50 U.S.C. app. § 2094.

15. DPA § 305, 50 U.S.C. app. § 2095.

16. DPA § 309, 50 U.S.C. app. § 2099.

17. DPA § 702, 50 U.S.C. app. § 2152.

18. DPA § 708, 50 U.S.C. app. § 2158.

19. DPA § 710, 50 U.S.C. app. § 2160.

20. DPA § 703, 50 U.S.C. app. § 2153.

21. DPA § 707, 50 U.S.C. app. § 2157.

22. DPA § 702(14), 50 U.S.C. app. § 2152(14).

23. DPA § 702(14), 50 U.S.C. app. § 2152(14).

24. Pub. L. No. 103-337, § 3412(a).

25. 42 U.S.C. § 5195a(b). "Cross Reference—The terms 'national defense' and 'defense,' as used in the Defense Production Act of 1950 (50 U.S.C. App. 2061 et seq.), includes emergency preparedness activities conducted pursuant to this title."

26. 42 U.S.C. § 5195a(a)(3).

27. 42 U.S.C. § 5195.

28. Defense Production Reauthorization Act of 2003, Pub. L No. 108-195 (Dec. 19, 2003).

29. 42 U.S.C. § 5195a(a)(3). "Emergency preparedness. The term 'emergency preparedness' means all those activities and measures designed or undertaken to minimize the effects of a hazard upon the civilian population, to deal with the immediate emergency conditions which would be created by the hazard, and to effectuate emergency repairs to, or the emergency restoration of, vital utilities and facilities destroyed or damaged by the hazard. Such term includes the following:

"(A) Measures to be undertaken in preparation for anticipated hazards (including the establishment of appropriate organizations, operational plans, and supporting agreements, the recruitment and training of personnel, the conduct of research, the procurement and stockpiling of necessary materials and supplies, the provision of suitable warning systems, the construction or preparation of shelters, shelter areas, and control centers, and, when appropriate, the nonmilitary evacuation of civil population).

"(B) Measures to be undertaken during a hazard (including the enforcement of passive defense regulations prescribed by duly established military or civil authorities, the evacuation of personnel to shelter areas, the control of traffic and panic, and the control and use of lighting and civil communications).

"(C) Measures to be undertaken following a hazard (including activities for fire fighting, rescue, emergency medical, health and sanitation services, monitoring for specific dangers of special weapons, unexploded bomb reconnaissance, essential debris clearance, emergency welfare measures, and immediately essential emergency repair or restoration of damaged vital facilities)."

30. *See* 50 U.S.C. app. § 2152(14), "national defense," quoted earlier.

31. 42 U.S.C. §§ 5196-5196d.

32. *Id.*

33. 42 U.S.C. § 5196(c): "Delegation of emergency preparedness responsibilities—With the approval of the President, the Director may delegate to the several departments and agencies of the Federal Government appropriate emergency preparedness responsibilities, and review and coordinate the emergency preparedness activities of the departments and agencies with each other and with the activities of the States and neighboring countries."

34. DPA § 704, 50 U.S.C.app. § 2154.

35. DPA § 708(c)(1), 50 U.S.C.app. § 2158(c)(1).

36. DPA § 708(j), 50 U.S.C.app. § 2158(j).

37. PRESIDENT'S COMMISSION ON CRITICAL INFRASTRUCTURE PROTECTION, CRITICAL FOUNDATIONS—PROTECTING AMERICA'S INFRASTRUCTURES (Oct. 1997) (President's Commission Report).

38. S. REP. NO. 108-156, *accompanying* S. 1680, 108th Cong. (2003), a bill to reauthorize the Defense Production Act. S. 1680 was enacted into law as the Defense Production Reauthorization Act of 2003, Pub. L. No. 108-195 (2003).

39. Defense Production Reauthorization Act of 2003, Pub. L. No. 108-195 (2003).

40. DPA § 702(2), 50 U.S.C. app. § 2152(2).

41. 50 U.S.C. app. § 2154(a) provides: "In general. Subject to section 709 and subsection (b), the President may prescribe such regulations and issue such orders as the President may determine to be appropriate to carry out this Act."

42. President's Commission Report.

43. S. REP. NO. 108-156, *supra note 37.*

44. Cf., Homeland Sec. Presidential Directive 7 (HSPD 7), Critical Infrastructure Identification, Prioritization, and Protection), ¶¶ 15, 18, and 29 (Dec. 17, 2003); Homeland Sec. Presidential Directive 9 (HSPD 9), Defense of United States Agriculture and Food (January 30, 2004).

45. 149 CONG. REC. H9417 (daily ed. Oct. 15, 2003).

46. U.S. Const., art. II, § 2, cl. 2. *See* Buckley v. Valeo, 424 U.S. 1, 125-26 (1976) (per curiam).

47. *See* Constitutional Limits on "Contracting Out" Department of Justice Functions under OMB Circular A-76, 14 Op. Off. Legal Counsel 94, 99 (1990) ("We emphasize that under Buckley private individuals may not determine the policy of the United States, or interpret and apply federal law in any way that binds the United States or affects the legal rights of third parties.")

48. HSPD 7, at ¶ 15.

CHAPTER 13

Integrating the Private Sector in Homeland Security Preparation and Response

by John Copenhaver

Introduction

Governments traditionally have viewed emergency management primarily as a governmental function: They have the responsibility to protect the "public health and safety." Therefore, they enact legislation that enables them to act in emergencies and they set up contingency plans to deal with potential catastrophic events. These roles have been further extended to efforts to meet serious threats from potential terrorist activities. In developing these plans and preparations, frequently governments give only secondary consideration to the role of the private sector.

Yet, the private sector has responsibility for much of this country's critical infrastructure—including utilities, transportation systems, and medical care—and private sector institutions are responsible for most of our nation's employment, income, and financial and economic activity. Thus private sector institutions are a critical part of any effort to prepare for and respond to catastrophic events. Damage to private facilities would have a major impact on employment and economic activity, and government must rely on the private sector for the resources needed to respond to and recover from catastrophic losses.

When such events threaten, governments mobilize their resources, create emergency command centers, assess damage to public infrastructure, remove debris blocking public roads, and help mobilize and coordinate emergency food, medical, and shelter programs. Governments use law enforcement and public safety officers to help prevent such events, and then to deal with their consequences.

Under the National Response Plan, representatives of numerous government agencies staff the "Emergency Support Functions" that provide the response efforts, expertise, and many of the resources required to address damage to energy, transportation, and communications infrastructure, as well as various other emergency needs.[1]

The governmental flavor of emergency management has grown stronger with the establishment of the Department of Homeland Security (DHS). If a catastrophic event involves terrorists, and the need to prevent and respond to the possible use of chemical, biological, or nuclear/radiological weapons of mass destruction, the preeminence of government's role to protect our nation from attack is manifest. In this environment, where governmental action is mobilized to prepare for and respond to catastrophic events, it almost would be possible to believe that government had no need to interact with the private sector in such emergencies. One might also assume that the private sector could fend for itself and needed no assistance—and, in fact, its resources would not need to be called upon to assist governmental efforts.

Actually, no state or local government can ignore the private sector, either in its emergency response planning or its response activities. Quite simply, government cannot protect our communities and our homeland either from terrorist threats or natural disasters, without also mobilizing the full support and involvement of the private sector.

This chapter describes the essential relationship between traditional governmental emergency management and the private sector—frequently corporate emergency preparedness and response—efforts that must be integrated effectively with governmental functions. The important lesson is that federal, state, and local governments need to build effective partnerships with corporate America, whose property, goods, workers, and businesses are often primary targets of such threats and whose significant resources are needed to respond to such emergencies.

The Importance of the Private Sector to Homeland Security

Our nation is built on a capitalist system of individual rights, private ownership of property, and private operation of business. Private commerce is not just the backbone of America—private business owns and operates the vast majority of the infrastructure, employs most of the population in communities across the nation, and produces almost all of the goods and services consumed in America today.

One simple fact is determinative: A majority of the infrastructure that makes the operation of this country possible—our power grids, communications networks, water and gas lines, transportation systems, and storage facilities, etc.—is owned and managed by the private, not the public, sector. In fact, estimates of just how much of our nation's critical infrastructure is privately owned range from 85 percent to more than 90 percent. This means that even though many disaster response programs are aimed at getting *government* running again,[2] protection of the health, safety, and welfare of the American people can be complete only if privately held infrastructure and businesses are functioning and secure.

Indeed, the most devastating component of the attacks on America that occurred on September 11, 2001, came in the destruction of New York's World

Trade Center—one of the world's great business centers—and not in the destruction of government buildings (although the Pentagon was hit, and either the Capitol or the White House also appears to have been a target). This symbol of the country's business economy, and what it represents to the world, was a primary target of those terrorists.

Economic infrastructure is clearly a principal target of terrorist attacks on our country, both here and abroad. In efforts to forestall a new government from succeeding in Iraq, insurgents there have targeted that country's oil pipelines and storage facilities, trying to disrupt what little commerce Iraq has left. Members of the al Qaeda network have repeatedly threatened further attacks on commercial airliners, forcing the aviation industry to make tremendous expenditures on security, the financial effects of which have daily impact our civilian traveling population. Today's terrorist targets are different from those of the pre-9/11 days—the business sector is now as much of a target as government institutions, officials, or historic and symbolic landmarks.

Moreover, measurements of the "economic resilience" of American communities in a post-disaster environment continue to point out the importance of involving the private sector in planning for and managing emergency responses. For example, Hurricane Andrew had a devastating impact on the town of Homestead, Florida. That town and its residents suffered tremendously from the aftermath of Andrew's landfall in August 1992. While the downgrading of the Homestead Air Force Base from full-time to reserve status shortly thereafter, in 1993, left the base's 595 acres mostly vacant and had a severe impact on the entire Homestead community, it was actually Andrew's devastation of the Homestead business community that has had the greatest lasting impact on the town's vitality. Even in 2005, more than twelve years after the event, Homestead is still working to recover its 1992 pre-Andrew tax base, without which it will continue to struggle to recover.

One essential reason for integrating the private sector in planning and responding to homeland security matters is that, in many communities across America, the resources that are available and could be used to help prevent disasters—as well as to respond to and mitigate their effects and recover from them—are more predominantly available from the private sector. U.S. corporations, such as Home Depot, frequently have made their goods available to government response workers and impacted homeowners to help facilitate recovery. Immediately after the events of September 11, 2001, corporate America began making donations of equipment for use by emergency responders in New York City. Indeed, the resources that can be brought to bear by the private sector to respond to an emergency often far exceed the local and state government resources, and also can be made available very quickly.

Another role that the business sector can play is through its workers who are part of the community. Businesses provide a conduit to pass information on preparedness and emergency response through to their employee base. With the majority of wage earners in almost every community employed in the private sector, a strong partnership with the business leadership can ensure good communication and coordination regarding matters of homeland security that are critical to state and local governments. In many communities, the largest businesses employ a high percentage of local workers. By enlisting the help of major employers, government can quickly and effectively "get the word out" to large numbers of community residents so they will have knowledge of potential events, as well as information about how to protect themselves and respond to emergencies.

Emergency Response: How Government and Private Sector Approach This Issue

To form functional partnerships in the homeland security arena, both government and business sectors need to understand how they differ in preparation for and responses to emergencies. In the government sector, the term "emergency management" is used to describe a specific range of activities. Preparation for emergencies in the government sector frequently involves developing plans for anticipated events, and then training government entities and their staffs to mitigate the potential impacts of disasters. Actions in anticipation of events can be structural (e.g., building a levee to redirect floodwaters) and nonstructural (e.g., buying homes in areas that flood repeatedly and turning the areas into parks or other greenspace applications that will not be harmed by future flooding). State and local governments also develop cooperative arrangements between governmental entities to come to each other's aid, and to share and coordinate public sector resources and personnel. Rarely, except for nonprofit entities that may provide some functions such as health care and medical facilities rather than government, do such agreements include private sector actors.

Within the private sector, the term "emergency response planning" frequently is used to describe the process by which businesses plan to address the immediate impacts of a potential event that threatens harm to its employees and/or corporate physical assets. The concerns often relate to how to continue to perform as a business entity in the face of such events. Subcomponents of corporate emergency response plans (ERPs) typically are threat-specific, such as fire, toxic spill, severe weather, or building collapse plans. These subcomponents address specific threats primarily because specific capabilities are required to address each threat, such as firefighting, hazmat response, collapsed building search and rescue, and the like.

Also, most corporate ERPs include evacuation plans that can range from very simple—for example, fire drills and "head to the nearest exit" plans—to comprehensive—for example, use of trained floor wardens and predesignated assembly areas, as well as institution of perimeter and internal security measures. These plans also can include provisions for building occupants to *stay* in the building to avoid dangers outside the building—known as shelter-in-place or "safe haven" plans—that include stockpiling of necessary food and emergency supplies.

Examples of such private sector planning were apparent in several firms that were impacted by the World Trade Center attacks. Some, but not enough, of the firms housed in the towers had adequate planning for the catastrophic events that actually occurred. Lessons from the earlier 1993 attacks on the World Trade Center—and lessons from other recent threats—were incorporated in many businesses' plans. For example, American Express was able to activate an alternate facility created in the days prior to the year 2000—when people were concerned that many financial systems would fail due the "Y2K" computer-programming glitch—to allow it to continue processing financial transactions. Yet while some firms had evacuation plans, others seemed to have none. Most firms gave inadequate attention to continuity of operations in the event the site in which the offices existed was destroyed. The ability to identify and locate personnel that might have been affected was also lacking for most companies.

While some differences exist between government "emergency management" and corporate "emergency response planning"—the former being concerned for the overall population and the latter being focused on the specific business involved—there are still many similarities and interdependencies between these sectors. Government entities look at the critical functions they perform and develop "continuity of operations" (COOP) plans to ensure that these critical functions, together with "essential personnel," will be available on a continuing basis. In the private sector, similar concerns drive businesses to engage in a planning process termed "business continuity planning." The business identifies processes and functions deemed critical to its health and survival, and develops specific plans, such as backing up critical records, having off-site record facilities, and ensuring protection of its workers.

A "business impact analysis" (BIA) is conducted that looks objectively at all the major business functions and processes within an entity. Then, an assessment is made of the impacts to the entity should a particular function or process be interrupted for some period of time. During this process, impacts may be calculated for several different lengths of interruption to illustrate the time criticality of the function/process.

Both government COOP initiatives and corporate BCP efforts focus on maintaining or quickly restoring functions that are mission-critical to the entities covered by the plans. While there are differences in the damages these sectors could suffer—private sector firms may face loss of market share, breach of contracts, and loss of competitive positioning, while governments face the inability to perform legislatively mandated responsibilities and services for the public sector—the fundamental planning components are much the same. These similarities offer opportunities for cooperation between these two sectors in preparing our communities against harm. This "common ground" should be part of shared planning efforts. For example, local governments can include key representatives from private sector providers of critical infrastructure in their COOP sessions, and vice versa. Government and private companies also can exchange relevant information on response priorities in settings such as "Local Emergency Planning Committees" (LEPCs), or even jointly staged exercises of both sectors' response plans—such as "tabletop" exercises or field simulations.

There are numerous examples of cooperation between the government and business sectors in the arena of homeland security currently taking place.

Back in the late 1990s, the Federal Emergency Management Agency (FEMA) launched a program, called "Project Impact," to bring together the government and business sectors in pilot communities across the country so they could work together to achieve disaster preparedness, mitigation, response, and recovery. FEMA provided "seed" money and expertise to selected communities to help grow capabilities at the community level, with local government and local businesses taking the lead in developing plans and projects designed to reduce community exposure to both natural and manmade hazards—true "homeland security." Although FEMA's "Project Impact" was discontinued, it clearly established the need for integrated efforts, and created the momentum for congressional enactment of a new pre-disaster mitigation program.[3]

Another source of cooperation and integrated efforts is through the LEPC structure mentioned above. These committees are comprised of individuals appointed by State Emergency Response Commissions and typically include elected government officials, as well as representatives from local first responders, media outlets, and healthcare providers. The membership roster of many LEPCs has grown in recent months. Now, representatives from key private sector employers, as well as owners of critical infrastructure, are included in LEPC meetings.

While LEPC membership is stronger in some jurisdictions than in others, the underlying concept remains sound. In some locations, LEPCs have expanded beyond their initial intent, and now address private sector storage and transportation of hazardous materials and the consequent need for government planners to factor the presence of those dangerous materials into local emergency plans. Each community needs to develop such levels of cooperation. State and local government attorneys can take a critical role in ensuring that such efforts are undertaken when they participate in emergency planning.

Additional efforts are now being made to "bridge the gap" between business and government preparedness efforts. Recent examples include the establishment of the Citizen Corps, which is a division within the USA Freedom Corps that focuses on coordinating volunteer activities aimed at community emergency preparedness, and the DHS "Ready for Business" initiative that seeks to encourage private and public sector partnerships in emergency preparedness.

In September 2004, there was a kickoff of "National Preparedness Month," highlighting participation in preparedness activities by all components of American communities, and the creation of a new foundation, the Global Partnership for Preparedness. The missions were "reducing risk, improving response, (and) safeguarding the future" through the implementation of highly focused partnerships between public and private sectors at the community level. This set of initiatives reflects the growing awareness of the need to integrate governmental and private sector preparations and responses to catastrophic events. These are welcome recognitions of the role of the private sector as a critical partner with government in the efforts to protect America.

As state and local government officials and their counsel come to recognize the importance of an integrated preparation and response system for homeland security, the private role that has been neglected and poorly defined can become more central to these efforts. Together, the public and private sectors can provide the needed responses that will improve our society's health and safety.

NOTES

1. The National Response Plan includes fifteen Emergency Support Functions (ESFs): ESF #1—Transportation; ESF #2—Communications; ESF #3—Public Works and Engineering; ESF #4—Firefighting; ESF #5—Emergency Management; ESF #6—Mass Care, Housing, and Human Services; ESF #7—Resource Support; ESF #8—Public Health and Medical Services; ESF #9—Urban Search and Rescue; ESF #10—Oil and Hazardous Materials Response; ESF #11—Agriculture and Natural Resources; ESF #12—Energy; ESF #13—Public Safety and Security; ESF #14—Long-Term Community Recovery and Mitigation; and ESF #15—External Affairs. Some states, in their own versions of the plan, have included additional ESFs, addressing, for example, emergency veterinary needs.

2. Private businesses, for example, are not eligible to receive assistance under most federal disaster relief programs. *See*, 42 U.S.C. §§ 5170-5193 (Titles IV and V of the Robert T. Stafford Disaster Relief and Emergency Assistance Act, as amended).

3. *See*, § 203 of the Disaster Mitigation Act of 2000, Pub. L. No. 106-390, 114 Stat. 1552 (2000).

APPENDIX

A Checklist for State and Local Government Lawyers to Prepare for Possible Disasters

by Ernest B. Abbott and Otto J. Hetzel

Preface

The American Bar Association's Section of State and Local Government Law has long recognized that state and local governments respond first to catastrophic events and must be prepared to do so. In 1995, the section, working through its Jefferson Fordham Society, sponsored the production of *Are You Prepared?*—a continuing legal education video describing the legal challenges that lawyers faced after the 1993 bombing of the World Trade Center and the catastrophic flooding along the Missouri River. Over the last decade *The Urban Lawyer*, a law journal published by the section, has provided a number of seminal articles dedicated to exploring emergency management law.[1]

In 2002, after the devastation caused by the attacks of September 11, 2001, and following the birth of the Department of Homeland Security, it was clear that the section could do more, so it created a new Committee on Homeland Security and Emergency Management specifically "to help state and local government lawyers prepare for and respond to the legal issues their client jurisdictions face from threats due to both natural and non-natural disasters and emergencies."

This checklist, first published as a draft in late 2002, has reached a wide audience of state and local government lawyers, federal lawyers who work on intergovernmental issues, practitioners in law firms that service state and local governments, clients that frequently work with those governmental bodies, and academics in such fields as public health, land use, urban development, and emergency management law.

The checklist incorporates legal issues that likely will result from emergency situations regardless of cause. Emergencies—and the legal issues they create for state and local governments—are triggered by all manner of catastrophic events. These catastrophes range from nonnatural "Homeland

Security" threats involving terrorists or weapons of mass destruction, to industrial or transportation accidents involving hazardous materials, to threats resulting from natural hazards of flood, fire, wind, earthquake, and disease. A municipality's fire and police services respond to all disasters and operate under legal authorities relating to emergency situations that are activated regardless of cause.

Although terrorist events involving weapons of mass destruction may raise unique emergency management issues—such as mass casualties, federal control over crime scenes, quarantines, decontamination, and coordination of police with military and intelligence officials—many of the legal issues surrounding disaster preparedness and response are the same regardless of the cause. The National Response Plan and the National Incident Management System—recently adopted at the direction of President Bush—both recognize that the nation is well served by its "all-hazards" approach to emergency management. With this approach, the capabilities that are developed in preparing for catastrophic terrorist events also will be available when communities, states, and the federal government react to natural disasters, which fortunately are more common than the nonnatural variety.

Similarly, our nation's preparedness for terrorist incidents is significantly enhanced when the response uses the same management systems and response plans that are regularly exercised in mobilizing for emergencies resulting from natural events. The nation's all-hazards approach to emergency management also is important for state and local government lawyers who do not have the luxury of specializing in catastrophic events of only one type.

When first publishing this checklist as a draft in 2002, the committee expressed the long-term hope that it could expand its efforts beyond a simple checklist of issues to development and dissemination of available resources with respect to those issues—for example, key cases, sample contracts, summary analyses, and experts willing to discuss the issues. We are pleased that several of the efforts of this committee have reached fruition. *The Urban Lawyer* has published several new pieces reflecting the committee's work. The section and the Jefferson Fordham Society, with the assistance of a generous grant from the Public Entity Risk Institute, have produced a new and updated continuing legal education video, *Are You Ready? What Lawyers Need to Know About Emergency Preparedness and Disaster Recovery*. Finally, the section has published this book in an effort to aid lawyers dealing with these issues.

We very much hope that this checklist will be of real assistance to state and local government lawyers as they help their clients prepare for, respond to, and recover from catastrophic events. We are continually looking for comments and revisions to provide even more thorough coverage of these issues and to help legal counsel become better prepared to handle these critical issues that directly affect our country's health and public safety.

I. Introduction

Before a disaster strikes, legal counsel should be prepared for the role they may be asked to play. Anticipating issues, policies, and legal questions that may arise, identifying the various actors with whom counsel may be involved, and knowing how counsel may need to relate to or advise them are obvious starting points. The checklist that follows is organized to help counsel work through the issues and identify topics for researching the laws, systems, and policies that may arise in the context of any type of disaster, whether unnatural or natural.[2]

Lawyers should try to determine in advance what roles they may be asked to play by their governmental or other affected clients and what is the likely scope of their specific responsibilities. The tasks requested of counsel will be dependent, at least to some extent, on the issues that the government officials and public, nonprofit, or private-sector officers being advised are likely to be encountering.

When a disaster strikes, unless some advance preparation has taken place, counsel may find that a number of the issues they are being asked to consider will be new to them. Moreover, if they had been better prepared, many options that might have been available for dealing with emerging issues may no longer be available. In addition, lawyers operating in the midst of a catastrophe may find their working conditions difficult, to say the least. The disaster may disrupt the infrastructure—computers, telephones, and Internet connections—that counsel normally would rely on to research and generate legal documents to address issues that arise. Given the scope of actions that could arise and the potential impact that terrorist-caused and major natural disasters may entail, preparation is essential. The following steps are many, but certainly not all, of those that should be taken to prepare for these disasters.

II. Prepare an Emergency and Disaster Response Handbook and Share It with Your Client

1. Research all relevant emergency powers for the jurisdiction.
   NOTE: Emergency management and homeland security now are exceptionally active areas for legislation at the federal, state, and even local levels. Legal research on the scope of emergency powers should be updated several times per year.
   a. Research, using phrases such as "disaster or emergency" and (specific jurisdiction or level of jurisdiction, such as "state, municipal, county, or town"). This should yield the bulk of the various laws, and possible interpretations of them, that deal with what a jurisdiction can do in times of disaster.
   b. Use legal indices of statutes. In the bound copies of the index to the general laws in your jurisdiction, look up such topics as "disaster," "emergencies," "war," "civil defense," and the like. This search likely will refer you to applicable laws as well.
   c. Check special acts for the particular jurisdiction. Many states pass special acts dealing with disaster responses.
   d. Check with the state and local government emergency preparedness agencies that already may have compiled many of these sources.
   e. Check for local laws, ordinances, and regulations on these topics.

2. Compile a handbook containing legislative authority and judicial decisions relevant to the variety of issues, policies, and systems that could arise in emergencies and disasters, and keep it current. Keep hard copies and electronic files on-site at the office but also at another off-site location.
3. Give client contacts copies of the materials for advance reference as part of disaster crisis management.
4. Develop and maintain as part of your handbook a list of resources where you can get legal assistance and information. Keep in your handbook a master list of names, addresses, telephone/fax numbers, and e-mail addresses of resources. One resource is the International Municipal Lawyers Association, which has a data bank of forms and materials submitted by members on disaster-related legal issues.
5. Set up a portion of your handbook to cover the various laws and related forms that deal with responding to disasters in your jurisdiction.
6. Have sample forms ready to cover any matters for which specific action cannot be taken beforehand, to allow for rapid response to issues that can be anticipated.
7. Develop an appendix of forms and have them in hard copy, on disk, and on CD so they can readily be adapted to any particular situation. Typical forms may include declarations of emergency, declarations of curfews, bans on liquor or gun sales, emergency petitions to a court, orders of closure, emergency purchase orders, etc.
8. Identify in your handbook sources of information regarding planning for and responding to disasters, best practices, model acts, and other sources for assistance with legal issues from such national organizations as the National Governors Conference, the League of Cities, Conference of Mayors, National Association of Counties, and the International Municipal Lawyers Association. The websites of several federal agencies—FEMA, DHS, and the Public Health Law Program of the Centers for Disease Control—also provide substantial resources for state and local government lawyers.

III. Authorities Available to Jurisdictions to Protect Public Health and Safety

1. Determine whether the emergency authority currently provided and the powers that can be exercised under it are sufficient to deal with the potential scope and range of nonnatural and natural disasters. Among the issues that must be determined is who has the legal authority to take action, for instance, to tear down dangerous buildings, to exceed appropriations, to purchase supplies, to use volunteers who will be certifiable as professionals and can come under sovereign immunity protections, to hire more workers, etc. For example, the following questions need to be answered:
   a. In times of disaster, who is in charge—the elected official or local governing body or board, or a previously appointed administrative

professional? Who has authority: the county executive, the city or town mayor or manager (and if so, does the mayor or manager need the approval of the council or the board of selectmen?), the designated emergency preparedness director, or the police or fire chief? Under Homeland Security Presidential Directive No. 5, President Bush directed every federal agency, where permitted by law, to withhold any federal preparedness funding to any state or community that had not adopted an incident command system consistent with the National Incident Management System (NIMS).[3] Counsel should review the community and state command systems to confirm that they comply with applicable law and NIMS requirements to be eligible for potential grants-in-aid.

b. Must there be a declaration of an emergency before the person(s) with authority can act? In many jurisdictions, public health officials have strong powers to protect public health and safety—for example, by detaining persons diagnosed with or exposed to a communicable disease in a quarantine or isolation facility—without a formal declaration of emergency. Issues of forced evacuation also may arise, and both the legal authority and policies that are used in such situations should be known beforehand and relevant instructions should be prepared beforehand.

c. When do laws become effective? Are there provisions for emergency laws to become effective sooner than nonemergency laws? What are the steps? Does it make a difference if it is a state or a local law? (There may be special posting requirements for emergency laws.) What procedures apply to renewing such provisions, if that becomes necessary?

d. Who has the authority to declare an emergency, and what laws, potential actions, and access to benefits are triggered as a result of who makes the declaration? What powers and authorities of the client jurisdiction are triggered by declarations by various officials—mayor, city or town manager, council or board of selectmen, police or fire officials, state emergency officials, or governor? Many jurisdictions have different types of declarations for which different officials are responsible. For example, a public health officer or commission may have authority to declare a "public health emergency."

e. What differences in declarations of an emergency apply to a local, a state, or a federally declared emergency? Generally, different rules apply to each type of declaration. For instance, whether it is a local, state, or federally declared disaster may affect the availability of loans, grants, and reimbursements from state and federal government sources.[4] Depending on the particularities of the jurisdiction's laws, the nature of the designation also may affect the scope of authority and actions that can be taken. Knowing the difference in advance will minimize claims after the disaster is over.

f. What issues of succession of governmental officials may arise in an emergency situation that could have implications for governments taking action (for instance, to declare an emergency)? Determine whether your state's constitution provides for the continuity of government in times of emergency. Are there succession powers and designations, and who makes those determinations?

2. If sufficient powers have not been provided, or are not clear, consider proposing necessary additional relevant authority to cover necessary responsibilities and tasks.

3. Determine whether powers are sufficient for public health and safety purposes in the context of the need for emergency responses. For instance, in times of disaster it often becomes necessary to require evacuations, quarantine persons, impose curfews, and restrict persons from access to certain areas, including public thoroughfares and buildings. Also, it may be advisable to impose other controls in emergency situations, such as banning sales of liquor and guns, and imposing price controls, if authorized.

4. Determine who has the authority to make these decisions, what steps must be taken to do so, and what documents are required to record properly the actions taken. As noted above, sample forms that can be adapted readily for these purposes should be prepared well in advance. Be aware of time limits and renewal procedures in drafting such documents.

5. Determine whether an evacuation plan exists, who determines the circumstances that can require population evacuations in the jurisdiction, and what grounds for evacuation are required and will need to be documented. The authority for most state or local evacuation orders stems from the state's police power. Evacuations generally are ordered by police or fire authorities based on a judgment that evacuation is necessary to protect the public health and safety (i.e., evacuation of a community affected by brush fires or the leak of a derailed tank car containing chlorine gas). Counsel should confirm which procedures and limitations apply to evacuation orders, and in so doing, should consider the legal and practical challenges of "mandatory" evacuations and any responsibility of the jurisdiction to protect property vacated/abandoned during an evacuation. Can there be forced evacuations and, if so, how are they to be implemented? Is the jurisdiction responsible to effectively evacuate special needs populations? Laws vary widely in terms of whether the government can force people to leave their property. Even if a jurisdiction does not permit forced or mandatory evacuations, it is a good idea to have ready a notice to give property owners advising them of the risks involved and the fact that the government may not be in a position to rescue them as events progress. Some jurisdictions give people who resist evacuation a preprinted waiver form and collect information from such people for purposes of notifying their next of kin.

6. Determine whether different legal requirements (and authorities of different agencies) will apply when allowing reentry to evacuated areas at the conclusion of the crisis. After evacuation, the evacuating authority must determine when it is safe to allow residents to return to their

homes and businesses. Who is responsible for determining when it is "safe"? What kind of public announcement will be made? Will decisions be left to police and fire officials in the area? Do other agencies have jurisdiction where trace amounts of chemical, radiological, or biological contamination remain?

7. Determine the scope and range of regulatory powers available to control operation of commercial establishments that may be required in emergencies and disasters, including access to and restrictions on the use of food service establishments, grocery outlets, etc.

8. Determine the applicability of existing curfew provisions, what grounds or events are required to impose such controls in emergencies and disasters, and how they are to be documented. For instance, what is the process to declare curfews and how are they to be justified? A review of the available legal decisions relating to curfews in a state is an essential starting point.

9. To the extent that law enforcement powers may pertain to your client, or to you, determine if a relevant range of potential acts of terrorism are sufficiently covered under applicable criminal laws to enable public safety officials to exercise necessary powers to act.

10. Considering the potential issues that may arise under possible biochemical terrorism scenarios, determine if authority is sufficient to protect residents. For instance, can persons within the jurisdiction be required to undergo tests for possible exposure to toxic substances? Can testing (possibly invasive) be ordered? Can treatment to protect them be ordered and then compelled—including, for instance, decontamination procedures? Can persons be required to take medication with protective agents that may involve injections or pills and that may entail some risk? Can use of various protective apparatus, such as biochemical breathing equipment and masks, be mandated?

   Assuming there is legal authority to require decontamination, medical testing, treatment, vaccination, quarantine, and isolation, what legal options are available to address an individual's refusal to consent, for example, to treatment? Can such persons be restricted in the area where they possibly were infected until appropriate procedures to ensure that they safely may enter back into the general society are implemented? If challenges occur, how and when would the individual be provided with whatever hearing might be required by constitutional due process protections?

11. Determine whether a sufficient range of related public health powers is available to prevent or to control contamination, to permit destruction of real and personal property that may constitute a potential hazard, and determine what compensation is required of government. What is the process for boards of health, governing officials/boards, public safety officials, building commissioners, fire departments, and others for making buildings or property safe or demolishing them, and where can such debris be disposed of? Inevitably, during an emergency, there will be a need for the government to restrict access to, raze, or board up

buildings or to clear property due to health and safety concerns. Even in times of emergency, there are special procedures that must be followed. A failure to follow the rules could lead to claims later on, even if the jurisdiction was justified in tearing down a dangerous structure. A failure to follow the legal requirements in times of an emergency likely will make the jurisdiction liable for damages. Different rules may apply to different officials who all may be authorized to take such action. Know the differences and the rules.

NOTE: By statute, federal assistance for debris removal is available only if the state or community arranges for an unconditional authorization to remove the debris and indemnifies the federal government against any claim arising from the removal of debris from private property.[5] It is important to observe appropriate procurement requirements when expecting reimbursement from federal funds. No more than the minimal essential work necessary to clear access should be undertaken using emergency procurement procedures. Wider cleanup can be accomplished through appropriate normal procurement processes.

12. Review the jurisdiction's police power authority related to the following matters:

a. Restriction and control of access to crime scenes or to areas subjected to biochemical or radioactive incidents having the potential of residual pollution of the area that will require abatement and cleanup.

b. Protection and control of access to infrastructure critical to the functioning of government and the generation and transmission of utilities, such as public buildings; transportation, including bridges, elevated highways, tunnels, and the like; water processing facilities; reservoirs; electrical and gas storage, generation, and transmission facilities; communication facilities; or other areas and systems subject to potential threats of harm.

Determine the level of threshold authority available to protect critical sites of governmental and public utility infrastructure, through such measures as authority to search vehicles, detain persons near critical sites for questioning, and restrict access to such critical areas while addressing applicable First Amendment, due process, and privacy rights. For example, know who has authority to impose emergency actions relative to water supplies, and what actions may be taken. These could range from the need to limit water consumption or divert water from one area to another because of drought conditions, to the need to protect water supplies, as well as other utilities, from corruption. Consideration must be given to handling situations where the water is not produced by the jurisdiction but, rather, is the property of a private utility.

c. Imposition of security measures, such as searches and restrictions on access to public gatherings including sports and entertainment events and to other areas requiring protection.

What is the process to set up roadblocks and vehicle searches in certain areas? What are the legal issues that may arise from stopping vehicles or people in public areas during an emergency? What are the community's procedures for responding to evidence of unrelated criminal activity (such as stolen property, drugs, and drug paraphernalia) discovered during a security search?

13. What restrictions are there on emergency action in certain areas, such as private roads, wetlands, waterways, private lands, utility easements, etc.? Under the wetlands laws of some states, before emergency work can be done in a protected area there must be approval of the emergency by the local agency having jurisdiction. Be familiar with the process for emergency work in such areas before you need to use it. Under what circumstances and conditions can entry be made on private property? Under what circumstances and conditions can private property—both real and personal—be taken or used during an emergency? What, if any, compensation may need to be given the owner for the loss of use or damage to such property?

IV. *Surveillance Authority and Protection of Security Information*

1. Determine the jurisdiction's authority to conduct surveillance activities. Government surveillance activities already have triggered issues with respect to use of closed-circuit video cameras, photographs, and aerial surveillance, as well as the extent of government's authority to impose restrictions or sanctions based on such surveillance. Consideration will need to be given to possible damage claims that could be made as a result of governmental actions.

2. Determine the jurisdiction's authority to institute background checks on individuals, use licensing documentation, and access public safety information in facilitating responses to potential threats to public safety. Justification required for restrictions on an individual's access to facilities and transportation modalities, and the basis for the denial, has been challenged in a number of decisions that lawyers should have adequate knowledge of in advising their clients. Maintaining the confidentiality of the information source also may be a problem depending on the source of the records used.

3. Determine what forms of communication during the onset of a disaster are available to jurisdictions that may be involved, and develop strategies for ensuring coordination of communications in such circumstances. Various client communication systems need to be shared by different departments and units of government that must act in a coordinated fashion in disaster situations. These systems should include access to legal counsel to obtain advice on issues that are likely to arise during the course of events when guidance may be requested.

   Recent federal preparedness grants, training, and exercises have focused on improving "interoperability of communications." The challenge extends far beyond compatibility of equipment and into the compatibility of incident command/management systems of multiple responders. The requirement that all communities be certified as compliant under the National Incident Management System by September 30, 2005, is intended to address interoperability concerns. Counsel may need to become familiar with the consequences in the event a community fails to comply or states that it is compliant but then demonstrates in an incident that it is not.

4. Determine who has authority to access and respond to various types of intelligence information from other levels of government. Determine those persons authorized to receive communications from other levels of government regarding intelligence matters and will be responsible for taking action upon receipt of such communications.

5. Determine who is to have access to intelligence information and how such information will be safeguarded from those without such authority. How will advance clearance to such communications be documented? Classified intelligence information cannot be provided to any person who does not possess valid clearance. Violation of this statute is a serious criminal offense.

   Only the federal government may grant security clearances. The Department of Homeland Security has ensured that the emergency management function of each state has at least one—and usually more than one—person who has been granted the security clearances necessary to review classified information about potential terrorist threats.

   Local officials without clearance should be aware of who is the "cleared" individual to contact about suspected events and whether there is any information (stripped of classified material) that can be provided to assist in response efforts.

6. Establish communication links and command authority with medical support systems, such as hospitals, doctors, and emergency medical services, and determine who such communications will be safeguarded. In an era of highly communicable diseases, bioterrorism is a potential basis for attacks on the population that will require careful management and difficult decisions regarding how information on conditions will be communicated.

V. Intergovernmental Joint Powers Agreements and Actions

1. Determine the scope of existing joint powers agreements with other governmental bodies, and determine whether those powers are sufficient to cover issues that may arise in allocation of manpower and resources and to ensure cooperation necessary to respond effectively to various types of disasters. Be familiar with existing joint powers agreements and mutual aid agreements. For instance, if there are mutual aid agreements, how are they activated?

2. Determine what existing policies and procedures have been agreed to by various governmental bodies under emergency plans required of jurisdictions in some states, and, more generally, concerning potential exercise of joint responsibility for dealing with disasters and whether

these powers are documented adequately regarding responsibility for responding to particular disasters. Review the article on Intergovernmental Agreements in the winter 2005 issue of *The Urban Lawyer*. Interstate mutual aid is frequently provided under the Emergency Management Assistance Compact, which 48 states have signed. A Draft Model Intrastate Mutual Aid Agreement has been developed by the National Emergency Management Association.

3. Identify existing coordination requirements among various levels of government in preparing for and responding to disasters, and determine whether they are adequate.

4. Review the jurisdiction's emergency plan and command structure for emergency management, as well as the client's role in both, to prepare to respond to client questions about legal authority for carrying out various actions for which the client's jurisdiction is responsible and to ensure effective cooperation among various jurisdictions at all levels of government.

VI. Disseminating Critical Information to the Public

1. Review the available communications systems for conveying information between government officials and the public for such matters as disaster alerts and management information, and determine how the authority to use such systems needs to be authorized and documented. Determine what procedures and legal approvals should be used before and during an emergency regarding what will be communicated when to alert and inform the public adequately about potential disaster situations and conditions.

2. Determine how dissemination of information to the public will be provided using cooperative local media outlets, radio, television, and cable technology for notifications, as well as the various warning systems and alarms that may be available in a jurisdiction, such as sirens, loudspeakers, etc. The lawyer's natural instinct may be to restrict communication to the public due to potential liability for providing inaccurate information. However, this instinct simply is wrong during emergencies. Information—coordinated among all responders and levels of government to ensure consistency—is absolutely critical to a successful emergency response. Members of the public must be advised what the problem is and how they can best protect themselves, their families, their property, and their livelihoods.

3. Set parameters on sharing intelligence and disaster information with the news media, and determine how much access to give citizens and the media to make inquiries of government officials or obtain access to government documents, intelligence information, or sensitive records (including those maintained by medical facilities and health care professionals).

4. Determine how freedom of information and open meetings laws will be applied to governmental information sources during periods of crisis

management and planning. What are the effects of an emergency declaration or situation on open meetings laws, public records laws, ethics
laws, etc.? For example, what are the requirements to hold an emergency meeting? Are on-site inspections considered meetings? Typical
open meetings laws provide exemptions from notice requirements in an
emergency. Know in advance what constitutes an emergency under the
law, and know what special steps must be taken. Consider procedures
needed to provide centralized and consistent treatment of these issues
by governmental clients and to give the media and the public advance
information about how such matters will be handled.

The balance between policies of openness in government and re-
stricting access to information that would be useful to those planning a
terrorist attack is still being developed. The Department of Homeland
Security is promulgating regulations implementing an exception to
FOIA contained in the Homeland Security Act of 2002, Pub. L. No. 107-
296, 116 Stat. 2229; this rule—which would preempt certain state open
records laws—may help clarify information issues.

VII. Establish Guidance for Administrators Regarding Administrative Functions during Emergency and Disaster Crises

A. Fiscal and Budgetary Matters

1. Determine what existing sources of funding can be used and what
   procurement requirements are applicable to emergency situations.
   For instance, who has authority to order emergency actions entail-
   ing governmental costs? Who determines the use and allocation of
   resources/reallocation of appropriated funds? What procedures must
   be observed, and how are they to be documented? What restrictions
   or limitations apply to such actions? Decide whether existing special
   emergency authority in this regard is sufficient, and propose changes if
   needed.
2. Determine whether current emergency procedures are sufficient to
   authorize funds and obtain access to budgetary resources that may be
   required, including whether normal limits and restrictions on spending
   will apply and who can make those decisions. The extent to which supplemental approvals will be required should be determined as well.

B. The Exercise of Fiscal Authority

1. Who has the authority to do what in times of disaster?
2. What limits are there on the authority of various boards, the city council, or executive officials in terms of exercising their typical authority?
3. Who has the authority to waive certain laws? In a disaster, some laws
   can be waived, but only with prior action by designated officials. Determine whether that authority exists in the jurisdiction, who can exercise

it, and what must be done. If a declaration or formal order must be is-sued, have sample forms readily available that can be filled in with the details.

4. Is there authority to exceed appropriations and basically disregard set budgets when there is an emergency situation, and who has the author-ity to do what is essentially emergency borrowing?

What limits are there on what the money can be spent on? Dealing with the issue of exceeding budgetary appropriations is often one of the first legal issues to arise. Some laws require a vote of various governing board officials. Others may require the approval of state officials, the obtaining of which can be problematic during disasters. Some laws may restrict or limit funds that exceed approved budget amounts, and limit how they can be spent. Conveying these limitations to your client will be essential.

5. Determine how reimbursement for emergency expenditures for re-sources can be obtained, what procedures are required to obtain such funding and from what sources of funds, and what restrictions apply.

C. Contracting and Procurement Procedures

1. Determine what contractual procedures are applicable during an emer-gency that allow for expedited procurement of necessary resources and personnel, including equipment, supplies, materials, food, shelter facilities, etc. Identify any special rules in contracting during times of a disaster and how they differ from the typical procurement rules. What triggers special contracting authority, if applicable? Is a declaration of disaster needed, and by whom? A related question is what rules for contracting and procurement are waived when there is an emergency?

What special actions must be taken to use the emergency rules? For example, are different actions required for certain types of emergencies? Who declares them? Are special filings required for actions taken un-der emergency laws? Are there limits on how much work can be done, such as a requirement that the work only go so far as necessary to abate the emergency temporarily? Some laws limit the emergency contract work to only the least amount of work needed to abate the emergency. Some laws require approval from state officials before normal contract rules can be waived. There also may be special requirements for filing certifications with the state when a contract has been entered into with-out the normal procurement process. Such special authority may be needed for:

   a. procurement of services, supplies, and materials (especially food, shelter, supplies, and medical supplies)
   b. public works projects (i.e., bridge repairs, road work, dams, etc.)
   c. public building projects (i.e., repairs, reconstruction, temporary structures, etc.)
   d. utility contracts (i.e., water, gas, etc.)

D. Handling Personnel Issues in an Emergency Situation

1. Determine how personnel can be hired in an emergency, how compensation is determined, and what worker rights will apply when increased governmental staff resources must be deployed.

2. Identify what personnel rules apply in times of disaster, such as hiring procedures, liability for employee actions, actions available under mutual aid agreements, calculation of benefits, wage-hour limits, etc. In responding to an emergency, a jurisdiction almost always will need more employees than it has. It is critical to know beforehand how to hire people in an emergency, particularly in view of civil service or local personnel code requirements. Other issues that may be affected are whether medical examinations are needed for employees hired in an emergency. Administrators may need to exercise care regarding hiring of persons who would not have been hired under normal circumstances who may then gain preferences or access to benefits not normally available to them by suddenly responding to calls for emergency employees.

3. Determine under what circumstances emergency appointments can be made, which in effect bypass normal hiring rules (civil service, collective bargaining, etc.). What restrictions are there on emergency employees performing the duties of other employees? Some laws restrict, for example, police performing the duties of fire fighters. Are there emergency exceptions? What special rules exist for calling into service employees who have already retired? (Retired employees may be a good source of additional workers when there is a disaster. However, there may be special restrictions on their returning to work, even in times of an emergency.) Other personnel issues also can arise. For instance, can an unpaid volunteer be considered an employee if he or she serves in an emergency situation? Even under normal circumstances, governmental jurisdictions often survive on volunteers. Their assistance becomes even more important during an emergency. However, there are a host of special problems and issues that arise with volunteers, including liability, licensing, credentialing, and management/supervision.

4. What special rules are there in terms of the number of hours/days an employee can work, and how are those rules applied in times of emergency? Often state and federal laws limit the number of consecutive hours or days an employee can work. Special rules may apply, however, in times of emergency. What are the rules of the Fair Labor Standards Act and the Family Medical Leave Act concerning emergency situations?[7] Are there comparable state laws to be considered?

How does the federal Uniformed Services Employment and Reemployment Rights Act of 1994 (38 U.S.C. § 4301 *et seq.*) affect employment practices when employees are called up for military duty when National Guard units are activated?[8] Are there comparable state laws to be considered? Some key—and not so key—employees may be called up for reserve duty during the time the jurisdiction also needs them. There are special rules on how soon they must return to work following release from military service in order to maintain their rights to their positions.

VIII. Liability of Governmental Units in Emergency Situations

1. Determine the extent of the municipality's potential for liability for injuries/medical expenses sustained by employees and volunteers or retirement/disability benefits for them in times of emergency. While there is usually little dispute that all that can (and some would argue should) be done should be attempted when people need to be saved from injury or death, administrators should at least know what the government's exposure will be if a volunteer is injured, the rescue of a victim fails, or a citizen's property is damaged. Another issue is the jurisdiction's potential liability for benefits to an emergency employee or to a volunteer's family should the employee or volunteer die while serving in the emergency. Similarly, to what extent is the jurisdiction liable for injuries/medical expenses or personal property damages sustained by employees from other jurisdictions, or for contributions to retirement/disability benefits for those employees from other jurisdictions coming to its aid in an emergency? Many of these issues are dealt with in the mutual aid agreements under which assistance is provided by other jurisdictions.

2. What are the special rules for dealing with hazardous substances in times of emergency? Are there environmental restrictions when taking action to dispose of materials, including debris, snow, water, etc.? Are piles of snow, which may have road salt or other chemicals mixed in, considered hazardous material for which special disposal rules apply? Environmental agencies have been known to cite (and fine) local governments for such acts as dumping snow (which has chemicals in it from the roads) into a body of water. Knowing where such material can be disposed of in advance could save a jurisdiction considerable costs, let alone embarrassment, if remediation becomes necessary.

3. Determine to what extent governmental liability will still apply in emergency and disaster management situations. For instance, to what extent is a jurisdiction liable for injuries/medical expenses/property damage *caused by* employees and volunteers in times of emergency? Further, will employees or volunteers be indemnified for any damage or injury they may cause? What if they are performing a task that normally requires a special license, and they do not have it because they are filling in during an emergency? Do the same rules apply, and to what extent is a jurisdiction liable for injuries/medical expenses/property damage sustained or caused by employees from other jurisdictions, or for contributions to their retirement/disability benefits as a result of those employees coming to the jurisdiction's aid? Typically, mutual aid agreements or laws provide that the entity providing the employees remains liable for payment, but the entity receiving the services has to

reimburse the entity sending the help. Different requirements might apply when the employees volunteer on their own time to help out in another jurisdiction.

4. What special liability rules apply in emergency circumstances? For instance, what are the jurisdiction's special liability rules that might apply to doctors, nurses, and other health care professionals, or to a "Good Samaritan" who comes forward to help people in times of emergency? State laws often provide special exemptions to liability by doctors, nurses, people with CPR training, etc. Knowledge of the application of such rules is likely to affect whether a jurisdiction enlists the assistance of such professionals.

5. What are the liabilities a governmental jurisdiction faces when entering on private property or taking or using private property during an emergency? The state laws that apply to government entering private property in times of an emergency can be critical regarding government liability. Those laws may be different if it is not a state-declared disaster. Photographs or videos taken of the area before, or at least while, work is being carried out may provide useful evidence to sustain government intervention. State eminent domain laws also may apply to such situations.

6. Determine what laws are subject to suspension during times of emergency. For instance, how are laws regarding statutes of limitations, Sunday or Blue Laws, waiver of minimum number of school days, local tax proceedings, and creditor/debtor laws affected by declarations of emergency? Special rules may even govern the use of vehicles (including all-terrain vehicles and snowmobiles) in times of emergency. Often there are special rules for using such vehicles on public streets during an emergency if authorized by the appropriate official. Such vehicles may be the community's only source of transportation in some disasters.

Special laws concerning rebates on taxes paid for property damaged during a disaster may apply during emergencies. (Some states have laws that provide for rebates of taxes when property has been damaged and the taxes were paid on the predamage value of the property.)

Special laws may apply to the valuation of property taken under eminent domain when the property was damaged in a disaster. Similarly, access to state funding may apply in times of emergency or to the time for repayment of loans.

Disaster relief organizations also may receive special treatment under state laws.

Contract provisions also can be affected by definitions concerning acts of God, disaster, emergency, etc. In some states, special laws establish a day or week for particular recognition of workers in disasters. Disasters also can affect the administration of the criminal justice system. Some municipal counsel also handle criminal prosecutions, so counsel need to know the rules regarding the effect of a delay on bringing someone before the court for bail or arraignment in times of an emergency, as well as the other nuances of criminal law in such circumstances.

Insurance provisions also can be affected by disaster situations. Know before disaster strikes what your insurance policies provide for coverage in times of an emergency. Remember, an emergency declaration may be helpful in getting state or federal aid, but it also may affect the level of insurance coverage that later can be obtained from the carrier. Similarly, "force majeure clauses" in existing contracts may need to be evaluated—ideally before, but certainly after, emergencies occur. Many construction project contracts may provide for extensions of time and releases from liability if there is an enemy attack, act of God, or other force majeure event. Many times, these clauses are left in contracts with little thought given to them. Since contractors often can obtain insurance to cover these contingencies, governments may want to consider excluding such clauses.

Access to governmental benefits also may be subject to disaster relief. Following 9/11, a number of bar associations and other legal agencies set up programs to help people deal with the paperwork needed for receiving benefits. There was, for example, an expedited process on receiving death certificates. Of course, it is important not to overlook appropriate verification requirements. It has been reported recently that a number of fraudulent cases have arisen involving people wrongly obtaining death benefits following 9/11.

IX. *Develop a Knowledge of Applicable Federal and State Government Laws, Regulations, and Authority in Handling Disasters, Both Nonnatural and Natural*

A. Key Federal Laws

1. The Robert T. Stafford Disaster Relief and Emergency Assistance Act, 42 U.S.C. § 5121 *et seq.*, as amended. This act deals with federally declared disasters and emergencies; it is a principal source of federal disaster assistance to state and local governments in times of disaster.
   a. Direct Federal Assistance: FEMA coordinates all assistance provided directly by the federal government in response to declared disasters and emergencies.
   b. Public Assistance Program provides federal grants of "not less than 75%" of certain emergency costs and of the "repair, restoration, reconstruction, or replacement" of public facilities and certain non-profit facilities.
   c. Individual and Housing Assistance provides funding for, and in some cases supplies, temporary housing for displaced households; and for federal funding of "immediate needs" of affected individuals and families.

    d. Postdisaster Mitigation Programs—particularly the Hazard Mitiga-
tion Grant Program.

    e. Predisaster Mitigation Programs—mitigation planning require-
ments and funding for predisaster mitigation.

    f. Emergency preparedness planning and exercising authorities. Gen-
eral requirements that affect local government eligibility for funding.

    g. Duplication of benefits.

    h. Ineligibility of for-profit businesses and the Legal Responsibility
Doctrine.

    i. Federal grant administrative requirements.

    j. Distinction between "costs" that can be eligible and "losses," such as
reduced revenues, that are not.

2. Small Business Administration

    a. SBA disaster loans for individuals and small businesses.

3. Specific departmental emergency programs.

    a. Department of Health and Human Services.

    b. Department of Transportation.

    c. Department of Housing and Urban Development.

    d. Environmental Protection Agency.

    e. Department of Agriculture.

4. National Flood Insurance Program

    a. Floodplain management.

B. State Laws

1. Local government lawyers should become familiar with the state laws
for dealing with both statewide and local emergencies. For instance,
know how the state militia or other such groups can be called in to help.
(Usually the law provides that local officials may request the National
Guard or militia to come and provide assistance; know whether a legislative body also must approve.)

NOTES

    1. *See, e.g.*, Alan D. Cohn, *Mutual Aid: Intergovernmental Agreements for Emergency Preparedness and Response 7*, 36 URB. LAW. 1 (2005); Ernest B. Abbott, *Representing Local Governments in Catastrophic Events: DHS/FEMA Response and Recovery Issues*, 37 URB. LAW. 467 (2005).

    2. The committee wishes to acknowledge with appreciation its use with his permission of the very thoughtful paper by James B. Lampke, Esq., town counsel of the Town of Hull, Mass., which he presented to the International Municipal Lawyers Association in April 2002, "Legal Issues for Municipal Counsel to Consider *Before* Disaster Strikes," as a starting point in developing this checklist.

    3. Homeland Security Presidential Directive 5, ¶20, (February 28, 2003), *available at* http://www.whitehouse.gov/news/releases/2003/02/20030228-9.html. The full text of NIMS is available at http://www.dhs.gov/interweb/assetlibrary/NIMS-90-web.pdf (last accessed March 15, 2005).

4. It is critical, regardless of who declares the disaster or whether it is declared at all, that such decisions be documented adequately, including the basis for all actions taken and the need for expenditure of funds for this purpose. After the dust settles, the affected jurisdiction will begin to look at loans, grants, and reimbursements, and unless careful records are kept all along, the task of documenting past actions becomes much more difficult. A process needs to be established in the beginning, even if it as simple as keeping a log of all actions and assigning one or two persons to maintain it.

5. 42 U.S.C. § 5173.

6. Alan D. Cohn, *Mutual Aid: Intergovernmental Agreements for Emergency Preparedness and Response 7*, 36 Urb. Law. 1 (2005).

7. *See, for example*, 29 C.F.R. § 553.25(c), regarding there being an exception to the rules on providing reasonable time off under the FLSA if there is an emergency situation.

8. The Veteran's Employment and Training Services section of the U.S. Department of Labor website (http://www.dol.gov) provides a wealth of information on this law, including downloadable and printable text.

INDEX